VOICES

FROM THE

RECONSTRUCTION YEARS,

1865–1877

Glenn M. Linden
Associate Professor of History
Southern Methodist University

HARCOURT BRACE COLLEGE PUBLISHERS

Fort Worth   Philadelphia   San Diego   New York   Orlando   Austin   San Antonio
Toronto   Montreal   London   Sydney   Tokyo

Publisher:	Earl McPeek
Acquisitions Editor:	David Tatom
Product Manager:	Laura Brennan
Project Editor:	Travis Tyre
Art Director:	Don Fujimoto
Production Manager:	Linda McMillan

Cover Photo: Freedman's Village, Arlington, Virginia
Cover Design: Candice Swanson
ISBN: 0-15-508456-9
Library of Congress Catalog Card Number: 98-84958

Address for orders:
Harcourt Brace & Company
6277 Sea Harbor Drive
Orlando, FL 32887-6777
1-800-782-4479

Address for editorial correspondence:
Harcourt Brace College Publishers
301 Commerce Street, Suite 3700
Fort Worth, TX 76102

Web site address:
http://www.hbcollege.com

Harcourt Brace & Company will provide complimentary supplements or supplement packages to those adopters qualified under our adoption policy. Please contact your sales representative to learn how you qualify. If, as an adopter or potential user, you receive supplements you do not need, please return them to your sales representative or send them to: Attn: Returns Department, Troy Warehouse, 465 South Lincoln Drive, Troy, MO 63379.

Printed in the United States of America

8 9 0 1 2 3 4 5 6 7   039   9 8 7 6 5 4 3 2 1

❧ CONTENTS ❧

Americans have always been better at winning a war than at winning the peace after a war. After a war begins, the objective is clear and simple—to organize the society on a war footing and to win the war as quickly and with as few casualties as possible. Whatever the differences about the causes of the war or the best way to conduct the war, the American people unite around the need to sacrifice toward the common goal. Few doubt that the result will be victory.

When the war is over, however, the situation becomes more complicated. No longer are citizens united around a simple, overarching objective. Instead, they usually disagree about the best way to ensure a lasting peace. Often the issues become a partisan matter with the two political parties taking opposing positions. This makes it difficult for the Administration to formulate a policy that commands the necessary popular support. The postwar years present special problems that are not easily resolved and often last longer than the war itself.

Two obvious examples of this pattern can be seen in the First World War and the Civil War. In the First World War, President Woodrow Wilson tried to avoid involvement in the European war, but when it became inevitable, he called a special session of Congress and asked it to support a "war to end all wars." Enthusiastically, Congress and most Americans supported his call, and, as wartime measures were put into place, opposition to the war faded into insignificance. A year and a half later, military victories brought the conflict to a successful conclusion. The nation, united and confident, had achieved a great win and looked forward to a successful peace.

After the war, however, President Wilson's efforts to gain support for his policies were unsuccessful. Despite his pleadings, the country remained outside the League of Nations and apart from its efforts to build a structure for world peace. The two political parties split over the issue, and the country remained only an observer of the peace process in the 1920s and 1930s. Americans came to believe that U.S. participation in the war had been a mistake. Thus, many Americans believed that the "war to end all wars" had ended in an unsatisfactory peace, and they had little confidence in any future war effort. This was to be a serious hindrance to President Roosevelt's efforts to stop totalitarianism in the late 1930s. Ironically, the "failure" of the "war to end all wars" meant that the United States could not help prevent the next great war—World War II.

Two generations earlier Abraham Lincoln, like Woodrow Wilson, also tried to avoid a war. However, when the Confederacy attacked Fort Sumter, Lincoln called for seventy-five thousand volunteers to put down the rebellion in the South. With the help of Congress, he was able to bring the North together and to keep it focused on winning the war. From the beginning, the objective was simple but powerful—to preserve the Union, whatever the cost. It was an idea that united all parts of the

North. However, it was not enough, and by the fall of 1862 Lincoln needed to broaden the aims of the war. Thus, he issued the preliminary Emancipation Proclamation on September 22, 1862, stating that slavery would be ended in those states still in rebellion on January 1, 1863. When his warning was not heeded, he issued the final Emancipation Proclamation. This was a controversial decision that slowly gained acceptance in the North over the next two years.

As Union armies plunged deeper into the South in 1863, Lincoln began to think seriously about how to restore the Union as quickly and with as little controversy as possible. On December 8, 1863, he announced his new plan—the "10 per cent plan." It stated that when, in any Confederate state, one-tenth of those who voted in 1860 took an oath pledging loyalty to the United States and also organized a new government that agreed to end slavery, that state could be restored to the Union. Three states—Arkansas, Louisiana, and Tennessee—accepted the offer and in 1864 applied for readmission. Congress, however, believing that the legislative, not the executive branch, should control Reconstruction, refused to seat the newly elected representatives.

On July 4, 1864, Congress passed the stringent Wade-Davis Bill, which mandated that no states would be readmitted until a majority of voters took an ironclad oath stating that they had never fought against the Union. Also, the states had to end slavery, disavow Confederate debts, and disfranchise Confederate leaders. President Lincoln decided not to sign the bill and killed it with a pocket veto and an accompanying explanation: "I am . . . unprepared, by a formal approval of this Bill, to be inflexibly committed to any single plan of restoration."

Throughout the last year of the war, Lincoln continued his moderate Reconstruction plan, while Congress refused to readmit any states that did not meet the standards of the Wade-Davis Bill. Neither was prepared to accept the validity of the other's claims.

One week after the war ended, Abraham Lincoln was assassinated. His successor, Andrew Johnson, accepted Lincoln's Reconstruction policy with few changes and was determined to carry it out. The Republican party, though somewhat divided, still maintained the Wade-Davis Bill as its model. Also, there were disagreements between the North and South over the role of the freedmen in the newly restored Union. In the North, there was growing support for civil rights and protection for the former slaves. Some even wanted slaves to have the vote. In the South, however, the large majority of whites opposed any extension of political or economic rights to the freedmen. Thus, the nation was deeply divided over the next steps to take. The result was to be a long, painful, and complicated process with an uncertain end. The war was over, but the problems of finding a lasting peace were only beginning.

Over the years, there have been collections of historical readings and documents on the Reconstruction years. These have been valuable in adding new information, such as documents, government papers, and newspaper articles. What has been missing, however, has been the firsthand accounts of those who lived during the period. It has been the experience of this author that students need to come into direct contact with persons of the past in order to understand the problems and the efforts to find satisfactory solutions. When this happens, students feel a new appreciation and empathy for the participants. In a measure, students are transported back into the past and can begin to think like those who lived in the Reconstruction years.

The emphasis in this book will be upon firsthand accounts of the Reconstruction years. Twenty-seven individuals have been included—five southern men, two southern women, eleven northern men, five southern blacks, and four northern blacks. Also included are several editorials and accounts written by Southerners during the counter Reconstruction period, excerpts from two biographies of scalawags (because their firsthand accounts were not available), and a number of letters written by black soldiers and their relatives after the war.

Some might argue that twenty-seven people cannot completely reflect the experiences of a generation of Americans in these critical years. This may be true, but the author believes that these people do provide valuable information that speaks volumes about the trials and tribulations of those who lived in the Reconstruction years. This book will not be the final word on the lives of these Americans nor of the Reconstruction years, but it is hoped that it will speak directly to the reader in a convincing manner about the challenges faced by Northerners and Southerners. In the final analysis, it will be up to the reader to determine the value of this information. At the very least, he or she will begin to appreciate the complexity of the issue of race, economics, and the postwar efforts to bring the North and South together.

The readings have been arranged chronologically, beginning with the first days after the war ended and culminating with the removal of federal troops from the South in 1877. The divisions are the traditional ones—moderate Reconstruction (April 1865–November 1866), radical Reconstruction (December 1866–1873), and counter Reconstruction (1874–1877). Inevitably, there will be some overlapping, particularly between periods two and three, because radical Reconstruction lasted longer in some states (South Carolina, Louisiana, and Florida) and shorter in other states (Virginia, Tennessee, and North Carolina).

As the reader begins studying the firsthand accounts, three main themes will appear and reappear throughout the book. The first is the great destruction done to the South. There are many graphic examples of damage done to the land and people of the South. The second is the new racial situation with freed slaves and Southern whites who were uncertain about how to deal with the new freedom. This is constantly repeated by whites and blacks, by men and women, by Northerners and Southerners. It was the beginning of a more egalitarian Southern society. The third concerns the continuing hostility between North and South. There seemed to be no end to the hatred and anger expressed by both sides.

It should be noted that the spelling and punctuation used in the diaries, letters, documents, and other accounts presented in this book, such as salutations with periods instead of commas or colons and ampersands ("&" instead of "and"), have been reproduced for the most part without change to the original.

(in order of appearance)

WILLIAM GILMORE SIMMS (1806–1870) was born in Charleston, South Carolina, the son of a poor immigrant tradesman. With little formal schooling, he served as an apprentice to an apothecary and in later years read law. He early on decided to be an editor and writer. In 1830, he purchased the *Charleston City Gazette* and supported the Union in the Nullification Controversy of 1832. He began to write poems and novels in these years; his best and most popular novel was *The Yemasse,* published in 1835. In the following years down to the Civil War, he wrote seven Revolutionary War romances; novels of crime, colonial history, and Spanish history; seventy short stories; and seventeen volumes of verse and criticism. During those years, he edited ten periodicals and continued to defend slavery. He was a vigorous supporter of the Confederacy during the war and was left virtually destitute at its end. The writings quoted in this volume come from a five-volume collection of his letters.

THE JONES FAMILY included Mary Jane Jones (1808–1869), her husband, Reverend Charles Colcock Jones (1804–1863), Charles Colcock Jones Jr. (1831–1893), and his wife, Eva (1841–1890). A number of letters from members of this influential family are included in this book.

Mary Jane Jones and her husband owned three plantations of thirty-five hundred acres in Liberty County, Georgia. The census lists their slaves at 107 in 1850 and 129 in 1860. She attended McIntosh Academy at Barsden's Bluff (1820–1823) and the academy of Abiel Carter in Savannah (1823–1827) and married Reverend Jones in 1830. Three of their children, including Charles Jr., lived to maturity. She was a woman of remarkable strength of character. Many commented on her energy, patriotism, and spirit. Her husband died in May 1863, and she continued to run the plantation until her death.

Charles Colcock Jones Jr. attended South Carolina College from 1848 to 1850 and the College of New Jersey (Princeton), from which he graduated in 1852. He went to Harvard Law School and received a degree in 1855. Active in politics, he became an alderman (1859–1860) and mayor of Savannah (1860–1861). During the war, he was a lieutenant colonel of artillery and served until the end of the war.

Eva Berrien Eve Jones was born in Augusta, Georgia. She attended several schools in Bethlehem, Pennsylvania and Washington, D.C. A bridesmaid at the marriage of her first cousin once removed, Ruth Berrien Whitehead to Charles Jones Jr. in 1858, she became Charles's second wife in 1863.

Mary Sharpe Jones Mallard was the daughter of Mary Jones. She married Robert Q. Mallard, a Presbyterian clergyman, in 1857 and had four children by the end of the war. While living in New Orleans, the family wanted Mary Jones to sell the plantation and live with them. Mary Robarts, the cousin of Mary Jones, was unmarried and lived in Marietta, Georgia.

The years of radical Reconstruction were difficult ones for the members of the Jones family but throughout, they continued to support each other. The excerpts in this book are from *The Children of Pride,* by Robert Manson Myers, editor, Yale University Press, New Haven, 1972.

GEORGE RICHARD BROWDER (1827–1886) was born on January 11, 1827, near Olmstead, Kentucky. His mother died within a few months after his birth, and his stepmother, Sarah L. Gilmer, the daughter of a Methodist preacher, carefully trained him in the Methodist faith. He was sent to a private school in the Olmstead community and later to the Male Academy in Clarksville, Tennessee, where he received a classical education. During these years, he decided to become a minister and was licensed to preach in 1846 by the quarterly conference of Logan Circuit. In October, he was admitted on a trial basis to the Louisville Conference of the newly organized Methodist Church of the South; he completed the requirements and was ordained a deacon in October 1848. Two years later, he married Ann Elizabeth Warfield; he had met her while at the Male Academy in Clarksville (she attended the Clarksville Female Academy). During the 1850s, he preached extensively but because of a sore throat he never accepted a regular appointment. Throughout the war, his physical problems continued to plague him. In 1861 he became a full-time minister but had to give it up for health reasons. His greatest personal tragedy was the death of his daughter, Sarah Virginia, in 1860. Two other children were born during the war: Luther in 1861 and Wallace in 1865. Drafted by the federal army in 1864, he secured a substitute. He had ten slaves during the war. From 1852 to 1886 Browder kept a diary, from which the excerpts in this book were taken.

DAVID GOLIGHTLY HARRIS (1824–1870) was the only son among seven children born to W. W. Harris and his wife, Elizabeth Golightly. He married Emily Jane Liles, the daughter of a slaveowning farmer, and began to farm acreage given to him by his father. He had ten slaves and cultivated as many as one hundred acres of land. He and his wife lived in the Piedmont region near Spartansburg, South Carolina with their eight children. He enlisted in the Confederate army and served from November 1862 until the end of the war. He was seldom involved in combat duty and occasionally hired a substitute in order to go home on furlough. He kept a journal from 1855 until 1870; that journal is the source of the selections used in this book.

FRANCES BUTLER LEIGH (1838–1894) was born in Philadelphia. Her father, Pierce Butler, was heir to a number of large and productive Georgia plantations. Her mother was the noted English actress, Frances Ann (Fanny) Kemble. They were married in 1835 and had two daughters, Sarah in 1835 and Frances in 1838.

Their marriage, a tumultuous one, resulted in divorce in 1849. The girls remained with the father; the mother continued her acting career. The girls visited the plantations regularly. Frances was happy in the South and accepted the necessity of the plantation system and slavery. Her sister, however, was very unhappy and finally refused to go south in 1856. On the eve of the Civil War, Frances and her father were in Charleston but returned to Philadelphia.

During the war, Pierce lived in the North with his daughter. He was staunchly pro-Confederate and was once arrested for gunrunning, although he was quickly released.

After the war, Pierce and his daughter Frances decided to return to Georgia and the old plantations. For the next ten years, Frances's life was closely connected to the plantation life and to the hundreds of former slaves in Georgia. The excerpts in this book are from *Ten Years on a Georgia Plantation Since the War* by Frances Butler Leigh, Richard Bentley & Son, London, 1883.

WHITELAW REID was born in 1837 in Zenia, Ohio. He wrote for newspapers before graduating from Miami University. He entered politics as an enthusiastic Republican and supported John C. Fremont in 1856 and Abraham Lincoln in 1860 for the presidency. During the Civil War he was a correspondent, receiving acclaim for his coverage of the battles of Shiloh and Gettysburg. As the war ended, he was one of three newspapermen who first entered the city of Richmond.

Less than one month later, he went with Chief Justice Chase and other officials who were sent south by President Johnson. This trip was intended to convince white Southerners of the necessity of enfranchising blacks. For two months Reid toured the South. He returned two more times on his own and finally returned to Washington, D.C., in May of 1866. At first he favored a lenient policy of pardon and restoration, but he shifted toward a tougher policy as a result of his last two trips. His final conclusions were important in the development of policy toward the South. (The excerpts in this book are from Whitelaw Reid, *After the War: A Tour of the Southern States, 1865–1866*, edited by C. Vann Woodward, Harper & Row, New York, 1965.)

SIDNEY ANDREWS was born in Massachusetts in 1835 and moved to Illinois in 1846. He worked as an assistant editor and later as editor of the Alton, Illinois *Daily Courier* in the 1850s. Working in Washington, D.C. during the war, he became a special correspondent in 1864 and the next year, he began a fourteen-week investigation of conditions in the South. He spent one and a half months in South Carolina, three weeks in North Carolina, and his last five weeks in Georgia. He attended each of the state conventions that were convening to restore the states to the Union. He regularly sent dispatches to the *Chicago Tribune* and the *Boston Advertiser*. His final conclusion was that the South was not yet ready for readmission. His advice was not well received by President Johnson. (The excerpts in this book are from the *Boston Daily Advertiser*, September–December 1865. His dispatches were also compiled in a book entitled *The South since the War as Shown by Fourteen Weeks of Travel and Observation in Georgia and the Carolinas*, published in 1866 by Ticknor and Fields, Boston.)

JOHN TROWBRIDGE was born in September 1827 in Ogden Township, Monroe County, New York. Always interested in language and the classics, he won a literary prize from the *Niagara Courier* in 1845. For a time he taught school and then became a writer. In the 1850s, he wrote several novels; one of the most successful was *Neighbor Jade Wood,* inspired by the experiences of Anthony Burns, a Negro slave whose trial had been a celebrated case in Boston. The novel became a stage play and had a long run in Boston. During the war, Trowbridge continued to write antislavery books and edited a magazine for younger people called *Our Younger Folks.* It was the forerunner of the Horatio Alger books.

In late summer 1865 L. Stebbins, a Hartford publisher, decided to send an observer through the former Confederacy to file a human interest report on conditions in the South. Trowbridge accepted the assignment with enthusiasm. For the next four months he toured the South and completed a 200,000-word manuscript of his travels. The excerpts in this book are from *The Desolate South, 1865–1866,* edited by Gordon Carroll, Little, Brown & Co., 1956.

MARSHALL TWITCHELL was born in Townshend, Windham County, Vermont, on February 29, 1840. His parents were Harvey Daniel and Elizabeth Scott Twitchell. Until the age of nine, he lived in Vermont. For two years he lived in Bedford, Quebec, and then moved back to his hometown, where he attended school until the age of sixteen. Then he taught school for several years while attending Leland Seminary until the beginning of the Civil War.

Twitchell served in the Fourth Vermont Regiment throughout the war. He was seriously wounded and left behind with the dead but survived. Posted to Texas after the war, he requested assignment to the Freedmen's Bureau in Louisiana. In the fall of 1865, he was sent to the village of Sparta in Bienville Parish in the upper Red River Valley, where he served for six months as a bureau agent. The excerpts in this book are from *Carpetbagger from Vermont: The Autobiography of Marshall Harvey Twitchell,* Ted Tunnell, editor, Louisiana State University Press, 1989.

JOHN W. DEFOREST was born in 1826 in Connecticut. He became a writer, but when the Civil War broke out, he enlisted. In *A Volunteer's Adventures,* DeForest kept a personal record of his participation in the war. His book has been compared to Stephen Crane's *Red Badge of Courage* for its vivid, accurate, and perceptive prose.

After the war, he applied for a commission in the Veteran Reserve Corps, which consisted of experienced soldiers who were disabled for active service. He served for one year, and when the corps was disbanded in July 1866, he transferred into the Freedmen's Bureau. Two months later, on October 1, DeForest was posted as an agent of the Freedmen's Bureau in Greenville, South Carolina, where he remained for fifteen months. The excerpts in this book are from *A Union Officer in the Reconstruction,* Cronshore & Potter, editors, Yale University Press, 1948.

ALBERT MORGAN was born in New York in 1842, raised in Wisconsin, and fought in the Union army during the Civil War. With his brother Charles, he decided to go to Mississippi after the war to raise cotton. They bought land, hired over one hundred freedmen in 1865 to work the land, and enjoyed some modest success in the early months. However, by 1867 the resistance by Southern whites resulted in their loss of property and about $50,000.

During radical Reconstruction, Albert became active in politics, first in the constitutional convention in Mississippi, then as a state senator for four years, and later as a sheriff and tax collector for Yazoo County. He was an active leader in the Republican party in those years. His marriage to a black schoolteacher from New York caused considerable controversy. His account of those years is entitled *Yazoo; or, On the Picket Line of Freedom in the South.* It was published in 1884.

PETER RANDOLPH was born (date uncertain) a slave on the Brandon plantation in Prince George County, Virginia. He taught himself to read and write and in 1847 was freed by the provisions of the will of his master (Carter Enloe). In Randolph's own words, "In order to gain the freedom given us by the provision of the will, it was necessary that we should leave the South and seek a new home in the North." On September 15, 1847, he left for Boston. In the next few years, he met many of the most prominent abolitionists and politicians—William Lloyd Garrison, John A. Andrews, Wendell Phillips, and Samuel May. Encouraged to write about his life as a slave, he wrote a small book entitled *Sketches of Slave Life,* which was circulated in Boston. Later he was licensed as a Baptist preacher in Boston, after which he was ordained in Brooklyn, New York and became a minister to the New Haven, Connecticut Baptist Church. He was a minister during the Civil War, and when it ended, he went back to Virginia, first to Petersburg and then to Richmond for four and a half years. He was active in efforts to help the newly freed slaves in Virginia during the early years of Reconstruction. Selections in this book come from his *From Slave Cabin to the Pulpit.*

JOHN ROY LYNCH was born a slave in 1847 on a Louisiana plantation. His Irish father had intended to free him and his family but died before completing his plans. John Lynch became free in 1863 when Union forces took over Natchez, Mississippi. Over the next few years, he learned photography and soon became manager of a local photography studio. In 1867, after passage of the Reconstruction Acts, he went into politics. Soon he was appointed justice of the peace. Later he was speaker of the Mississippi House of Representatives and became a congressman in the last years of Reconstruction. Selections in this book are from *The Autobiography of John Roy Lynch.*

GIDEON WELLES (1802–1878) was born in Glastonbury, Connecticut, the son of Samuel and Ann Welles. He attended the Episcopal Academy at Cheshire, Connecticut and the American Literary, Scientific, and Military Academy at Norwich, Vermont. He was part owner and editor of the *Hartford Times* for ten years. He was elected as a Democrat to the office of state comptroller of public accounts and in the late 1840s was chief of the Bureau of Provisions and Clothing for the Navy. In the 1850s he left the Democratic party because of the slavery issue and helped organize the Republican party in Connecticut.

During the Civil War, he was secretary of the Navy and contributed to the Union victory. When the war ended, Welles became a confidant of Andrew Johnson and was strongly opposed to the policies of the Republican party in 1866 and 1867. In 1868 he returned to the Democratic party. Four years later, he became a liberal Republican and in 1876 supported Samuel J. Tilden in his unsuccessful efforts to win the presidency. The excerpts in this book come from volumes 2 and 3 of *The Diary of Gideon Welles*.

GEORGE TEMPLETON STRONG (1820–1875) was a lawyer in New York City, a graduate and later, a trustee of Columbia University, and a supporter of the Whig party until the 1850s. In the late 1850s, he became a strong supporter of the Union. During the Civil War, he was treasurer of the United States Sanitary Commission, an organization that cared for the wounded, sent food and supplies to soldiers, and compiled a directory of the sick and wounded in army hospitals. On a number of occasions, he met with President Lincoln.

When the war ended, Strong was forty-five years of age and in poor health. Still, he carried a full share of the legal work in the law firm of Strong, Bidwell and Strong and to be active in a variety of philanthropic areas. Strong continued to be a careful observer of political matters, with an abiding interest in the Reconstruction policies of the postwar years. Fortunately for posterity, he kept detailed entries in a diary until his death in 1875. The excerpts in this book are from his four-volume diary.

FREDERICK DOUGLASS (1817?–1895) was born a slave in Maryland. He taught himself to read and write, and in 1838 he escaped to the North by taking a train from Baltimore to New York. During the 1840s, Douglass was an active abolitionist, and by the time of the Civil War he was probably the best known black man in the United States.

At the start of the war, he was critical of Lincoln's policies, especially the President's reluctance to allow black men to fight. However, the issuance of the Emancipation Proclamation made Douglass a warm supporter of Lincoln's policies. He campaigned actively for Lincoln's reelection to the presidency in 1864.

When the war ended, Douglass considered retirement but soon became a vigorous champion of black rights, including suffrage. He was tireless in publishing and speaking on behalf of black rights. The excerpts in this text are from two books— *The Life and Writings of Frederick Douglass*, vol. 4, and *The Frederick Douglass Papers*, vol. 4, edited by John W. Blassingame and John R. McKivigan.

RUTHERFORD B. HAYES (1822–1893) was born at Delaware, Ohio, the son of Rutherford Hayes, a farmer, and Sophia Birchard Hayes. He attended several private schools before going to Kenyon College; later he spent a year and a half at Harvard Law School. During the 1850s, he became interested in politics and supported presidential candidates Winfield Scott in 1852, Fremont in 1856, and Lincoln in 1860. Hayes served in the Civil War as a soldier and a judge-advocate, trying court-martial cases; by the end of the war he was a major general.

In October 1864, he was elected by a large majority to the House of Representatives, where he was a loyal member of the Republican caucus. Reelected in 1866, he was asked to run for governor of Ohio in 1867. He served two terms and campaigned actively for Grant. He ran for Congress in 1872 and was defeated because of the party split. In 1875 he was again elected governor. The next year, he ran for President of the United States and was finally chosen on March 2, 1877, by one electoral vote, 185–184. The excerpts in this book are from his *Diary and Letters*, vol. 3.

HIRAM RHODES REVELS was born of free parents in Fayetteville, Cumberland County, North Carolina and claimed September 27, 1827 as his date of birth. He attended various schools and seminaries and Knox College in Bloomington, Illinois. Ordained a minister in the African Methodist Church, Revels carried on religious work in Indiana, Illinois, Kansas, Kentucky, Tennessee, Mississippi, and Maryland in the years before the Civil War. During the war, Revels assisted in recruiting two regiments of Negroes in Maryland, served as a chaplain of a Negro regiment, and organized churches in Mississippi. Settling in Natchez, Mississippi after the war, he served as an alderman and a member of the state senate in 1870. He was chosen to fill the unexpired U.S. Senate term of Jefferson Davis from February 27, 1870 until March 3, 1871. Revels was the first black to serve in the U.S. Senate.

RICHARD BROWN ELLIOTT was born in Boston on August 11, 1842. He attended the High Holborn Academy in London, England in 1853 and was graduated from Eton College, England in 1859. Admitted to the bar, Elliott practiced law in Columbia, South Carolina after the war. In 1868 he was a member of the state constitutional convention and also a member of the state House of Representatives from July 6, 1868 to October 23, 1870. From 1869 to 1871 Elliott was assistant adjutant general of South Carolina. He was elected as a Republican to the Forty-Second and Forty-Third Congresses and served from March 4, 1871 until his resignation on November 1, 1874.

JOSEPH HAYNE RAINEY was born in Georgetown, South Carolina on June 21, 1832. He received a limited education and worked as a barber until 1862, when upon being forced to work on Confederate fortifications in Charleston, he escaped to the West Indies, where he remained until the war ended. After the war Rainey returned to South Carolina and became involved in politics. He was elected a delegate to the state constitutional convention in 1868 and served as a state senator until he resigned in 1870 to be elected to the Forty-First Congress to fill the vacancy created when the House of Representatives declared the seat of B. Franklin Whittemore vacant. Rainey was the first black to be elected to the House of Representatives, was reelected four times, and served from December 12, 1870 to March 3, 1879.

CHARLES HAYS (1834–1879) was the son of a wealthy Alabama planter. He attended the Greene Spring School, Franklin College, and finally the University of Virginia. He returned home and received his inheritance at the age of twenty-one. He became a wealthy man, and by the time of the Civil War, he had one hundred slaves and a net worth of $112,500.

During the first two years of the Civil War, Hays served as a Confederate officer at the battles of Shiloh and Chickamauga. Upon the death of his stepfather in the fall of 1863, he returned home to run the plantation. Later that year he married Cornelia Ormand. Several months later he returned to active duty and served until the end of the war. He sought and received a pardon from President Johnson on September 12, 1865. Selections in this book are from a biography by William W. Rogers Jr., *Black Belt Scalawag*.

JAMES ALCORN (1816–1894) was born in Illinois. His parents soon moved to Salem, Kentucky where his father struggled to make a living. James received some education and went to Cumberland College in Kentucky for a year. Two years later, in 1838, he received a license to practice law. Unhappy with his prospects in Kentucky, Alcorn moved to Mississippi in 1844. Soon he was a cotton planter and southern Whig. Successful in local politics during the 1850s, he served in the Confederate army during the war, reaching the rank of general. When the war ended, Alcorn prepared to pick up the threads of his life and to bring Mississippi back into the Union with as few changes as possible.

He was a Whig and a conservative who soon saw that there would be many distasteful changes. He was, however, prepared to accept the new freedom of Negroes and to look for ways to manage that reality. Perhaps a new party could be created to work with the federal government, secure financial aid, and control the newly freed slaves. The task would be more difficult than he envisioned. Excerpts in this book are from a biography by Lillian Pereyra, *James Lusk Alcorn, Persistent Whig*.

RICHARD HARVEY CAIN was born in Greenbriar County, Virginia, on April 12, 1825. Six years later he moved with his father to Gallipolis, Ohio, where he attended school. Cain became a minister and led a congregation in Brooklyn, New York during the Civil War. In 1865 he moved to South Carolina and settled in Charleston. During Reconstruction, Cain was a delegate to the constitutional convention of South Carolina, a member of the state senate from 1868 to 1872, and a manager of a newspaper in Charleston in 1868. He was elected as a Republican to the Forty-Third Congress and served from March 4, 1873 to March 3, 1875.

JAMES THOMAS RAPIER was born a free black in Florence, Lauderdale County, Alabama, on November 13, 1837. Educated by private tutors, he studied law in Canada and was admitted to the bar after the war. Rapier became a cotton planter and then was appointed a notary public by the governor of Alabama. Rapier attended the first Republican convention held in Alabama, and in 1867 he was a member of the state constitutional convention. He was unsuccessful in a campaign for the office of secretary of state in 1870; the next year he was appointed assessor of internal revenue. Rapier was elected as a Republican to the Forty-Third Congress and served from March 4, 1873 to March 3, 1875.

BLANCHE K. BRUCE was born a slave in Prince Edward County, Virginia on March 1, 1841. His master's son taught him to read. In 1850 Bruce moved to Missouri where he lived until the middle of the Civil War when he freed himself and founded a school for black refugees. After the war he went to Oberlin College for one year and then moved to Mississippi in 1867. In the next few years, Bruce became a member of the Mississippi Levee Board and the sheriff and tax collector of Bolivar County. He was elected as a Republican to the U.S. Senate and served from March 4, 1875 to March 3, 1881. Bruce was the first black man to serve a full term in the U.S. Senate.

JAMES SHEPHERD PIKE was born in Maine in 1811. A success in business, he became a correspondent for the *Portland Advertiser* and the *Boston Courier,* and in the 1850s, the Washington correspondent for the *New York Tribune.* During the Civil War, he was minister resident to the Hague, serving from 1861 to 1866. The remaining years of his life were devoted to writing and to collecting and publishing his earlier correspondence. In 1874, he published *The Prostrate State: South Carolina under Negro Government,* the result of his observations of the workings of the Reconstruction government in South Carolina; a Dutch translation was also published in 1875.

EDWARD KING was born in Massachusetts in 1848. At the end of the Civil War, he became a reporter for the *Springfield Daily Union.* Two years later, he joined the staff of the *Springfield Republican* where he served (until 1870) as a reporter, subeditor, and editorial writer. After Dr. J. G. Holland of the *Springfield Republican* became editor of *Scribner's Monthly,* he invited King to travel through the southern states and gather materials for a series of articles on the effects of the Civil War, the economic situation in the South, and interesting features of the landscape and social life. The tour lasted until 1874, and the articles published by *Scribner's* appeared in book form in 1875. This was twice reprinted in 1875 in England as the *Southern States of North America.*

PART I

MODERATE
RECONSTRUCTION

CHAPTER 1

CONDITIONS IN THE SOUTH, 1865–1867

"Have we not fallen upon sad, sad times?"

— CAROLINE JONES, April 30, 1865

William Gilmore Simms

As the Civil War ended, Southerners began to consider the losses suffered in the four-year conflict. Few lost as much as or sank more quickly into poverty than William Gilmore Simms, one of the most important writers in the antebellum South. The son of a poor immigrant tradesman, Simms had risen rapidly to a position of affluence and leadership. Thus, during the war he was a strong supporter of slavery and the Confederacy. However, the war destroyed his society and with it his place in society; he was near destitution with nine persons to support on a mere $10 per week. Most of his letters in these years dealt with his impoverished condition. Writing from Columbia, South Carolina, to a friend in the North, Simms poured out his sad story and asked for help.

Columbia, S. C.
June 13, 1865.

My dear Lawson.

I have a chance of writing you, but only a few moments. I have written you repeatedly, by parties going north, mostly returning soldiers, but half doubt whether you have received any of my letters. If you have not you have yet to learn that my house, newly rebuilt, has been destroyed by Sherman's army; my stables, carriage house, barns, gin house, machine and threshing houses; in short every building of any value; my mules, horses, cattle driven off & carried away, or butchered; my wagons,

3

ploughs, implements, all destroyed; and I am here, temporarily destitute, without money to spare to telegraph you. I am sleeping in a garret, so are my daughters, Mary L. & Chevillette. Augusta, with her own daughter, & my two little boys are living with Mrs. Rivers at the little village of Bamberg, with barely bread enough to support life. I earn here a small pittance weekly, by editing a paper, newly started in this place, which does not yet pay. Two weeks ago, I was summoned by telegraph to my son, Gilmore, who lay dangerously ill, in the town of Chester, some 65 miles off. He had typhoid fever. I had to borrow the money, a trifle, to eke out the little I had, in order to get to him—had to travel in a wagon, all the railways being destroyed. I found him delirious, raving, & without sleep for 5 days. By the blessings of the Good God he is spared; and the crisis terminated favorably. I left him convalescent & out of all danger, but too feeble to travel, and had to leave him, to see to my duties here & my other children. Thirty of my negroes were carried off by Sherman's Army; the rest are at work, after a fashion, but greatly needing my presence & help; and I have still my lands, and some of my property to see after. Yet I lack the means to get home again. The railroads destroyed, the horses & mules carried off, it is only at long intervals that an opportunity offers for travel, and it requires money—which I have not. . . . You have been apprised that I am a widower; that I have lost the one precious companion of 27 years. I have 3 boys & 3 daughters left. Gilmore has had several narrow escapes, & bears the marks of four desperate wounds, & has lost the middle finger of his left hand. . . . Among my losses is my library, 10,700 vols! My books! My books! My heart is ready to break when I think of them. I have had nothing new, in the way of books for four years. My friends here, by the way, the very wealthiest are incapable of helping me, or I should not call upon you & my friends at the North. They have the will, but are as helpless as myself. But enough. I will tell you all, when I am more calm. . . .

Yours Ever as Ever,
W. Gilmore Simms.

———————

Two months later, he again referred to his diminished situation.

To Evert Augustus Duyckinck
Columbia, S.C.
Augt. 12, 1865.

My dear Duyckinck.

Since your first letter, I have had no other from you. I have written you two in reply to it, and now address you the third. All these letters have to be despatched by private hand, as we have neither post office nor regular mails. It is quite probable that the hurry & remissness of the parties, by whom my letters were sent, may have occasioned their failure. One of them, addressed to Godey, has been returned to me through the Charleston P.O. in consequence of the nonpayment of stamps. Not a stamp is to be had here for love or money. Cover me a few, if you please. Our only communications with the surrounding country, are by a few miserable wagons; and it is only now & then that we hear of a citizen going to the North. I forward this by a hand, which, I trust, will secure its safe delivery either to yourself in person, or at your post office. He promises me to procure the stamps when he shall reach some town where they are to be had. In my first letter I sufficiently described to you my wretched situation. I have lost every thing but my lands. I have barely a sufficiency of clothes—chiefly homespun—for decency; and with 9 persons to support, my whole income is but $10 per week, and, until I can get means to get away from this place, & to find a comfortable shelter for my little ones, I can do nothing better. With a little help from Lawson, I have sent off all my family to Barnwell, where my eldest son is striving to make some outhouses habitable. My eldest daughter, Mrs. Roach, with her husband and one child, and with my two youngest boys, are about to go thither in a few days. I have succeeded in buying them 50 bushels of corn, & hope to procure a little bacon for them, and with this they must make out. . . . Here, I write in a borrowed room. My chamber in a garret, being under the *leads,* as in Venice, is almost killing, day & night. In fact, I mostly sleep in an open piazza, on a mattress spread on the floor, and free to the incursions of the musquitos, to say nothing of other insect invaders. Verily, that I can write or think at all, is wonderful. I need a few hundred dollars to buy lumber, for building 3 rooms at the plantation—need a couple of mules for hauling lumber & material—need crockery, clothes, bedding, &c. My hat, a vile thing, cost me $400. My shoes, the commonest farmers, which pain me as I walk, cost $300. My son, just recovering from typhoid, comes home to me naked. But you can conceive all. If the publishers could make me these advances, I could begin the world anew, and set my wheels & springs in motion. I am conscious of no diminution of powers. My health is good   my frame vigorous, and, once restored to peace of mind,—freed from the terrible anxieties about my children, which now afflict & keep me sleepless, I believe that I could do better things in letters than I have ever done before. I have my brain seething ever and anon, with fresh conceptions, over which I brood at intervals, with a loving mood of meditation which makes them grow upon me, until the images become as familiar to the eye, as they have been to the mind. You suggest to me a part in politics. It may be that I shall take your advice. My neighbours have applied to me to go to the Convention. This I have declined; but have told them that if sent to the Lower House in the Legislature, where much good & fresh work is to be done, I will go, provided they do not ask me to canvas the country. . . . See if your publishers & patrons of Literature have magnanimity enough to give present employment, and a small credit, to one, who after 40 years service in the field of letters, may well consider himself a veteran—one not broken down in the service, but wretchedly out of repair.—I am also greatly in need of Books,—have had nothing to read for 4 years. My library gone—& no books for study. Can you not have some sent me—"Care of John Russell, Charleston"—to await my orders. Please write to J. T. Fields on this subject.—But, I pause. I hesitate! May I not be trespassing too much on our ancient friendship? Has the war chilled you towards your Southern friends? Has politics killed Literature? Where are you? Speak! What are our present relationships. At all events, may God forgive & be with you in mercy.

Yours as Ever.
W. Gilmore Simms.

Recovering his spirit, Simms made plans to travel north to secure assistance. He was anxious to see his old friend "after four, nearly five, dreadful years."

Columbia, S. C.
Oct. 1. 1865.

My dear Duyckinck.

. . . I propose to go down to the plantation, where I shall stay some week or 10 days, return, & proceed from Columbia to the North. I hope to be in N. Y. & to see you somewhere about the 20th. or 25th. inst. I told you in previous letters that I had been appointed by the Masonic bodies of this place, the Chairman of a Commission to represent them in the Northern cities in the hope to procure some assistance. I prepared their memorial, a copy of which I will send or bring you. They are to raise the necessary funds for the Commission—not so easy a matter in a place so utterly stript of resources. Lawson authorizes me to draw on him for $100—the amt. of a dft from Widdleton. Wretched as this return is, the money enables me to send off by wagon, all the little luggage, clothing, bedding & furniture which I have here, to my children on the plantation. Of 16 Bedsteads, I have 1 left; so, in proportion of mattresses & feather beds. We have not a chair or a table. Not a knife or fork; hardly a cup or plate or tumbler. And such things we cannot buy. Our basins for washing are of tin, made out of tin, saved amid the ruins of Columbia. We have literally nothing left us but our lands, & how to dispossess the negroes is the problem. They will no longer work. They steal. We can scarcely keep a horse or mule, unless in a lodge directly beneath your chamber, under the muzzle of a gun. They are perishing by thousands of exposure, drunkenness, starvation & all brutal practices. The old are deserted by the young. Sons abandon their fathers, mothers their infants, all to crowd to the cities where they quarter themselves for rations on the Government. They are daily convicted of robbery, & murders are frequent. But I will tell you all when we meet. . . . After four, nearly five, dreadful years, it will give me the greatest pleasure to meet with you again. But say as little as possible to me about the war, and my miserable Country. . . .

Yours as Ever
W. G. S.

The Jones Family

The Jones family encountered many of the same problems that Simms experienced—the frustration and humiliation of a lost war ("a joyless future of probable ignominy"), the uncertainty over how to work with the newly freed slaves ("one day they work, and the next day they come to town"), and severe economic losses from inflation and thievery ("every vestige of bacon we owned in the world stolen from us a few days ago"). It was a world turned upside down. Family members desperately tried to help each other cope with the new conditions.

In a letter on April 30, 1865, from Augusta, Georgia (less than one hundred miles from Simms in Columbia), Caroline Jones poured out her frustrations to her mother-in-law, Mary Jones:

. . . We are almost paralyzed here by the rapid succession of strange and melancholy incidents that have marked the last few weeks—the sudden collapse of our tired and trusted General Lee and his army, about which, sad as it is, I can feel no mortification, for I know he did all that mortal man could do; then the rumors of peace, so different from the rapturous delight of a *conquered peace* we all looked forward to; then the righteous retribution upon Lincoln. One sweet drop among so much that is painful is that he at least cannot raise his howl of diabolical triumph over us. . . . Have we not fallen upon sad, sad times? . . .

We are suffering here extreme embarrassment from the derangement of currency consequent upon the war—or rather peace—news. Days ago Confederate money, according to the *government* gold standard, was 100 to 1. Today gold is 300. We got rid of all of ours speedily, the Doctor investing six months' pay in bacon and flour. You will be grieved to hear that our storeroom was broken into and one-third of our flour and every vestige of bacon we owned in the world stolen from us a few nights ago. It is our first misfortune of the kind, and but that now it is irreparable we should not feel it so much, so many others having suffered much more severely. I have taken the hint and moved what little I had left upstairs into the garret.

———————

Two months later, on June 13, 1865, another daughter-in-law, Eva Jones, wrote in a similar vein to Mary Jones:

It is with sad and heavy hearts we mark the dark, crowding events of this most disastrous year. We have seen hope after hope fall blighted and withering about us, until our country is no more—merely a heap of ruins and ashes. A joyless future of probable ignominy, poverty, and want is all that spreads before us, and God alone knowing where any of us will end a life robbed of every blessing and already becoming intolerable. You see, it is with no resigned spirit that *I* yield to the iron yoke our conqueror forges for his fallen and powerless foe. The degradation of a whole country and a proud people is indeed a mighty, and all-enveloping sorrow. . . .

I suppose you have learned even in the more secluded portions of the country that slavery is entirely abolished—a most unprecedented robbery, and most unwise policy. So it must appear even to the ignorant. I know it is only intended for a greater humiliation and loss to *us*, but I should think that even the powerful and unconscientious conqueror would reap the ill effects of so unguarded a movement. However, it *is* done; and we, the *chained witnesses*, can only look on and draw inferences and note occurrences—"only this and nothing more." There has been a great rush of the freedmen from all families in the city and from neighboring plantations. Adeline, Grace, and Polly have all departed in search of freedom, without bidding any of us an affectionate adieu. All of Dr. Joe's servants have left save Titus and Agrippa and children, I think he told me. . . . We have lost many of our servants, but a sufficient number have remained to serve us, and as yet these appear faithful and anxious to please. On our plantation everything is "at sixes and sevens." One day they work, and the next they come to town. Of course no management of them is allowed. Our Yankee masters think that *their* term of slavery having expired, that the shackles they have abandoned, more firmly riveted, will do for us their former owners. And we meekly bow the head, receive chains and insults, and observe a mute and most submissive demeanor. Veritably like lambs we are led to the slaughter, and like sheep before the shearers we are dumb. And they *shear* ahead—in a manner most wonderful to behold.

A month later, on July 14, 1865, Eva continued her lament:

. . . **W**ell, we are all down here as poor as poverty can make us. Besides the freeing of our Negroes (which deprives us of the greater part of our property, of course), the Yankees and Negroes together have stolen every piece of meat we had (about one hundred and seventy pieces), and we have not a *ham* even left. Then a variety of mules, sheep, and hogs; so altogether we are in a forlorn condition. I expect before long to become a very efficient chambermaid and seamstress, though the latter comes very hard to my poor unused fingers. Our ménage has been frightfully reduced; and of our numerous throng there remains a seamstress (who has had to lay aside her old calling to become cook, washer, and chambermaid) and one who attends to everything else about this unfortunate establishment. . . . To crown my misfortunes, which persistently attack me from all sides, Charlie and I had been laying aside carefully every few cents of specie that we could gather; and most tenderly did I keep it locked and laid away. To no one would I breathe of my few gold and silver dollars, when what was my surprise and despair the other day to find that my wardrobe had been *entered with a false key* and my forty-three dollars in specie gone—vanished, abstracted!

'Twas ever thus from childhood's hour:
I've seen my fondest hopes decay.

One of our freedwomen expects shortly to enter the holy estate of matrimony, and has therefore indulged in some extravagancies and petty fineries. The question arises: Whence came the "filthy lucre" to purchase these indulgences? And my empty wardrobe echoes emphatically: *"Where?"*

Two weeks later, on July 28, Charles wrote to his mother, Mary Jones, about a disconcerting incident in the family.

. . . Mrs. Eve has been sued by three of her house servants for wages—a most unwarrantable procedure. The truth is that unless something is done here, great annoyance will occur. We will all have to recognize the fact at once that our former slaves have been set free, that we have no further legal claim upon their services, and that if they continue with us we must pay for services rendered. The amount of the compensation will of course depend upon each particular case. I am just writing Mr. Fennell a full letter on the subject. . . .

Your affectionate son,
Charles C. Jones, Jr.

Three days later Mary wrote to the northern officer in charge of the Atlanta area, General James II. Wilson, asking for help:

General, . . .

After the advance of the army and occupation of Savannah, although left in great destitution, I still hoped to remain with the servants at home and do the best we could to sustain life, but found myself and them in such circumstances of peril from marauding bands of Negroes (that had occupied the adjoining counties and sea islands and were continually returning to steal the little that remained) that we were finally compelled to leave, and did so through the assistance of kind friends from abroad, upon whose kindness and charity they have subsisted to the present time.

These people are now desirous of returning to their former home, and I am desirous of aiding them to do so; but as you will see from the above recital, I am powerless to do so. I am reduced from affluence to penury, so far as any available support for them or for myself remains; and if I cannot obtain assistance, they too must be numbered among the millions suddenly made homeless and friendless. My distress is not more for myself than for them. My honored husband, Rev. C. C. Jones, D.D., expended his talents, his energy, his fortune, his exalted piety in devoted efforts to benefit the Negro race. His record is on high, and the good he accomplished in their elevation and true conversion to God will meet an eternal reward. These servants have composed our household, and I would gladly do something to promote their future welfare. But as I have said, I am without the means of assisting them.

The request I prefer is twofold. Will you give me transportation for two families of Negroes, or as many as desire to return (they will be from fifteen to twenty in all, many of them children), from Thomasville on the Savannah, Albany & Gulf Road to No. 3 (McIntosh Station), Liberty County, in the month of October, when I understand the road will be completed? The government have repeatedly aided the destitute or those who applied for agricultural purposes. Can you assist me in obtaining either horses or mules for plantation use, or direct me to any source by which they can be thus secured?

General Wilson, if you have favored my letter with a reading, I fear I have overtaxed your courtesy. I trust your forbearance will be exercised.

Very truly yours,
Mary Jones.

———————————————

Mary Jones began to think about the possibility of taking the oath of loyalty to the United States. She would have to swear that she had not voluntarily aided the Confederacy. Taking the oath would protect her rights to the family plantations. Her main concerns were to keep the land and to get reliable labor. Neither was easy to accomplish. On August 18 she wrote to Charles of her concerns.

My dear Son, . . .

Robert has taken the oath; and as I have several interests to represent, would it not be well for me to do so at once before I go to the low country, where I may not have the opportunity of doing so, and yet might be put to some trouble about our landed property there if there should be any attempt at confiscation? Do write me about this if you can get a reliable *private* opportunity of doing so. I am suspicious of all communications *by mail.*

I have made a written contract with Flora to remain with me until the end of the year, and your sister and Robert have made contracts with their servants. They *all* design returning to Liberty, but will wait until the railroad to Savannah is finished. I am distressed at the thought of Lucy's leaving, for I fear your sister and her little children will miss her sadly. I would do anything in my power to retain her, but your sister thinks if she stays against her will she would be worse than useless. Tenah and her increasing family would be a burden in town. I mean to inform them plainly if they come below it must be to labor and be subject to control, either at Montevideo or Arcadia. I think they have an idea of possession. With regard to cultivating Montevideo, I will be compelled to increase the force there to do so successfully; and if I can do so from those who have lived there and are now at Indianola, I would prefer it to strangers. But of this we can arrange when you come down. Do write me what report Stepney brings when he returns. . . .

Ever your affectionate mother,
Mary Jones.

—————

George Browder

Some three hundred miles away in south central Kentucky, George Browder, a Methodist minister, considered the changed conditions in his home state. During the war he owned slaves and was sympathetic to the South. However, Browder accepted northern control and, when drafted in 1864, paid for a substitute to take his place. After the war he was concerned about the cruelties inflicted on the South. He was especially unhappy with the freeing of the slaves. He lost money and reliable labor. Opposing the continuing punishment of the South, he feared the impact of racial change that might give the vote to the freedmen.

April 10 — . . . I have looked to the results of this war as a providential settlement of the great slavery question, either in its establishment or its demolition. I think the northern states will yet be scourged, for unnecessary cruelties & oppression to the Southern people. There is a great grief in the South & great exultation in the north to night.

April 12—Rain! wind! thunder! What a storm last night! The fences are washed away again & the streams are all flooded, the 3rd time in a few weeks. Cousin Rose says the Heavens are weeping over Lee's surrender! . . .

May 28—We had a good love feast. At 3 I baptized 17 negroes & administered the Lords supper to a large crowd. I have not seen so many negroes together for a long time. White federal soldiers sat promiscuously among them & seemed to feel on terms of equality. A small company of colored troops are recruiting and taking in some.

A negro boy of James M. Graham, struck his master with an axe on Thursday or Friday, & came into town & enlisted in the negro company. The sheriff demanded him for civil law, & the Lieut. declined to give him up, without orders from higher Military officers. Quite a sensation exists in the community. A small negro boy in uniform on the street cursed and abused the whole town & the white people generally. A spirit of revenge is gaining ground.

May 29—Mr Graham is dead, & the people begin to clamor for the blood of the negro who murdered him. Threats are rife on the street, & it is said that an anonymous letter persuaded the Lieut. that he had authority to deliver the culprit to the sheriff, so he gave him up & the citizens guarded him to the dungeon, while the negro troops beat a speedy departure from the town. I was glad to see them leaving.

June 1— . . . To day our Gov. calls upon the people to fast & pray for the pardon of our sins, which he says "have culminated in the assassination of Abraham Lincoln." It is right to observe days of humiliation & prayer. We have greatly sinned before God & ought to be sorry, but I do not think the assassination of Mr Lincoln a national sin. I think the nation at large was opposed to such a procedure. Our nation has sinned in elevating wicked men to office, North & South. . . . Many of our statesmen are corrupt, God-defying sinners, & I fear that many of those who call the people to pray for pardon are themselves blasphemous, and drunkards.

June 6—The people are rather desponding, and altho the rebellion is crushed, we apprehend much trouble from our government officials about their negro policy. They either know nothing of negro character, or care nothing for the welfare of both white & black in the south. Genl Palmer who has charge of this department ignores the laws & constitution of our state & rules with military power. Even the ballot box is indirectly threatened, unless the state will vote with the radical part. . . .

July 5—Excessively hot—almost made myself sick putting up a horse rake for father. As I was working my tobacco a voice called out—"Do you want help?" Hanson who was with me cried out Uncle George! Uncle George! and there sure enough was George Warfield come at last! Then came Helen—running & jumping—& then came Lizzie—in full speed & we had a most joyful meeting. Dear boy—almost four years in the war—wounded & starved, worn out & often ragged, yet coming home pure & faithful & sound in mind & morals! Thank God. And dear Frank too—brave & daring, honorable & true—in many battles & skirmishes, long marches—& dangerous raids, long confinement in different prisons—often poorly clothed & barely fed at all—has come back looking well & cheerful—hailed with joy & love by father, mother, brothers & sisters—kindred & friends. Oh how we have all prayed to God for their preservation & how thankful we ought to be for their safe return! . . .

July 20— . . . There is some sensation in regard to Genl Palmers being interrupted by a negro woman in his radical speech. Dr Keene first & then Dr Evans was arrested, charged with inciting her to offer the indignity to the Military ruler of Ky, but when it was shown that the negro was crazy, they were released, and apologies made. Genl Palmer ought not to object to negro equality. . . .

On Monday 7th of Aug—the election was held in Ky. There was great excitement—illegal oaths—arrest & military interference, all failed to make Ky vote for the constitutional amendment [Thirteenth Amendment ending slavery rejected by a two-to-one margin]. . . .

December 4—A much desired rain! Our poor cross, hired *Mary* has been in an ill humor for two or three days & to day is in bed. Several remarks lead to the belief that she is much more contrary than sick. Poor Negroes! I pity them in the delusion & ruin the yankee has forced upon them. If changing the status of the race be God's will I say Amen—but to my eyes certain ruin awaits the race under the new programme. Many of them remain with their masters. Many return & beg to be taken back as they were before—but the majority are restless—indolent, discontented, seeking constant changes—& not knowing what to do with their freedom. It is to be hoped that the experience of years will improve their condition. It is estimated that 1,000,000 have perished since the war—25 pr ct!

January 1, 1866—. . . On Christmas morning as usual, the children were up early shouting "Christmas Gift" and eagerly examining the stockings full of candies, cakes, nuts, toys &c. that Good Santaclaus had provided.

Through the week there was quiet. The negroes were running about from house to house trying to make bargains for the years work.

A great many, both men & women applied to me. Our *Abram* vowed that he would not leave me—but his poor worthless wife is a great trouble to him. The young people have been having parties & Christmas trees—& there is altogether more cheer & hope than most people anticipated. Robert & Hanson are in ecstacies over a new knife & a new gun and feel great that they have each shot a bird—& Robert is proud to have killed a squirrel in the top of a tall tree—& when I shot two fine wild ducks at a long range—they thought the gun was grand.

Abram & *Mary* have gone—and we had a houseful of company Sunday unexpectedly. I have hired a man (Uncle Bells *Henry*) & his wife (*Kate Sydnor*) on reasonable terms & they move in to day. I hauled up their furniture Saturday. I pay *Henry* 150. & feed the family & clothe *Kate*—they pay their own doctor. Negro men are hiring 120. to 175. in different neighborhoods & women without children at 5. to 7. pr month—while women with two or three children work for food & raiment. Most of them in this neighborhood are hiring to their former owners, but many do not feel free unless they change homes. Many are roving about troubled to find employment and many others do not wish to work . . .

February 7—James had trouble with an insolent contraband & I went with him to see the boys Father, *Henry Bailey*, who directed James to correct him. George Duerson was present. . . .

February 13—Heard that the old negro *Henry Bailey* had been informed that he could make James pay for whipping his son and intended to arraign him & me before the Freedmens Bureau. I was on my way to pay him for the months work his boy had done—though not worth much, for he is very trifling, but when I heard that he had threatened me with the Bureau I declined to see him for the present . . .

February 14—I went to town on business. I saw the agent of the Bureau who assured me that a case as *Henry Baileys* could not result in any damage to the parties accused because he had consented to the whipping of his boy. . . .

May 1—. . . Yesterday morning we finished planting corn, have now planted forty acres. The pastures now are green, the woods are full of verdure & flowers, the corn is coming up beautifully & the oats are promising. Fruit trees are loaded with abundant crops & we have every indication of plenty in our land. Peace seems coming on. The president has declared the war at an end & a general amnesty is expected. President Johnson is gaining favor rapidly with conservative men, while the radicals & disorganizers are deserting him. He has vetoed two egregiously unconstitutional bills, the Freedmens bureau & the Civil Rights. The latter congress passed over his head by expelling a member & taking advantage of the illness of two others (Senators) in order to get the necessary majorities. Rebels who hated Andy Johnson with a perfect hatred now endorse & support him. . . .

David Harris

As the war came to an end, David Harris, a Confederate veteran, was apprehensive about the future. The new economic situation seemed too severe: There was little food to eat— "a little corn & a little meat." He feared that this situation would soon lead some people to violence and thievery. At the same time, Harris knew that slavery would soon end and that he would have to tell his slaves that they were free. How, then, would he get reliable workers in the future? He was also angry about the continuing occupation by Union troops— "We are conquered & the feet of the conquars/sic/ are on our necks." The future, indeed, looked very bleak.

May 27 *[1865].* It is almost frightful to look at the effects of the late storm. The boards are split & some of them knocked off the houses. The trees are almost denuded of their leaves & little branches. Some of the young trees are badly injured. I am pastureing the mules on the rye and will soon put them in the wheatfeild. No fruit nor cake for us this year. This is sad disappointment to us, in this, our day of need. Nothing in the world to eat, but a little corn & a little meat, only half rations at that. "Misfortune never come alone" & Famine follows war. I have read of the time that Tried mens souls, I think that this is the time that tries mens souls, pockets and his bowels at the same time. The Lord only knows what is to be of the fate of our unlucky country. I much fear that the worst is yet to come. Raids, mobs, & thefts is the order of the day. It seems that our unfortunate country is drifting to ruin as fast as the Tide of Destruction can carry it. Our currancy has entirely failed. No one will take a "Confederate dollar" for anything (An hundred dollars would not buy a good drink). We have no other money, consequently the prices have suddenly fallen flat. All trading is done by bartering. For everything that is sold, provision is demanded & no one have provision to give. All is at a stand still & wondering what will be done next. All anxious to see, yet all fearing to know. . . .

June 5. . . . [Major General Quincy Adams] Gillmore (A Yankey) has issued a proclimation freeing all the negroes. I do not think it will have much effect. . . .

However, the next day, Harris reported the loss of one of his slaves:

York disappeared on yesterday morning. I suppose that he has gone to the yankey. I wish they would give him a good whipping & hasten him back. This is the begining of negro trouble. I think they are making trouble for themselves."

———————

A week later, on June 14, Harris was still concerned:

There is much talk about the negroes being free. Some have gone to the yankeys. I have heard mine say nothing on the subject. They are at work as usual (except York, who has been gone some time). I expect there will be some confusion about freeing the negroes, but I do not anticipate much trouble. It is about as cheap to hire help as to work your own negroes.

July 24. . . . There is much talk about freeing the negroes. Some are said already to have freed them. There is much apprehension of confusion & distress arising from the emancipation of the negroes. Provisions are still scarce, & the negroes are now stealing, & it is feard they will steal every thing they can lay their hands on. It is said that many have already been killed in this State & it is thought that it is only the begining

July 25. Still warm & dry. Went to the Factory for the wool. Brought home 90 lbs & left a bag-full uncarded. Heard that Mr J Bomar Senior was freeing some of his negroes. . . .

August 14. Went to the village & found the citizens in a gloomy frame of mind on account of ugly state of affairs in the political wourld. Indeed it is a most gloomy time. We are conqucred & the feet of the conquars[*sic*] are on our necks. We must submit to all they require & have no redress. Alas! A decree has gone forth from the Yankeys, that we must say to our negroes that they are free. If they stay with us, we are to pay them, & not drive them off nor correct them. The negroes seem to receive a higher place in the yankey opinion than the white people. Negroes are permitted to do & say what they please & the white man has but little favours shown them.

August 15. To day I told my negroes they were all free & requested all to go. . . .

September 4. Went to the village, it being Sale-day and election-day for the Convention. There was some dozen or 15 yankeys at the village, regulating matters between the negroes & the whites, & administering the oath of allegeance to the United States. I did not take the oath & will not until circomstances compel me. . . .

September 16. Gwinn & I went to the village in haste & came home in haste without any reason for so doing. Yesterday the free negroes had a picnic at the village & seem to be enjoying their freedom to the utmost. The most of them are not disposed to work & the white men seem to be disposed to let them do just as they please & dare not to open their mouths to oppose them. I have much work that I need done but find it a hard matter to hire. . . .

September 23. . . . The negroes had a jubilce yesterday at the village. The yankees and the negroes going hand in hand. They hoisted the United States flags. The Yankey yoke is in our teeth. . . .

October 22. Saturday. This, as usual has been a very busy day. All hands has been "rushin" to make up the negroes cane. Their crops are small, but it is a little fortune to them. The weather is still fine. We have had but one rain in a long time. So far it has been a remarkable fall for gathering in our years work. The most of my land is rented to white men, & I am trying to make arangement for the next year. I am afraid to risk the negro the first year of his freedom. I think they had better tast their freedom awhile & then they may be more reasonable. My Buffalo-crop is still to gather. We are prepairing to have a big corn-shucking as soon as I can get my crop togather. . . .

November 24. . . . In this district several negroes have been badly whipped & several have been hung by some unknown persons. This has a tendency to keep them in their proper bounds & make them more humble. . . .

December 19. . . . As my negro[es] will all be free after Christmas, if they leave me (as I suppose they will) I will not have so many to feed. I do wish the negroes would all go to the Yankeys & stay with them until they all got their satisfaction. Between the negro & yankey, we are certainly in an humble and awkward situation, & what makes it much worse, there is no hope of a situation that will be more pleasant. The yankey Congress has refused to admit our members to a seat with them & so we are to have no representation at all. . . .

December 25. . . . The negroes leave to day to hunt themselves a new home while we will be left to wait upon ourselves. It may be a hardship; but I hardly think it will. I do think that we can do without them as well as we have with them. . . .

January 1 [1866]. This is the [first] time I have made this date & made a mistake at the first effort. Yesterday I went to the village, and from the village to fathers plantation to try to make some arangement with some negroes to work the land that I had rented to Mr Brewten who had rented this, but at a late date concluded that he had rather not take it. Now I am put to much trouble to find some suitable person to work it. While at the village, I saw many negroes enjoying their freedom by walking about the streets & looking much out of sorts. The negroes all desire to farm & to work by the job, but none seem disposed to be hirelings, or to work by the day. Poor things. They are more to be pitied than blamed. They are like a bird out of the cage & no [know] not what to do. Ask who you may, "What are you going to do?" & their universal answer is "I dont know." To day was Sales day. The streets was filled with negroes, mud & water. The roads was about as muddy & wet as they could well be. I was both amused & vexed to day while talking with the negroes. They are all afraid of perishing but do not like the idea of loosing their freedom by hireing. . . .

January 6. . . . My negroes have all left me but Elifus. He has concluded to live with me this year on the Camp Place & work for me until the crops are made & take one third of what he makes. This thing of trading with free negroes is very annoying. They do not know how to arange for themselves & do not like to trust the white people. They are in a destitu[t]e situation & do not know what to do. . . .

February 4. . . . I am not well pleased with the way our free negroes are putting in their time, but do not know how to help it. These are surely times of trouble. The yankeys are occasionly killing some Southern man, & we must put up with it, whether we like it or not. . . .

June 9. . . . I have had much trouble hiring free negroes. They are not disposed to work for fair wages but soon get tired and want to try some other place. This morning I told Wilson that I could not feed his horse any longer. Corn is so scarce that it can not be had for two dollars in gold. I told him that his horse must die and our crop must be lost rather than give him any more corn from my crib. . . .

June 16. . . . The weather is still warm and we have good seasons just when we want them. Our crops are very promising at this time and if they so continue, we will all have plenty to live upon for the next two years. With our present prospects, if it was not for our yankey masters, with their odious laws and the taxes which they impose, we would be a prosperous people once again. There is no improvement in our political status. The Northers Congress have all law making in there own hands & the more they oppress us the better they seem to like it. . . .

July 6. My Birth-Day. To day I am 45 years old and not much better than I was just 45 years ago. I have journalized on my birth-day for many years, & hope that I will be permitted to do so for many years to come, but such luck is granted to but few. The last five years of my life has been an eventful one. In that time I have witnessed many an exciting scene and spent many a troublesome hour at home & abroad in peace & in war. I once thought that when the war was over & I was safe at home again, that I would be Oh so well satisfied, but I find that there is as but little hope for happiness now as there was before. The Political World is in a terible ugly situation, & no one can tell the consequences. It seems as if we are to be totaly ruin[ed] in money matters as well as in everything else. . . .

Frances Butler Leigh

During the war, Frances Butler Leigh and her father lived in Philadelphia. Pierce Butler was arrested on suspicion of gunrunning early in the war but was soon released. For the remainder of the war father and daughter were sympathetic to the Confederacy. In the spring of 1866 they returned to take possession of several Georgia plantations. The changes were beyond anything that they had imagined. Preoccupied with the severe economic conditions, they faced the problem of getting the former slaves to work the land. Arrangements were made to pay the freedmen for their work. The first chapter in Frances's book is aptly entitled "Chaos."

The year after the war between the North and the South, I went to the South with my father to look after our property in Georgia and see what could be done with it.

The whole country had of course undergone a complete revolution. The changes that a four years' war must bring about in any country would alone have been enough to give a different aspect to everything; but at the South, besides the changes brought about by the war, our slaves had been freed; the white population was conquered, ruined, and disheartened, unable for the moment to see anything but ruin before as well as behind, too wedded to the fancied prosperity of the old system to believe in any possible success under the new. And even had the people desired to begin at once to rebuild their fortunes, it would have been in most cases impossible, for in many families the young men had perished in the war, and the old men, if not too old for the labour and effort it required to set the machinery of peace going again, were beggared, and had not even money enough to buy food for themselves and their families, let alone their negroes, to whom they now had to pay wages as well as feed them.

Besides this, the South was still treated as a conquered country. The white people were disfranchised, the local government in the hands of either military men or Northern adventurers, the latter of whom, with no desire to promote either the good of the country or people, but only to advance their own private ends, encouraged the negroes in all their foolish and extravagant ideas of freedom, set them against their old masters, filled their minds with false hopes, and pandered to their worst passions, in order to secure for themselves some political office which they hoped to obtain through the negro vote. . . .

———

As Frances and her father traveled south and talked with friends, she sensed a profound sadness. So much had changed. The old way of life was gone. Still, there was gratitude that father and daughter had returned to Georgia.

I can hardly give a true idea of how crushed and sad the people are. You hear no bitterness towards the North; they are too sad to be bitter; their grief is overwhelming. Nothing can make any difference to them now; the women live in the past, and the men only in the daily present, trying, in a listless sort of way, to repair their ruined fortunes. They are like so many foreigners, whose only interest in the country is their own individual business. Politics are never mentioned, and they know and care less about what is going on in Washington than in London. They received us with open arms, my room was filled with flowers, and crowds of people called upon me every day, and overwhelmed me with thanks for what I did for their soldiers during the war, which really did amount to but very little. I say this, and the answer invariably is, 'Oh yes, but your heart was with us,' which it certainly was. . . .

———

It had been six years since the Butlers had seen their former residence, a splendid house worthy of a wealthy family, with more than four hundred slaves. Now it was barely a shell of its former self.

I wish I could give you any idea of the house. The floors were bare, of course, many of the panes were out of the windows, and the plaster in many places was off the walls, while one table and two old chairs constituted the furniture. It was pretty desolate, and my father looked at me in some anxiety to see how it would affect me, and seemed greatly relieved when I burst out laughing. My bed was soon unpacked and made, my tub filled, my basin and pitcher mounted on a barrel, and I settled for the rest of the night.

The next morning I and my little German maid, who fortunately takes everything very cheerily, went to work, and together we made things quite comfortable; unpacked our tables and chairs, put up some curtains (made out of some white muslin I had brought down for petticoats) edged with pink calico, covered the tables with two bright-coloured covers I found in the trunk of house linen, had the windows mended, hung up my picture of General Lee (which had been sent to me the day before I left Philadelphia) over the mantelpiece, and put my writing things and nick-nacks on the table, so that when my father and Mr. J—— came in they looked round in perfect astonishment, and quite rewarded me by their praise. . . .

The response of the freedmen, when they returned, was heartwarming to Frances and her father. Many had come great distances to be back on the old plantation. They had been waiting for their old master.

The negroes seem perfectly happy at getting back to the old place and having us there, and I have been deeply touched by many instances of devotion on their part. On Sunday morning, after their church, having nothing to do, they all came to see me, and I must have shaken hands with nearly four hundred. They were full of their troubles and sufferings up the country during the war, and the invariable winding up was, 'Tank the Lord, missus, we's back, and sees you and massa again.' I said to about twenty strong men, 'Well, you know you are free and your own masters now,' when they broke out with 'No, missus, we belong to you; we be yours as long as we lib.'

Nearly all who have lived through the terrible suffering of these past four years have come back, as well as many of those who were sold seven years ago. Their good character was so well known throughout the State that people were very anxious to hire them and induce them to remain in the 'up country,' and told them all sorts of stories to keep them, among others that my father was dead, but all in vain. One old man said, 'If massa be dead den, I'll go back to the old place and mourn for him.' So they not only refused good wages, but in many cases spent all they had to get back, a fact that speaks louder than words as to their feeling for their old master and former treatment. . . .

Despite the freedmen's affection for their former owners, it was difficult to reestablish the old patterns of work. The blacks professed their desire for work, but it was slow in coming.

And, of course, contracts—year-long legally binding labor agreements—had to be drawn up.

     M y father was quite encouraged at first, the people seemed so willing to work and said so much about their intention of doing so; but not many days after they started he came in quite disheartened, saying that half the hands had left the fields at one o'clock and the rest by three o'clock, and this just at our busiest time. Half a day's work will keep them from starving, but won't raise a crop. Our contract with them is for half the crop; that is, one half to be divided among them, according to each man's rate of work, we letting them have in the meantime necessary food, clothing, and money for their present wants (as they have not a penny) which is to be deducted from whatever is due to them at the end of the year.

    This we found the best arrangement to make with them, for if we paid them wages, the first five dollars they made would have seemed like so large a sum to them, that they would have imagined their fortunes made and refused to work any more. But even this arrangement had its objections, for they told us, when they missed working two or three days a week, that they were losers by it as well as ourselves, half the crop being theirs. But they could not see that this sort of work would not raise any crop at all, and that such should be the result was quite beyond their comprehension. They were quite convinced that if six days' work would raise a whole crop, three days' work would raise half a one, with which they as partners were satisfied, and so it seemed as if we should have to be too. . . .

In May 1866, as the weather became hot and uncomfortable, Frances and her father moved to one of their plantations on St. Simon's, a sea island fifteen miles away. The freedmen were happy to see the old master, quickly agreed to conditions, and went back to work. However, the local Freedmen's Bureau officer was unhappy with the arrangement and tried to stop it.

     T hey still showed that they had confidence in my father, for when a miserable creature, an agent of the Freedmen's Bureau, who was our ruler then, and regulated all our contracts with our negroes, told them that they would be fools to believe that my father would really let them have all the crops they had planted before he came, and they would see that he would claim at least half, they replied, 'No, sir, our master is a just man; he has never lied to us, and we believe him.' Rather taken aback by this, he turned to an old driver who was the principal person present, and said, 'Why, Bram, how can you care so much for your master—he sold you a few years ago?' 'Yes, sir,' replied the old man, 'he sold me and I was very unhappy, but he came to me and said, "Bram, I am in great trouble; I have no money and I have to sell some of the people, but I know where you are all going to, and will buy you back again as soon as I can." And, sir, he told me, Juba, my old wife, must go with me, for though she was not strong, and the gentleman who bought me would not buy her, master said he could not let man and wife be separated; and so, sir, I said, "Master, if you will keep me I will work for you as long as I live, but if you in trouble and it help you to sell me, sell me, master, I am willing." And now that we free, I come back to my old home and my old master, and stay here till I die.'" This story the agent told a Northern friend of ours in utter astonishment. . . .

———————————

It was now clear to many southern whites that their cherished way of life was forever gone. What would take its place was still a mystery. How long it would take to bind up the wounds from the war no one knew. It would depend to a large degree upon the response of the North to the new situation. Those Northerners traveling to the South or living in the South would have an important role in determining what that response would be.

CHAPTER 2

THE SOUTH AS SEEN BY WHITE NORTHERNERS: JOURNALISTS, FREEDMEN'S BUREAU OFFICERS, AND A CARPETBAGGER

"The whole body politic was as wax.
It needed but a firm hand to apply the seal."

—WHITELAW REID

Whitelaw Reid

In the fifteen years after the Civil War, more than two hundred writers traveled to the South. Some were foreigners, but the bulk of them were Americans. Their focus was upon the major issues of the time—particularly the physical condition of the South, the loyalty of ex-Confederates, and the treatment of the freed slaves.

Three journalists who went south in 1865 and 1866—Whitelaw Reid (three times), Sidney Andrews (one time), and John Trowbridge (one time)—published books of special interest. Their books have been accepted as among the best accounts of conditions after the war. Each will be discussed at some length in this section.

Whitelaw Reid, a correspondent for several Ohio newspapers during the war and one of the first three newspapermen to enter Richmond, took three tours of the South in the first year after the war. His first tour in May and June 1865 was in the company of Chief Justice Salmon Chase and numerous dignitaries in a ship provided by President Johnson's orders and with a special pass signed by Johnson. His second tour was in the fall of 1865, and his third began in January 1866 and ended in May of that year.

His first impressions were formed in North Carolina, where the bitterness of southern women toward Yankees and the problems faced by the newly freed slaves soon became apparent. When Reid reached Mobile, he found that former Rebel soldiers had fully accepted their defeat but were uncertain about their property rights and their position under the law. He believed that the South was waiting for the settlement terms but that time was running out.

At a dinner party at General Hawley's, and subsequently at a little party, later in the evening, we saw and heard a good deal of the feelings of the people. The women are very polite to Yankee officers in particular, but very bitter against Yankees in general. Negro troops are their especial detestation; and for the monstrosity of attempting to teach negroes to read and write, they could find no words to express their scorn. A young officer told me that he had been "cut" by some ladies, with whom he had previously been on very cordial terms, because they had seen him going into one of the negro schools! The men of North Carolina may be "subjugated," but who shall subjugate the women? . . .

Negroes are already beginning to congregate here from the surrounding country. They do not wish to trust their old masters on the plantations; and, without any definite purpose or plan, they have a blind, but touching instinct, that wherever the flag is floating it is a good place for friendless negroes to go. Others are hunting up children or wives, from whom they have long been separated. Quite a number have been located on plantations, and these are working better than could be expected; but the uncertainty of their tenure of the land, the constant return of the old proprietors, and the general confusion and uncertainty as to the ownership of real estate, under the confiscation and abandoned-property laws, combine to unsettle both them and the Superintendents of Freedmen, who are trying to care for them. . . .

The Wilmington negroes have no faith in the ready assent to the proposition that slavery is dead, which all the old slaveholders give. They say—and the negro refugees, all, and some of the whites bear them out in it—that in the country slavery still practically exists. The masters tell them that slavery is to be restored as soon as the army is removed; that the Government is already mustering the army out of service; that next year, when the State is re-organized, the State authorities will control slavery. Meantime, the negroes are worked as hard as ever—in some cases a little harder—and they have no more protection from the cruelty of the whites than ever.*

*Numerous instances were told, while I was at Wilmington, but the following case, related by Colonel Boynton, occurred farther in the interior:

"Here in Salisbury, two prominent men are on trial by a military court, for killing a negro, and one of the wealthiest, most refined and respectable young ladies in all this section, is under twenty thousand dollars bonds to appear and answer for shooting a negro woman with her own hands. Miss Temple Neeley is considered one of the belles of the State. The family is very wealthy, aristocratic, and all that, and stands at the very top in this section. Her mother was flogging a little negro child, when the mother of the child interfered to protect it. Miss Neeley stepped up, and, drawing a revolver from her pocket, shot the negro woman dead, firing a second ball into the body. She was arrested, and will be tried by a military court. The papers here are defending her, and trying to stir up the old feeling toward the slaves, and excusing her under the black laws of the State." . . .

Continuing his trip south, Reid found white Southerners in Savannah, Georgia, to be proud and sullen.

To the Northern reader, Savannah, Charleston, Wilmington, Richmond, have always seemed important names; and while never unconscious that none of them were New York, or Boston, or even Baltimore, yet he has nearly always associated with them the idea of large population, fine architecture and general metropolitan appearance. Nothing better illustrates the pretentious policy of this latitude, which has been always successful in being accepted at its own valuation. Savannah, for example, which is a scattered, tolerably well-built town of twenty thousand inhabitants, about the size of Oswego or Utica, in New York, or Dayton or Columbus, in Ohio, has aspired to be the "metropolis of the South Atlantic coast;" and by dint of their perpetual boasts, Georgians had actually succeeded in making us all regard it very nearly as we do Cincinnati, or Chicago, or St. Louis. A Savannah shopkeeper was indignant, beyond description, at a careless remark of mine. I had asked the population of the place, and, on being told, had answered wonderingly, "Why, that isn't more than a thousand ahead of Lynn, the little town in Massachusetts, where they make shoes and send Henry Wilson to the United States Senate." The shopkeeper swept off the counter the articles he had been showing me, and, with an air of disdain, said he would like to count profits on goods by the arithmetic Yankees used in estimating the population of their nasty little manufacturing holes.

But the people in general were exceedingly polite, though one could now and then detect the sullen air which showed how hard it was to bear the presence of the Yankees. It was evident that they felt conquered, and stood in silent and submissive apprehension, awaiting whatever course the victors might see fit to pursue, and ready to acquiesce, with such grace as they might, in whatever policy the Government should adopt. Surely, now is the golden opportunity for a statesman to shape and mold these Southern institutions as he will. Shall it not be improved? . . .

When Reid reached Mobile in early June, Rebel soldiers could be seen everywhere. They clustered on the corners or mingled about the bars and hotels.

. . . They still wore their uniforms, for the best of reasons—they had no other clothes to wear; but nothing could have been more unexceptionable than their general conduct. "I tell you, sir," exclaimed one of our Generals, in a burst of enthusiasm, "I tell you, they are behaving splendidly. In fact, sir, these Rebel soldiers are an honor to the American name."

"You've whipped us," said one of their officers, with whom I had been carrying on a desultory conversation, "and you did the work thoroughly. I think too much of the bravery of our army and of my own honor to admit that we would have surrendered if we had *not* been thoroughly whipped. Of course, then, we've had enough of it. If we hadn't, we'd have fought on. As we had, we mean to d——-n politics, try and get some clothes, and go to making money."

Nearly all the old inhabitants of Mobile were in the city when it fell, and very few had yet procured the means, even if they had the desire, to leave. Stores that had been closed for months, or even years, were being reopened, in the hope that the antiquated stocks of goods might bring in some trifle in a currency no longer worthless, to supply the wants of the family. A large furniture store was pointed out, where the owner had sold enough to supply himself with the immediate necessaries of life, and had then closed again, declaring that he wouldn't sell another article till fall. His explanation gives a curious glimpse into the condition of the people. Everybody, he said, wanted to buy, and nobody had any money. When they began to sell their lands or their cotton, and get money, he was ready to resume business; but till then, it would ruin him to have his store open. If he refused credit, he would make all his old customers enemies; if he gave credit, he would soon be bankrupt. To save himself from destruction, there was absolutely no way but to bolt his doors and put up his window-shutters! . . .

―――――――

At the end of his two-month trip to the South, Reid saw an opportunity for a successful Reconstruction disappearing. He blamed President Johnson's proclamation on May 23 for changing the expectations of Southerners who were becoming less willing to cooperate and resisting northern efforts.

The months of May and June were the chaotic period of the returning Rebel States. All men were overwhelmed and prostrated under the sudden stroke of a calamity which the fewest number had anticipated. Many had believed the war hopeless, but nearly all had thought their armies strong enough, and their statesmen skillful enough, to extort from the North terms that would soften away, if not conceal, the rugged features of utter defeat. They expected the necessity of a return to the Union, but they hoped to march back with flying colors, with concessions granted and inducements offered that would give them the semblance of a victory. Studious encouragement had been given from the Rebel Capital to such hopes; and outside of Virginia there were scarcely a dozen men in a State who comprehended the straits to which the Confederacy was reduced in the winter of 1864–65, or were prepared for the instantaneous collapse of the spring.

The first feelings were those of baffled rage. Men who had fought four years for an idea, smarted with actual anguish under the stroke which showed their utter failure. Then followed a sense of bewilderment and helplessness. Where they were, what rights they had left, what position they occupied before the law, what claim they had to their property, what hope they had for an improvement of their condition in the future—all these were subjects of complete uncertainty.

Here was the opportunity for a statesman to grasp. I speak advisedly, and after a careful review of our whole experiences through the months of May and June, in all the leading centers of Southern influence, when I say that the National Government could at that time have prescribed no conditions for the return of the Rebel States which they would not have promptly accepted. They expected nothing; were prepared for the worst; would have been thankful for anything.

In North and South Carolina, Georgia, and Florida, we found this state of feeling universally prevalent. The people wanted civil government and a settlement. They asked no terms, made no conditions. They were defeated and helpless—they submitted. Would the victors be pleased to tell them what was to be done? Point out any way for a return to an established order of things, and they would walk in it. They made no hypocritical professions of new-born Unionism. They had honestly believed in the right of secession. The hatred of Yankees, which had originally aided the conspirators in starting the movement, had grown and strengthened with the war. Neither the constitutional theory nor the personal hate of their lives could be changed in a day, but both were alike impotent; and having been forced to abandon the war, they longed for the blessings which any peace on any terms might be expected to bring in its train. With unchanged faith in the constitutionality of their secession, they were ready to abandon or ignore it, at the requirement of the victors. Fully believing the debts of their Rebel Government legal and just, they were prepared to repudiate them at a hint from Washington. Filled with the hatred to the negroes, nearly always inspired in any ruling class by the loss of accustomed power over inferiors, they nevertheless yielded to the Freedmen's Bureau, and acquiesced in the necessity for according civil rights to their slaves. They were stung by the disgrace of being guarded by negro soldiers; but they made no complaints, for they felt that they had forfeited their right of complaint. They were shocked at the suggestion of negro suffrage; but if the Government required it, they were ready to submit.

The whole body politic was as wax. It needed but a firm hand to apply the seal. Whatever device were chosen, the community would at once be molded to its impress. But if the plastic moment were suffered to pass—!

So we found public feeling everywhere along the Atlantic coast. So, by the common testimony of all, it was found throughout the limits of the rebellion, down to the period when the terms of the President's North Carolina proclamation came to be generally understood. On the Gulf we caught the first responsive notes given to that proclamation by the revived Southern temper. By the time we reached New Orleans the change was complete; the reaction had set in. Men now began to talk of their rights, and to argue constitutional points; as if traitors had rights, or treason were entitled to constitutional protection. They had discovered that, having laid down their arms, they were no longer Rebels, and could no longer be punished; as the thief who is forced to abandon his booty is longer a thief, and may laugh at penitentiaries. As Mr. Randall Hunt dextrously put it, "We withdrew our Representatives from Congress, and tried to go out of the Union. You went to war to keep us in. You have conquered; we submit, and send back our Representatives. What more do you want?" The President had lustily proclaimed treason a crime, but the Southern people took his actions in preference to his words, and were confirmed in their own view that it was but a difference of opinion on a constitutional point, in which, under the circumstances, they were ready to yield.

Not less marked was the reaction on all points connected with the negro. He was saucy and rude; disposed to acts of violence; likely, by his stupid presumptions, to provoke a war of races, which could only end in his extermination. In all this the Freedmen's Bureau encouraged him, and thus became solely a fomenter of mischief. The presence of negro troops tended to demoralize the whole negro population. Negro evidence would make courts of justice a mockery. As to negro suffrage, none but the black-hearted Abolitionists who had brought on this war, and were now doing their best to provoke a second, would dream of seriously asking the South to submit to so revolting a humiliation.

The mistake of the last four or five years had been the one against which Henry A. Wise had warned them in the beginning. They ought to have fought for their rights within the Union. That they must do now.

Sidney Andrews

Sidney Andrews spent three months — September, October, and November of 1865 — in North Carolina, South Carolina, and Georgia as a correspondent of the Boston Daily Advertiser *and* Chicago Tribune. *He traveled by sea, railroad, and stagecoach. Though his major concern was the political situation and the possibility of early readmission to the Union, Andrews noted the great destruction of the land, the problems faced by blacks and whites in working together, and the continuing bitterness of many Southerners. His dispatches regularly appeared during the fall of 1865.*

Charleston,
Sept. 9, 1865.

A city of ruins, of desolation, of vacant houses, of widowed women, of rotting wharves, of deserted warehouses, of weed-wild gardens, of miles of grass-grown streets, of acres of pitiful and voiceful barrenness — that is Charleston, wherein rebellion loftily reared its head five years ago, on whose beautiful promenade the fairest of cultured women gathered with passionate hearts to applaud the assault of ten thousand upon the little garrison of Fort Sumter!

"The mills of the gods grind slow, but they grind exceeding small." Be sure Charleston knows what these words mean. Be sure the pride of the eyes of these men and women has been laid low. Be sure they have eaten wormwood, and their souls have worn sackcloth. "God's ways seem dark, but soon or late they touch the shining hills of day." Henceforth let us rest content in this faith; for here is enough of woe and want and ruin and ravage to satisfy the most insatiate heart—enough of sore humiliation and bitter overthrow to appease the desire of the most vengeful spirit. . . .

———————

In the same dispatch, Andrews referred to several conversations concerning the situation since the war.

I took a long walk yesterday with a former Charlestonian—a man who left here in the first year of the war, and returned soon after our occupation of the city. "You Northern people," said he, "are making a great mistake in your treatment of the South. We are thoroughly whipped; we give up slavery forever, and now we want you to quit reproaching us; let us back into the Union, and then come down here and help us build up the country and make the South what God intended she should be." . . .

On the surface, Charleston is quiet and loyal, and I do not doubt that the more intelligent citizens are wholly sincere in their expressions of a desire for peace and reunion. The city has been humbled as no other city has been; and I can't see how any man, after spending a few days here, can desire that it shall be further humiliated merely for revenge. Whether it has been humiliated enough for health is another thing. Said one of the Charlestonians on the boat, "You won't see the real sentiment of our people, for we are under military rule; we are whipped, and we are going to make the best of things; but we hate Massachusetts as much as we ever did." This idea of making the best of things is one I have heard from scores of persons. I find very few who hesitate to frankly own that the South has been beaten—"We made the best fight we could, but you were too strong for us, and now we are only anxious to get back into the old Union and live as happily as we can," said a large cotton factor. I find very few who make any special profession of Unionism, but they are almost unanimous in declaring that they have no desire but to live as good and quiet citizens under the laws.

For the first two months of our occupancy of the city scarcely a white woman but those of the poorer classes was seen on the street, and very few were even seen at the windows and doors of the residences. That order of things is now, happily, changed. There doesn't yet appear to be as much freedom of appearance as would be natural, but very many of what are called the "first ladies" are to be seen shopping in the morning and promenading in the evening. They, much more than the men, have contemptuous motions for the negro soldiers; and scorn for Northern men is sometimes apparent in the swing of their skirts when passing on the sidewalk. One doesn't observe so much pleasantness and cheerfulness as would be agreeable, but the general demeanor is quite consonant with the general mourning costume. A stroller at sunset sees not a few pale and pensive-faced young women of exquisite beauty; and a rambler of the evening not infrequently hears a strain of touching melody from the darkened parlor of some roomy old mansion, with now and then one of the ringing, passionate airs with which the Southern heart has been fired during the war. Mothers yet teach their children hate of the North, I judge, for when I asked a bright-eyed girl of half a dozen years, with whom I walked on a back street for a block or two, whose girl she was, she promptly answered, "A rebel mother's girl," and the phrase "nasty Yankee boy" seems to be the strongest taunt among some of the street children. Patience, good people who love liberty, patience—this petty woman's spite will bite itself to death in time. . . .

────────────

In a later dispatch from Orangeburg, Andrews observed the situation with respect to the Negro:

Orangeburg C.H., S.C.,
Sept. 12, 1865 . . .

Coming up in the cars from Charleston I had for seat-mate part of the way one of the delegates to the convention which meets at Columbus tomorrow. He was a very courteous and agreeable gentleman, past middle age, and late the owner of twenty-two negroes. He was good enough to interest me at some length in respect to the character of the negro. "You Northern people are utterly mistaken in supposing any thing can be done with these negroes in a free condition. They can't be governed except with the whip. Now on my plantation there wasn't much whipping, say once a fortnight, but the negroes knew they would be whipped if they didn't behave themselves, and the fear of the lash kept them in good order." He went on to explain what a good home his negroes always had—laying stress on the fact that they never had to care for themselves, but were always tenderly cared for both in health and sickness, "and yet these niggers all left me on the day after the Federals got into Charleston!" I asked where they now are, and he replied that he hadn't seen anybody but his old cook since they ran away, but he believed they were all at work except two who had died. Yet I am told constantly that these ungrateful wretches, the negroes, cannot possibly live as free people. . . .

I scarcely talk with any white man about the negroes, who fails to tell me how anxious many of them are to return to their old houses. In this ride from Charleston I heard of not less than eleven in this condition, and mention has been made to me here in Orangeburg of at least a score. The first curious circumstance is, that some of them are allowed to return; and the account is, that I can't find any of those desirous of returning. I presume I have asked over a hundred negroes here and in Charleston if they wanted to go back and live with their old masters as slaves, or if they knew any negro who did desire to return to that condition, and I have yet to find the first one who hesitates an instant in answering "No." I spoke of this difficulty I have in finding a single negro who loved slavery better than he does freedom to an intelligent gentleman whom I met here last evening, a member of the Rhett family. "I am surprised to hear that," said he, "but I suppose it's because you are from the

North, and the negro don't dare to tell you his real feeling." Riding with an ex-confederate Major, we stopped at a home for water. The owner of the property, which was a very handsome one, was absent, and it was in charge of a dozen negroes, former slaves of the proprietor. "Now here," said the late officer, "here is a place where the negroes always had the pleasantest sort of a home—every thing to eat, and drink, and wear, and a most kind master and mistress." Pompey, aged about twelve, came to bring us the water. "Pompey," said the Major, "Pompey, how do you like your freedom?" He hung his head and answered, "Dun know, massa." "O, well, speak right out, don't be afraid; tell us just how it is, now," said he again. Whereupon Pompey: "Likes to be free man, sah, but we's all workin' on yer like we did afore." "That's right, Pompey," said I, "keep on working; don't be a lazy boy." "It won't do," said the Major, "he'll grow up idle, and impudent, and worthless, like all the rest." "No, sah," answered Pompey, "I'se free nigger now, and I'se goin' to work."

═══════

The next month in North Carolina, Andrews was bothered by the consumption of tobacco, which seemed to him to be a distinctive mark of the state's "civilization":

Wilmington,
October 14, 1865. . . .

The amount of tobacco consumed by the people is beyond all calculation. I hardly exaggerate in saying that at least seven tenths of all persons above the age of twelve years use it in some form. Nearly every man and boy smokes or chews, and very many of them do both, while the country women chew and smoke to some extent, and women of all classes "dip." When I saw old Solon Shingle come into the witness box to tell the story about his famous "bar'l o' apple sass" I thought the manner in which he disposed of his quid of tobacco the nastiest piece of business I should ever see. I was mistaken. To see a man take it from his mouth and put it in his hat when he goes to breakfast is by no means uncommon. I have even seen men lay it under the edge of their plate at dinner; and one of the leading delegates in the convention held an immense quid between the thumb and finger of the hand with which he abundantly gesticulated during a ten-minutes speech! Could nastiness go further? And do not these things mark the civilization of a people? In South Carolina, though seeing all classes, I did not once observe a white woman "dipping" snuff; but in this State I have seen scores—I should scarcely exaggerate if I said hundreds. I saw them in Charlotte, the first town at which I stopped, within an hour after my arrival; and have seen them in every place I have visited since—"dipping" in the porches of their own houses, on the streets, and, twice, in the public parlors of hotels. If barbaric life has a filthier and more disgusting custom than this, may I be excused from seeing it. . . .

═══════

In his travels, Andrews observed the low value that Southerners placed on labor. Too often labor was considered to be degrading. This attitude had to be changed.

Greensborough,
Nov. 25, 1865. . . .

If there is one thing more needed in the whole South—in those three States, I mean, which have come under my observation—more needed here than loyalty, it is respect for labor as labor—not merely respect for it as a means of sustaining life; but respect for it as a branch of Divine economy, respect for it as a means of human elevation. And if there is one thing more needful than to teach the man of the South that labor is noble, it is to teach the woman of the South that labor is not degrading. Therefore, as one who would see the problem of man's capacity wrought out in this country to most beautiful results, I welcome the necessity which the course of the negro has forced upon so many women here. Let them work—let them *begin as children and learn to do housework.* It is pitiful that, in this age and in this country, one should find occasion to say what is thus impliedly said; but we shall not see the full fruit of the war till labor is dignified in every town and village of the whole South. . . .

———————————

Andrews spent all of November and the first week in December traveling in Georgia. He had a harrowing experience in Albany, where his life was threatened and he left town to avoid violence. Then he visited Andersonville, with its great military prison; Columbus and the state elections; Atlanta, where the marks of Sherman's army could be clearly seen; Greensboro; and Augusta. The twelve-week trip ended in Savannah, where, in his December 4 dispatch, he summarized his impressions of the last five weeks. Two matters continued to trouble him—shortages of food and the continuing conflict between Negroes and whites.

Savannah,
Dec. 4, 1865. . . .

. . . there is a scarcity of food everywhere—in many whole counties the merest necessaries of life are all any family have or can afford, while among the poorer classes there is great lack of even these. Of course this poverty falls most hardly on the negroes. General Tillson reports something less than twelve hundred pauper blacks in the State, but I know he will find them by the thousand as soon as the cold weather comes if he has agencies in most of the counties. But the suffering will not by any means be confined to the blacks. Hundreds of the "cracker" families will have a hard fight to keep the lean wolf of starvation from the doors of their wretched cabins; and not a few of those who before the war never knew any want, will now know that sharpest of all wants—the want of food. . . .

The complaint that the free negro will not work is even more common than in South Carolina. There I found many persons anxious to argue the point—anxious to show me why he would not work; but here the fact is assumed in a somewhat lofty manner that precludes discussion.

That the negro will not work simply because he is free, is the most insolent of all the humbugs of Southern society. Thus, a Macon gentleman who has a plantation below Albany told me of his experience. He was in the army of Johnston, and came home in the early part of June. He heard that many planters were losing their help, and at once went down to his plantation, called his negroes together, made them a little speech, told them they were free, and could go where they pleased, said he would be glad to have them remain where they were, and would pay them fair wages for fair work. Some conference followed, resulting in arrangements mutually satis-factory. The negroes were faithful to their work all through the season, he has fairly set off to them their share of the crops made, and every thing on his plantation has prospered. . . .

Andrews's last dispatch was sent on December 7, 1865. Because Congress was to meet in Washington, D.C., and the southern states wanted to be readmitted, he did not mince his words:

On Shipboard,
Dec. 7, 1865.

If the representatives elect from the Southern States have been admitted to their seats in Congress, then, indeed, has the South been victorious. . . .
. . . the conclusion of the whole matter is, that a very grave mistake, not to say a criminal blunder, has been committed, if the Southern Representatives have been admitted into Congress. . . .

By the end of his three-month tour Andrews had become disturbed by the lack of freedom and safety in the South. Travelers from the North were in danger if they spoke their minds openly.

Freedom of speech and safety of person are very far from being hon-ored in all sections of these States. I believe they have been won in the cities and large towns, and on the main lines of railway travel; but any Northern man who goes into the country, whether for business or pleasure, whether as a resident or a trav-eler, must walk and talk circumspectly. If he undertakes to maintain radical senti-ments on the negro question, his friends will probably find him dead some morning—shot from behind, as is the custom of the country. The leading men of each of these States generally invite immigration from the North, and they are honest and sincere in their expression of desire for the influx of new life. They will, I am sure, do all they can to make the States safe and inviting for immigrants. In time even Georgia will be as free as New York; but at present the masses of the people have little disposition of wisdom for Northerners. The ex-rebel soldiers are everywhere the best disposed class of citizens, and if they alone constituted any given State, I should expect peace and order and freedom to freely abound at once. The bad classes are, all the women, most of the preachers, nearly all the young and middle-age men who did not go in the army, and many of the young rebel staff officers and officers who didn't see active service. . . .

Andrews worried that those who opposed the war had little chance of being elected to office.

The . . . fact [that] almost every candidate was defeated who didn't "go with the State" during the war is one of serious import. It indicates just the spirit that leads Wade Hampton [former Confederate general, planter, and political leader], to say to his friends, "It is our duty to sustain the President so long as he manifests a disposition to restore all our rights as a sovereign State." It is the spirit of defiance to the nation—of sullen antagonism to the idea of national unity—of determined opposition to the principle of national sovereignty. So long as it prevails we can hope for no sound peace. It will not again marshal armies in the field—the common people have had enough of war; but it will stimulate sectional bitterness, encourage neighborhood animosities, embroil the desires and longings of the whole people. . . .

There was still a need for the Freedmen's Bureau. The safety of the Negroes and of Northerners required its continuance. Reconstruction would take more time.

For the abolition of the Freedmen's Bureau and the removal of the military the mass of citizens of the three States is very anxious—though protests had been made from some localities against the withdrawal of the troops till after the holidays, and in some quarters of South Carolina there is even a demand that they shall be retained there indefinitely. The truth is, that the whites of the low country of that State are afraid of the negroes—their numbers in many parishes being scarcely one-fourth as great as those of the blacks. But every interest of the negroes requires that the Freedmen's Bureau shall not only not be abolished but be more vigorously administered, and more energetically sustained by the government and the nation, than heretofore; and the safety of the officers and agents of that bureau, no less than the well-being of the negroes, the furtherance of good order everywhere, the protection of Northern immigrants in many sections, and the inculcation of a sound national sentiment among all classes, requires that the States be still kept under military control, and that more attention be paid to the enforcement of discipline among the soldiers.

Possibly we were wrong to hope that one season could sow the grain of reconstruction and gather its gristage of good order and fair respect for human rights. At least this season has not done that. I am sure the nation longs for nothing else as for honest and heroic peace; yet let not the representatives of the nation mistake this longing for weakness of faith or faintness of purpose in respect to the final triumph of justice.

John Trowbridge

John Trowbridge began his four-month trip in the South in August 1865. He was anxious to see the South and the places that he had heard about since 1861. He was especially interested in the battlefields but wanted to see other sights also—the condition of the defeated people, the situation of the freed Negroes, and the temper of the southern mind.

In Charleston, West Virginia, he found an old acquaintance who was pleased to see "a loyal face in that nest of secession":

"They are all Rebels here—all Rebels!" he exclaimed, as he took his cane and walked with me. "They are a pitiably poverty-stricken set; there is no money in the place, and scarcely anything to eat. We have for breakfast salt fish, fried potatoes, and treason. Fried potatoes, treason, and salt fish for dinner. At supper the fare is slightly varied, and we have treason, salt fish, fried potatoes, and a little more treason." . . .

My friend concluded with this figure: "The war feeling here is like a burning bush with a wet blanket wrapped around it. Looked at from the outside, the fire seems quenched. But just peep under the blanket and there it is, all alive, and eating, eating in. The wet blanket is the present government policy; and every act of conciliation shown the Rebels is just letting in so much air to feed the fire."

Passing through Washington, D.C., Trowbridge noticed large numbers of Southerners at his hotel, at the attorney general's office, and at the White House. It was one of the president's reception days. Southerners who wanted to be pardoned were waiting for the president's office to open. They had to take an oath pledging loyalty to the Union and support for emancipation; taking the oath meant restoration of all property rights except slaves. While they waited, Trowbridge was singled out by several of the Southerners:

"You are not a Southern man?" said one of the crowd, singling me out.

"No," said I. "I am a Yankee. What have you done to be pardoned for?"

"I am worth over twenty thousand dollars; that's my difficulty."

"And you aided the Rebellion?"

"Of course"—laughing. "Look here!"—his manner changed, and his bright dark eye looked at me keenly—"what do you Northerners, you Massachusetts men particularly, expect to do now with the niggers?"

"We intend to make useful and industrious citizens of them."

"You can't!" "You never can do that!" "That's an absurdity!" exclaimed three or four voices; and immediately I found myself surrounded by a group eager to discuss that question.

"The nigger, once he's free, won't work!"

"No," said another. "He'll steal, but he won't work."

"I pity the poor niggers, after what you've done for them," said a third. "They can't take care of themselves; they'll starve before they'll work, unless driven to it; and in a little while they'll be exterminated, just like the Indians."

"I don't think so," I said. "The Negro is very much like the rest of us in many respects. He won't work unless he is obliged to. Neither will you. So don't blame him. But when he finds work a necessity, that will drive him to it more surely than any master."

"You Northerners know nothing of the Negro; you should see him on our plantations!" . . .

Of these men, one was from Georgia, one from North Carolina, and others from Florida and Virginia, yet they all concurred in the opinion, which no argument could shake, that the freedmen would die, but not work. . . .

———————

In Spotsylvania, Virginia, Trowbridge found a Union officer lying on a lounge, sick with fever. Learning that the officer had been in command of the post for some time, Trowbridge asked him why the citizens were so eager to save the government the expense of feeding the poor:

"It is very simple: they wish to get control of the business in order to cut off the Negroes. They had rather have the assistance the government affords withdrawn altogether than that the freedmen should come in for a share. It is their policy to keep the blacks entirely dependent upon their former masters, and consequently as much slaves as before."

"You hear many complaints that the blacks will not work?"

"Yes, and they are true in certain cases: they will not work for such wages as their late owners are willing to give. In other words, they will not work for less than nothing. But when they have encouragement they work very well in their fashion—which is not the Yankee fashion, certainly, but the fashion which slavery bred them up to. The masters have not yet learned how to treat their old servants under new conditions. They cannot learn that they are no longer slaves. That is one great source of trouble. On the other hand, where the freedman receives rational, just and kind treatment, he behaves well and works well, almost without exception."

"What do you think would be the effect if our troops were withdrawn?"

"I hardly know; but I should expect one of two things: either the freedmen would be reduced to a worse condition than before, or that they would rise in insurrection." . . .

On a boat going down the Mississippi River a well-dressed couple came aboard, asking for a stateroom.

. . . Terrible was the captain's wrath. "God damn your soul," he said, "get off this boat!" The gentleman and lady were colored, and they had been guilty of unpardonable impudence in asking for a stateroom.

"Kick the Nigger!" "He ought to have his neck broke!" "He ought to be hung!" said the indignant passengers, by whom the captain's prompt action was strongly commended.

The unwelcome couple went quietly ashore and one of the hands pitched their trunk after them. They were in a dilemma: their clothes were too fine for deck passage, and their skins were too dark for a cabin passage. So they sat down on the shore to wait for the next steamer.

"They won't find a boat that'll take 'em," said the grim captain. "Anyhow, they can't force their damned nigger equality on to me!"

Afterwards I heard the virtuous passengers talking over the affair. "How would you feel," said one with solemn emphasis, "to know that *your wife was sleeping in the next room to a nigger and his wife?*" . . .

In Vicksburg, Trowbridge found evidence of severe hatred of supporters of the Union:

An unrelenting spirit of persecution, shown towards Union men in Mississippi, was fostered by the reconstructed civil courts. Union scouts were prosecuted for arson and stealing. A horse which had been taken by the government, and afterwards condemned and sold, was claimed by the original owner and recovered—the quartermaster's bill of sale, produced in court by the purchaser, being pronounced void. The government had leased to a Northern man an abandoned plantation, with the privilege of cutting wood upon it at forty cents a cord: the Rebel owner returns with his pardon and sues the lessee for alleged damages done to his property by the removal of wood, to the amount of five thousand dollars; a writ of attachment is issued under the local court, and the defendant is compelled to give bond to the amount of ten thousand dollars, or lie in jail. Such cases were occurring every day. . . .

━━━━━━

Several days later, in Natchez, Trowbridge talked to a planter who had educated his slaves and was willing to work with them.

A Louisiana planter from Lake Providence—and a very intelligent and well-bred gentleman—said: "Negroes do best when they have a share of the crop; the idea of working for themselves stimulates them. Planters are afraid to trust them to manage, but it's a great mistake. I know an old Negro who, with three children, made twenty-five bales of cotton this year on abandoned land. Another, with two women and a blind mule made twenty-seven bales . . . I was always in favor of educating and elevating the black race. The laws were against it, but I taught all my slaves to read the Bible. Each race has its peculiarities: the Negro has his, and it remains to be seen what can be done with him. Men talk about his stealing: no doubt he'll steal, but circumstances have cultivated that habit. Some of my neighbors couldn't have a pig but their niggers would steal it. But mine never stole from me because they had enough without stealing. Giving them the elective franchise just now is absurd; but when they are prepared for it, and they will be some day, I shall advocate it." . . .

━━━━━━

Trowbridge was pleased to find thousands of blacks being educated in Macon, Georgia. There, unlike the efforts in Vicksburg, where it was difficult to lease buildings for freedmen schools, numerous schools for blacks of all ages were being used for education.

There were four freedmen's schools in Macon, with eleven teachers and a thousand pupils. There was a night school of two hundred children and adults, where I saw men of my own age learning their letters, and gray-haired old men and women forming, with slowness and difficulty, with the aid of spectacles, the first characters in the writing book. The teachers were furnished by the American Missionary Association—the freedmen paying for their own books and for fuel and lights.

Mr. Eddy, the superintendent and an old experienced teacher, said to me: "The children of these schools have made in a given time more progress in the ordinary branches of education than any white schools I ever taught. The eagerness of the older ones to learn is a continual wonder to me. The men and women say, 'We work all day, but we'll come to you in the evening for learning. We're dull, but we want you to beat it into us!'" . . .

━━━━━━

Trowbridge continued to find examples of freedmen who were being educated despite severe resistance from white Southerners.

I found the freedmen's schools in Georgia supported by the New England Freedmen's Aid Society and the American Missionary Association. These were confined to a few localities—principally the large towns. The opposition to freedmen's schools on the part of the whites was generally bitter; and in several counties schoolhouses had been burned and the teachers driven away on the withdrawal of the troops. Occasionally, however, I would hear an intelligent planter remark: "The South has been guilty of the greatest inconsistency in the world, in sending missionaries to enlighten the heathen and forbidding the education of our own servants."

At Augusta, I visited a number of colored schools, including a private one kept by Mr. Baird, a colored man, in a little room where he had secretly taught thirty pupils during the war. The building, containing a store below and tenements above, was owned and occupied by persons of his own race; the children entered by different doors, the girls with their books strapped under their skirts, the boys with theirs concealed under their coats, all finding their way in due season to the little schoolroom. I was shown the doors and passages by which they used to escape and disperse at the approach of white persons. . . .

It was my original intention to speak of the various schemes of reconstruction claiming the consideration of the country. But they have become too numerous and are generally too well known to be detailed here. The Southern plan is simple: that the states lately so eager to destroy the Union are now entitled to all their former rights and privileges in that Union. Their haste to withdraw their representatives from Congress is more than equaled by their anxiety to get them back in their seats.

They consider it hard that at the end of the bloodiest civil war that ever shook the planet, they cannot quietly slip back in their places and take up once more the scepter of political power.

Often, in conversation with candid Southern men, I was able to convince them it was hardly to be expected that the government, emerging victorious from such a struggle and finding its foot on that scepter, should take it off with alacrity. And they were forced to acknowledge that, had the South proved victorious, its enemies would not have escaped so easily.

This plan does not tolerate the impediment of any Congressional test oath. When I said to my Southern friends that I should be glad to see those representatives who could take the test oath admitted to Congress, this was the usual reply: "We would not vote for such men. We had rather have no representatives at all. We want representatives to *represent* us, and no man *represents* us who can take your test oath. We are Rebels, if you choose to call us so, and only a good Rebel can properly represent us."

This is the strongest argument I have heard against the admission of loyal Southern members to Congress. And if the white masses of the lately rebellious states are alone, and indiscriminately, to be recognized as the people of those states, it is certainly a valid argument.

"It is enough," they maintained, "that a representative in Congress takes the ordinary oath to support the government; *that* is a sufficient test of his loyalty"—forgetting that, at the outbreak of the Rebellion, this proved no test at all.

Such is the Southern plan of reconstruction. Opposed to it is the plan on which I believe a majority of the people of the loyal states are agreed, namely, that certain guarantees of future national tranquillity should be required of those who have caused so great a national convulsion. But as to what those guarantees should be, opinions are divided, and a hundred conflicting measures are proposed.

After four months of travel, Trowbridge reached the conclusion that the South should not be readmitted until " . . . all men are equal before the law."

For my own part, I see but one plain rule by which our troubles can be finally and satisfactorily adjusted; that is, the enactment of simple justice for all men. Anything that falls short of this falls short of the solution of the problem.

The "Civil Rights Bill"—enacted since the greater portion of these pages were written—is a step in the direction in which this country is inevitably moving. The principles of the Declaration of Independence, supposed to be our starting point in history, are in reality the goal towards which we are tending. Far in advance of our actual civilization, the pioneers of the Republic set up those shining pillars. Not until all men are equal before the law, and none is hindered from rising or from sinking by any impediment which does not exist in his own constitution and private circumstances, will that goal be reached.

Soon or late the next step is surely coming. That step is universal suffrage. It may be wise to make some moral or intellectual qualification a test of a man's fitness for the franchise; but anything which does not apply alike to all classes is inconsistent with the spirit of American nationality.

But will the Southern people ever submit to Negro suffrage? They will submit to it quite as willingly as they submitted to Negro emancipation. They fought against that as long as any power of resistance was in them; then they accepted it; they are now becoming reconciled to it; and soon they will rejoice over it. Such is always the history of progressive ideas. The first advance is opposed with all the might of the world until its triumph is achieved; then the world says "Very well," and employs all its arts and energies to defeat the next movement, which triumphs and is finally welcomed in its turn.

But are the emancipated blacks prepared for the franchise? They are, by all moral and intellectual qualifications, as well prepared for it as the mass of poor whites in the South. Although ignorant, they possess, as has been said, a strong instinct which stands them in the place of actual knowledge. That instinct inspires them with loyalty to the government, and it will never permit them to vote so unwisely and mischievously as the white people of the South voted in the days of secession.

Moreover, there are among them men of fine intelligence and leading influence by whom, and not by their old masters, they will be instructed in their duty at the polls. And this fact is most certain—that they are far better prepared to have a hand in making the laws by which they are to be governed than the whites are to make those laws for them.

How this step is now to be brought about is not easy to determine; and it may not be brought about for some time to come. Meanwhile, it is neither wise nor just to allow the representation of the Southern states in Congress to be increased by the emancipation of a race that has no voice in that representation; and some constitutional remedy against this evil is required.

The present high price of cotton, and the extraordinary demand for labor, seem providential circumstances designed to teach both races a great lesson. The freedmen are fast learning the responsibilities of their new situation, and gaining a position from which they cannot easily be displaced. Their eagerness to acquire knowledge is a bright sign of hope for their future. By degrees the dominant class must learn to respect those who, as chattels, could only be despised.

Respect for labor rises with the condition of the laborer. The whites of the South are not by choice ignorant or unjust, but circumstances have made them so. Teach them that the laborer is a man, and that labor is manly—a truth that is now dawning upon them—and the necessity of mediation between the two races will no longer exist.

Then the institutions of the South will spontaneously assimilate to our own. Then we shall have a Union of states not in form only but in spirit also. Then shall we see established the reality of the cause that has cost so many priceless lives and such lavish outpouring of treasure. Then will disloyalty die of inanition, and its deeds live only in legend and in story. Then breaks upon America the morning glory of that future which shall behold it the Home of Man, and the Lawgiver among the nations.

The conclusions reached by the three northern journalists pointed toward a more severe Reconstruction of the South. All were Republicans and were impatient with the pace of present efforts. Sidney Andrews stated clearly the necessary conditions for readmission: ". . . make haste slowly in the work of reconstruction; temper justice with mercy . . . keep military control of these lately rebellious States till they guarantee a republican form of government; scrutinize carefully the personal fitness of the men chosen therefrom as representatives in the Congress of the United States; and sustain therein some agency that shall stand between the whites and the blacks and aid each class in coming to a proper understanding of its privileges and responsibilities."

Marshall Twitchell

Marshall Twitchell, a Union officer during the war, wanted to serve in the Freedmen's Bureau in Louisiana. He had been in Texas since the end of the war and was anxious for a change. The idea of helping in the Reconstruction process appealed to his idealism.

*Believing in the rights of Negroes, he found himself deeply involved in the day-to-day rela-
tionships between the freedmen and their former owners. At the same time he was surrounded by thousands of former Confederate soldiers who had no love for the new
government. It was his duty to enforce the new laws, which dramatically changed the rela-
tionships between blacks and whites in the South. It was a far more challenging duty than
he had ever imagined.*

After a few days, in full uniform I reported to Commissioner Conway.
The careless dress and unmilitary manners at his headquarters gave me my first lesson of the semi-civil duties of my new assignment. It was here that I was introduced
to Edward W. Dewees, a boyish-looking fellow in civilian dress and, it seemed to me,
much too young for a chief of detective police. I little thought of the dangerous and
exciting future which would bind us together like brothers.

I was informed at headquarters that I was to be appointed provost marshal and
agent of the Freedmen's Bureau for the parish of Bienville or Claiborne, that I might
have my choice. I selected Bienville and received my orders, dated October 24, 1865.
I drew a fine black Morgan horse from the quartermaster department and, with an
order on General A. J. Smith for troops, started up the river for Sparta, the parish
seat of Bienville. The boat was a little stern-wheel, so loaded with passengers that
nearly all the men had to sleep on the floor. I was the only one in uniform and consequently came in for a good share of notice. The first annoying speech which I
overheard was at Alexandria. As I passed by some workmen, one spoke, motioning
his head towards me, and said to a comrade, "There goes one of our bosses."

General Smith endorsed my order for the troops and sent me on to
Shreveport. . . .

I went out into the country twice to assist in making contracts between freedmen
and their employers. Once [I visited] upon the plantation of Mr. Howell, whose
brother was afterwards killed at Coushatta. After this last journey I came to the conclusion that the story which the officers had been telling me, "that it was not safe to
go through to Minden without a guard," was partly to keep me there for the purpose
of making their own duty lighter. So one morning I ordered my horse and with a
single orderly set out through the swamp for Minden, which I reached before dark.
I learned there that a few days before, Captain Graff had been sent down from Minden with a detachment to Sparta; consequently, I would have nothing to do but to
go on the next morning and relieve Captain Graff.

I reached Sparta the next afternoon without incident and the next morning received the command, stores, and supplies from Captain Graff, and he at once returned to Minden. I now found myself twenty-five miles from the nearest military
post in command of a detachment of United States Colored Infantry, about twenty
men with horses for only about fifteen.

I was surrounded by a community in which there were at least one thousand disbanded Confederate soldiers, all having no love for the government which had just
vanquished them and of which I was the representative. There was an intense bitterness against the colored soldiers, once their slaves but now, under my direction,

their masters. In case of needing assistance, I was without telegraph, railway, or water connection. The government of the people was entirely with me, with no authority from which to receive instructions nearer than New Orleans, to which place a paper could not go at that time in less than five days. I am free to confess that had I known beforehand what my position was to be, I should have remained with my regiment.

I selected for my office the room in the courthouse which had formerly been used as the jury room. My men quartered in a vacant house about ten rods from there. My first work I thought should be to attend to the occupants of the jail. I found no charges against anyone among the captain's papers and asked the sergeant what that girl whom I had seen there was in jail for. He said he did not know, so I ordered her before me and inquired the reason. She could not tell but said that Mrs. Pearce was mad at her anyway, and she presumed that was the cause for her being arrested.

Mrs. Pearce was the wife of Lieutenant Governor Pearce, the most prominent [man] in town. The governor was absent, and this girl, reported to be his illegitimate daughter, usually received marks of Mrs. Pearce's disapproval of her existence whenever the governor was gone. I walked over to Mrs. Pearce's and as she declined to make any complaint against the girl, I immediately released her, thereby emptying the jail.

———————

One of Twitchell's most important duties was to explain the new employer-employee relationship that had to be accepted by all whites and blacks. Also he ordered that any severe punishment for the former slaves had to be agreed upon by the Freedmen's Bureau.

I then commenced a study of my instructions concerning the parish and people around me. My duty was to inform both black and white of their changed relations from master and slave to employer and employee, giving them the additional information that it was the order of the government that old master and old slave should remain where they had been [and] work as usual in the harvesting of the crop, at which time I would fix the pay of the ex-slave in case he and his former master did not agree about the amount. I expected all to obey and should not hesitate to enforce obedience from both employer and employee. Corporal punishment must not be restored by the planters, but all cases requiring extreme measures must be reported to me for settlement.

I now came to the question as to how this should be made known to the people scattered over the entire country, two-thirds of them unable to read and no paper published through which I could reach the others. While [I was] pondering over this question, the sergeant came in and informed me that a great many men were coming into town from the country and he feared that something was going to happen. Directing my company to stay at their quarters, I hailed the first man I met with the question of what was the occasion of so many being in town? He informed me that the Masonic lodge met there that day. I at once made myself known as a member of that order and secured the services of the Masons—who, then as now, included all the leading elements of society in Bienville Parish—to give notice to all the people that I would be at five different villages in the parish the next week and would there give both black and white their instructions. The notice was faithfully distributed. The gatherings at each place were so great that no attempt was made to get them into any public building, but I spoke to them from the veranda of some house.

The first dispute sufficiently grave to require any investigation was the case of a white man who had struck his old foreman with a stick. I immediately sent a mounted orderly to his plantation with an order for him, the black man, and two colored witnesses to report at my office the next morning; and as the distance was considerable, he [the planter] was directed to furnish the three black men with mules.

The first man I saw in the morning was the plaintiff. In answer to my question of why he walked to town, he said the old master was mad and he was afraid to ask him for a mule. In due time the others arrived and I commenced the proceedings. I found a large audience of spectators curious to see how I was going to manage a case in which all the different powers of legislature and court were combined in one person, who was also the judge.

I ordered the sergeant to take the defendant and witnesses out of the room, then called upon the plaintiff to state his case. After this the defendant was called in for the same purpose, then the first witness. To my relief I found that they all agreed so well that I was having no difficulty in arriving at the facts.

In substance, the planter had three times repeated an order to his foreman in regard to a fence to keep the hogs from the corn. The last time, upon finding the hogs in the field, he had struck him with a stick, but without inflicting any personal injury.

As he was there I thought I would call in the other witness. To my great surprise he made out a case of such bad treatment that I think the plaintiff must have wondered that he was alive. I could see in the audience that there was the most intense interest as to what my decision would be; even the negroes showed much curiosity about the matter. The planters felt that their crops could not be gathered if their hands could obey or not as they might choose.

I told the plaintiff that the defendant had no right to strike him but that he had done him no injury, which was more than I could say of the corn crop which had suffered by his disobedience of orders, and that I would warn him not to again disobey a proper order, and the defendant not to again use a stick; and [I] dismissed the case so far as they were concerned. I then turned to my lying witness and told him that as a slight punishment for the lies he had told me he could walk home and allow the plaintiff to ride his mule. This decision seemed to the people as unique as it was just and gave to all a feeling of relief and confidence. My treatment of the lying negro had so much in it of the comical that it became a standard threat when one was telling a large story for someone to say, "Look out now or you will have to walk home."

For the next three months I was engaged in settling disputes, generally trivial, between the people and explaining to ex-master and slave their respective rights under the new order of things. My disapprobation of lying, as shown in my first case, had in my opinion great effect in lightening my work. It was very rare that I found occasion to go outside of the interested parties to arrive at the facts. In dealing with cases, riding over the parish, and coming in contact with all the different classes of people, it was an exceptional day that I did not find something new or have some of my preconceived ideas swept away. I found the mulattoes did not owe their existence to the white men nearest the social equal of the colored but, on the contrary, to the very highest in social and official life. So far as the forms of religion were concerned, there seemed to be a good percentage of the people Christians.

As I came into dinner one day, I heard my landlady talking in language not very choice to one of the negro girls. We were all seated at the table, and I was wondering how, in her high temper, she was going to ask a blessing, as was her usual custom, when she suddenly dropped her head and said, "Lord bless our food if I be mad," and then continued her scolding. . . .

Twitchell continued to ride around the county. He gained respect for the non-slaveholders, for their honesty, industry, and law-abiding character. They seemed to be free from what he considered "the vice" of slavery.

One day, upon returning from a visit in the country, I found the town in the highest state of excitement. The soldiers were in their quarters with rifles in hand, while many of the citizens were also armed and all parties anxiously waiting for my arrival. I made a rapid investigation and discovered that the cause of the difficulty was in itself so small that it was almost impossible to discover exactly what it was. The people complained only of one man by the name of Harris. The soldiers admitted that insulting language had been used by him, but said that the citizens had threatened to attack all of them. I ordered Harris to remain in his quarters until I had made an examination of the citizens as to what had caused the insulting and threatening language from both parties.

The next morning the sergeant reported to me that Harris had packed his knapsack and said he was going to Shreveport. I had decided in my mind that to send him back to his regiment would be the best thing to do, on account of the ill feeling between him and some of the people, which seemed to be altogether personal. I could not permit the citizens to use threatening language to the soldiers, although they claimed that no threats were made, only against Harris for his insulting language. But Harris could not be allowed to walk off to Shreveport without my order, and I did not believe that he would seriously make the attempt.

Shortly after the sergeant left my room, Mr. Love, a citizen, stepped to my door and informed me that Harris, with his rifle, had left and was going towards Shreveport. I immediately ran out and told him to halt and ordered him back to his quarters. He brought his rifle to the ready, but before he could bring it to his shoulder, he fell from a shot coming from behind me. Love had followed me out, and when Harris brought his rifle to the ready, had fired, as he swore, to save my life, saying that I had no idea of the desperate character of Harris. Love was arrested and taken to Shreveport, examined, and released. I have no doubt but that Love believed that Harris was going to shoot me, but I have always been in doubt whether he [Harris] was preparing to shoot me or whether he had seen Love and was getting ready for him.

The arrest of Love, in connection with bad whisky, had the effect of giving me a little annoyance the next afternoon. A drunken desperado met me on the street and commenced complaining about the presence of negro soldiers, flourishing his revolver until he had exhausted my patience. I told him to put it up and come over to the grocery with me. When I said to the barkeeper, "Here is a customer of yours whom you will certainly lose if he annoys me any more today," I think the deliberate coolness with which I informed them that after that notice I should kill him made even his drunken brain perceive that his provocations must cease.

During my boyhood I had heard and read of the palatial residences with splendid furnishings and luxurious living of the Southern planter, and as I had thus far seen dwellings hardly comfortable, without a carpet on the floor, [the inhabitants] living generally on corn and bacon, I was beginning to entirely disbelieve these early stories. I received a call one day from the son of one of the wealthiest planters, with the request from his father that I come out to his plantation (eighteen miles) and divide the crop. I thought that this would give me an opportunity of witnessing the rich Southern planter in the splendor of his home surroundings. We reached the place just at sundown. It was a large one-story log house with the usual chimneys at each end of the outside and a broad piazza across the entire front, no better than the other planters' houses which I had visited. I at first thought it must belong to the overseer and made up my mind that if I was to be the guest of the overseer instead of the planter, they would learn before I was through with them that I was master, not servant. An old white-haired gentleman met us at the gate and was introduced by his son.

I found the house had but four rooms, all upon the first floor, with nothing overhead nearer than the shingled roof, the chairs all homemade with split bottoms, tableware of the cheapest kind, forks of iron, none of them ever having had more than two tines, and with knives [that] had evidently been in use for many generations, no carpets, nor in fact any evidence of splendor, luxury, or hardly comfort. I never afterwards attempted to find any realization of my boyhood fancies of Southern splendor.

John DeForest

In the fall of 1866, John DeForest was appointed as a Freedmen's Bureau officer in Greenville and Pickens Counties, South Carolina. Unlike Marshall Twitchell, before the war he had lived for several years in the South—South Carolina—where he courted a northern woman who lived in the South, married her, and with her made frequent trips to the

South in the years before the war. In fact, he was on the last steamer to leave Charleston before the fall of Fort Sumter. During his service in South Carolina, his wife remained in New England, where she could watch over the education of their son, Louis Shepard DeForest. Committed to racial equality, DeForest tried to make the Reconstruction measures work in South Carolina. However, neither blacks nor whites easily understood what to do. It was a constant challenge to him. However, he began to enjoy the southern way of life, especially its literary activities.

I had been adjutant-general of the Veteran Reserve Corps, and when that ceased to exist I was placed on duty in the Bureau of Refugees, Freedmen and Abandoned Lands, commonly called the Freedmen's Bureau.

On the 2d of October, 1866, I took charge of the sub-district of Greenville, South Carolina, with the official title of Acting Assistant Commissioner. My satrapy [jurisdiction] consisted of the two counties of Greenville and Pickens, and was subsequently increased by the addition of the county of Anderson, the whole including a surface of some three thousand square miles and a population of perhaps eighty thousand souls. My capital was the little borough of Greenville, situated in the northwestern part of the state, two hundred and seventy miles from Charleston, and within sight of the lower extension of the Alleghenies.

In population and wealth Greenville was then the third town in South Carolina, ranking next after Charleston and Columbia. It boasted an old and a new courthouse, four churches and several chapels, a university (not the largest in the world), a female college (also not unparalleled), two or three blocks of stores, one of the best country hotels then in the South, quite a number of comfortable private residences, fifteen hundred whites and a thousand or so of other colors.

The neighboring scenery is varied and agreeable, and picturesque highlands are not far away. In a latitude of rice and cotton, but with an elevation of one thousand feet above the sea, the climate has a winter which resembles a Northern November, and a summer which is all June.

The officer whom I relieved said to me, with an expression of good-natured envy, "You have the best station in the state."

His eulogium referred more particularly to the inhabitants. He went on at some length to declare that they were orderly, respectful to the national authorities, disposed to treat the Negroes considerately, and, in short, praiseworthily "reconstructed."

"The worst social feature is the poverty," he added. "There are numbers of old Negroes who are living on their bankrupted former masters. There are four hundred soldiers' widows in the district of Greenville, and six hundred in that of Pickens. You can imagine the orphans."

Such was my field of duty. . . .

DeForest found the new labor system to be confusing to both blacks and whites. He tried to explain it to them and then to enforce it. It was not an easy task.

Most of the difficulties between whites and blacks resulted from the inevitable awkwardness of tyros [novices] in the mystery of free labor. Many of the planters seemed to be unable to understand that work could be other than a form of slavery, or that it could be accomplished without some prodigious binding and obligating of the hireling to the employer. Contracts which were brought to me for approval contained all sorts of ludicrous provisions. Negroes must be respectful and polite; if they were not respectful and polite they must pay a fine for each offense; they must admit no one on their premises unless by consent of the landowner; they must have a quiet household and not keep too many dogs; they must not go off the plantation without leave. The idea seemed to be that if the laborer were not bound body and soul he would be of no use. With regard to many freedmen I was obliged to admit that this assumption was only too correct and to sympathize with the desire to limit their noxious liberty, at the same time that I knew such limitation to be impossible. When a darkey frolics all night and thus renders himself worthless for the next day's work; when he takes into his cabin a host of lazy relatives who eat him up, or of thievish ones who steal the neighboring pigs and chickens; when he gets high notions of freedom into his head and feels himself bound to answer his employer's directions with an indifferent whistle, what can the latter do? My advice was to pay weekly wages, if possible, and discharge every man as fast as he got through with his usefulness. But this policy was above the general reach of Southern capital and beyond the usual circle of Southern ideas.

One prevalent fallacy was the supposition that the farmer could, of his own authority, impose fines; in other words, that he could withhold all or a part of the laborer's pay if he left the farm before the expiration of his contract. The statement, "You can not take your man's wages for July because he has refused to work for you during August," was quite incomprehensible from the old-fashioned, patriarchal point of view.

"But what am I to do with this fellow, who has left me right in the hoeing season?" demands a wrathful planter.

"You have no remedy except to sue him for damages resulting from a failure of contract."

"Sue him! He ha'n't got nothing to collect on."

"Then don't sue him."

Exit planter, in helpless astonishment over the mystery of the new system, and half inclined to believe that I have been making game of him. I could, of course, have sent for the delinquent and ordered him to return to his work; but had I once begun to attend personally to such cases I should have had business enough to kill off a regiment of Bureau officers; and, moreover, I never forgot that my main duty should consist in educating the entire population around me to settle their difficulties by the civil law; in other words, I considered myself an instrument of reconstruction.

The majority of the complaints brought before me came from Negroes. As would naturally happen to an ignorant race, they were liable to many impositions, and they saw their grievances with big eyes. There was magnitude, too, in their manner of statement; it was something like an indictment of the voluminous olden time—the rigmarole which charged a pig thief with stealing ten boars, ten sows, ten shoats, etc. With pomp of manner and of words, with a rotundity of voice and superfluity of detail which would have delighted Cicero, a Negro would so glorify his little trouble as to give one the impression that humanity had never before suffered the like. Sometimes I was able to cut short these turgid narratives with a few sharp questions; sometimes I found this impossible and had to let them roll on unchecked, like Mississippis. Of course the complaints were immensely various in nature and importance. They might refer to an alleged attempt at assassination or to the discrepancy of a bushel of pea vines in the division of a crop. They might be against brother freedmen, as well as against former slave owners and "Rebs." More than once have I been umpire in the case of a disputed jackknife or petticoat. Priscilly Jones informed me that her "old man was a-routin' everybody out of the house an' a-breakin' everything"; then Henry Jones bemoaned himself because his wife Priscilly was going to strange places along with Tom Lynch; then Tom Lynch wanted redress and protection because of the disquieting threats of Henry Jones. The next minute Chloe Jackson desired justice on Viney Robinson, who had slapped her face and torn her clothes. Everybody, guilty or innocent, ran with his or her griefs to the Bureau officer; and sometimes the Bureau officer, half distracted, longed to subject them all to some huge punishment. Of the complaints against whites the majority were because of the retention of wages or of alleged unfairness in the division of the crops.

If the case brought before me were of little consequence, I usually persuaded the Negro, if possible, to drop it or to "leave it out" to referees. Without a soldier under my command, and for months together having no garrison within forty miles, I could not execute judgment even if I could see to pronounce it; and, moreover, I had not, speaking with official strictness, any authority to act in matters of property; the provost court having been abolished before I entered upon my jurisdiction. If the complaint were sufficiently serious to demand attention, I had one almost invariable method of procedure: I stated the case in a brief note and addressed it to the magistrate of the "beat" or magisterial precinct in which the Negro resided. Then, charging him to deliver the letter in person and explaining to him what were his actual wrongs and his possibilities of redress, I dismissed him to seek for justice precisely where a white man would have sought it. Civil law was in force by order of the commanding general of the department; and the civil authorities were disposed, as I soon learned, to treat Negroes fairly. Such being the case, all that my clients needed in me was a counselor.

"But the square [squire] won't pay no sawt 'tention to me," a Negro would sometimes declare. To which I would reply: "Then come back and let me know it. If he neglects his duty we will report him and have him removed."

Of the fifty or sixty magistrates in my district I had occasion to indicate but one as being unfit for office by reason of political partialities and prejudices of race. New

York City would be fortunate if it could have justice dealt out to it as honestly and fairly as it was dealt out by the plain, homespun farmers who filled the squire-archates of Greenville, Pickens, and Anderson.

But the Negro often lacked confidence in the squire; perhaps, too, he was aware that his case would not bear investigation; and so, instead of delivering my letter in person, he often sent it by a messenger. As the magistrate could not act without the presence of the complainant, nothing was done. A week or fortnight later the Negro would reappear at my office, affirming that "dese yere Rebs wouldn't do nothin' for black folks no-how."

"What did the squire say?" I would ask.

"Didn' say nothin'. Jes took the ticket an' read it, an' put it in his pocket."

"Did you see him?"

"No. I was feared he wouldn' do nothin'; so I sont it roun' to him."

"Now then, go to him. If you have a story to tell, go and tell it to him, and swear to it. I shall do nothing for you till you have done that."

And so the process of education went on, working its way mainly by dint of general laws, without much regard to special cases. As this is the method of universal Providence and of the War Department, I felt that I could not be far wrong in adopting it. But even this seemingly simple and easy style of performing duty had its perplexities. Magistrates rode from ten to thirty miles to ask me how they should dispose of this, that, and the other complaint which had been turned over to them for adjudication. Their chief difficulty was to know where the military orders ended and where civil law began; and here I was little less puzzled than they, for we were acting under a hodgepodge of authorities which no man could master. I had files of orders for 1865, and 1866, and 1867; files from the Commissioner, and from the Assistant Commissioner, and from the general commanding the department; the whole making a duodecimo volume of several hundred closely printed pages. To learn these by heart and to discover the exact point where they ceased to cover and annul the state code was a task which would have bothered not only a brevet major but a chief justice. My method of interpretation was to limit the military order as much as might be, and so give all possible freedom of action to the magistrate. . . .

―――――――――

DeForest was constantly surprised by the desire of freedmen to go somewhere else. There could be many reasons, but usually it was to find or to visit a family member. Sometimes it was to take a vacation.

For nothing were the Negroes more eager than for transportation. They had a passion, not so much for wandering, as for getting together; and every mother's son among them seemed to be in search of his mother; every mother in search of her children. In their eyes the work of emancipation was incomplete until the families which had been dispersed by slavery were reunited. One woman wanted to rejoin her husband in Memphis, and another to be forwarded to hers at

Baltimore. The Negroes who had been brought to the up-country during the war by white families were crazy to get back to their native flats of ague and country fever. Highland darkeys who had drifted down to the seashore were sending urgent requests to be "fotched home again." One aunty brought me her daughter, who suffered with fits, and begged me to give them "a ticket" to Anderson so that they might consult a certain famous "fit doctor" there resident. Others desired me to find out where their relatives lived, and send for them.

In short, transportation was a nuisance. I believed in it less than I believed in the distribution of rations and in modes of charity generally. It seemed to me that if the Negroes wanted to travel they should not insist on doing it at the expense of the nation, but should earn money and pay their own fare, like white people. I learned to be discouragingly surly with applicants for transportation papers and to give them out as charily as if the cost came from my own pocket. I claim that in so doing I acted the part of a wise and faithful public servant.

From the class properly known as refugees—that is, Unionists who had been driven from their homes during the war by the Rebels—I had no requests for transportation. Not that they were few in number; the mountains near by Greenville were swarming with them; but they had the Anglo-Saxon faculty for getting about the world unassisted. The mean whites, those same "low-down" creatures who bored me to death for corn and clothing, were equally independent of aid in changing their habitations. The "high-toned" families which had fled to the up-country from the cannon of Dupont and Gillmore also made shift to return to their houses in Charleston or their plantations on the sea islands, without any noticeable worrying of government officials. The Negroes alone were ravenous after transportation.

I soon found that many of my would-be tourists were chiefly anxious to enjoy that luxury, so dear to the freedman's heart, "going a-visiting." A woman would obtain transportation of me on the plea that she wanted to rejoin a child in Charleston whom she had not seen for ten years and who was suffering for her care; then, having enjoyed a sufficient amount of family gossip in the city, she would apply to the Bureau officer there to save her from starvation by returning her to Greenville. I became wickedly clever in fathoming this deceit and used to ask in a friendly way, "When do you want to come back?"

"Well, Mars'r, I doesn't want to stop mo'n a fo'tnight," would perhaps be the answer.

"Ah! if that is all," I would lecture, "you had better wait till you want to stay for good, or till you have money enough to pay for your own pleasure excursions."

It was necessary, I thought, to convince the Negroes of the fact that the object of the government was not to do them favors, but justice; and of the still greater fact that there is very little to get in this world without work.

Planters who were about to remove to more fertile regions sometimes asked transportation for their Negroes, on the ground that these latter would be benefited by the change of locality and that it could not be effected without government assistance. Of course this seemed rational; and I understood that aid of this sort was freely rendered by some Bureau officers; but I rejected all such applications. Grant one, grant a thousand; and the government would be bankrupt. At last a general order from the Commissioner sanctioned transportation for this purpose; but the planter's application must be approved by the Assistant Commissioner of the state where he resided and by the Assistant Commissioner of the state to which he proposed to emigrate; he must give satisfactory security that he would feed and pay his hands; he must then get the approval of the Commissioner. What with postal and official delays these preliminaries generally consumed at least a month; and as the planting season pressed, this complicated circumlocution was usually abandoned before it was completed, the applicant either giving up his migration or conducting it at his own expense. Whether the result were intended or not, it was a good one. In so vast and fertile a region as the South the industry which can not succeed alone rarely deserves success. Charity is either an absolute necessity or an absolute evil.

Although I received no precise instructions as to visiting the various portions of my district, it was probably presumed by my superiors that I would make occasional tours of inspection, and so attend to local disorders on the spot where they occurred. I did not do this; I made but a single journey of above fifteen miles; I did not absent myself more than a single night from my station, except once when summoned to Charleston. My satrapy, it must be remembered, contained two state districts or counties, and eventually three, with a population of about eighty thousand souls and an area at least two thirds as large as the state of Connecticut. Consider the absurdity of expecting one man to patrol three thousand square miles and make personal visitations to thirty thousand Negroes.

Then I had no assistant to attend to the complainants who constantly presented themselves at my office. They averaged five a day, or a total of something like two thousand during my fifteen months of duty. Moreover, they came from distances of five, ten, twenty, and even thirty miles. I planted myself firmly in Greenville and let my world come to me. Toward the end of my term of service an order was promulgated to the effect that Bureau officers should thereafter "travel more" and that they should regularly visit the important points of their districts, giving previous notice of their tours to the inhabitants. Knowing what labor this signified and how impossible it would be to perform it in any satisfactory manner, I welcomed the decree from the headquarters of the army which mustered all volunteer officers out of the service, and declined an appointment as civilian agent of the Bureau. How far and with what good result my successors performed their tourist labors I should be glad to know. . . .

After a few months DeForest began to enjoy his work. It was not demanding and provided him with chances to observe the southern way of life. Sometimes it even involved literary activities, a special favorite of his.

Thus far I have sketched my duties; I must now describe my pleasures. At two o'clock, after from three to five hours of labor or lounging, I closed my office and rarely had positive need to open it again during the day. Having breakfasted at eight on beefsteak, bacon, eggs, and hominy, I now fortified myself with a still more substantial dinner and looked forward to a sufficiently solid tea. The manner in which my host of the Mansion House kept up his hotel and supplied a praiseworthy table on a clientage of five permanent boarders and from five to ten weekly transients was to me one of the greatest financial phenomena of the age. The same amount of "faculty" exerted in New York City during the last seven or eight years would have made Mr. Swandale a Croesus. In a region of miserable hotels, where the publican seems to consider it a part of his contract to furnish his board-crs with dyspepsias, I considered myself amazingly lucky in finding such fare as honored the Mansion House.

It was a large building and had been a flourishing stand of business in the prosperous old times of Greenville, when the merchants of Charleston and the planters of the low country came up every summer to breathe the wholesome air and enjoy the varied scenery of this mountain district. There had been a great ballroom—later an apothecary's shop—and in it there had been gayeties of proud ladies and "high-toned gentlemen"—later paupers. Occasionally a representative of this impoverished gentility, a transitory Rutledge, Pinckney, Grimke, Hayward, or Ravenel, passed a night under the roof, finding cause, doubtless, for sad meditations in the contrast of the present with the past. The Trenholms, a comparatively parvenu race, but famous since the days of secession, were there repeatedly, on their way to and from their country seats in western North Carolina.

Laying down the huge and sorrowful volume of the past, I emerge from the Mansion House and proceed upon my constitutional. There were some sights worthy of a glance, and perhaps of a smile, in the eight or ten brief streets of the village. There were the two or three leisurely gentlemen who "did the heavy standing round," one in front of his favorite grocery and another at his pet corner. There were those wonderful acrobats, the cows, who climbed into market wagons after ears of corn and bunches of fodder. There were occasional soldiers—staggering, noisy, quarrelsome, and slovenly, if they had been lately paid off; otherwise, quiet even to demureness, buttoned from waist to chin, and brushed as clean as dandies. Women of the low-down breed, in the coarsest and dirtiest of homespun clothing, and smoking pipes with reed stems and clay bowls straddled by with so mannish a gait that one doubted whether they could be hipped after the feminine model. The young ladies of the respectable class were remarkably tall, fully and finely formed, with good complexions, and of a high average in regard to beauty. The men were of corresponding stature, but in general disproportionately slender, and haggard from overuse of tobacco. At least half of the villagers and nearly all of the country people wore gray or butternut homespun; even Governor Perry, the great man of the place, had his homespun suit and occasionally attended court in it.

The Negroes are not so numerous as the whites, but there is a wonderful number of variously colored youngsters about, generally in an uproarious excitement of playing or fighting. These youth are getting to be nuisances, and I am on the look-out for the first punishable malefaction among them, meaning to call on the Council to fine and imprison the noisiest. Twice, late at night, I have been so infuriated by their persistent screaming and swearing that I have opened my window and ordered them to go home and, on receiving a hoot of defiance, have sallied out, cane in hand, only to find the street solemnly quiet. Many of them are children without parents, who have run away from farm labor to enjoy the festivities of the village, and are living Heaven alone knows how and growing up to be merely vicious and indolent.

One urchin of eight or ten presents a fearful example of what may come from overmuch happiness. He has his hat half full of brown sugar and is eating it with an ecstatic rolling of the eyes; discovering some boys at the next corner, he is taken with the idea of joining them and claps his hat upon his head; then, seized with dismay, he snatches it off and exhibits an embarrassing topknot of commingled wool and sugar. Whether the Negro will not use his newly won social and political blessings with some equally discomforting result is a grave question.

The country around Greenville is hilly, sufficiently wooded, and affords a number of pleasant walks. I established three or four rounds for myself, going out on one road and returning by another, the trips varying from three to eight miles. I walked alone; no young man would like to be seen much in my company; the Southerner so forgetting himself would not be smiled upon by woman. I do not think that the hatred of Northerners was seriously bitter; but it was a fashion set by the aristocracy, and Mrs. Grundy [one marked by prudish conventionality] is everywhere potent. However, I could not personally complain of inhospitality on the part of the elder and solider citizens. Yankee, military officer, and Bureau agent as I am, I was invited to breakfasts, dinners, teas, and picnics. It is my belief that, if I had set my heart upon it, I could have made a footing in Greenville society. I did not, because my chief did not want his officers on familiar terms with the citizens, and because I dreaded to be hampered by the hospitality of men against whom I might be called upon to urge complaints.

A certain judicious and popular post commandant once said to General Robinson, temporarily in charge of the department, that he should consider it a favor to be allowed to remain at his present station, adding that he could easily have the request supported by a petition of citizens.

"By Jove!" answered the general, "you bring me such a paper, and I'll order you off immediately. I don't think, by Jove! that it looks well for an officer to be such a favorite with people whom it is his business to govern. It may be all right, but it doesn't look well."

One of the hospitalities offered to me was so great a temptation that I could not decline it. There was a literary club in Greenville; it had weekly essays and discussions and provided the public with lectures; it had a reading room also and a list of some thirty American and English periodicals. To this library I was made welcome and allowed to draw as a member. It must be noted that a Southern village differs from a Northern one of the same magnitude in possessing a larger class of leisurely people; and consequently, notwithstanding its mania for politics and cotton, Southern society has a considerable element which is bookish, if not literary. Besides this set, Greenville had the professors of a university and of a female college, so that it was able to claim rank as the Athens of the up-country, thereby exciting much envy and bitterness among less pretentious communities.

There were other amusements in Greenville. There were concerts of native talent, in which I noted two unusually fine singers of operatic music, one of them a pretty girl of barely fourteen. There were two circus visitations, various afflictions of Negro minstrelsy, a series of grievances from a vagrant dramatic company, a wizard, and a magic lantern. The Baptist church, a most aggressive and money-getting institution, had two admirably managed fairs and a succession of ice-cream entertainments, for the purpose, as I was given to understand, of paying off a mortgage on its steeple. At one of these fairs there was exhibited a fabulous beast called the Gyascutus, who howled and shook his chains to the great terror of an audience of freedmen, but also with much pecuniary benefit to the cause of religion. Whether he was one of the beasts seen by Daniel I did not learn.

Knowing the general poverty of the citizens, I wondered at this succession of recreations. I thought of the desperate Florentines, in the time of their plague, who put on their best apparel and passed their days in festivity. I am inclined to believe that in eras of supreme misfortune the mass of men are disposed to become wasteful and to seize recklessly upon every chance of enjoyment. The Negroes, who were the poorest class in the community, were the most given to entertainments. It was wonderful to see the great circus tents crowded with this bankrupt population, and especially wonderful to note that fully one half of the spectators were freedmen, all screaming in happiness without a cent in their pockets.

The drollest evening that I passed in Greenville was at a magic-lantern exhibition. The pictures illustrated Bunyan's *Pilgrim's Progress* and were horrible enough to have been designed by Apollyon himself in mockery of that almost sacred narrative. The exhibitors were two "muscular Christians," who had precisely the tone and bearing of professional roughs, and whom I suspected of being Baltimore plug-uglies. The contrast between their blood-tub intonation, as they explained the designs, and the pious gravity of the story which was illustrated kept me in a paroxysm of laughter. The climax was reached when we beheld a blue and white Christian meeting three greenish angels.

"Here you see the three shining ones," expounded the plug who stood beside the curtain. "As Christian goes up the hill with his burden he meets the three shining ones. One of them takes him by the hand and says to him—What the h–ll are you doing?"

This last phrase was a loudly whispered aside, addressed to the operator in rear of the curtain, who at that moment extinguished the lantern, perhaps in lighting a cigar from its hallowed flame.

In the years after the war, Freedmen's Bureau officers were in a very difficult position. As Northerners and former army officers, they were charged with meting out justice in the South at a time when white Southerners questioned their motives and resisted their efforts. It required a Solomon-like wisdom to find solutions that would be acceptable to both sides. Unfortunately, President Johnson's lack of support for the bureau made its work more difficult. Still, many officers hoped that the true story of conditions in the South would be made known to the northern public. They believed that this could lead to a better situation in the South.

Albert Morgan

Albert Morgan and his brother Charles, veterans of the Union army during the war, decided to remain in the South when the war ended. Charles had talked to many planters while he served in the armies of George Thomas and William Sherman. He asked his brother to be a partner in raising cotton in Mississippi. Albert gladly agreed. Both were happy that the war was over and were ready to begin leading a normal life raising cotton. They believed that blacks should have equal rights and were prepared to work with them. Soon the brothers found out that few Southerners agreed with them and that even fewer welcomed their efforts to raise cotton in the South. They were unprepared for the hatred and anger expressed toward them by southern whites. In time this hostility would become a serious problem.

It was early autumn when we landed at Vicksburg, 1865. Nearly every steamer from above brought large quantities of freight and many prospectors like ourselves. The town was astir with young life, and new vigor everywhere manifested itself. New stores and new residences were building, the levees were being repaired, and, though the works of the two armies had been dismantled, they had not yet been leveled down.

The caves in which the citizens had taken refuge during the siege and the point where Pemberton met Grant and arranged the terms of surrender were objects of great interest to all strangers. The hotels were full; they overflowed, and we had been obliged to seek accommodation in a private family, known to our agent to be highly respectable, but so reduced in circumstances by the war that they were willing to accept such means of gaining a livelihood. . . .

We had spent about a month examining such as we could hope, from the description of them in the hands of the agent, might meet our requirements, without success, when one day Mrs ——, the only other guest of our hostess, received a letter from a "dear old friend" of hers, living "up the Yazoo," at Yazoo City, announcing that she had been "utterly ruined by the war"—all her slaves had run off with the first Yankee troops that came into that section. . . .

———————

Albert spent a day examining a nearby plantation and returned to a boardinghouse where he was rooming. Quickly it became an uncomfortable experience.

On returning next day from my visit to the plantation, I observed there were a good many men in and about an old barn-like structure some distance back from the river bank. A shed at the landing, this structure, and my shelter were the only buildings I could see. My landlady told me they were holding "co't" there that day.

She had already spread a table for fifteen or twenty guests, who soon after began to gather around it. I thought they returned my salutations gruffly, and that they appeared curious about me. At each end of the table was a large bottle of whisky, which was offered to me, but I declined, saying I never drank anything.

This resulted in a request, which was more like a demand, for my name. One appeared to be the leader, asked me where I came from, and what my business there was. This I frankly made known to them, and then the "late war" became the only topic of conversation. Finally, the spokesman announced that "no Yankee radical could ever come into that county, make a crop and get away with it," and the crowd joined in abusive personal epithets.

It occurred to me that I ought to get away from them; but how? There was no boat, nor would there be until the following morning, perhaps not then. I resolved to try and shame them. So rising, I said I had indeed been in the Federal army, and had never yet been ashamed of the fact. I was there for the purpose of engaging in a legitimate business enterprise, as I had a right to do, and concluded by saying, that if they really possessed any of that "chivalry" they claimed as peculiar to the Southern character, they would not have treated an utter stranger as they had done me. Then I left the table, and passed into the only other room in the building. A thin board partition divided me from them, and, although their talk was in a much lower key than before, I could hear most of it.

When they had finished their meal, the leader, whom they called Major, came in, apologized to me and quite warmly urged me to "accept the hospitalities of my home, sir, such as it is," etc., assuring me of his "personal protection," and concluded with a hint that he might, after all, determine to lease his own plantation, or, we might find one in his neighborhood that would suit me.

It was "agreed" that he should send his "boy," with the Major's "own saddle horse," for me in the morning, and we separated; he for his home, while I took the steamer, which happened to be on time early next morning, for Vicksburg.

The fact is, after they had all gone I had a brief consultation with my landlady, and concluded that would be the safer course for me. For, while so much of their talk as I had been able to hear was about me, she assured me their plan was to decoy me to the country, where they would be in waiting, and hang me to a tree by the roadside. During the presence of her guests this woman had been in full sympathy with them, so far as I could see. But no sooner were we alone than she manifested great concern for my safety.

I related this experience to different Southern men, whom I saw on my return to Vicksburg, and each one declared they were "some irresponsible, worthless fellows" who had, probably, never been in the Confederate army, and I ought not to heed anything they said or did.

Nevertheless they were in attendance at court, some of them as jurymen. Nearly all wore the Confederate gray, and carried pistols.

Two days afterward Charles returned. He took occasion to see Mrs.——at once, and inform her that he had rented Tokeba for three years, subject to my approval.

She was "perfectly delighted." . . .

Albert's efforts to hire freedmen were not appreciated by southern whites, but he was successful.

I had not been long engaged in the work of hiring the labor for Tokeba before it became evident to me that my manner toward freed people was being unfavorably commented upon by the "best citizens."

Occasionally, some planter in town on similar business as my own, observing me in conversation with a group of freed people, would stop, and, after listening a short while, speak to some one he might know and ask who I was. Upon being informed he would mutter: "I thought so;" then walk on a few steps, halt, turn about, scowl gloomily upon us, and always turn finally to go away, with a nervous jerk of his head or shoulder, or some deprecatory wave of the hand. . . .

Another cause of ill-feeling toward me I discovered to be in the fact that, whereas I was succeeding beyond my expectations in re-stocking Tokeba, many old planters, or their overseers, were not having any success at all, and it was being acknowledged on all sides, what indeed had been feared by the native planters, that the freedmen preferred to hire to the "new-comers," even at less wages than native planters were offering. This fact was made a pretext for unfriendly criticism of the means employed by the new-comers to "entice the nigros from their masters," as it was called.

The fact is, I did not have to use persuasion at all. My chief difficulty was to select from the great number willing to go with me the very best, and, unlike most of the natives, I inquired into the habits of the men and women who offered; whether they were given to drunkenness or other vicious practices, and it was whispered about that I had applied another test, to wit, whether they could read or write! But this rumor, I was satisfied, was started by some wag for a jest. . . .

———————

Northern whites who went South disagreed over the degree to which the South had accepted its defeat and over the possibility of another effort at secession. Clearly there was smoldering resentment and often active resistance to northern efforts to work with blacks, to start schools for them, or to treat blacks as equals. What was less certain, to both Northerners and Southerners, was how the former slaves would act. Would they be willing to work, or would there be disruption and violence? The response of the newly emancipated slaves was still unknown.

CHAPTER 3

THE SOUTH AS SEEN BY BLACK SOUTHERNERS, 1865–1867

"Slavery chain done broke at last."

—NEGRO SPIRITUAL

Peter Randolph

When the war ended, Peter Randolph, a black minister of a Baptist church in New Haven, Connecticut, decided to return to his home state of Virginia. On his journey he stopped in Baltimore, where he found out that Lincoln had been assassinated. Remaining in Baltimore until after the funeral, he hastened to City Point and then to Richmond. There he found a place "suited for the work" of helping the newly freed slaves.

The response of blacks to the changed conditions was much different than that of south- ern whites. As Peter Randolph remembered, "The colored people from all parts of the state were crowding in at the capital, running, leaping, and praising God that freedom had come at last." Many others undoubtedly had similar sentiments. For many freedmen it was a time of hope and optimism, and Randolph was swept along by their enthusiasm.

On my arrival at Richmond [in May 1865], I was met at the Rocketts, by Filds Cook, and carried to the house of Mr. John Adams, who had cognizance of my coming. He was one of the most prominent colored men in the city, having been a freeman before the war, and was in fair circumstances. Being in his hands I was taken good care of, and was able to proceed at once to the needed work. The scene that opened before my eyes as I entered Richmond cannot be accurately described by word or pen. The city was in smoke and ashes, that is, a goodly part of it, for the Confederacy, on taking their departure, fired the city rather than let it fall into the hands of the Union forces.

The colored people from all parts of the state were crowding in at the capital, running, leaping, and praising God that freedom had come at last. It seems to me I can hear their songs now as they ring through the air: "Slavery chain done broke at last; slavery chain done broke at last—I's goin' to praise God till I die."

Many of the old people had prayed and looked forward to this day, but like Moses they were permitted to see it afar off, and not enter it.

The place was literally full of soldiers, "Yanks" and "Rebs."

The armies were breaking up and returning home. Richmond was the great centre for dispersions, all hours, day and night was the marching of regiments, going and coming. The sight of some of these would bring tears to the dryest eyes, as they beheld men wounded, maimed in every possible shape and form that could be mentioned. And many of these, like the poor colored people, were truly glad that the war was over.

The city of Richmond did not have accommodations enough for this great mass of colored people, so many were gathered on the suburbs and taken care of in the best way possible under the circumstances.

One of these principal camps, where the people were huddled in temporary structures, was called Schinnborazzo. Here I spent a part of my first Sunday in Richmond, and preached to a large congregation. Religious services were held in these camps all day, and several other preachers were present and readily lent their service. Among these was Rev. John Jasper, who has distinguished himself since, as the famous "Sun do move preacher." This was the first time I had the pleasure of meeting him. His preaching was much more excitable than mine, and seemed to effect the people in a way that I could not. This scene, and the day's work, was very impressive upon me, and made me feel and sympathize with these folks only as one who had been in slavery, could feel and sympathize.

It had been argued by some that, if the Negroes were set free they would murder and kill the white people. But instead of that, they were praising God and the Yankees for life and liberty. . . .

At the same time Randolph saw mistreatment of the freed slaves by northern soldiers and former owners. This bothered him, and he brought the need for their protection to President Johnson's attention.

. . . I am sorry to say here, that the treatment of some of the soldiers toward the poor colored people was indeed shameful. For the slightest provocation, and sometimes for no cause whatever, the butts of their guns and bayonets were used unmercifully upon them.

The colored people held indignation meetings, resolutions were passed, and a delegation appointed to lay this whole matter before President Johnson. I was the instigator of the meeting being called. And not until these steps were taken did the colored people have rest from the ill-treatment of the soldiers.

This, also, must be said, relative to these soldiers: the most of them who committed these depredations were from the Middle States, and sympathizers with the South. They seemed to be mad because the "negger" was free, and took the authority given them by the wearing of the blue to express it.

The petition of the colored men was noticed by the President, and remedied by General Schofield. In addition to the Provost Marshal's, where soldiers were disciplined, bureaus were established for the freedmen, where they could be heard and assisted. The true condition of the colored people at this time will never be written. When I arrived at Richmond, I had letters of introduction from Governor Andrew to Governor Pierpont, and also to General Schofield. I was appointed by the General to issue tickets or passes, and distribute them to the people, in order that they might get what provisions and clothing there was for them through the agency of the bureau. It was a sight to behold to see these hungry souls crowding in at my office to obtain the slips of paper that was to give them the necessities of life. The Freedman's Bureau also took the place of the Court House, to protect and settle all difficulties that might arise among the people.

In this particular some of the incidents were heartrending, the most severe cases being where the former master and slave were concerned. Some of the masters were very reluctant in giving up their servants, and tried to defraud and rob them out of their freedom, and many of the slaves had to run away from their masters to be free. It is true that the proclamation had been accepted, and Lee had surrendered his sword to Grant, but some of the white people still contended that "these are my neggers."

———————

When the Freedmen's Bureau met, Randolph was occasionally called to help the freedmen. One case especially bothered him.

. . . One sad case I will here mention—a colored girl about eighteen years of age, who was brought before the bureau, with a charge against her former master. She had been shamefully whipped and her back burned with a hot iron. I well recall the words of General Merrett, who was at the time the president of the bureau.

As he beheld the condition of this girl, he exclaimed, "What is this!" The officer who had her in charge said, "It is the devil." An eye-witness who was present photographed the back of this girl, and it can be had if my readers would like to see it. . . . This simply illustrates the condition of things that I speak of, and also the necessity and work of the Freedman's Bureau.

The Freedman's Bureau was only a temporary arrangement intended to help relieve the condition of the ex-slaves. While it had the means to do so it was inestimable to the poor and needy. But soon the sources of supply failed and the important work was abandoned. This made the suffering and needs of the people more intense than ever. Many had to go back to their former masters to work or starve, and many of the whites tried to make the Negroes feel that freedom was worse than slavery.

In slavery times the masters would see to it, that the slaves were fed—that is, with such as they had to give them, but now, they would see them starve. It is not hard to understand this state of affairs, when one thinks of the situation; here the whites were smarting under their defeat, the Negroes, who were their main support, were taken away from them as slaves and goods of chattel, but still remained at their doors. The unvented wrath they had for the Yankees, for meddling with their pet institution, was poured out on the poor Negroes.

John Lynch

Unlike Peter Randolph, who had been free since 1847, John Lynch became a freedman in 1863 when Union troops occupied Natchez, Mississippi. In order to find his mother, from whom he had been separated for over a year, Lynch decided to cross the picket lines and search for her in Natchez. She had been anxiously waiting for his arrival fearing that he was dead or had been carried off by Confederate soldiers. Finding her safe, he began his new life as a free man in a society that was rapidly collapsing around him. Now Lynch's basic concern was to find a job to support his mother and other family members. With the help of northern white schoolteachers he received enough education to get a job in the photography business.

The problem of making a living was the one that was before me. I was without means and without an education. The only capital I possessed was youth, health, and a determination to win the race of life. My mother occupied two small rooms in a frame building in Market Street, which building had been converted into flats. Several other families occupied apartments in the same building. My brother had secured employment at army headquarters, as an attendant upon General W. Q. Gresham, the general in command of the Union troops there at that time. As the result of an effort covering about ten days, I finally succeeded in securing employment as a dining-room waiter in a private boarding house at a monthly salary of five dollars. This was a small salary, but I felt that I had to do something to assist my mother in her efforts to make ends meet. Rent, which was unreasonably high at that time, had to be paid promptly at the end of each month, otherwise we would be without a place to lay our heads. My mother was an excellent cook and in that capacity she frequently earned a good sum of money in the course of a month, but the employment was not continuous and permanent, hence the income from that source was uncertain and doubtful. It was absolutely necessary, therefore, that my brother and I should do something to assist in meeting the expense of the home.

My work at the boarding house was not at all satisfactory to me, hence I decided to remain there but one month; when I was paid off at the end of the first month I received four dollars instead of five, one dollar having been deducted, as I was then informed, because one or two knives and forks had disappeared, for which it was alleged I was responsible. After thinking the matter over I came to the conclusion that I was fortunate in that an amount equal to the whole month's salary had not been thus detained. I next found employment as a cook for a company of the Forty-ninth Illinois Volunteers Regiment of Infantry. No fixed sum as a salary was agreed upon. I remained there until the regiment was ordered away, which covered a period of about six weeks. When the regiment was about to leave and while bidding good-bye to the men for whom I had faithfully worked, I was made the happy recipient of the snug sum of two dollars as compensation in full for the services I had rendered. Of this I did not complain and found no fault, because I felt that I had rendered some service to a few of those who had contributed something to the salvation of the Union and the abolition of slavery.

I next found employment in the same line with a small detachment at army headquarters where I remained about three weeks, at the end of which time I was paid five dollars. Before leaving them I had secured employment as pantryman on the government transport *Altamont,* at a stipulated monthly salary of twenty-five dollars. The *Altamont,* it was thought, would remain in the Natchez harbor until the cessation of hostilities. In point of fact, it remained there until shortly after the assassination of President Lincoln. I shall never forget the distressing scenes that took place on the vessel when the news of that terrible tragedy was received. Our hearts were broken, our heads were bowed in grief, and every eye was moistened with the tear of sadness and sorrow. We all felt that the country's greatest statesman had been stricken down at the hands of a cowardly assassin and that his taking off had produced a grave and perplexing situation, the outcome of which no one could foretell or conjecture. . . .

For a time Lynch was employed as a printer and later in the photography business of which he became the manager. He was becoming successful and respected.

This employment proved to be the opportunity of my life. It marked the beginning of a somewhat eventful career. As soon as I commenced work for Black, I decided to renew my efforts to acquire an education, which had been neglected during the preceding five years. But since I was obliged to be at my place of business every day, it was not possible for me to attend any other than a night school. Such a school was then being conducted by several teachers from the North. I decided to attend this school and was assigned to a class that was in charge of Mr. and Mrs. Charles M. Bingham of New York, both of whom seemed to take an especial interest in me. The school continued for about four months from the time I commenced. At the end of that time I could compose and write a pretty good letter. Composition, grammar, and spelling might have been very imperfect; still it was a letter that could be read and understood. But my occupation happened to be favorable for private study. I had my books at my place of business. It frequently happened that I had time enough to devote two and, some days, as many as three hours to private study during the course of the day. Among the books that I carefully read and studied was one on parliamentary law, which I found to be of great advantage to me in after life. I also kept myself posted on the current events of the day by reading newspapers and magazines. I was especially interested in the proceedings of Congress, for it was just about that time that the bitter fight was going on between Congress and President Johnson.

I also received, in an indirect way, some valuable assistance from the white public school. My place of business was in Main Street. The white public school was across the alley in the rear of this building. I could easily hear the recitations that were going on in the school across the way. I would sometimes sit in the back room for hours and listen with close attention to what was going on in the school across the alley. I could clearly and distinctly hear the questions asked by the teacher and the responses given by the class or individual pupil. In fact, I was sometimes so much absorbed that I would imagine, for the time being, that I was a member of the class and was eager to answer some of the questions. I could also see and read the problems in arithmetic that were on the blackboard that was directly in front of where I was sitting, the knowledge and information thus obtained proved to be of great assistance to me.

Freedmen

As conditions grew worse in the South, many freedmen and freedwomen looked to the North for economic assistance. In Vicksburg, Mississippi, freedmen adopted a resolution to help a freedmen's store that had kept prices down since January 1865.

At a meeting in the presbyterian church April 17, 1865, of the self supporting Freedmen of the Post of vicksburg *[sic]*, the following preamble and resolutions were proposed and unanimously adopted,

> Whereas the military authorities of this Department have kindly established for us a freedmen's store, with a view to better our condition, protect us from extortion, and place the means of subsistance within our reach, and whereas; a subsequent order has been issued, the effect of which is to deprive us, in a great measure, of these benefits, therefore be it

∽   RESOLVED   ∞

> That the Freedmen's store kept by Ellet and Huggins . . . is regarded by us as the most direct, the most feasible, and the most substantial effort that could be made for our relief . . .

That through this instrumentality the prices of all the necessaries of life have been greatly reduced, and a better chance given us to support ourselves by industry and economy. . . .

That we have therefore heard with sorrow and regret that subsequent orders have been issued, requiring us to obtain a permit to purchase at that store before goods can be obtained, thereby imposing such a heavy tax upon our time as to deprive us, in a great measure, of the benefits which we believe were intended to be conferred upon us.

∽ RESOLVED ∾

That this shall be our petition to the military authorities, requesting them to rescind special order No 83, par IV, and allow us to purchase our goods as heretofore, without this great annoyance and inconvenience. . . .

Several months later, on June 15, 1865, a group of Mississippi freedmen and freedwomen who had worked on the Robinson plantation petitioned the supervising agent of the Treasury Department.

Your petitioners would respectfully shew, that they are men of colour of African decent *[sic]*, who have been recognized by their late owners as free, under the proclamation of President Lincoln, and as freed-men are labouring for their own support and benefit, and that of their families; that about the close of the late military campaign in the state of Mississippi, the Rebel Soldiers were permitted to seize, or did, in their own strenght *[sic]*, seize upon, and convey away, what remained in this locality of the Cotton that had been purchased by the Rebel Government of Richmond; that said Cotton from having been exposed for one year without any shelter, had wasted & become rotten & worthless to the extent of 5/6th of its bulk and value, and that out of what was left by said Rebel Soldiers, or not burnt, your petitioners picked by hand, & with arduous labour, separated from the decayed & decaying Cotton, conveyed to the nearest Gin, repacked, rebaled & repressed, to the extent of Twenty six (26) Bales Cotton, which they herewith surrender upon your authority, to Erskine & Co, agents, & James Davis, Govermt aid, to be delivered to you at Memphis

Your petitioners respectfully alledge that they have by their labour saved what would have been entirely lost to the Government, by natural decay & exposure, or otherwise, as can be verified by an inspection of what remains, where this was saved; and they respectfully claim the most liberal compensation allowable under the circumstances, for their own benefit & to discharge obligations to others, (independent of their late owner,) incurred in thus saving, conveying to gin, repacking,

covering & repressing said Cotton. And your petitioners will ever pray &c   Signed
by Jno M. Dingall, in behalf of, & by request of,
[36? signatures]

Conditions for the freedmen after the war were dramatically different. The slavery chain in-
deed had been broken. However, the growing resistance of white Southerners to any
significant change in the status of blacks began to alarm many in the North. Also the efforts
of the Johnson government to admit the former Confederate states to the Union seemed to be
premature. Slowly northern attitudes shifted toward support for more extreme measures to
guarantee the fruits of the war—preservation of the Union and protection of the rights of
blacks in the South.

CHAPTER 4

REACTIONS OF WHITE AND BLACK NORTHERNERS TOWARD THE SOUTH

"They gave us the bullet to save themselves;
they will yet give the ballot to save themselves."

—FREDERICK DOUGLASS

Gideon Welles

Gideon Welles, secretary of the navy and a member of Lincoln's cabinet throughout the war, was called to Lincoln's bedside as the president slowly died. Welles recorded his feelings in his diary.

The President had been carried across the street from the theatre, to the house of a Mr. Peterson. We entered by ascending a flight of steps above the basement and passing through a long hall to the rear, where the President lay extended on a bed, breathing heavily. Several surgeons were present, at least six, I should think more. Among them I was glad to observe Dr. Hall, who, however, soon left. I inquired of Dr. H., as I entered, the true condition of the President. He replied the President was dead to all intents, although he might live three hours or perhaps longer.

The giant sufferer lay extended diagonally across the bed, which was not long enough for him. He had been stripped of his clothes. His large arms, which were occasionally exposed, were of a size which one would scarce have expected from his spare appearance. His slow, full respiration lifted the clothes with each breath that he took. His features were calm and striking. I had never seen them appear to better advantage than for the first hour, perhaps, that I was there. After that, his right eye began to swell and that part of his face became discolored.

Senator Sumner was there, I think, when I entered. If not he came in soon after, as did Speaker Colfax, Mr. Secretary McCulloch, and the other members of the Cabinet, with the exception of Mr. Seward. A double guard was stationed at the door and on the sidewalk, to repress the crowd, which was of course highly excited and anxious. The room was small and overcrowded. The surgeons and members of the Cabinet were as many as should have been in the room, but there were many more, and the hall and other rooms in the front or main house were full. One of these rooms was occupied by Mrs. Lincoln and her attendants, with Miss Harris. Mrs. Dixon and Mrs. Kinney came to her about twelve o'clock. About once an hour Mrs. Lincoln would repair to the bedside of her dying husband and with lamentation and tears remain until overcome by emotion.

[April 15.] A door which opened upon a porch or gallery, and also the windows, were kept open for fresh air. The night was dark, cloudy, and damp, and about six it began to rain. I remained in the room until then without sitting or leaving it, when, there being a vacant chair which some one left at the foot of the bed, I occupied it for nearly two hours, listening to the heavy groans, and witnessing the wasting life of the good and great man who was expiring before me.

About 6 A.M. I experienced a feeling of faintness and for the first time after entering the room, a little past eleven, I left it and the house, and took a short walk in the open air. It was a dark and gloomy morning, and rain set in before I returned to the house, some fifteen minutes [later]. Large groups of people were gathered every few rods, all anxious and solicitous. Some one or more from each group stepped forward as I passed, to inquire into the condition of the President, and to ask if there was no hope. Intense grief was on every countenance when I replied that the President could survive but a short time. The colored people especially—and there were at this time more of them, perhaps, than of whites—were overwhelmed with grief.

Returning to the house, I seated myself in the back parlor, where the Attorney-General and others had been engaged in taking evidence concerning the assassination. . . .

A little before seven, I went into the room where the dying President was rapidly drawing near the closing moments. His wife soon after made her last visit to him. The death-struggle had begun. Robert, his son, stood with several others at the head of the bed. He bore himself well, but on two occasions gave way to overpowering grief and sobbed aloud, turning his head and leaning on the shoulder of Senator Sumner. The respiration of the President became suspended at intervals, and at last entirely ceased at twenty-two minutes past seven.

A prayer followed from Dr. Gurley; and the Cabinet, with the exception of Mr. Seward and Mr. McCulloch, immediately thereafter assembled in the back parlor, from which all other persons were excluded, and there signed a letter which was prepared by Attorney-General Speed to the Vice-President, informing him of the event, and that the government devolved upon him. . . .

[April 19.] The funeral on Wednesday, the 19th, was imposing, sad, and sorrowful. All felt the solemnity, and sorrowed as if they had lost one of their own household.

By voluntary action business was everywhere suspended, and the people crowded the streets. . . .

There were no truer mourners, when all were sad, than the poor colored people who crowded the streets, joined the procession, and exhibited their woe, bewailing the loss of him whom they regarded as a benefactor and father. Women as well as men, with their little children, thronged the streets, sorrow, trouble, and distress depicted on their countenances and in their bearing. . . .

[April 21.] . . . We hurried on, reached the Capitol, and entered the rotunda just as Mr. Gurley was commencing an earnest and impressive prayer. When it was concluded, the remains were removed and taken to the depot, where, in waiting, were a car and train prepared for the commencement of the long and circuitous journey of the illustrious dead to his last earthly resting-place in Springfield, in the great prairies of the West. . . .

———————

In a series of meetings with his cabinet, the new president, Andrew Johnson, began to consider reconstructing the South. Welles's position continued to be consistent support for readmitting the former Confederate states and opposition to the granting of suffrage to the freedmen. Believing that the war was over, he deplored the continuing hatred expressed by the North toward the South. As can be seen by Gideon Welles's account, significant differences were emerging over the treatment of the former Confederates.

*M*ay *[?]* . . . The subject of reestablishing the Federal authority, and of a reorganization of the State governments in the insurrectionary region was discussed. . . .

At the Cabinet-meeting the plan of asserting the Federal authority and of establishing the State government in Virginia was fully considered. . . .

May 9, Tuesday. . . . The condition of North Carolina was taken up, and a general plan of organization intended for all the Rebel States was submitted and debated. No great difference of opinion was expressed except on the matter of suffrage. Stanton, Dennison, and Speed were for negro suffrage; McCulloch, Usher, and myself were opposed. . . .

This question of negro suffrage is beset with difficulties growing out of the conflict through which we have passed and the current of sympathy for the colored race. The demagogues will make use of it, regardless of what is best for the country, and without regard for the organic law, the rights of the State, or the troubles of our government. There is a fanaticism on the subject with some, who persuade themselves that the cause of liberty and the Union is with the negro and not the white man. White men, and especially Southern white men, are tyrants. Senator Sumner is riding this one idea at top speed. There are others, less sincere than Sumner, who are pressing the question for party purposes. On the other hand, there may be unjust prejudices against permitting colored persons to enjoy the elective franchise, under any circumstances; but this is not, and should not be, a Federal question. No one can claim that the blacks, in the Slave States especially, can exercise the elective franchise intelligently. In most of the Free States they are not permitted to vote. Is it politic, and wise, or right even, when trying to restore peace and reconcile differences, to make so radical a change,—provided we have the authority, which I deny,—to elevate the ignorant negro, who has been enslaved mentally as well as physically, to the discharge of the highest duties of citizenship, especially when our Free States will not permit the few free negroes to vote?

====

George Templeton Strong

George Templeton Strong, a successful New York attorney and acute observer of economic and political events, became more and more bitter toward the South. As stories about resistance and violence by white Southerners and the mistreatment of blacks became known, he began to express more radical views—criticism of white Southerners and support for limited black suffrage. The more the South resisted, the more certain many in the North were that a more severe Reconstruction was needed.

June 1, Thursday. Most shops and offices closed, this being the national day of mourning for the President's murder. Attended service in Trinity Church awhile. . . .

Jefferson Davis, "yeoman," as his indictment presumes to style him, is, or soon will be, at Washington awaiting arraignment and trial in due course of law. He is reported to say that "the United States will never hang him," but his past mistakes should make him hesitate about any more predictions. His prophesyings of four years ago have proved disastrous to himself and to all who put faith in him. He told his people that the North would never undertake a war against secession and that France and England would have to become active allies of the South or perish for want of cotton. His people believed this flattering tale and rebelled. Most of them regret it just now!

June 10. . . . The *World* and other papers publish letters from Southern correspondents stating that Southern Niggerdom refuses to work for wages, holding freedom to mean the right to support by government, or by somebody, without labor. I suppose these statements true as to the course adopted and the theory held by some of our Africo-Americans. We cannot wonder that they should take up any delusion whatever, after being studiously and systematically assimilated to brutes by the legislation of their masters, generation after generation, for so many years. There are predictions of a social or servile war, a war of races, but it is unlikely. If the Negroes go to work and earn their living, they will fall naturally into their proper place, and hold it to the great advantage of all parties. If they decline to do so, they will starve and perish and disappear, and emigration will supply the labor needed to develop the wealth of secession soil. . . .

June 20. . . . The political pots of Washington are simmering ominously and are not unlikely to reach boiling heat before long. Advanced Republicans grumble over

President Andrew Johnson's reconstruction policy, and say he is selling his party, after the manner of dirty old Tyler, twenty-five years ago. I do not "see it in that light," and have faith in the President's judgment and honesty. But a split in the party seems certainly coming, and Copperheads [Northern Democrats who opposed the Union's war policy and favored a negotiated peace] chuckle over the prospect, to my serious aggravation. Next winter will probably find Sumner, Wilson & Co., organized as an opposition, and "conservative" Republicans sustaining the Administration, in alliance with Northern "democrats" and malignants and restored penitent Congressmen from the Carolinas, with bowie knives about their persons. Next session of Congress will be an anxious time. "Darkey Suffrage" is a dark and troublesome question, and it must be met. That freedmen, who have as a class always helped the national cause to the utmost of their ability, at risk of their lives, should have political rights at least equal to those of the bitter enemies of the country who are about to resume those rights, sullenly and under protest, only because they are crushed, coerced, and subjugated, is (abstractly considered) in the highest degree just and right. But the average field hand would use political power as intelligently as would the mule he drives. The current phrase that "those who have helped the country with bullets should be permitted to help it with ballots" is mere nonsense. . . . Were I President, I should aim at securing political rights to property-holding Ethiopians and to such as could read and write. . . .

———

By the middle of the summer Strong believed that the South had accepted its defeat and waited uneasily for the terms of readmittance to the Union. Though reports on conditions in the South were mixed, he thought they were encouraging. Southerners had accepted defeat, and radicals did not have enough support for their extreme position.

July 15. . . . The South is quiet and passive. But there are abundant signs that the old plantation spirit ("Plantation Bitters"?) of truculence and lawlessness is not dead but sleeping, or rather shamming dead. It takes more than one licking to cure a bully. The World and the News and their rapidly diminishing train of followers continue wailing over a violated constitution. There has been only outrage after outrage for the last four years, and the series continues. What fools they are! Of course, subordination of government to the Constitution and to law is good— very good—among the very best things. But it's not the only good thing. To save the country is also good. To prevent Jeff Davis from chasing Lincoln out of Washington in 1861 was an object of some public importance. Emergencies are certainly conceivable that justify a little unconstitutionality. Perhaps our recent experiences are of that class. . . . In A.D. 1865, the situation is wholly changed once more. The whole South is in a state of subjugation, indignation, emancipation, ruination, and starvation. It's a chaos of hostile elements mitigated and quieted by bayonets, a collection of acids and bases hardly restrained from fizzing into furious disastrous reaction at any moment. Our constitution-framers never dreamed of this state of affairs and made no provision for it. One would think it most desirable to get the South into good order again without delay. . . .

August 9. . . . Reports from the South continue to be mixed, but on the whole, not discouraging. Newspapers generally say, in substance: "We are thoroughly whipped; only a lunatic would dream of further struggle against government. We cannot be expected to be jolly and jubilant over our defeat and suppression, but we must take things as they come and make the best of them. The best thing for us is to acquiesce in our failure, save what we can out of the general wreck, try to reorganize the ruins of society, and submit in good faith and without reservation to the national rule imposed on us by the chances of war, and get ourselves restored to our normal place in the national system as soon as may be." . . . Of course, there are signs of gall and bitterness, breaking out sometimes into overt acts of ruffianism. But the wonder is they are so few. . . .

September 8. . . . It would not be easy now to draw a line between Democrats and Republicans, Conservatives, and Radicals, unless in regard to Negro suffrage—and that's a question to be left to the Southern States themselves, and not a national issue. Were it national, I think the Radicals, so-called, would be beat on it.

News from the South continues contradictory. The South has made up its mind most fully to submit. The South is hushed in grim repose and only waiting a chance to rebel again. Niggers are generally fairly treated when they engage to work and keep their bargains. Niggers are being flogged, hanged, and shot by their late masters everywhere, no matter how they behave—and so on. Probably there are abundant facts to support each of these statements. But the refusal of the Mississippi Constitutional Convention to repeal the ordinance for the secession of that state, and its adoption (six to one) of a resolution declaring that ordinance null and void *ab initio* [from the beginning] is a controlling and significant fact. If that cut-throat state have undergone so radical a change of heart, we may hope that all the wayward sisterhood will bring forth fruit meet for repentance. No Southern State seemed more irreclaimably given over to a reprobate mind than Mississippi only a year ago, unless possibly South Carolina. And South Carolina is today the worst-whipped state of them all. She lies stunned and passive, without energy enough to get on her legs and try to resume her place in the ranks. . .

Frederick Douglass

As the war ended, Frederick Douglass, now in his forty-eighth year, considered retiring from public life and enjoying a life of leisure. Friends had encouraged him to take a well-earned rest. For a brief time he agreed but soon realized that his voice and pen were needed to lead the newly emancipated slaves. His work would continue for another thirty years until his death in 1895. Through these years his position remained clear—the abolitionists' work was not over until the black man received the ballot. Until that day the South would continue to try to find a way to limit black rights. Thus, a premature return of the South to

political power would be disastrous. On May 10, before the American Anti-Slavery Society,
Douglass argued successfully for its continued activity on behalf of blacks and against the
motion of William Lloyd Garrison to dissolve the society. The motion failed—118–48.

      Slavery is not abolished until the black man has the ballot. While the
Legislatures of the South retain the right to pass laws making any discrimination between black and white, slavery still lives there (applause). As Edmund Quincy once
said, "While the word 'white' is on the statute-book of Massachusetts, Massachusetts
is a slave State. While a black man can be turned out of a car in Massachusetts, Massachusetts is a slave State. While a slave can be taken from old Massachusetts, Massachusetts is a slave State." That is what I heard Edmund Quincy say twenty-three or
twenty-four years ago. I never forget such a thing. Now, while the black man can be
denied a vote, while the Legislatures of the South can take from him the right to
keep and bear arms, as they can—they would not allow a negro to walk with a cane
where I came from, they would not allow five of them to assemble together—the
work of the Abolitionists is not finished. Notwithstanding the provision in the Constitution of the United States that the right to keep and bear arms shall not be
abridged, the black man has never had the right either to keep or bear arms; and
the Legislatures of the States will still have the power to forbid it, under this Amendment. They can carry on a system of unfriendly legislation, and will they not do it?
Have they not got the prejudice there to do it with? Think you, that because they are
for the moment in the talons and the beak of our glorious eagle, instead of the slave
being there, as formerly, that they are converted? I hear of the loyalty at Wilmington, the loyalty at South Carolina—what is it worth?

    MR. MAY—Not a straw.

    MR. DOUGLASS—Not a straw. I thank my friend for admitting it. They are loyal
while they see 200,000 sable soldiers, with glistening bayonets, walking in their midst
(applause). But let the civil power of the States be restored, and the old prejudices
and hostility to the negro will revive. Aye, the very fact that the negro has been used
to defeat this rebellion, and strike down the standards of the Confederacy, will be a
stimulus to all their hatred, all their malice, and lead them to legislate with greater
stringency towards this class than ever before (applause). The American people are
bound—bound by their sense of honor (I hope by their sense of honor, at least by
a just sense of honor), to extend the franchise to the negro, and I was going to say,
that the Abolitionists of the American Anti-Slavery Society were bound to "stand still
and see the salvation of God," until that work is done (applause). Where, where shall
the black man look for support, my friends, if the American Anti-Slavery Society fails
him? ("Hear, hear.") From whence shall we expect a certain sound from the trum-
pet of freedom, when the old pioneer, when this Society that has survived mobs, and
martyrdom and the combined efforts of priest-craft and state-craft to suppress it,
shall all at once subside, on the mere intimation that the Constitution has been
amended, so that neither slavery nor involuntary servitude shall hereafter be allowed in this land? What did the slaveholders of Richmond say to those who objected to arming the negro, on the ground that it would make him a freeman? Why,

they said, "The argument is absurd. We may make these negroes fight for us; but while we retain political power of the South, we can keep them in their subordinate positions." That was the argument; and they were right. They might have employed the negro to fight for them, and while they retained in their hands the power to exclude him from political rights, they could have reduced him to a condition similar to slavery. They would not call it slavery, but some other name. Slavery has been fruitful in giving itself names. It has been called "the peculiar institution," "the social system," and the "impediment," as it was called by the General Conference of the Methodist Episcopal Church. It has been called a great many names, and it will call itself by yet another name; and you and I and all of us had better wait and see what new form this old monster will assume, in what new skin this old snake will come forth next (loud applause).

———————

In late September Douglass was honored by the dedication of the Douglass Institute for the intellectual and moral development of black youth in Baltimore. On this occasion he spoke at length of the challenges that still remained for black people in the United States.

My friends, the present is a critical moment for the colored people of this country; our fate for weal or for woe, it may be yet for many generations, trembles now in the balance. No man can tell which way the scale will turn. There is not a breeze that sweeps to us from the South, but comes laden with the wail of our suffering people. Heaven only knows what will be in store for our people in the South. But dismal as is the hour, troubled and convulsed as are the times, we may congratulate ourselves upon the establishment of this institution. It comes as a timely argument on the right side of the momentous questions which now agitate the nation. It comes at a time when the American people are once more urged to do from necessity what they should have done from a sense of right, and of sound statesmanship. It is the same old posture of affairs, wherein our rulers do wrong from choice and right from necessity. They gave us the bullet to save themselves; they will yet give the ballot to save themselves. My hope of the future is founded just where it was during the war. I always said that I had much faith in the virtue of the great North, but that I had incomparably more in the villainy of the South. The South is now on its good behavior, we are told. They have been invested with powers merely to see how they will use them. If they do certain things, we are told, it will be well, but if they do certain other things—well, somebody will interfere. Very well. I expect to see the rebels consistent with their whole past. They are sworn now as at the beginning of the war, and with like results. They take the oath to support a Government they hate. They are sure to abuse the power given them, and I believe there will be virtue enough in the country, when it shall see that the loyal whites can only be saved by giving the ballot to the negro, to do the thing now called impossible. . . .

———————

The following month, on October 8, Douglass, anxiously awaiting the convening of the Thirty-Ninth Congress, wrote his abolitionist friend, Gerrit Smith:

I wish you could be in Congress this winter, for Congress is now to determine whether all that has been fairly purchased by the patriots' blood of the North, and by the brave Negroes of the South, shall be given back again to the spoilers of the Nation. . . .

Two months later Douglass again wrote to Gerrit Smith of his concerns:

We must demand Suffrage, but rejoice if we can get the Slave code abolished, and future ones made impossible.

Gideon Welles

Gideon Welles continued to watch the changing political situation. He was uneasy over the growing extremism.

September 28. . . . Little of importance has transpired during the month. The rebellious States are reorganizing their governments and institutions,—submitting to results they could not arrest or avert. In the Free States, political conventions have been held and movements made to revivify old parties, and, on the part of the extremists, or Radicals, an exhibition of intense hate towards the Rebels which bodes mischief has manifested itself. . . .

October 11. The elections in Pennsylvania, Ohio, and Iowa come in favorable, though the vote and the majorities are reduced from the Presidential election. . . .

October 12, Thursday. . . . The Radicals of Massachusetts are preparing to make war upon the President. This is obvious, and Sumner has been inclined to take the lead. . . .

Rutherford B. Hayes

The Thirty-Ninth Congress convened on Monday, December 4. Three days earlier the Ohio Republicans caucused to decide their strategy. The next day the entire Republican party caucused. Rutherford B. Hayes, a newly elected congressman from Ohio, participated in these momentous decisions that laid the basis for radical Reconstruction. His experiences as a soldier during the war made him a staunch Republican. He voted with his party on every major vote. He did not trust the Democratic party and was unwilling to readmit the South at the present time. There was more for the South to do before it earned the right to regain its former status. The rights of the freedmen could be protected only by the party that won the war. He kept a diary and wrote his wife and friends regularly.

December 1, 1865. . . . A caucus of the Ohio Union delegation held at Mr. Delano's rooms tonight. . . . It was our first, and a very agreeable and harmonious, meeting. Mr. Delano, chairman, stated the object to be to consult as to candidates for the offices of the House of Representatives, and as to matters connected with the organization of the House. It was agreed to support Mr. Colfax for Speaker and Mr. McPherson for Clerk, they being the old officers and having no opposition. . . .

We agreed to oppose the admission of any delegate from the Rebel States for the present. . . .

General Schenck gave notice that he would propose an amendment on the first opportunity by which representation would be based on suffrage. All seemed to acquiesce. On General Schenck's suggestion I offered the resolution, with *educational test or condition* added. Adopted with two negatives. . . .

December 2. . . . The general caucus [of Republican members] tonight a pleasant thing. Mr. Morrill of Vermont, an intelligent merchant who put the vote, "*Contrary-minded* will say no," presided. Thad Stevens made the important motions. A committee of seven reported resolutions to be submitted to the Senate and House, providing for the appointment of a Joint Committee of Fifteen, nine for the House, six for the Senate, to report as to the status of the Rebel States and whether they were in a condition to be represented; and in the meantime all members from those States to be kept out. . . .

December 4.—We organized the House according to programme. Mr. Brooks [Democrat], of New York, undertook to make some opposition but the previous question settled him. Brooks is a pleasant speaker, and a gentlemanly, agreeable man, judging by appearances. Thad Stevens, grim-looking, cool, with a ready wit, perfect courage, and the sort of independence which long experience, assured position, and seventy years of age gives an able man. He seems to be leader of the House.

My Darling: . . . So far I have no very decided feeling about the life I am leading. With my family here, pleasantly homed, I would like it well. As it is, I find nothing very gratifying in it and nothing decidedly the contrary. My quarters are well chosen. . . . I eat two meals a day wherever hunger overtakes me. . . .

Thus far the noticeable men on our side of the house are Thad Stevens, Judge Kelley, and Roscoe Conkling, and on the Democratic side, James Brooks. Stevens is over seventy, sharp-faced, grim-looking. . . . The only blemish in his puritanical, severe appearance is a brown wig. He is witty, cool, full of and fond of "sarcasms," and thoroughly informed and accurate. He has a knack of saying things which turn the laugh on his opponent. When he rises everyone expects something worth hearing, and he has the attention of all. You remember his speech on confiscation. He is radical throughout, except, I am told, he don't believe in hanging. He is leader.

Judge Kelley of Philadelphia talks often; has studied rhetoric and elocution, and, I am told, is theatrical overmuch, but so far his little short speeches have been exceedingly well delivered.

Roscoe Conkling of New York State delivers measured sentences in a grave, deliberate way that is good.

James Brooks, former Know-nothing leader, speaks pleasantly and is the leader of the Democrats; has, of course, to talk for Buncombe [for mere show or popularity]. . . .

December 12.—Today the credentials of Mr. Maynard and other claimants to seats from Tennessee were referred on motion of Mr. Raymond to the Joint Committee of Fifteen, proposed by the Stevens resolutions. Several attempts were made which by implication gave them some official recognition. These the Union men with a few exceptions voted against, and [they] were all defeated. A motion was then carried by the vote of all except thirty-five Union men to admit these gentlemen under a resolution containing no allusion to their official character, making it purely a courtesy on the part of the House. For this I voted. Seeing there was division among the Ohio and other Union members, I voted to lay it on the table, thinking a little delay and consultation would lead to entire unanimity. The first thing is to keep together, united and harmonious. I am glad to see that this duty is generally recognized.

―――――――――

Gideon Welles

The day before the convening of Congress, on December 3, Gideon Welles discussed his concerns with President Johnson about the growing radicalism of Congress. He was worried about the potential for conflict. He continued to be distressed in the early days of the new year.

December 3. Told the President I disliked the proceedings of the Congressional caucus on Saturday evening. The resolution for a joint committee of fifteen to whom the whole subject of admission of Representatives from States which had been in rebellion [should be referred] without debate was in conflict with the spirit and letter of the Constitution, which gives to each house the decision of election of its own members, etc. Then in appointing Stevens, an opponent of State rights, to present it there was something bad. The whole was, in fact, revolutionary, a blow at our governmental system, and there had been evident preconcert to bring it about. The President agreed with me, but said they would be knocked in the head at the start. There would be a Representative from Tennessee who had been a loyal Member of the House since the War commenced, or during the War, who could present himself, and so state the case that he could not be controverted. I expressed my gratification if this could be accomplished,—knowing he alluded to Maynard,—but suggested a doubt whether the intrigue which was manifest by the resolution, the designation of Stevens, and Colfax's speech had not gone too far.

Congress organized about the time this conversation took place. Maynard was put aside, I think by concert between himself and the Radical leaders. The resolution introduced by Stevens passed by a strict party vote. In the Senate, Sumner introduced an avalanche of radical—and some of them absurd—resolutions. These appeared to have absorbed the entire attention of that body, which adjourned without the customary committee to wait upon the President and inform him that Congress was organized. This was not unintentional. There was design in it. . . .

December 13, Wednesday. The Radicals have been busy. They are feeling their way now. The President has been deceived, I think, in some persons in whom he has confided, and the patronage of the government, without his being aware of it, has been turned against the Administration. . . .

January 8. The Members of Congress since their return appear more disposed to avoid open war with the President, but yet are under the discipline of party, which is cunningly kept up with almost despotic power. I am confident that many of those who are claimed as Republicans, and who are such, are voting against their convictions, but they have not the courage and independence to shake off the tyranny of party and maintain what they know to be right. The President and the Radical leaders are not yet in direct conflict, but I see not how it is to be avoided. When the encounter takes place there will be those who have voted with the Radicals, who will then probably go with the President, or wish to do so. This the leaders understand, and it is their policy to get as many committed as possible, and to get them repeatedly committed by test votes. . . .

January 13, Saturday. I had this P.M. quite an animated talk with Senator Sumner . . . we got on to the question of Reconstruction. I was anxious to get an inside view of the movements and purposes of the Radicals, and in order to do this, it would not do to put questions direct to Sumner, for then he would put himself on his guard, and be close-mouthed. I therefore entered into a discussion, and soon got him much interested, not to call it excited. We went over the ground of the status of the States,—their political condition. He, condemning unqualifiedly the policy of the President, said, while he would not denounce it as the greatest crime ever committed by a responsible ruler, he did proclaim and declare it the greatest mistake which history has ever recorded. The President, he said, was the greatest enemy of the South that she had ever had, worse than Jeff Davis; and the evil which he had inflicted upon the country was incalculable. All was to be done over again, and done right. Congress, he says, is becoming more firm and united every day. . . .

George Templeton Strong

George Templeton Strong was satisfied with the organization of Congress in December and with keeping "Southern members . . . out in the cold a little longer . . ." He worried about the efforts of Thaddeus Stevens and Charles Sumner to make war on Johnson's Reconstruction policy but began to think that they might be right.

January 19. The House has passed the bill for Negro suffrage in the District of Columbia, and by a two-thirds vote. I think the Senate will pass it, and I do not expect a veto from Johnson. The whole question is full of difficulties and conflicting rights. No statesman ever had a more knotty problem set him by destiny. But whatever doubts there may be as to South Carolina and Mississippi, I approve of Negro suffrage in the District, for it will de-Southernize and nationalize the atmosphere of the national capital. . . .

January 25. . . . *How* shall we deal with our Southern malignants? What shall we do with them? We cannot afford to let them back into the Congressional seats they left so unceremoniously and defiantly and truculently five years ago. We cannot leave our black soldiers, now mustered out, to the mercy of their late masters. We have the Southern wolf or hyena by the ears. Letting go would be ruinous. Holding on awhile is inconvenient. I prefer to hold on awhile, as the less of two evils, and belong (I suppose) to the Radical Party. It seems clear that no Northern man, no Yankee, can live at the South in any moderate safety yet. Negroes are oppressed, tortured, and murdered by their *ci-devant* [former] owners. We may have to undertake another civil war. If we do, it will be waged in most grim and bitter earnest, with no scruple about the summary hanging of rebels and traitors. Troubles and taxes have taught us much. We disincline to hang J. Davis because he and we were equally untaught as to the value of civil order and the criminality of rebellion, five years ago. We know better now. Woe to the next gentleman that sets up a rebellion. . . . .

February 1. Every symptom of Southern temper is bad. It seems to grow worse rather than better. The South is crushed for the time, but the more bitter and vindictive for its humiliation, and fuller than ever, even, of sectional, anti-national, traitorous impulses. Nothing but physical exhaustion keeps the Southern Hyena from instantly flying at our throats again. The beast is whipped into temporary submission, but utterly untamed. It will not be domesticated in our day, if ever.

"Stern looks the Fiend, as frustrate of his Will,
Not half sufficed, but greedy yet to kill."

There is a quarrel among his keepers, much to be regretted. The Republican party is cracked, and the crack is spreading and widening. Andrew Johnson seems more and more inclined toward what is called conservatism, and Raymond leads a "Conservative" party in the House. His party is small, but will grow in the sunshine of executive favor. The "Radicals" are firm. I am sure their doctrine is gaining ground with the people. Every change I notice in anyone's political sympathies is that way.

Almost every one has changed a little during the last six months, and become a little more Radical or Conservative. The constitutional amendment (as to the basis of representation) passed the House yesterday, 120 to 46. Expediency, abstract right, and common sense agree in calling for some amendment of the Constitution there anent, and this seems a judicious amendment. The President is said to disapprove it. The Hon. Thaddeus Stevens belabored the President in debate yesterday, loudly, coarsely, and unwisely. Brooks, Win Chanler, and the Devil chuckled over Stevens's oratory, no doubt. . . .

Frederick Douglass

While the debate over Reconstruction raged in Congress, a delegation appointed by the National Convention of Colored People, an organization from thirteen states meeting in Washington, D.C., called on President Johnson. At the meeting on February 7, George Downing, chairman, and Frederick Douglass made brief remarks, which were followed by a response from Johnson.

Mr. George T. Downing then addressed the President as follows:

> We present ourselves to your Excellency to make known with pleasure the respect which we are glad to cherish for you—a respect which is your due as Chief Magistrate. It is our desire for you to know we come feeling that we are friends, meeting a friend. We should, however, have manifested our friendship by not coming to further tax your already much burdened and valuable time; but we have another object in calling. We are in a passage to equality before the law. God hath made it by opening a Red Sea. We could have your assistance through the same. We come to you in the name of the United States, and are delegated to come by some who have unjustly worn iron manacles on their bodies—by some whose minds have been manacled by class legislation in States called free. . . .

Following upon Mr. Downing, Mr. Fred. Douglass advanced and addressed the President, saying:

> Mr. President:—We are not here to enlighten you, sir, as to your duties as the Chief Magistrate of this Republic, but to show our respect, and to present in brief the claims of our race to your favorable consideration. In the order of Divine Providence you are placed in a position where you have the power to save or destroy us; to bless or blast us. I mean our whole race. Your noble and humane predecessor placed in our hands the sword to assist in saving the nation, and we do hope that you, his able successor, will favorably regard the placing in our hands the ballot with which to save ourselves.

We shall submit no argument on that point. The fact that we are the subjects of Government, and subject to taxation, subject to volunteer in the service of the country, subject to being drafted, subject to bear the burdens of the State, makes it not improper that we should ask to share in the privileges of this condition.

I have no speech to make on this occasion. I simply submit these observations as a limited expression of the views and feelings of the delegation with which I have come.

☞ RESPONSE OF THE PRESIDENT ☜

. . . I say that if I have not given evidence that I am a friend of humanity, and especially the friend of the colored man in my past conduct, there is nothing that I can now do that would. I repeat, all that I possessed, life, liberty, and property, have been put up in connection with that question; when I had every inducement held out to take the other course, by adopting which I would have accomplished perhaps all that the most ambitious might have desired. If I know myself, and the feelings of my own heart, they have been for the colored man. I have owned slaves and bought slaves, but I never sold one. I might say, however, that practically, so far as my connection with slaves has gone, I have been their slave instead of their being mine. Some have even followed me here, while others are occupying and enjoying my property with my consent. For the colored race my means, my time, my all has been perilled; and now at this late day, after giving evidence that is tangible, that is practical, I am free to say to you that I do not like to be arraigned by some who can get up handsomely rounded periods and deal in rhetoric, and talk about abstract ideas of liberty, who never perilled life, liberty, or property. This kind of theoretical, hollow, unpractical friendship amounts to but very little. While I say that I am a friend of the colored man, I do not want to adopt a policy that I believe will end in a contest between the races, which, if persisted in, will result in the extermination of one or the other. God forbid that I should be engaged in such a work!

Now, it is always best to talk about things practically, and in a common-sense way. Yes, I have said, and I repeat here, that if the colored man in the United States could find no other Moses, or any Moses that would be more able and efficient than myself, I would be his Moses to lead him from bondage to freedom; that I would pass him from a land where he had lived in slavery to a land (if it were in our reach) of freedom. Yes, I would be willing to pass with him through the Red Sea to the Land of Promise—to the land of liberty; but I am not willing, under either circumstance, to adopt a policy which I believe will only result in the sacrifice of his life and the shedding of his blood. I think I know what I say. I feel what I say; and I feel well assured that if the policy urged by some be persisted in, it will result in great injury to the white as well as to the colored man. . . . .

The colored man went into this rebellion a slave; by the operation of the rebellion he came out a freedman—equal to a freedman in any other portion of the country. Then there is a great deal done for him on this point. The non-slaveholder who was forced into the rebellion, and was as loyal as those who lived beyond the limits of the State, was carried into it, and his property, and in a number of instances, the lives of such, were sacrificed, and he who has survived has come out of it with nothing gained but a great deal lost.

Now, upon a principle of justice, should they be placed in a condition different from what they were before? On the one hand, one has gained a great deal; on the other hand, one has lost a great deal; and, in a political point of view, scarcely stands where he did before.

Now, we are talking about where we are going to begin. We have got at the hate that existed between the two races. The query comes up, whether these two races, situated as they were before, without preparation, without time for passion and excitement to be appeased, and without time for the slightest improvement, whether the one should be turned loose upon the other and be thrown together at the ballot-box, with this enmity and hate existing between them. The query comes up if right there we don't commence a war of races. I think I understand this thing—and especially is this the case when you force it upon a people without their consent. . . .

Each community is better prepared to determine the depository of its political power than anybody else, and it is for the legislature, for the people of Ohio to say who shall vote, and not for the Congress of the United States. I might go down here to the ballot-box to-morrow and vote directly for universal suffrage, but if a great majority of the people said no, I should consider it would be tyrannical in me to attempt to force such upon them without their will. It is a fundamental tenet in my creed that the people must be obeyed. Is there anything wrong or unfair in that?

MR. DOUGLASS (SMILING.)—A great deal wrong, Mr. President, with all respect.

THE PRESIDENT.—It is the people of the States that must for themselves determine this thing. I do not want to be engaged in a work that will commence a war of races. I want to begin the work of preparation, and the States, or the people in each community, if a man demeans himself well, and shows evidence that this new state of affairs will operate, he will be protected in all his rights, and given every possible advantage by that community when they become reconciled socially and politically to certain things. Then will this new order of things work harmoniously; but forced upon the people before they are prepared for it, it will be resisted, and work inharmoniously. I feel a conviction that driving this matter upon the people, upon the community, will result in the injury of both races, and the ruin of one or the other. God knows I have no desire but the good of the whole human race. I would it were so that all you advocate could be done in the twinkling of an eye, but it is not in the nature of things, and I do not assume or pretend to be wiser than Providence, or stronger than the laws of nature. . . .

God knows that anything I can do I will do. In the mighty process by which the great end is to be reached, anything I can do to elevate the races, to soften and ameliorate their condition I will do, and to be able to do so is the sincere desire of my heart.

I am glad to have met you, and thank you for the compliment you have paid me.

MR. DOUGLASS.—I have to return you our thanks, Mr. President, for so kindly granting us this interview. We did not come here expecting to argue this question with your Excellency, but simply to state what were our views and wishes in the premises. If we were disposed to argue the question, and you would grant us permission, of course we would endeavor to controvert some of the positions you have assumed.

MR. DOWNING.—Mr. Douglass, I take it that the President, by his kind expressions, and his very full treatment of the subject, must have contemplated some reply to the views which he has advanced, and in which we certainly do not concur, and I say this with due respect.

THE PRESIDENT.—I thought you expected me to indicate to some extent what my views were on the subjects touched upon in your statement.

MR. DOWNING.—We are very happy, indeed, to have heard them.

MR. DOUGLASS.—If the President will allow me, I would like to say one or two words in reply.

THE PRESIDENT.—All I have done is simply to indicate what my views are as I supposed you expected me to, from your address.

MR. DOUGLASS.—My own impression is, that the very thing that your Excellency would avoid in the Southern States can only be avoided by the very measure that we propose, and I would state to my brother delegates that because I perceive the President has taken strong ground in favor of a given policy, and distrusting my own ability to remove any of those impressions which he has expressed, I thought we had better end the interview with the expression of thanks. (Addressing the President.) But if your Excellency will be pleased to hear, I would like to say a word or two in regard to that one matter of the enfranchisement of the blacks as a means of preventing the very thing which your Excellency appears to apprehend—that is a conflict of races.

THE PRESIDENT.—I repeat, I merely wanted to indicate my views in reply to your address, and not to enter into any general controversy, as I could not well do so under the circumstances.

Your statement was a very frank one, and I thought it was due to you to meet it in the same spirit.

MR. DOUGLASS.—Thank you, sir.

THE PRESIDENT.—I think you will find, so far as the South is concerned, that if you will all inculcate there the idea in connection with the one you urge, that the colored people can live and advance in civilization to better advantage elsewhere than crowded right down there in the South, it would be better for them.

MR. DOUGLASS.—But the masters have the making of the laws, and we cannot get away from the plantations.

THE PRESIDENT.—What prevents you?

MR. DOUGLASS.—We have not the simple right of locomotion through the Southern States now.

THE PRESIDENT.—Why not, the Government furnishes you with every facility.

MR. DOUGLASS.—There are six days in the year that the negro is free in the South now, and his master then decides for him where he shall go, where he shall work, how much he shall work—in fact, he is divested of all political power. He is absolutely in the hands of those men.

THE PRESIDENT.—If the master now controls him in his action, would he not control him in his vote?

Mr. Douglass. — Let the negro once understand that he has an organic right to vote, and he will raise up a party in the Southern States among the poor, who will rally with him. There is this conflict that you speak of between the wealthy slaveholder and the poor man.

The President. — You touch right upon the point there. There is this conflict, and hence I suggest emigration. If he cannot get employment in the South, he has it in his power to go where he can get it.

In parting, the President said that they were both desirous of accomplishing the same ends, but proposed to do so by following different roads.

Mr. Douglass. — (on turning to leave, remarked to his fellow delegates:) "The President sends us to the people, and we will have to go and get the people right."

The President. — Yes, sir; I have great faith in the people. I believe they will do what is right.

Gideon Welles

Twelve days after meeting the Negro delegation, President Johnson called a special cabinet meeting to discuss his decision to veto the Freedmen's Bureau Bill. Welles was pleased with his decision, whereas the cabinet was divided in its sentiment.

February 19, Monday. Attended special Cabinet-meeting this morning, at ten, and remained in session until about 1 P.M. The President submitted a message which he had prepared, returning the Freedmen's Bureau Bill to the Senate with his veto. The message and positions were fully discussed. Seward, McCulloch, and Dennison agreed with the President, as did I, and each so expressed himself. Stanton, Harlan, and Speed, while they did not absolutely dissent, evidently regretted that the President had not signed the bill. Stanton was disappointed. Speed was disturbed. Harlan was apprehensive. The President was emphatic and unequivocal in his remarks, earnest to eloquence in some portion of a speech of about twenty minutes, in which he reviewed the intrigues of certain Radical leaders in Congress, without calling them by name, their council of fifteen which in secret prescribed legislative action and assumed to dictate the policy of the Administration. The effect of this veto will probably be an open rupture between the President and a portion of the Republican Members of Congress. How many will go with him, and how many with the Radical leaders, will soon be known. Until a vote is taken, the master spirits will have time to intrigue with the Members and get them committed. They will be active as well as cunning. . . .

February 20, Tuesday. The Cabinet was pleasant and harmonious on the matters before it to-day, though outside rumors make them divided. Much excitement exists in Congress and out of it on the subject of the veto. The dark, revolutionary, reckless intrigues of Stevens manifest themselves. In the House, the bigoted partisans are ready to follow him in his vindictive and passionate schemes for Radical supremacy. Radicalism having been prevalent during the War, they think it still popular.

On the vote which was taken to-day in the Senate, the veto was sustained and the bill defeated there not being the requisite two thirds in its favor. Morgan, Dixon, Doolittle, and four or five others with the Democrats, eighteen in all against thirty. Violent and factious speeches were made in the Senate, and also in the House. Stevens, as I expected he would, presented his schemes to oppress the South and exclude the States from their constitutional right of representation. Such men would plunge the country into a more wicked rebellion, one more destructive of our system of government, a more dangerous condition than that from which we have emerged, could they prevail. . . .

February 22, Thursday. Washington's Birthday . . . There was a large gathering of the citizens to-day at the theatre to approve the veto, and they subsequently went to the Executive Mansion, where the President addressed them in quite a long speech for the occasion.

February 23, Friday. The papers of this morning contain the reported speech of President Johnson yesterday. It is longer than the President should have delivered,—if he were right in addressing such a crowd. His remarks were earnest, honest, and strong. One or two interruptions which called out names I wish were omitted. . . .

I told the President I was sorry he had permitted himself to be drawn into answering impertinent questions to a promiscuous crowd and that he should have given names of those whose course he disapproved. Not that his remarks were not true, but the President should not be catechized into declarations. Yet it is the manner and custom in the Southwest, and especially in Tennessee, to do this on the stump. . . .

February 24, Saturday. . . . The President says there has been a design to attempt impeachment if he did not yield to them. I am inclined to believe this has been talked of among the leaders, but they would not press a majority of their own number into the movement.

———————

George Templeton Strong

George Templeton Strong supported the veto of the Freedmen's Bureau Bill but worried about the growing division within the Republican party. He was especially offended by the speeches and remarks of Johnson, which struck him as unpresidential.

February 20. Today's sensation was Johnson's veto of the Freedman's Bureau Bill. It seems a tough paper, not easily to be answered. It goes far toward demonstrating certain provisions of the bill not only impolitic and open to most mischievous abuse, but plainly repugnant to the Constitution. Johnson states his objections clearly and cogently. Had he contented himself with stating them, all but a few extremists would heartily approve this message (though the New York World's delectation over it disgusts all who love the nation more than they love the South). But after giving his sufficient reasons for this veto, in statesmanlike style, Johnson goes out of his way to lecture Congress for not letting in Southern Representatives, wherein I think he shows himself impertinent, and what's worse, radically unsound. I am sorry, for I do not want to lose my faith in Andy Johnson.

February 22, Thursday. . . .The "Freedmen's Bureau" bill failed of a two-thirds vote in the Senate (30–18), so the "Radicals" are defeated, and you can distinguish a Copperhead a hundred yards off by the light that beams from his countenance. Confounded be their breed! The veto was wise, but I wish it did not give these caitiffs such keen enjoyment. H. W. Beecher says in the course of a long lecture or address defending it and the President's general policy, that an executive officer declining power and patronage so immense as Congress offered Johnson by this bill is something new under the sun. It's quite true. But the more extreme Republicans in both Houses are furious. Senator Anthony of Rhode Island writes Mrs. Charley Strong in depths of despair. "The party is broken up," he says. "No such scene in the Senate since Buchanan's time, when Senators from seceding states were going out." But he is an easy man to scare. It is clear, however, that moderation and temper are needed to keep the party from a split, and that "Radical" leaders have shewn little sign of either, since this bombshell burst among them.

February 23. . . . This [conservative] meeting was significant. It shewed that discord in the National or Union party (i.e., the North, *minus* Copperheads) is beginning to formulate itself. But far more significant was Mr. President Johnson's long speech yesterday at the White House addressed to a mob that waited on him and asked for a few remarks. It is a very long speech and full of repetitions. Its bouquet seems to me (as to others) to be that of Old Bourbon, largely imbibed by the orator just before taking the rostrum. Anyhow it is bad, egotistical, diffuse, undignified, intemperate, unwise, and sure to do great mischief. He avowed himself at war with radicalism, and denounced Sumner of the Senate and Stevens of the House and Wendell Phillips, who is a mere private lecturer and sophist (if you will), as disunionists and traitors. He talked of Senators going about "with assassination in their hearts," and of his own indifference to such hypothetical designs; of the exceedingly moderate sum he needed for food and raiment, and talked much bosh beside.

This speech is a national calamity. It hurts us badly, and it will disgrace us abroad. . . . Neither party has shewn a trace of temperance or conciliatory disposition. And war being now declared, I fear it is manifest that the "Radicals" of Congress first drew the sword. This may result in an impeachment of the President within thirty days!!! . . .

March 1. All indications are that Johnson's policy gains ground with the people, and that the extreme Left in Congress is losing heart. But Southern representatives will have to "stand disconsolate," . . . There is still a working majority to keep them "out in the cold." Sooner or later the gates must open, I suppose, for we cannot always hold these barbarians as a conquered people. Their representatives will have to be admitted, and the wolves swarm in to help the dogs guard the sheepfold. What will happen then? . . .

March 2. . . . Extreme Republicans denounce A. Johnson most savagely. "When he dies," quoth——, "there will be one comfort. Judas Iscariot will not be quite so lonesome!!!" Another says, "It's bad enough to have a tailor for President, but a drunken tailor, and a drunken Democratic tailor, is beyond endurance." I see nothing to justify such extravagant bitterness. . . .

Rutherford B. Hayes

Hayes was disturbed by the veto of the Freedmen's Bureau Bill. He wished for a reconciliation between Congress and the President, but he was slowly losing hope.

. . . February 28, 1866.

Dear Uncle:—I don't know whether I have written to you since the veto or not. Many of our good men still hope that we may retain the President, but it is a very faint hope, scarcely more than a wish that he may return "to the bosom of his family," as Lucy says. The general impression is, however, that Rebel influences are now ruling the White House and that the sooner Johnson is clear over, the better for us. Almost all are for going forward with business and measures in the usual and proper way without excitement or abuse. . . .

Yours,
R. B. Hayes.
S. Birchard.

. . . February 28, 1866.

Dearest:—You left me last evening, and I am already half homesick about it. Possibly I would not have thought of it so feelingly, but the sight of these gloves put me in mind of it. What a happy time we have had! Six weeks of real, genuine old-fashioned love.—Love to Grandma and the boys all.

Affectionately,
R.
Mrs. Hayes.

. . . March 2, 1866.

Dear Uncle: . . . We are not quite sure yet whether Andy is with us or against us—in a party sense, I mean. Doctrinally, he is against us on many things and with us on a few. . . .

Sincerely,
R. B. Hayes.
S. Birchard.

. . . March 4, 1866.

My dear Uncle:—We are still not clear as to the chances of harmony with the President. He no doubt differs and has all along avowedly and openly differed with us on some important matters. At the time of his unfortunate talk on the 22nd he seemed to be surrounded and possessed by all manner of evil influences. He now seems to feel that he was misled and is really anxious to conciliate. If he signs [the] Civil Rights Bill [defined blacks as U.S. citizens and guaranteed certain civil rights] and the Tennessee Resolution which will both pass soon, the chances are that a complete rupture will be avoided. Otherwise, otherwise. It is an interesting time to be here and I enjoy it very much now,—the last three weeks more than ever before. My ever hopeful temper is a good thing in these perplexing and exciting times. . . .

Sincerely,
R. B. Hayes.
S. Birchard.

. . . March 17, 1866.

Dear [General] Force:— . . . I could argue with you on the wisdom and justice of what Congress is doing with our erring sisters if I knew exactly your points. The truth is, Congress has done next to nothing yet on that subject, and can give good reasons for not having yet done anything. The position held by the majority is this: The Rebel States having gone into insurrection and lost their lawful State Governments, it is for the law-making power of the Nation to say when (or whether) such new State Governments have been set up as ought to be recognized. Is not this sound? Granting this, ought we to recognize any State Government which does not *undertake,* at least, to afford adequate protection to Union people and freedmen? And further, is there evidence showing such State Governments except in Tennessee and possibly Arkansas? . . .

Sincerely,
R. B. Hayes
General M. F. Force,
Cincinnati.

. . . March 22, 1866.

My Darling:— . . . A. J. [the president] is now being tried by another test—the Civil Rights Bill. If he signs it he gets into the bosom of the family again. If not, more worry. . . .

Affectionately, ever your
R.
Mrs. Hayes.

. . . [March] 29, 1866.

Darling:— . . . A. J. [the President] getting into a bad row of stumps; not in the bosom of his family any longer, I suspect.

    Yes, it is lonely and bad. I begin to think that I ought to quit a "biz" which separates me from you so much. . . . Love to all.

Yours,
H.
Mrs. Hayes.

George Templeton Strong

The veto of the Civil Rights Bill bothered George Templeton Strong greatly. He was losing faith in Johnson and in his policies.

    March 28. . . . Another veto! A. Johnson has put his foot on the Civil Rights Bill. So the crack spreads and widens. His message is less strong than that against the Freedmen's Bureau, but very able, perhaps sound, possibly a little disingenuous. I fear that these vetoes shew Johnson's sympathies and prejudices to be wrong and dangerous. I am losing my faith in him, by no logical process, but by instinctive distrust of any one who is commended by the Express and Daily News and World, the London Times, and the Richmond papers. . . .

    April 2, Monday. . . . The loose, reckless denunciations of the President as without personal honesty and integrity which I hear uttered by "Radicals" (with whom I, on the whole, sympathize) tempts me to wish it may not be so. They are chargeable with most bitter intolerance and uncharitableness. But the opposing party, the Democrats and Copperheads of the *World* and the *Express* and *Daily News,* sin against charity no less, and are, moreover, utterly dead (and rotten) in all the trespasses and sins of political profligacy. . . .

    April 5. . . . They are jawing away at the veto in Congress and making much use of the *argumentum ad hominem* founded on Mr. President Johnson's talk when a

Senator and disgusted with old Buchanan's exercise of the veto power. This is small business. The "Radicals" are strong on the merits, but they will fail to override the veto. . . .

━━━━━━━━━━

Gideon Welles

Gideon Welles supported the veto of the Civil Rights Bill; his advice had been asked for by President Johnson. The cabinet and the Congress were more divided over this action than ever. Welles worried about the conservative Republicans and the pressures to be brought upon them to override the veto.

March 26, Monday. Senator Doolittle called at my house last evening on the subject of the Civil Rights Bill, which it is now well understood, outside, will meet an Executive veto. Doolittle has an elaborate bill of his own which he proposes to submit. Something, he thinks, must be done. His bill is, perhaps, somewhat less offensive than the one which has been passed by both houses, but the whole thing is wrong and his plan has the same objectionable machinery as the other. I frankly told him that the kind of legislation proposed, and which Congress was greedy to enact, was not in my view correct, was sapping the foundation of the government and must be calamitous in its results. We went together to Senator Morgan's and talked over the subject an hour or more with him.

The President convened the Cabinet this A.M. at ten and read his message returning the Civil Rights Bill with his veto. . . .

April 6. . . . The Senate by a vote of 33 to 15 this evening overrode the veto on the Civil Rights Bill. Wright of New Jersey was in his seat, but Dixon was not. Morgan, unexpectedly to me, and, I think, to most persons, voted with the majority. The vote of M. was one of calculation, not of conviction. I shall be disappointed if he does not lose rather than gain by the step he has taken. Such is usually the righteous termination of calculations made by scheming and ambitious men who consent to do wrong. In this instance M. may have had honest reasons. It is true he voted for the passage of the bill, but that was, as he has said to me, without much consideration given to the law, and, in repeated interviews and conversations since, he had left the impression on my mind that he should sustain the veto.

General and Mrs. Grant gave their last reception for the season this evening. Being somewhat indisposed, I did not propose to attend, but Edgar had not returned and there was no one to accompany Mrs. Welles and her friend, and I was, consequently, under the necessity of going, though afflicted with a severe headache. The party was in some respects unlike any of the season, and there was present not only a numerous but a miscellaneous company of contradictions. There had been some pre-understanding on the part of the Radicals, or a portion of them, to attend and to appropriate General Grant, or at least his name and influence, to themselves. But, most unexpectedly to them, as I confess it was to me, the President and his two daughters appeared early, and Montgomery Blair and some of his ladies were also on hand. There came also Alexander H. Stephens, Vice-President of the late Confederacy, so called. When, therefore, Thad Stevens, Trumbull, and others, not exactly homogeneous though now acting together, came in, they were evidently astonished and amazed.

Stevens, though a brave old stager, was taken aback and showed himself discomfited. Trumbull betrayed surprise. I was not in a condition to circulate much in the crowd, but heard repeatedly, amid the exultation over the vote of the Senate, expressions of vexation that there was such a strange attendance here. . . .

General and naval officers, as well as politicians, were present, with most of the foreign ministers.

May 29. . . . The Senate, after many caucuses on the part of the Republican members, have an amendment of the Constitution modified from that reported by the *con*struction, or *ob*struction, committee. This amendment may be less offensive than that which passed the House by excluding one of the States from any voice or participation, but it ought not to receive the sanction of the Senate. Yet I have little doubt that it will and that the canvassing has been a process of drilling the weak and better-minded members into its support. Disgraceful as it may seem, there is no doubt that secret party caucus machinery has been in operation to carry through a Constitutional Amendment. Senators have committed themselves to it without hearing opposing arguments, or having any other discussion than that of a strictly party character in a strictly private meeting. Of course this grave and important matter is prejudged, predetermined.

Rutherford B. Hayes

Rutherford Hayes was pleased by the passage of the Civil Rights Bill over the president's veto. He was becoming hopeful for the future.

. . . April 8, 1866.

My dear Darling:—The last week is the only one since you left that you would have enjoyed here particularly. The Connecticut election early in the week was an enjoyable thing. The passage of the Civil Rights Bill in the Senate over the veto was a most exciting and delightful thing—such enthusiasm was manifested. Things have improved here. The general feeling is hopeful, loyal, and patriotic. A great change from that [of February] 22nd, when treason crept out and triumphed. The next thing was the great party at Grant's the night of the passage of the Civil Rights Bill. All our side was there in great spirits, Trumbull, Stevens, and all. The President stood between General and Mrs. Grant. Vice-President (Rebel) Stephens stood near. Montgomery Blair, etc., etc. Old Thad shook hands cordially with Andy. Andy presented him to Mrs. Grant. It was the happiest gathering I have seen. Andy looked and behaved very well indeed.

Affectionately ever, your
R.
Mrs. Hayes.

. . . April 12, 1866.

Dear Mother:—The appearance of things here has improved decidedly since the passage of the Civil Rights Bill over the veto. Both President and Congress feel better. After growling at each other a long time, they have come to blows and that being over they are nearer being friends again. . . .

Affectionately,
R. B. Hayes.
Mrs. Sophia Hayes

May 15.—The [Republican] policy is to leave to the States the question of suffrage. But in the District and the Territories it is for Congress to lay down the rule. Now, colored people are citizens of the United States. In some States they are allowed to vote, in some they are not. And in the places where all the States are interested, it is right to treat all citizens alike. When they [the people of the Territories] come to form State Governments, I leave it to the people to say, as in Colorado.

Besides, in the District [of Columbia] and in Territories they [the citizens] have no political power.

My decided preference: Suffrage for *all* in the South, colored and white, to depend on education; sooner or later in the North also—say, all *new* voters to be able to write and read.

━━━━━━

One of Hayes's sons died of scarlet fever on May 24, 1866. It had appeared that the son would recover, so Hayes went back to Washington.

*M*ay *24, 1866.* . . . A week ago he seemed so much worse that I was dispatched that he was sinking. I came home a week ago tomorrow. I found him low and was prepared for the worst. He was a very handsome child; abundant waving light hair; very large blue eyes and a broad, full forehead. He looked like my sister Fanny. His corpse reminds us of hers. [He was nineteen months old.]

━━━━━━

For the next month Hayes referred to this loss in his letters. Then his attention shifted back to politics.

. . . June 6, 1866.

My Darling:—I knew you would feel more keenly the loss of the dear boy when you got home, and in the quiet hours were reminded of his loss. My chief consolation is found in thinking of the good ones we have left. . . .

Andy is *thought* to be more conciliatory in his feelings, but nothing is very certain in that quarter. There are certainly some good indications. . . .

Affectionately, ever yours,
R.
Mrs. Hayes. . . .

. . . . June 14, 1866.

My Sweet Wife: . . . We passed the plan of Reconstruction as it came from the Senate. No man elected, or claiming to be, Union, voted against it. . . .

Yours ever,
H.

Gideon Welles

In June of 1866 supporters of President Johnson began to organize a National Union Convention to meet in Philadelphia in August. It was an effort to bring conservative Republicans and Democrats together to win seats in Congress in the fall. It was hoped that this would give President Johnson sufficient strength to sustain his vetoes of Republican Reconstruction measures. Gideon Welles was one of the early planners of this effort.

June 18, Monday. Senator Doolittle brought me last evening the rough draft of a proposed call for a national Union convention which he had prepared. Some of the points were well put, but there was too much restriction, too much fear that we should have men we did not care to fellowship with, although we might agree on present issues. To this I excepted, but my strongest point was the omission to meet and present the real issue,—our objections to the proposed change of the Constitution which has passed the two houses of Congress.

"What," said I, "are the reasons for calling a convention at this time? Is it not because the faction in Congress, assisted by schemers out of Congress, have concocted a scheme under party excitement and by party machinery to change the Constitution in important particulars, and that by a snap judgment Governor Curtin has addressed a circular letter to the Governors of the several States, inviting an immediate convening of the State legislatures to adopt the proposed change, before the people can have an opportunity to express an opinion? An alarm should be sounded, warning the people of the movements that are being made to alter the organic law, and insidiously change the government." . . .

I called on McCulloch, who agreed to come to my house this evening and go with me to the President. When he called, I detailed the conversation with Doolittle, told him of my apprehensions, and dwelt emphatically on the subject of the Constitutional changes as the true basis of action, and our sounding the bugle-note of warning to arouse the people. My earnestness and the facts excited him, and we went to the President.

We spent an hour in a free and unrestricted conversation with the President. McCulloch, full of the views which I had urged, advised that the President should at once issue a proclamation after the manner of Jackson in regard to nullification, appealing to the people. . . .

August 4, Saturday. The Philadelphia movement is gaining strength, but at the same time encountering tremendous and violent opposition from the Radicals. I trust and think it will be successful, but the convention will be composed of various elements, some of them antagonistic heretofore, and the error is in not having distinctive principles on which these prevailing opposing elements can centre. The time has arrived when our countrymen must sacrifice personal and mere organized party hostility for the general welfare. Either the Radicals or the Government are to be overthrown. The two are in conflict. . . .

August 11, Saturday. . . . Many delegates from the South to the Philadelphia Convention are in the city on their way thither. Generally they seem in good spirits and cheered with the prospect of a restored Union. So far as I have conversed with them they are of right tone and temper. . . .

August 20, Monday. Many calls to-day from delegates who have been to Philadelphia. . . .

Most of these men, as well as those whom they represent, have been connected in some degree with the Rebellion, but they submit and acquiesce in the result with grace, and I believe with sincerity. But the Radicals are filled with hatred, acrimony, and revenge towards them, and would persist in excluding not only them but the whole people of the South from any participation in the government. For four years war was waged to prevent them from going out; now the Radicals would wage as fine a war to shut them out.

George Templeton Strong

George Templeton Strong believed that the Philadelphia convention was controlled by Copperheads. It would bring southern rebels into "brotherhood and communion" with traitors in the North. All of this could result in violence.

July 2. Monday. . . . our affairs are in no comfortable state. "Recon-struction" makes little headway, and party discords grow more and more bitter. No Congress was ever so berated as this. There are special backers of Johnson who think he has failed and thrown away his chances for want of decision at the right moment. Do they mean that he should have taken the advice of the Daily News and followed the example of Cromwell? They decline to say. There is to be a formal bolt from the Republican party. A convention is called for August 14th in which "every state" is to be represented. It will probably generate an intermediate anti-radical, semi-Copperhead faction, styling itself "Conservative"; in fact, the party of "the King's friends." Meanwhile, Southern arrogance and brutality have revived, lifted up their ugly heads, and seem nearly as rank as ever. The First Southern War may prove not the last. These blind barbarians are actually protesting against immigration of Northern capital. They fear the debasement of "their people." Free speech is hardly less perilous among them today than it was six years ago. Slavery being dead (we may hope it is), improvement in Southern manners is now possible. But it has not yet begun. . . .

July 26. . . . The town is very dull. People are interested only in the foreign news and in the Philadelphia Convention that is to be held next month. This convention will be a "bolt" from the Republican party in the interest of the President's peculiar policy. . . .

July 30, Monday. . . . Congress has adjourned. Whether its "Radical" majority has done the country good or ill will be more apparent twenty years hence. But Andrew Johnson has played his cards badly. He might, I think, have prevented this split in the national party to which, as I hope and believe, he belongs. . . .

August 1 . . . . The people of New Orleans have been cutting up rough. There was a "Convention" dispersed by rioters. Some forty people were killed. It was almost a rebellion. A. Johnson's course in the premises seems to have been unwise. I begin to fear that Sumner and Stevens may be right about him. A few more outrages like this will teach all Northern men (Copperheads excepted) that these Southern wolves are not yet so humanized as to be fit to share the government of the sheepfold. Will this generation of Southerners ever be fit for it, brought up as they have been under the ruffianizing influence of slavery? . . .

August 7. . . . The feud between Johnson and the "Radicals" grows more and more deadly every day, and threatens grave public mischief. His "Philadelphia Conven-tion" seems likely to receive into brotherhood and full communion the Woods and Vallandighams of the North, and also any and every bitter rebel from the South who may call himself half-converted to a toleration of the national government, though avowedly so half-converted by the *vis major* [stronger power] and by nothing else. I am becoming an anti-Johnsonite, though with slow, unwilling steps. His policy seems to me wrong, and his practices bad. I fear the memories of his boyhood, when he was a Southern "poor-white," are ineradicable, and that he stands in awe of the chivalry. Yet his course from 1860 to 1865 does not look like it. . . .

August 15. . . . Philadelphia Convention in session. Fernandy Wood and Val-landigham decline to take their seats, lest they should thereby diminish and weaken the moral influence of the Convention. A good and hopeful sign. But if the

Convention do its work, the Woods and Vallandighams and Seymours will be our chief rulers next year. All the patronage and power of Johnson's administration will be used against the Republican party, to which (and to John Wilkes Booth) Johnson owes his great place.

August 19, Sunday. The Philadelphia Convention has adjourned, after a smooth session. All debate was discouraged and suppressed. It would have been dangerous and revealed deep latent elements of discord between the South and the country. Southern gentlemen were politic enough to sit mute and bide their time. The Convention has put forth a strong, well-written address. Not a difficult thing to do, for the constitutional argument of the Johnsonists is unanswerable, except by the proposition that *Salus Populi Suprema Lex* [the welfare of the people is the supreme law] . I predict that the fall elections will sustain the President. He has a strong case on the merits; the Radical project of Negro suffrage must find little favor with any but theorists, and the great law of reaction will tell in his favor. Perhaps it may prove best that the President's policy prevail. But I find my faith in A. Johnson growing daily weaker. . . .

Gideon Welles

During late August and early September, President Johnson traveled as far west as Chicago speaking in defense of his policies. Accompanied by Ulysses Grant, Admiral David Farragut, Gideon Welles, and other notables, he made an unprecedented attempt to win support for the coming fall elections. It was an effort to convince northern voters to vote for conservative candidates. Instead it was a political disaster. Gideon Welles recorded his impressions of the tour after his return.

September 17, Monday. Returned on Saturday, the 15th, from excursion with the President. Our route was via Baltimore, Philadelphia, New York, West Point, Albany, Auburn, Niagara Falls,—where we spent our first Sunday,—Buffalo, Cleveland, Toledo, Detroit, Chicago,—where we remained Thursday the 6th inst.,—Springfield, Illinois, Alton, St. Louis,—where we spent our second Sunday,—Indianapolis, Louisville, Cincinnati, Columbus, Pittsburg[h], Harrisburg, Baltimore, home. We only traveled by daylight, excepting when coming from Louisville to Cincinnati by steamer. . . .

The President made brief remarks at nearly every stopping-place to the crowds which assembled to meet and welcome him. . . .

The President spoke freely, frankly, and plainly. For the first three or four days I apprehended he would, if he did not forbear, break down, for it seemed as though no one possessed the physical power to go through such extraordinary labor day after day for two or three weeks. I therefore remonstrated with and cautioned him, but he best knew his own system and powers of endurance. He felt, moreover, that he was performing a service and a duty in his appeals to his countrymen, and desired to address them face to face on the great issues before the country. It was the method to which he had been accustomed in Tennessee and the Southwest, and he believed it would be effective in the North.

I was apprehensive that the effect would be different, that his much talking would be misapprehended and misrepresented, that the partisan press and partisan leaders would avail themselves of it and decry him. I am still apprehensive that he may have injured his cause by many speeches; but it is undeniably true that his remarks were effective among his hearers and that within that circle he won supporters. . . .

Speeches to a few crowds—or the same speech, essentially, to many crowds—are not in themselves, I fear, sufficient. In the mean time there is want of sagacity, judgment, and good common sense in managing the party which supports him. Candidates who are Copperheads, *i.e.*, who opposed the Government during the War, cannot become earnestly engaged or really enthusiastic supporters, yet the Radical Republicans hold back while this class is pressed forward. Such advocates can gain no recruits. There is a kinder feeling among Republicans towards beaten Rebels than towards Copperheads. But these last pay court to the President in the absence of the greater part of the Republicans, who have become Radicals. It is not strange while the Radicals conspire against him that he assimilates with those who, if they opposed his election, now doubtingly sustain his policy. It is out of sympathy and charity to them. They, however, are still selfish partisans and are unpatriotic and in adherence to mere party policy and a President they did not elect. . . .

At Cleveland there was evidently a concerted plan to prevent the President from speaking or to embarrass him in his remarks. Grant, I think, had been advised of this, and it affected him unfavorably. They did not succeed, but I regretted that he continued to address these crowds. Although it is consistent with his practice in Tennessee, I would rather the Chief Magistrate would be more reserved, and both Governor Tod and myself suggested to Seward that it was impolitic and injudicious, but Seward did not concur. He said the President was going good and was the best stump speaker in the country. The President should not be a stump speaker.

At Chicago and St. Louis the reception was magnificent. There was in that of the latter place a cordiality and sincerity unsurpassed. We were met at Alton by thirty-six steamers crowded with people and were escorted by them to St. Louis.

There was turbulence and premeditated violence at Indianapolis more than at any other and at all other places. At Indianapolis I became convinced of what I had for some days suspected,—that there was an extreme Radical conspiracy to treat the President with disrespect and indignity and to avoid him. Morton, who had early been obsequious to him and was opposed to negro suffrage and Radical demands, had become a Radical convert. He fled from us as we entered Indiana,—so of the little Governors of Ohio and Pennsylvania, who were purposely absent when we arrived at Columbus and Harrisburg.

Louisville gave us a grand reception. . . .

George Templeton Strong

Strong attended Johnson's speech in New York City on August 29 and was not impressed with it. He was becoming more critical of Johnson and his policies.

*A*ugust 20. . . . Morning papers full of political bitterness. The *Tribune* calls A. Johnson "Judas"—"Judas Johnson." That is mere Billingsgate, I think. Were he a politic scoundrel, he would make fewer speeches (imitating Grant's most popular talent for silence) and would not have declined by his veto the vast power and patronage offered him by the Freedmen's Bureau Bill. The Philadelphia Convention was clearly a most important transaction. If the so-called Radicals go into the fall campaign as advocates of Negro suffrage, they will be badly beaten. Their only true ground is a change in the basis of Congressional representation such as will put the voter of South Carolina on equal ground with the voter of New York. On that position they may succeed. . . .

August 29. Sultry and lowering. The city upside down, looking for the advent of A. Johnson, who is making a progress to Chicago. All vehicles ordered out of Broadway. My omnibus broke down in Center Street, and I had to walk home through ill-flavored side streets. Turned into Broadway at Bleecker Street. Broadway full of people, sidewalks lined by a continuous crowd. Windows and housetops fully occupied. I saw no shops closed, however. Johnson came along at last, preceded and followed by a large militia-escort. With him were Seward and Welles, Grant and Meade and Farragut, and a lot of notables besides. There was much cheering and waving of hats and handkerchiefs. It was what is called in newspaper English "an ovation." I did not quite like the President's bearing as he stood in his barouche [carriage]. His bows were a little too assiduous and too lowly, like those of a basso called before the curtain, not such as to become the Chief Magistrate of a great nation. But that may be hyper-criticism.. . . .

August 30. . . . At Union League Club tonight . . . The temper of the club seems most decidedly radical, and of an extreme radical type. Many foolish extravagant things were said against the President and applauded with enthusiasm. It seems to me senseless to call him a usurper—wicked and cowardly to speak of him as having been elevated to the Presidency by the late J. Wilkes Booth. But his dealings with this New Orleans "Convention" are certainly prima facie against him. I hope and believe—or incline to believe—they were a mere mistake or blunder. Why does he not neutralize their effect by vigorous action there or elsewhere, in Texas, for instance, where *ci-devant* rebel soldiers are shooting a score of suspected Union men every week?

September 3. . . . The Club did me the honor to make me one of their delegates to the Convention that met at Philadelphia this morning. Had I gone, I should have gone in very good company . . . But it is quite out of my line. I should have done no service. And though on the whole I prefer the policy of Congress to that of the President, I do not want to take part in proceedings that will doubtless endorse an extreme "radical" policy . . . Johnson is letting off one or two stump speeches every day as he travels westward. He makes himself too cheap thereby, and he says, moreover, many things that are not convenient. He descends to abuse of Congress, and suggests the most dangerous notion that this is not legally a Congress, because certain states are not represented therein. If so, *he* is no legal President, for the same states cast no electoral votes in 1864. All this will do him no good. *Demos* rejects any one who presents himself as agitator without decent disguise. . . .

September 4. . . . Here is a bad business at Cleveland (Ohio), disgraceful to the country and an omen of evil. The President harangued the mob there as usual, and a most weak, egotistical harangue he seems to have delivered. The mob, or part of it, interrupted and insulted him with cheers for Congress and the like. The President lost his temper, scolded, abused those who interrupted him as cowards who had stayed at home during the war, and pretenders to patriotism, talked about hanging Thaddeus Stevens, and so on, and disgraced himself profoundly. So reports tonight's *Post,* which is on the President's side, but I hope it is untrue. If true, it is nearly as bad as the memorable Inauguration speech a year and a half ago, which the *World* and other papers insisted was delivered by the "boorish tailor" under the inspiration of strong waters. . . .

September 5. . . . The President "progresses" and speechifies. Every speech costs "my policy" many votes, I think. No orator has used the first personal pronoun in all its cases (I—me—my) so freely . . . It is an unhappy mistake and may paralyze all his efforts to do the country service. I believe his intentions honest, whether his policy be wise or unwise, but this exuberance of egotism will surely weaken his influence. Seward helps him little. His auxiliary harangues are smart and plausible, but very shallow. Seward is a clever politician and has often secured many votes, but he has never secured any deep general faith in his sincerity and single-mindedness. . . .

September 12 . . . . The Republicans have carried Maine by 30,000 majority, gaining largely on the vote of 1864, in spite of the office-holder influence. . . . On the whole, I think I am a "Radical." I have wavered between the President's policy and that of Congress. But A. Johnson's stump-philippics have uprooted all my faith in him. He is doubtless honest, but he wants common sense, to say nothing of statesmanship and decency.

Frederick Douglass

The Southern Loyalists' Convention met in Philadelphia in 1866. It was the response of radical and moderate Republicans to the more conservative National Convention organized by Andrew Johnson that had met in Philadelphia the month before. The loyalists' convention reached a crisis on September 6, 1866. Efforts to adjourn the convention were finally successful at 2 P.M. However, it was reconstituted as a mass meeting at which time the abolitionist orator Anna Dickinson and then Frederick Douglass addressed the large audience. Douglass's speech may have caused the group to pass a resolution calling for federal laws to establish suffrage and equality by law.

I ask you to enfranchise the negro. The honor of the nation demands it. He has fought your battles when you called him to the war; now you turn your backs on him when the contest of blood is over! Oh! for a little Southern honor here in the North, that these loyal men may not be turned over to the merciless care of those men who sought to destroy the nation! (Cheers.)

The earth yields as richly and as readily to the black as to the white man; the sun shines as brightly upon him as upon his white brethren. We are American citizens, and merely ask to be treated as well as foreigners and aliens. We have watered the land with our blood and our tears, and we are ready to do it again. (Cheers continued.) Events form with rapidity and we scarcely comprehend their significance. Ten years ago he was a marked man for his utterance of sentiments that are now freely uttered in the face of day. The grand gathering in our city was animated by the same spirit that was murdered down in New Orleans. (Cheers.) Andy Johnson was to be our Moses (applause); but he has taken the back track. (Applause.) Without principles or friends, for no men or set of men can be said to love Andrew Johnson (applause), and if he lives to the end of his term he shall go down to eternal infamy. He deceived his own party, and when his party fell to pieces, from sheer rottenness, he clung to the rottenest end of it. (Cries of "hit him again," and laughter.)

When a man says he is afraid of universal suffrage, he is either a knave or a fool. (Applause.) It is nonsense to argue that because the right of suffrage be granted to the black man, he be admitted to equal social rights. As well might the rich merchant ask the vagrant to his table, and the society of his family. (Applause.) The negro asks only for his civil rights: to have the right to be protected in his own family. (Applause.) Color shall never by the example of the Constitution be a criterion of the right of liberty. (Applause.)

The Declaration says all men—all men are equal. God made of our blood all nations of men. The United States were included. There is some truth in the slavery of races, some have degenerated. But every race, even the Anglo-Saxon, has been at one time held in slavery. The enslaved Saxon and Sciavon [Scandian], and German were down then, they are up now. The time will come when the negro will be up. (Applause.) But they say the negro is too ignorant to vote, and they would vote as somebody told them to. Well, if they did, they would do just as you white men do. (Applause.)

If the Union party do not inscribe universal suffrage upon their banners before long, the Democratic party will. (Applause.) A candidate for Congress took occasion to see what relation the colored minister bore as a citizen of Rhode Island, and took occasion to say to his congregation that they should vote when they got his papers. (Applause.) The citizen the black man will vote where his interests will be most sacredly guarded. If the negroes know enough to fight, they know enough to vote. If he fights against his country's enemies, foreign and domestic, he has a right. A negro sober knows as much as a white man drunk. (Applause.) A negro knows as much sober as Andy Johnson in any condition you may name.

Johnson is afraid of [a] war of races. Abolition has been denounced as provoking the slave to cut his master's throat. A man has held his slave and kept his earnings for years and years, and then calls him to him and says, "Now, John, I am tired of taking your earnings, and I will treat you now as a man and leave you to the enjoyment of your earnings, and your wife and children." Is it reasonable that slave would fly at his master's throat for so doing?

Rutherford B. Hayes

On October 1, Rutherford Hayes wrote a letter to Guy Bryan, a friend with whom he corresponded occasionally. Hayes had been campaigning for some time and was nearing the end. Renominated easily for a second term in the House and certain to be reelected in one week, Hayes tried to explain to a Southerner his views on the importance of the election of 1866.

Cincinnati,
October 1, 1866.

My dear Guy:—Your letter of the 18th came duly to hand. It finds me in the midst of an unusually exciting political struggle. The election is next week. I am a candidate for re-election and expect to succeed by a large majority. I will bore you with only a few words on politics.

I think the election will show that the people are resolved to adopt the Congressional plan of Reconstruction. It does not *"disfranchise"* anybody in the South. It disqualifies for holding office those who have been leaders—the *old* office-holders. All young men are qualified although implicated in Rebellion. The disqualification probably applies to no man in your State who is now under twenty-seven or eight years of age. Recollect too that the disqualification can be removed in any case by a two-thirds vote of the Senate and House. That vote will be obtained in all cases in a few years, if peace and loyalty are restored in the South. You have, of course, seen our plan. I send you one of my electioneering speeches which contains the different sections, and let me frankly say *that if we carry these elections, this plan contains the best terms you will ever get—and they should be promptly accepted.* The young men are with us almost universally. The life and energy of the North is with us. If the elections are against us, we shall submit. If they are *for* us, the Democracy will submit. We shall be united in any event. Do not be again deceived with the hope of Democratic help in a further struggle. I hope you will give the Congressional plan a fair hearing. If we succeed you must adopt it, if you regard your own welfare. . . .

If we succeed in the elections now pending, don't be deceived by Andy Johnson. The North will be far better united during the next struggle, if unhappily there is one, than during the last. Johnson and his office-holders will be "a mere snap—a flash in the pan." Ten thousand majority in Ohio is as good for practical purposes as a unanimous vote. We shall be united in action. We shall submit, if the majority is clearly against us. Our adversaries will submit, if it is otherwise. My last word is, don't let Andy Johnson deceive you. He don't know the Northern people.

As ever,
R.
Guy M. Bryan,
Texas.

George Templeton Strong

George Templeton Strong was still hopeful about the fall elections. He hoped that congressmen who were opposed to Johnson's policies would be elected. On occasion he expressed uncertainty, but his mood improved as the elections drew near.

September 30, Sunday. . . . It seems admitted by everyone that the President's indiscretions have blighted his "policy" and mired his party. We shall see how that is next November. I fear the "President's party" is the old malignant "Democracy," most falsely so-called. He is certainly active in displacing Lincoln's appointees and putting very bad Copperheads into office as postmasters, collectors, and the like. I want to think well of Johnson. The statements on which one's opinion of him must be founded are obscure and conflicting. But I begin to fear that his name is destined to infamy. . . .

October 10. Election news from Pennsylvania and other places is good. The national majorities fall off a little in large cities like Philadelphia and Cincinnati, for they have to contend against the Administration. The post office and the custom house and the navy yard have always been formidable reservoirs of ballots. They are reinforced now by an army of internal revenue assessors, collectors, cashiers, clerks, and detectives. These officials are the semi-Johnson party. The old Democratic Copperhead party seems a little numerically stronger from the alliance of these hirelings. But I guess the country sees the case aright and understands it. . . .

November 10. . . . Tuesday's elections were a victory, thank God. We were routed in the city [New York], of course, but Fenton is reelected by a majority of near 15,000. All the states that voted on that day (New Jersey included, Maryland and Delaware excepted) voted a condemnation of the President's "policy." Another Congress will be controlled by a two-thirds majority of so-called Radicals, and competent to override any presidential veto. May it use its great power with discretion and moderation. The ex-rebel states seem utterly to repudiate the "Constitutional Amendment." Rather than ratify it, they will remain without representation. That is bad, and full of peril. But it would be far worse and more dangerous to open the doors of Congress to Wade Hampton and Robert Lee.

Gideon Welles

By mid-October Gideon Welles was losing hope of success in the fall elections. He even stopped regular diary entries after October 13. On November 17, Welles sat down to record the events of the day. With sadness he wrote of the overwhelming defeat of Johnson and his Reconstruction policies and despairs of the future.

October 9, Tuesday . . . Called in at the White House about 10 o'clock P.M. The President had about half a dozen telegrams from Philadelphia, which gave gratifying accounts of the results of to-day's voting in that city. If the rest of the State comes in with corresponding gains, Clymer will be elected. I am, I confess, agreeably disappointed in Philadelphia. It has done better than I expected; still I have doubts of general success. We may gain one or two Members of Congress. It is reported that we have gained the Fifth District. No returns from Pittsburg[h] and the West up to the time I left, almost eleven o'clock. The President is in good spirits and Randall full of confidence,—hoping too much, for there is a good deal of bad material and much political debauchery in Pennsylvania.

October 10, Wednesday. The election returns this morning are adverse and render it doubtful whether the Administration will hold its own. Still the result, so far as I have seen particulars, is quite as satisfactory as I expected. I think there will be a gain for the real Union, or Administration, cause. Had the Democratic Party been more wise and liberal, the result might have been different and better. But there has been an attempt to revive the old Democratic organization, instead of joining in the new issues, and to have very pronounced Democrats—Copperheads, or men of extreme anti-War feeling—for candidates. The rebuke to them is deserved, but it is sad that so good a cause should be defeated by such vicious, narrow partisanship. . . .

November 17, Saturday. Several weeks have elapsed, and many interesting incidents have gone which I wished to note, but, employed through the days and until late at night, have not had the time. The fall elections have passed, and the Radicals retain their strength in Congress. False issues have prevailed. Nowhere have the real political questions been discussed. Passion, prejudice, hate of the South, the whole South, were the Radical element and ailment [*sic*] for reestablishing the Union. Equal political rights among the States are scouted, toleration to the people of the South denied. The papers and orators appealed to the Northern public to know if they would consent to have the Rebels who had killed their fathers, brothers, sons, etc., brought into power. President Johnson was, and is, denounced as a traitor because he does not repel and persecute the beaten Rebels. The passions of the people are inflamed to war heat against the whole South indiscriminately, while kindness, toleration, and reason are discarded and the Constitutional changes and all real political questions are ignored. . . .

Now that the elections are over on this superficial, evasive, and skulking fight, this after-war feeling which has been prolonged and renewed for party purposes on the one hand, and this pitiful attempt to revive a defunct and deservedly defeated organization on the other hand, the Radicals say the people have decided on the Constitutional questions and indorsed the changes, when in fact they were never brought out.

Senator Grimes writes me that if the President does not take the present terms, harder ones will be proposed,—that never was more leniency shown to conquered by conquerors. These are the sentiments and views of our prominent legislators and statesmen.

I replied that the beaten Rebels were our countrymen, amenable, individually, to our laws; that as many as might be thought proper could be tried and punished if found guilty. That, the Rebellion being suppressed, no terms could be made, for no authority existed on their part to appoint negotiators, as would be the case had we conquered a foreign country. Here the Constitution and laws must do the work. If they are weak and insufficient, the fault was ours as much as theirs, and we must do the best we can under the circumstances.

But it is useless to attempt to reason with embittered partisans. The great scheme of the Radicals is to inflict vengeance on the whole South indiscriminately, regardless of their legal and constitutional rights. This was the steady aim of the centralists through the whole of the late long session; this is their present purpose, though such a scheme is subversive of the Government and the Union. . . .

The stage was now set for a more extreme Reconstruction policy. All of the efforts of President Johnson had been in vain. The Republicans in Congress had more than a two-thirds majority in each house and could pass over his veto any measure they desired. The Republican party did not have a specific plan, but soon it became clear that the president's plan was doomed and that harsher measures intended to protect the freedmen and to ensure that the South would never again secede would be passed. The hostility toward the South grew dramatically in the congressional campaign. Voters had decided that the president's plan was unacceptable. Only time would tell how severe the new measures would be. Few could have guessed that they would lead to the first impeachment of a president and to his near removal from office.

PART II

RADICAL

RECONSTRUCTION

When Congress reconvened in early December 1866, it was in an angry mood. Southern states had rejected the Fourteenth Amendment (only Tennessee ratified it in 1866). This meant that the amendment would not pass without southern states changing their votes. There was a growing desire to punish the South for its refusal to accept the results of the war.

In March 1867, Congress passed the Great Reconstruction Act for the ten states that had not accepted the Fourteenth Amendment. This new program ended state governments in the South and divided the South into five military districts. An army general was appointed for each district and given wide police powers with the authority to use troops to maintain order. The Great Reconstruction Act mandated new conventions to change the old state constitutions in order to make them acceptable. Those delegates elected to the conventions had to include blacks and to exclude all ex-Confederates who were barred from holding office under the provisions of the Fourteenth Amendment. The new state constitutions had to provide for black suffrage, be ratified by a majority of a state's voters, and, finally, be accepted by both houses of Congress. Also each state had to ratify the Fourteenth Amendment. Until all of these requirements had been met, the South was subject to the rule of the federal government. The veto of the Reconstruction bill by President Johnson was quickly overridden, and the program became law.

At the same time Congress passed two acts designed to stop President Johnson from interfering with Reconstruction. The Tenure of Office Act, restricting the power of the president to remove cabinet members without the approval of the Senate, was easily passed. Also the army appropriation act of March 2, 1867, required that military orders go through General Grant, who was in favor of the new Reconstruction measures. The president's vetoes were overridden, and the acts became laws.

The efforts of President Johnson to challenge the Reconstruction acts, particularly the Tenure of Office Act, resulted in his impeachment in early 1868. The House of Representatives passed an impeachment bill, and the Senate met to decide whether or not to convict him. The trial lasted eleven weeks, from March to May. During those weeks the president stopped criticizing Congress and promised to enforce the Reconstruction acts. Johnson's conviction was defeated by one vote, a two-thirds majority being necessary for his removal from office. His national political career was over, and he remained in office until March 4, 1869.

Radical Reconstruction measures were in place from 1867 until the middle of the 1870s. Northerners generally supported these policies, hoping that they would end the conflict with the South and protect the freedmen. Southerners, on the other hand, were less united—some went along with the hated measures, whereas others fought them every step of the way. The Ku Klux Klan became an important part of the response of Southerners to the new political reality of radical Reconstruction. The Klan was determined to maintain white supremacy at any cost. It was willing to punish any Negroes who committed "crimes," to discipline those who sought social equality or were "insolent," and to keep Negroes within their "proper" social bounds. After 1867 the Klan broadened its purposes to include political opposition to Reconstruction. It was this new political cause with its promise of success that drew many upper-class and conservative political leaders into tacit approval or actual membership. Thus, the Klan became the terrorist arm of the Democratic party, providing a convenient way to do what many southern whites felt had to be done.

The North watched uneasily as reports of violence poured in from the South. Should it pass new laws to enforce the Reconstruction acts, or would the original policies work if given sufficient time? Few were certain that they had the answer.

The reader will note that the three major themes mentioned earlier continue to appear in the following readings on radical Reconstruction. By 1867 the first theme, the great destruction to the South done by the North, was still referred to by many writers, but because conditions were better and other issues more important, it was of less immediate concern. The other two themes—the escalation of hostility over congressional Reconstruction and the requirement that black males participate in the politics of the South—became matters of even graver concern. New levels of violence were reached as Southerners resisted all efforts to enforce the Reconstruction acts. However, Northerners insisted on protecting civil and political rights for blacks in the South. This meant building state governments that included black as well as white voters and officeholders. There was no backing down from this commitment by Congress while the southern whites refused to accept the northern demands or to cooperate with efforts to enforce the laws. Thus, southern whites preferred to waive the right to vote rather than be forced into a political process so repulsive to them. There seemed to be no chance of compromise. ■

CHAPTER 5

THE ATTITUDES OF TWO NORTHERN WHITES TOWARD RADICAL RECONSTRUCTION

"Congress seems going ahead with vigor."

— GEORGE TEMPLETON STRONG

George Templeton Strong

George Templeton Strong, a practicing lawyer in New York City, carefully watched the impending crisis with growing anxiety. He was worried that the Democratic party, working with Andrew Johnson and the South, would soon return to power. His anger with the South grew more extreme with every passing day. He began to refer to white southern "aristocrats" as "floggers of women and vendors of babies." He believed that the freedmen in the South could be counted on to support the needed Reconstruction measures.

November 26. . . . Political affairs seem troubled. The Constitutional Amendment [Fourteenth Amendment] will not be adopted. It is dead, and its death is generally recognized. A. Johnson shews no disposition to conciliate Congress or to make any concession. He is refractory and lavishes his official patronage on Copperheads of the worst and most "septic" type. Congress will meet in bad humor. Its extreme "Radicals" will get up an impeachment if they can. A. Johnson disgraces his high place and deserves to be impeached, but these ultraists, as, for example, B. F. Butler, are no less violent in talk and revolutionary in aspiration than A. Johnson himself. They must be careful not to bring on a popular reaction. To retain public favor they should be most studiously moderate and dignified in all their action. If they undertake to out-scold or out-babble A. Johnson or to put him down by extreme measures, our popular weathercock will soon be pointing the other way. . . .

December 3, Monday. . . . "Extras" at two o'clock with President's message. It urges admission of Southern Congressmen temperately and fairly. The Congressional majority seems ready to go all lengths against the President. The temper of its caucus at Washington last Saturday was bad and ominous. I trust they may remember that it is excellent for the Republican or Radical Party to have a giant's strength, but tyrannous to "use it like a giant," and (what will touch them more nearly) that such use thereof may bring about a calamitous revulsion of public feeling.

December 13. . . . Congress seems going ahead with vigor. It is quite clear that the Southern States (so-called) spurn and repudiate the Constitutional Amendment, and Congress seems disposed to try another method of reconstruction, which will cut up Southern institutions, root and branch. . . .

Gideon Welles

Gideon Welles, observing the same events from his vantage point as secretary of the navy in the cabinet, had a very different view. A close adviser to the president, Welles agreed with Johnson's policies and was deeply suspicious of the growing power of Republicans and their complete control of both houses of Congress. For him the question was becoming a constitutional one. He feared that the actions of radicals could lead to impeachment and the removal of President Johnson from office. He continued to oppose all measures that would give blacks civil rights or the vote.

December 4, Tuesday. . . . The extreme Radicals in Congress and some of their newspapers are very vindictive and revolutionary. Their language in regard to the President is such as shows the unfitness of the Members for their places, and the columns of the press are disgraceful to the country. . . .

December 6, Thursday. . . . At the Radical, or as they now call it, the Republican, caucus,—since the Radicals have absolute control of the organization,—last evening, the measures for the session were reported upon and decided, the minority of the caucus surrendering their convictions, their duty, and their oaths to the decision of the party majority. These men have no deference for the Constitution. Parliamentary or Congressional deliberation is trampled under foot. . . .

December 7, Friday. . . . Sumner has introduced some resolutions which are revolutionary and wholly regardless of the Constitution. There is manifest intention to pull the Republic to pieces, to destroy the Union and make the Government central and imperious. Partyism, fanaticism rule. No profound, comprehensive, or enlarged opinions, no sense of patriotism, animates the Radicals. . . .

What will Congress do? is a question often put and never answered satisfactorily. The Constitutional Amendment cannot be adopted by the required majority of the States. But as States are excluded from Congress in disregard or defiance of the

Constitution, the same Radicals can with as much authority exclude them from satisfying or passing upon the constitutional changes. . . .

If the Southern States should be put to the ban by Congress and declared Territories, the Radicals will not have even then accomplished their purpose. . . . Andrew Johnson must be disposed of and impeachment must be effected. . . .

December 12, Wednesday. Negro suffrage in the District is the Radical hobby of the moment and is the great object of some of the leaders throughout the Union. . . . Most of the negroes of the District are wholly unfit to be electors. With some exceptions they are ignorant, vicious, and degraded, without patriotic or intelligent ideas or moral instincts. . . . As a community are too debased and ignorant. . . .

December 24, Monday. . . . The talk and labor are of Reconstruction for this is the engine by which they hold power, yet not a man among that great number of elected Radicals appears to know or be able to define what he means by Reconstruction. The States were for a time, while the Rebellion was going on, antagonistic. Those in rebellion were out of their proper relation to the Government. But the Rebellion has been suppressed. War has ceased and those of our countrymen who were in arms are, and have been for eighteen months, pursuing their peaceful avocations. Each State has its executive, its legislative, and its judicial departments, and the whole of machinery of government is in full operation; the State and municipal laws are in force; everything in each of the States is as perfect and complete as it was ten years ago before the Rebellion, saving and excepting their right to representation in Congress, which is denied them by the Radicals who want to reconstruct and govern them. There is nothing to *re*-construct. If Congress will forbear longer to *ob*struct, the country will move on quietly and prosperously. . . .

—————

In the early months of 1867 Gideon Welles continued to advise President Johnson to veto the bills establishing military government in the South and the Tenure of Office Act. However, his advice on military appointments was not always accepted.

March 2, Saturday. The President is greatly pressed with business. Sent in to-day his two vetoes. That on the establishment of military governments over the ten States was received with deep interest. The opinions of a majority of the Republicans are undoubtedly against the principles of the bill, but they have not the independence and moral courage to act in conformity to their convictions and confront the Radicals. Party subjection overpowers them. Thad Stevens and the discipline of the caucus are potent. . . .

March 5, Tuesday. . . . A question came up as to the power and jurisdiction of the military governors who were to be placed in charge of the Southern States. Stanton said they must be subordinate and accountable to their superiors who were in charge of the military departments. . . . I put the distinct question whether, if there were conflicts of opinion between the military governor and his superior,—as for instance if the brigadier governor of Georgia and Alabama should take a position, or issue an order which was disapproved by Major-General Thomas, in command of that military department, would he override and annul the order of the military governor? Stanton said General Thomas' order would control. I questioned it . . .

On March 12 Welles found out that his recommendation on the appointments of military officers had not been accepted. In his frustration he wrote two days later:

M*arch 14, Thursday.* . . . . The want of prompt and decisive action on the part of the President, who is deceived by Stanton [secretary of war], aided by Seward [secretary of state], who supports Stanton, we both lamented. It has made the Administration a failure and transferred power from the Executive to Congress which is now omnipotent and unrestrained. On every hand the Executive has been hedged in and crippled. . . . Seward has the ear and the confidence of the President, and is the man who by his efforts and representations retains Stanton. These two men have sacrificed the President. He has permitted it and thereby made his Administration impotent.

These were difficult days for Gideon Welles. His advice was not always taken, and the cabinet was increasingly divided in its recommendations. Andrew Johnson was faced with a challenge to his authority as he tried to control the Reconstruction of the South.

George Templeton Strong

After an initial flurry of interest in November and December of 1866, George Templeton Strong seldom mentioned the great events of congressional Reconstruction in the early months of 1867. His occasional references to these political events suggest strong support for congressional policies and fear that the Democratic party working with President Johnson and the South might return to power.

J*une 22, Saturday.* The illustrious Andrew Johnson arrived here last evening. He was received with the honors due his great place. A July session of Congress seems inevitable. Monied men talk of trouble to be caused by this session. I suppose there is no doubt that a financial panic and crash will come before long, and that repudiation of the national debt is not unlike to come next.

June 30. . . . . A. Johnson the Pig-headed is just closing another stumping tour. His utterances as itinerant evangelist of "My Policy" have been copious and characteristic. But he has kept himself tolerably sober this time. May a quorum of both houses appear at Washington July 3rd, for Johnson is doing South and North immense mischief every day, and needs a little more Congressional snubbing. . . .

August 5. . . . The political event of the last week is the Tennessee election, wherein "Conservatism" was smitten hip and thigh by the so-called Radicals, led by the refined and amiable Brownlow. A large class of white Tennesseans were disfranchised, and the freedmen voted the "Radical" ticket. Hence, we infer the triumph of a Republican ticket in every Southern State, even in South Carolina itself. The nigger vote seems likely to carry every state of them. What a bitter dose for their arrogant aristocracy of only seven years ago! Was there ever a more tremendous and searching social revolution? I know of none since the *noblesse* of France were crushed by the *canaille* of Paris. . . .

It is terrible to think of the sum total of arrogance, insolence, arbitrary power thus unhorsed and paralyzed, at least for the present, and of the humiliation of the *ci-devant* aristocrats and floggers of women. Floggers of women and vendors of babies, those were the functions on which the welfare of their social system depended. Of course, there were excellent and exceptional households whose slaves suffered nothing of the kind, unless when the sheriff intervened in the interest of a creditor, and put up nigger poppa, and nigger mamma, and nigger baby as three several lots. But the social system of "the South" has been founded on crime and oppression for years and years. The South is suffering and will long suffer for that great crime. We are suffering for our acquiescence in it. Hence my taxes and impoverishment. . . .

August 8. . . . Washington affairs look squally. A. Johnson writes Stanton that important public considerations would induce him to accept the resignation of the Secretary of War should it be tendered. Stanton replies, with equal urbanity, that important public considerations induce him to hold on to his secretaryship till Congress meets. The correspondence, as printed in this morning's papers, is remarkable for its brevity and condensation, or concentration. That is a rare virtue with our public men. They seldom economize on words. These two letters are models. War to the knife has seldom been declared with such distinctness and such brevity. Whether the President can decapitate the Secretary under the "Tenure of Office" Act seems uncertain. I should say he could. If he can do it, he will, for his pigheadedness is infinite. . . .

September 3. . . . Affairs at Washington do not improve. A. Johnson grows more pigheaded every day, and more sympathetic with the *ci-devant* aristocracy of the South. I fear the instincts of the village tailor—the "poor white"—survive in the acting President of the United States. Thank God, Grant seems sound, as witness his letter on Sheridan's removal. Were he unsound, no one can guess what wild revolutionary scheme A. Johnson might contemplate. . . .

Gideon Welles

Gideon Welles worried about the actions of the radicals toward President Johnson's amnesty and pardoning policies. He feared that these actions would lead to impeachment and a presidency forever weakened.

September 11, Wednesday. The Radicals are full of sensation and malignity over the "Amnesty" Proclamation. They see in it incipient monstrosities, and the leaders declare that the President shall now certainly be impeached. He has pardoned Rebels, as he had the undoubted right to do so, and this will allow them to vote, which Congress had no authority to prevent. . . .

September 12, Thursday. The *New York World* to-day has a very ungenerous and in a political view I think injudicious article, casting off President Johnson, for whose acts, they claim, the Democrats are not responsible, declaring he is the Republican President, etc.,—all for party, nothing for country.

Such a course is calculated to and ought to injure any party. . . .

September 25 . . . There are indications that the sense and reason of the people are moving in the Northern States, I trust in the right direction, but partyism is stronger than patriotism. The extreme Democrats seem to consider their obligations to party greater than to their country. In this respect they are surely better than the Radicals, who are partisan in the extreme. The Democrats do not, however, in all their excitement, ignore or trample on the Constitution, as the Radicals do, in order to attain party ends. . . .

October 1 . . . At this time, when the Radicals are breaking down all constitutional barriers,—confounding and ignoring all rights, State, Federal, Departmental, and individual,—it is the duty of those who are in position to be cautious but courageous, to abstain from assumptions, but to fearlessly assert the powers with which they are invested.

Congress is disposed to usurp all the powers of government, and take into its own hands not only the making but the execution of the laws,—to adjudicate and carry into effect its judgments. The President has passively submitted to have the executive department step by step encroached upon and crippled. Concession and submission have been advised, until the Government is a mass of weaknesses, losing its character.

George Templeton Strong

Strong foresaw Democratic successes at the polls in the North in the fall of 1867. However, he still had high hopes for Republican victories in the South and control of both houses of Congress despite the uncompromising opposition of white Southerners. He was not disappointed.

October 17. . . . Our political prospects are unchanged. The Democrats seem safe to carry the state. But they carried the state in the black days of November, 1862, and we survived the calamity somehow. Though their probable victory next month will be a serious misfortune to the country, we must not forget that the world has been moving during the last seven years, and that even "Democrats" (a few inveterate old Copperheads excepted) have moved with it, in spite of themselves. They are no longer what they were. Their position is now in advance of that held by the Republican rank and file and by Republican leaders in January, 1861. . . .

October 30. . . . Elections have just been held in Virginia, Alabama, and Louisiana. The freedmen voted for a reconstruction convention in each state. The whites were against it (preferring continuance of military rule), and the freedmen have prevailed. In Alabama and Louisiana the whites were apathetic and kept away from the polls, but in Virginia they put forth all their strength. It was in vain, for very many ex-rebels are still disfranchised in spite of A. Johnson, and Cuffee outnumbers his late master in power of vote. So it looks as if the two races were to be henceforth hostile and antagonistic. This is not very surprising, all things considered. But the *ci-devant* slaveholders could have done much to avert the calamity by tact and conciliation. Instead of this, they have, by all accounts, treated the freedmen as their natural enemies, and studiously displayed hatred and contempt toward them, which must have been nearly as galling as the tyranny of the old regime, and under the new state of affairs, wholly intolerable. Perhaps this is quite natural, too. Even now they are trying to make matters still worse, if possible. In Virginia, the hands employed in mines and factories and on farms are being discharged by wholesale "for voting the radical ticket." An inviting field for immigration! Unpromising enough two years ago, this development of irreconcilable social discord has made it the last region on earth in which a sane white mechanic or laborer would choose to live, or a Northern or European capitalist to invest a dollar. And for this, Southerners may thank their own blind, arrogant self-will, their inveterate obstinacy of pride and bad temper

This antagonism will make the black race masters of the South, unless something unforeseen prevent it. Very bad for the ex-chivalry, and not very good for us at the North, or for the nation. It may keep us unsettled for an indefinite period. . . .

———————

Gideon Welles and George Templeton Strong differed in fundamental ways over the new congressional Reconstruction program and its enforcement. Welles thought it to be misguided and to be resisted in all possible ways. To him, it was a subversion of the constitutional process. Strong, however, believed that the program was necessary to complete the work begun by the war—that of ensuring that secession was forever dead and that the freedmen would enjoy the full rights of citizenship. Thus, Welles recommended the vetoing of Reconstruction bills and cooperation with the Democrats to resist their passage, whereas Strong enthusiastically supported the bills and began to consider the possibility of new immigration to the South in order to make it a more hospitable place for white labor and capitalist investment. These two positions appeared to be irreconcilable.

Of greater importance, however, was to be the response of southern whites to the new laws. Their attitude and their response to the laws on a day-to-day basis would largely determine the success or failure of the northern efforts. The immediate response of the South was not surprising or encouraging.

CHAPTER 6

SOUTHERN WHITE RESISTANCE TO RADICAL RECONSTRUCTION

Are we not in a deploreable situation
to have negroes making laws for us[?]

—DAVID HARRIS

William Gilmore Simms

As radical Reconstruction began, William Gilmore Simms, partially recovered from the despair of the first months of the postwar years, focused his anger on "the despots" in the North—the members of Congress. Their policies were causing a general famine in the South. Unless these policies were changed, thousands would die. He continued to be frustrated by his inability to earn a "decent living" and by creditors who were bothering him for money that he did not have. He felt that Reconstruction policies must be repealed or else the white population would be driven out or perish.

To William Hawkins Ferris
Charleston,
Nov. 27. [1866]

My dear Ferris.

. . . . No news here—all dull, & monstrous scarcity of money. The people generally begin to say—"D——n restoration! Who cares for it. We are out of the Union. We are willing to stay out!" So much for your radicals. Nor will they stand to be driven against the wall. They will not suffer the South to be made a Poland or an Ireland of! *Nous Verrons* [we will see] . . .

Adios
W. Gilmore Simms . . .

To Evert Augustus Duyckinck
Charleston, S. C.
December 13. 1866.

My dear Duyckinck.

. . . All of my children, with this exception [daughter resides with her husband, Major Rowe] are with me here in the city, where my eldest son is now reading law, trying to make up for lost time. He left college at 18 to join the army, and has lost five years of his student life. Every thing is gloomy here. The prostration is complete. The crops are a general failure—there is no money in the country, and we anticipate a general famine. God be with you & yours in mercy.

Yours Ever truly
W. Gilmore Simms. . . .

To Evert Augustus Duyckinck
Charleston,
Jan 25 [1867]

My dear Duyckinck.

. . . I write, as you see, editorials in all our city papers, which yield me my liquors & cigars, and at present nothing more. All of these Journals are struggling up with difficulty & barely keep above water. The country as well as city seems wholly stript of money. My own embarrasments, in spite of all my exertions are very great and increasing, and recently I have been & am still suffering physically. I fortunately paid off, at an early period of the war, what I thought the whole of my own & the indebtedness of the plantation—some $10,000, but some few creditors, of small amounts, could not be found. They now rise up in judgment against me, and I am compelled to divide with them my present earnings, all of which are absolutely necessary to my own & the support of my family. This affects seriously my capacity to do good work. It keeps me harrassed anxious, and diseases my mind. . .

Ever Affectionately Yours
W. Gilmore Simms. . . .

To William Hawkins Ferris
Charleston,
7 March 1867.

My dear Ferris.

. . . Suffering in body, as I have been, the suffering of mind is still very far greater. You need not be told of the doings of our despots in Congress. If your own people submit, it is very clear that we must also. Not that we shall *accept* the conditions imposed upon us. We may submit, as a conquered people to the chain, but we shall not hug it, nor embrace the knees of the Conquerors. We shall only loathe them the more, and feel ourselves at all times free of all obligations. But on this subject, I prefer to say nothing. My personal and domestic anxieties continue to distract me, and leave me no leisure for the consideration of affairs of State. . . .

Adios!
W. Gilmore Simms. . . .

To Evert Augustus Duyckinck
Charleston,
March 21, 1867

My dear Duyckinck.

. . . We are all deeply immersed in gloom. Business is utterly at a stand. The produce of the country is wholly exhausted—the provisions nearly so; there is no money, & what the planters have borrowed at prices ranging from 30 to 60 per ct. on a mortgage of their plantations is equivalent, in 19 of 20 cases, to the utter abandonment of the lands. All these men are not only ruined by the operation but utterly destitute. Congress, however, has kindly relieved us from all obligations, of whatever kind, by recognizing secession as a legitimate right, recognizing us as enemies who have been conquered, & to be treated with the *Vae Victis!* [woe to the conquered]. It is well. Congress demands submission, and does not & can not expect loyalty. We have realized the usual fate of all Republican systems within the historical period. First after the Republic, comes the Democratic, the next natural step is the Ochlocratic [rule by the mob], and, the one man power, the Despot follows, as the sparks fly upward. According to the present Congress not one of your Northern States is in possession of a Republican form of gov. God save you, *mon ami.*

Yours Ever
W. Gilmore Simms. . . .

To Robert Barnwell Rhett, Jr.
Midway, Barnwell District.

[c. May 6, 1867]

As far as I can see, there is no possible escape from general famine, in which all will suffer, many perish. In a precinct of fifty miles in this district, there is not more than one planter in fifty who has corn enough to last him a single month; not more than one in two hundred who has enough for two months; none that have any that can last three months; and of these there is hardly more than five in the hundred who will be able to supply themselves with provisions of any sort, unless by borrowing money on mortgage, not only of the growing crop, but of the lands, and at such a rate of interest that no crop they can make can possibly save them from ruin. A great many will almost or quite starve, unless they can get help from some other resources than their own. Briefly, the famine which now threatens the land is all over the land, and no one region can help the other. The mules and horses, especially when owned by the negroes, and upon which the hope for next year's crop must greatly depend, are dying of work without food. They literally drop down in the harness, and much the same sort of a picture may be drawn of the humans, white and black. Life is prolonged solely by spasmodic efforts and all sorts of expedients, day by day, the parties not regarding any sacrifice which will yield the means of daily subsistence to their families. Unless the charities of the outer world are more prompt and more bountiful I do not see what is to avert the fate of thousands to whom the peck or bushel of corn, which suffices for a week, must simply prolong the agony of a death by inches. . . .

To William Hawkins Ferris
Woodlands, S. C.,
June 8, 1867.

My Dear Sir:—

. . . Our country is filled with widows and with orphans. Among these there are thousands who never clamor about their privations—*who suffer and are silent!* But it is impossible wholly to conceal the fact that they do suffer. I have applied your handsome donation almost wholly to this class of persons in our country Districts—my own especially. And all of these, and their circumstances, are wholly within my knowledge. Most of them are persons who have been habitually independent—free of care— accustomed to indulgence—living in comfort, if not in the enjoyment of absolute affluence. Many of them now are not merely destitute of help, and the attendance of ordinary servants, but, as I believe, suffer from a want of the simplest and most wholesome food. Your donation will be made to relieve from much privation: will afford comforts to revive an exhausted nature, to encourage a rapidly declining hope, to say nothing of a *faltering faith.* What I say of the *few* of whom I speak, is, I am sad to say, the truth as respects our whole country, and I see no prospect of change or relief. The South, unless the Government shall rise to that highest wisdom in government, which is magnanimity, *is destined to be the incubus of the Union.* The wisdom of government can only be shaped by the morals of society. If your people generally, could feel as those do who, like yourselves, are prepared to recognize humanity, irrespective of politics and party, there would be no difficulty. . . .

Very respectfully,
Your obedient and obliged servant,
W. Gilmore Simms. . . .

To Evert August Duyckinck
Charleston,

17 Nov. '67

. . . My boys at the plantation have, like most others of this country, made a failure in cropping, not making half a crop. The Fates still look upon us with an evil eye, and few of us, but apprehend that the denouement of the drama here, will be massacre. Unless the Congress shall repeal the reconstruction acts, the white population of the South must be driven out or perish. . . .

W. Gilmore Simms. . . .

George Browder

George Browder, a Methodist minister in Kentucky, was forty years of age when radical Reconstruction began. He was unhappy with the severe treatment of the South and with the new freedoms given to the freedmen. How could Negroes be given the vote while their former masters were disfranchised? How long would the southern states be held as conquered territory? When would this unfair treatment end? The future looked very dark to him.

March 4 [1867]—This day the new Congress goes into effect. Our state is not represented at present. The Southern States are out, & the most extreme, unjust, illiberal, & radical measures prevail in Congress. The president vetoes, but the party is powerful & carry measures over the veto. The future is dark. . . .

July 4—Day once sacred in the annals of freedom. What strange sights do you behold this day in the Land of Washington & Patrick Henry? Military law superior to civil authority! News papers suppressed, courts overthrown, judges removed, citizens imprisoned, property confiscated, elections controlled by military authority. Negroes admitted to suffrage & their masters disfranchised. The Southern states held as conquered provinces & the public confidence destroyed! The good people ground down with oppressive taxation, & nine states not allowed representation in the national council! Verily the shouts of jubilation that once rung in these states, will be few or feigned to day.

The Maximilian dynasty in Mexico has failed in the defeat & capture of the invader, & the last papers report that he has been shot by order of the Liberals under Juares. Poor Mexico. Poor America. . . .

April 14, 1868—Three years ago this day, President Lincoln was assassinated. The excitement of that day is almost repeated now in the trial & impeachment of Andrew Johnson. He will almost surely be expelled for trying to preserve the constitution against radical schemers. The country is in a deplorable state and growing worse. Clouds are darker & denser.

I am sorry I have so long neglected my diary as many important events have transpired and the influence of the political troubles has been sadly felt in the moral & spiritual growth of the church. Since my last entry, I have had better health than for some time previous.

Bishop Pierce reappointed me to the Elkton circuit, & I went on the first Sabbath to fill the first appointment at Hadensville. I was kindly greeted at all points & the brethren seem & say they are delighted with my return to the work. . . .

August 2 [1869]—Election day. The laborers stopped work to go to town. I voted *against* the additional school tax—because the fund is insufficient to educate the children & is a bone of contention & source of strife.

August 7—This afternoon the children & grown people have taken great interest in the eclipse of the sun—which was almost total—only a small part of the face of the sun being visible. Some of the fowls sought the roost & a few stars were very faintly discernable. . . .

August 14—A new thing in our neighborhood occurred to day. A negro Barn Dance! This is almost an insult to the moral sense & sentiment of our community. The dance was on Wm Gaines' land. My workmen stopped business to attend the frolic. . . .

January 20, [1870]—My hired man *Isham* was disrespectful to my wife & I rebuked him very sharply. Just before breakfast, we discovered our barn on fire—just in time to save it. The damage was slight but the peril was great & the smoke of burning tobacco stalks made us quite sick for a time. . . .

April 25—For the first time in Kentucky negroes are allowed to vote—they nearly all vote radical. I voted for Genl Lewis, democrat, to fill the place of Mr Golladay, resigned.

May 20—To night at nine oclock a precious little daughter was born to us, our eighth child. I feel truly grateful to our Heavenly Father that the crisis is past & Lizzie is doing so well. Dr Hutchings & my mother were with us. The Lord is better than our fears. I call the child "Lizzie." . . .

September 17—Sad day to our house! Our dear little Lizzie died this morning at break of day. She died calm & easy. God be praised for granting thus much of our prayer. Dear little sufferer—thy pains are over now. While thy natural eyes are glazed in death—thy spirit eyes behold "The king in his beauty & the land that is afar off." She had mild blue eyes slowly deepening into dark color, fair complexion—benignant—amiable countenance—beautiful form & regular features. Her expression was very sprightly & caused frequent remarks. She noticed more than any of our children of her age—up to the time of the fatal illness. Even when almost worn out with pain & fever she would force a smile in response to our coaxing. Dear one—sleep on till the resurrection of the just. May our sad bereavement drive us nearer to the cross of Christ.

We buried our precious babe near her little angel sister Ginnies grave. Home is dreary without her.

David Harris

David Harris, a farmer in South Carolina, disliked Reconstruction but was certain that it would not affect him. Unfortunately, he was unsuccessful in his farming and had to lease his land to white and black tenants. Still, it was impossible to pay his taxes and debts. Finally Harris was forced to begin selling his own land; it was a bitter pill to swallow.

Ironically, when General Gilmore on June 5, 1865, issued a proclamation freeing the Negroes in South Carolina, Harris wrote in his diary, "I do not think it will have much effect." Later he realized that he had been very wrong. Soon Negroes were voting and active in support of the new Reconstruction policies. Political prospects were worse than ever. His last diary entry was on March 5, 1870. He could write no more.

November [1, 1866]. Went to the village to do a little buisness and to hear what was going on at Court. Yesterday they had a negro witness on the stand. This is the first instant of the kind in the History of South Carolina. What has the war reduced us to? . . .

December 3. Sale-Day. Went to the village & sued Warren Smith (Freedman). I never expected being under the necessity of sueing a negro, but such is the case. This is about the first man I ever sued and hope it will be the last as it is a disagreeable [way] to make money. . . .

December 23. . . . At present, we have but one negro on the place (A man named Pascal [Spencer]). He has been at work on the millers' house, Hauling fire-wood, feeding stock &c. He is to farm with me next year. I think he will prove a good hand. . . .

December 31. This is the last page of my journal and this is the evening of the last day of the year. The old year is bidding us a cold farewell, for the ground is covered with a mantle of snow. All is still, cold and frozen. Not the least sign of a thaw is visable. Not a drop of melted snow or ice can be seen. All is ice. But as the wind is calm, the cold is not so disagreeable.

Renters are hunting farm[s]. Hirelings are hunting homes. Much moveing is being done and going to be done. But few negroes will remain in their old homes. Some move of choice, others are compelled to go. My three tenants have yet to move. I want them to give place to my new ones so that with the New Year we can all begin anew and try to survive another year.

But poor crops have been made this year. Corn is very scarce, and many families are even now without corn. I pitty them but can not help them much. I have [a] good lot of corn in the crib, 15 hogs in the pen and a nice lot of firewood under the shelter. We have good fires this cold weather, good health and plenty to eat. How will it be next Christmas? . . .

March 25 [1867]. . . . My upland on this place I have rented to a Freedman, named Paschal Peak. I am to furnish him with a horse & tools. He is to give me standing rent. 50 bushels corn for one feild. One bag cotton weighing 400 lbs and ⅔ of another feild &c. I think I have rented my land for about as much as I usually made with my negroes and mules. . . .

April 5. Court Week. . . . Much sueing have been [done during] this court, while,

I, with others recived a benefit. I was greived to see negroes put upon the stand as witnesses. This is but one of the fruits of being conquered. . . .

May 1. May Day, but no festivaties. . . . My tenants are much troubled to procure corn. Having but little credit & little money & dependent entirely on buying. I am trying hard to supply their wants. . . .

May 31. Went to the village to pay my taxes. Paid $22.29 for my share of the Confederacy. . . .

July 9. Reading Novels & doing but little else. . . .

August 25. . . . Sunday. Hail storm. Rain storm and wind storm. To day we have been again visited by one of those distructive hail-storm that are becoming so common in this locality. Though the hail extended but a short distance, the distruction is great. My tobacco & fodder is almost an entire wreck. My land is badly washed and much damage done generally. Gwinn's cotton & young corn is almost entirely destroyed. His loss is heavy, & he seems to feel it. Many of my fruit-trees are blown down &c. . . .

August 28. Gwinn Harris & several negroes are at work fraimeing the cotton-gin. I give the negroes 20 cts per day in specie & feed them. They work well & seem satisfied with their pay. I pay them pun[c]tually every Saturday evening. This seems to gratify them much & makes them willing to work for me when they will not work for other persons. For some days, I have been working too hard for my strength. I get so tired & so sore that it pains me to move in the morning. . . .

Efforts to register white and black voters in South Carolina in 1867 were only partially successful. Blacks registered in large numbers (over eighty thousand), whereas whites registered in considerably smaller numbers (forty-six thousand). Two-thirds of the counties (twenty-one) had large black majorities, whereas the other ten had white majorities. Men like David Harris refused to register in 1867 because it didn't seem to matter—the blacks would win anyway. Soon attention shifted to the Black and Tan Convention in January in Charleston. For the first time blacks sat alongside whites as lawmakers—writing the new constitution for South Carolina.

September 6. This is Second Round of Regeristring [registering] at the village. I am too busy to go to register. In fact I do not care to register at all. Some of us do not know what to do about regeristering but think it perhaps the best to let the yankeys do all such things as they please & quietly submit to the yoke put upon us & not to put it on ourselves. . . .

September 13. This as usual has been a busy week so far. The hired negroes & Mr Meadows have been engaged weatherboarding the mill. The Saw mill part should have been closed some time ago, but I was waiting to get able to saw my own lumber. Now, that the saw is at work, I am progressing with my work tolerably well. I am paying the negroes 20 cents per day (Specia) & Meadows 50 cts. I have dismissed Gwin for the present, his price being too high for such coarse work. Building a Negro house. As I had a chimney all ready build [built] and part of the logs ready, I determined to rebuild Jud[y]'s house. So at it we went, built the house in one day. . . .

September 29. . . . We are having many hard trials to contend with in the poor world. Our political prospects are worse than they were in the days of the war. Everything is in a gloomy fix & is seeming to get worse. Negro sumpremacy is the bone. . . .

October 5. . . . I learn that the negroes almost to a mas [mass] has joined the league headed by some of the indifferant white men. I am very fearful that [there] will be serious difficulty between the white men and negroes. . . .

October 7. Sales Day. Went to the village. There to find a great many persons both white & black all doing little or nothing. The crowds of negroes are increasing every day at all public places. . . .

November 10. . . . Times are hard indeed. No money. Credit is all gone & provision are even now (in the fall) hard to make or to buy. The negroes have but little. . . .

November 17. . . . Our crops are generally bad, and the free negroes are not disposed to work & to be economical. The Union-Leage is doing much injury to the negroes. . . .

December 25. . . . Mr Carter has sowed a part of the Camp Place. Carter had aranged to remain another year, but he fell so far behind with his rent that I thought it best for him to try another place. This throws the Camp Place on my hands again. Many negroes are wanting the place, but I fear to trust any of them for fear I will be deceived again. . . .

January 13 [1868]. . . . Our Black and Tan members have gone to Charleston to meet in Convention on tomorrow. There the negroes are to make laws to rule white people. For bid it, Fates. I am confident the Northern Democrats will soon oust these negroes & radicals then we will have a white man's government again. . . .

January 26. . . . I am anxious to hear from the Negro Convention. Are we not in a deploreable situation to have negroes making laws for us[?] My family have good health and plenty to eat so far. All well. . . .

February 6. Sale Day. Went to the village through mud and mire. There was many persons there like myself (doing but little unless it was complaining of hard times & the doing of the Convention). We all think ourselves in a most awful situation, our government being in the hands of ignorant negroes. But little property sold to day. . . .

February 14. . . . Every one seems to be wild on the subject of paying & collecting debts. The political world is in such a whirlpool of excitement that no one seems to know what to do, or what to think or expect. All are wondering what will turn up next & all are [wondering] what the *Convention will do*. My own affairs are in a tolerable train with the exception of a *few* Big debts that [hover] over me like an incubus. *Happy is the man who ows no man any thing. Remember that boys*. . . .

━━━━━━━━━

The place of "negroes" in the new political process in the South continued to trouble Harris. He could not see them as political or social equals. Nor was he certain that the freedmen should be allowed to work land owned by whites. He was not making money and worried about his own financial future.

February 26. Rainy weather & has been for several days and nothing doing. Fine time to sit by the fire & read the papers & see what the negro Convention is doing with us. . . .

April 12. . . . The negro question is still the all important subject of political excitement. Next week [we] vote on the adoption or the refusal of the Constitution. I think the State will go radical. But the District will not. . . .

April 14. Election to day to Ratify the Constitution. The negroes are jubilent over their expected conquest & the whites are all down in the mouth. Willie, James & I are going to the election to vote & to see what is going on.

April 15. The boys & I went to the Constitutional election yesterday. The day was very cold for the time of the year & the road was very wet & muddy. There was not so many persons present as I expected & not so much exitement. . . .

April 17. . . . I have to day engaged W Walden to do some work that Barnett had contracted to do. I am worn out & disgusted with his laziness & he is about as good as some of the other baptist brothering. I beleive that negroes are more reliable as regards their working contracts than the white men. . . .

June 20. . . . The people say that they are going to sow less wheat & manure the land so as to make the same on less land. In fact, the farmers are talking of working less land & almost entirely discarding the Radical Negro race. They will do as the day labourors but not as managing farmers. . . .

August 4. On Monday, the boys & I went to the village. There was a great many persons there & not much buisness doing. The Democrats held a meeting & tried to devise some plan to better our conditions if they can. The Democracy seems to be much on the increase. . . .

August 17. . . . Since I came home, I have heard that a negro was hanged at church until he was almost dead. The negro used insulting language to a white woman. . . .

October 9. Went to the village for Miss Virginia. The people at the village are almost as low in spirits as we in the country are. Some of us are begining to think that the radicals are going to elect their candadats for the Presadency. . . .

October 31. . . . The excitement concerning the presidents election has much abated. It is thought that [Ulysses S.] Grant will be elected & we must bide the conciquence*[sic]*. . . .

November 3. The long expected election Day has at length arived & as if by general concent we admit that U.S. Grant is to be our future President. There has not been the excitement that I expected. The election has passed off quietly in this Dst [District]. . . .

December 13. Sunday. This has been Court-week & a poor court it has been. Monday & Tuesday I was at the village & suffered more than a little with cold. I saw a negro on the Grand Jury. That was the first time that I have seen that humbling & disgusting site. Ignorant negroes to decide important cases between white men. How intolerable! . . .

January 21 [1869]. Time is passing on, but my journal *is not.* For some reson, I know not what, but I am getting [tired] of journalizing. Having no better reason, I will call it laziness & let it go for what [it] is worth & will begin again and see how long I can keep it up. . . . My freedmen are all working away. But they have no horses that can be called horses & I fear they will come out of the little end of the horn. . . .

February 2. The fine weather has finaly left us. To day it has *Rained* incessently. Cold rain at that, a bad day indeed. I have intended to commence getting saw-logs to re-cover the Golightly Bridge, but the day was so bad that the hired-hands did not make their appearance. I am to recover this bridge for two dollars per hundred foot. . . .

March 27. . . . The weather has been wet of late & now the ground is too wet to plow & I am trying to do some hauling when we can not plow. I am so poor that I can not own a full team of my own. So I find much inconveanance [inconvenience] when I have hauling to do. I do think that I must contrive to raise myself a team, or quit farming. I had thought that my renters would do their own hauling, but they are all so poor that they can not even do their own plowing. Negroes will not do to rely upon as croppers. They will not [plan] far enough ahead to do any good. Paschal has a coal-kiln on hand & all my hands are busy. Sold to Dr [Samuel B.] Jones a lot of brick at a cent each. A good price. Patrick & I are trying to arange to make brick this coming summer. . . .

May 18. To day we have finaly planted the lot around the gin. The land has been so wet for some days that we could not plow. There has been much rain lately, & the freshet has injured my Buffalo Bottom. Much damage would have been prevented if my hired negroes had fulfilled their contracts and had cleared out & cleared off the banks of the creek. I am getting tired of negro farmers. They are only calculated to worry the owner & injure his land. . . .

May 28. . . . My freedmen are generally behind with their work. But as they are to pay me stated rent, I am not much interested. I find it impossible to make them fulfill their contracts as regard the work they are to do. I am getting out of patience with the rascals. . . .

June 17. . . . This is tax time. We are nearly all on our head about them. They are so high & so little money to pay with. . . .

July 6. My Birth Day. To day I am forty-eight years old. Whenever I record a birthday, [I] wonder if I shall ever record another. One time must be the last, but no one can tell when that shall be. . . .

August 2. . . . *Taxes. Taxes.* With much ado, I have paid my taxes ($81.57). (This is enough to kill any poor man.) . . .

August 14. . . . This week I baled Leve (a negro) out of jail. He has promised to work four months for me. I have taken a mortgage on his crop to keep him from runing off & leaving me to pay his bond $100.00. . . .

February 27 [1870]. . . . This year I have but two families of negroes on my land and they are to pay me standing rent (to wit Prince & Patrick). . . .

March 5. . . . Taxes has come again & as usual, little or no money.

━━━━━━━━

The Jones Family

Mary Jones continued to try to run the plantation in Montevideo, Georgia. As a widow, she had to rely heavily on her manager, Mr. Broughton. He was not a strong disciplinarian and continued to ask for more money, which she could ill afford. Members of the family tried to keep her spirits up. Her daughter, Mary Mallard, urged her to leave the plantation and move to New Orleans. It was a hard decision. Mary did not want to lose the family home. Slowly her resources drained away. Her greatest anxiety was a possible war of the races because of the many reported meetings of freedmen nearby.

Mr. Charles C. Jones, Jr., to Mrs. Mary Jones
New York,
Sunday, March 3rd, 1867

My very dear Mother, . . .

All reports we have from the South are gloomy. I have endeavored in vain to effect a sale of our real estate. Parties here do not wish to invest at the South when so many better lands, and at cheaper rates, are offered in the West. The passage of this Reconstruction Bill over the President's veto also complicates matters very materially. . . .

Ever your affectionate son,
Charles C. Jones, Jr.

Mrs. Mary Jones to Mrs. Mary S. Mallard
Montevideo,
Monday, March 4th, 1867

My dearest Daughter,

To think over three weeks have passed since I wrote you a line! Your precious letters are a great comfort to me. They cheer my spirits and divert my thoughts from the daily pressure of care and perplexity, which I do assure you do not diminish.

I have felt at times that I must give way. The contract made is of the simplest kind and at the lowest rate—one acre to the women and two to the men, and the ground plowed, only corn and cotton planted; and yet they dispute even the carrying out and spreading the manure, and wanted a plowman extra furnished. And the fences are not yet made up, or the land prepared for planting. Mr. Broughton, too, appears very unwilling to give himself any trouble to enforce their contract. I sometimes feel that things cannot continue at their present rate, and this morning had a decided talk with him. He has accumulated business and not added one to the force here, but asked for higher wages. I have to give four hundred dollars, with no increase of force and diminished quantity of labor. I could do no better. The contract was at his suggestion, and I presume he thought it would save him trouble, of which he is evidently afraid. Gilbert is very faithful, and so is Charles. They are the exceptions. . . .

Ever, my darling child, your affectionate mother,
Mary Jones. . . .

Mrs. Mary Jones to Mrs. Mary S. Mallard
Montevideo,
Friday, March 15th, 1867

My darling Child,

I have just returned from a very hurried business visit to Savannah, weary and feeling very sad. All things conspire to make me so, especially the return of this most sorrowful period of my life. Oh, how long, how long it has been since your dear father
was taken from us! I feel at times as if I must die from the weight of grief which
presses on my heart. The unshared burden! Here I am utterly alone. The good-
ness of God alone comforts and sustains my poor soul with a conviction that for the
present I am in the path of duty, and hoping to accomplish the cherished wish of
my heart.
     . . . You know I lost all my mules, even to the little colt (Dove's last representative).
I will not by a great deal meet my last year's expenses, and our provision crop was so
short I fear many on this place will soon be in want. The freedmen—nearly all of
them—went to Savannah for their money; and although they need *bread,* almost all
of them, Gilbert tells me, bought either a musket, double-barreled gun, or revolver!
They all bear arms of some sort in this county. Such is the limited nature of my contract on this place for the present year—with no increase of laborers, but great increase of the manager's salary, and evident *decrease* of effort on his part—that I have
really very little hope of realizing anything from the place the present year. The only
advantage is the protection of the place in view of sale; but such is the state of the
country even *that* may not be advisable, although if a good offer presented, I do not
think I would hesitate. . . .

Ever your own loving mother,
Mary Jones. . . .

Mrs. Mary Jones to Mrs. Mary S. Mallard
Montevideo,
Monday, April 22nd, 1867

My darling Daughter, . . .

[April] 23rd. Yesterday was a great mass meeting (political) of the freedmen at New-
port Church. I am told there never was such a turnout in this county. They were addressed by Rev. Campbell, the former governor of St. Catherines, now owner of
Belleville plantation (McIntosh County), where he has a colony of his own color
(black) . . . . They erected a stage under the trees near Mr. Law's monument, and
had three flags (U.S.) displayed over their heads. Campbell urged them to hold fast
to the Radicals and give the Democrats a wide berth. This is the onward progress to
(I fear) a war of races.
     And yet I am more hopeful than I have been for a long time. I think the bill
of our governor, and that of the governor of Mississippi, will test if we have any

semblance of a constitution or any law in the land. I believe the whole government to be nothing more nor less than a great stranded whale, whose flounderings are just beginning to appear. I must believe that He who ruleth in the army of heaven and among the inhabitants of earth is about to defeat the counsels of the wicked and bring to confusion the iniquity of this nation. I do feel at times a *strange hopefulness.* . . .

[May 15th] . . . *Last night* there was a large meeting and registering of names at Riceboro. A Yankee Negro the speaker. Assurances given that the coming year forty acres of land would be given to each, and our lands confiscated and given to them, to whom they justly belonged. All here were present. A fearful state of things! Where will it end? . . .

Ever, my dearest child, your affectionate mother,
Mary Jones. . . .

Miss Mary E. Robarts to Mrs. Mary Jones
Marietta,
Monday, August 26th, 1867

My dear Cousin, . . .

The chains seem to be tightening every day. General Pope issued an order to withdraw the appropriation by the state to Franklin University on account of a speech delivered by one of the students. Threatened to close the college or convert it into barracks, but this has not been done. Exercises will be resumed, faculty supported by pay of the students. . . .

Your ever affectionate cousin,
Mary E. Robarts. . . .

Mr. Charles C. Jones, Jr., to Mrs. Mary Jones
New York,
Wednesday, October 30th, 1867

My very dear Mother, . . .

I have endeavored in vain to interest a single purchaser. Parties will not buy, and for very good reason. Who does wish to buy in a county in such an unhappy condition as that in which our beloved South now is, and in a climate far from healthy during the warm months of the summer? I must confess my heart is very heavy when I think of the present and the future of the South. I have no doubt but that Reason, at present dethroned, will eventually resume her sway; but intermediately what commotions may come before the white race regains its suspended supremacy? Who can tell? No one will wish to be there who can reside elsewhere. My impression is, my dear mother, that it would be best to sell out all the stock and perishable property at Montevideo and rent the place if a responsible party presents himself.

Negroes and Negro labor are so entirely unreliable that a sum certain is far better than a speculative interest in the results of labor. . . .

Your affectionate son,
Charles C. Jones, Jr. . . . .

Mrs. Mary Jones to Mrs. Mary S. Mallard
Montevideo,
Tuesday, November 19th, 1867

My darling Child, . . .

It is true, my child, this county is in ruins. The people are becoming poorer and poorer; I know not what is to become of them. My situation here is just this: one bale of cotton and about twenty bushels of corn made by the freedmen employed. Gilbert, whom I hired, has made me some more corn, but one-third is rotten. No rice at all, nor potatoes to speak of. And a salary of four hundred dollars to pay the manager! I had a talk with him last night and offered to turn everything into his hands, but he will not hear to it; and although I have furnished everything besides for his support and comfort in health and sickness, and he has really done nothing so far as labor is concerned on the place, he has not the honor or conscience to say he is willing to share in any degree the total loss of the year. I am totally at a loss what to do with the place, and am trying to sell cattle and sheep to meet expenses.

And now you must write me the best way of going to New Orleans, and what it will cost to take me there. If I only had the means, would send you just what you need to furnish your house. I must send you the Brussels carpet and a bedroom carpet and some bedding if no more. Would you be willing to pay the express on the carpets? Write me candidly and at once and tell me, my precious child, *when* you expect to be sick. I must bring on your father's papers; I could not leave them. All else—books, pictures, bedding, etc., etc.—must remain. Charles will be here 1st of January, and I could not leave before he comes. I am so much perplexed and distressed at my situation, and leaving the place unprotected (for Mr. Broughton will not manage for us again); and if I can get Mr. Alexander, I will do so. *Do write immediately; I have not a moment to spare.* . . .

Ever your loving mother,
Mary Jones.

Mrs. Mary S. Mallard to Mrs. Mary Jones
New Orleans,
Tuesday, November 26th, 1867

My dear Mother, . . .

I am truly sorry to hear of the deplorable condition of affairs at Montevideo. Would Mr. Alexander be willing to rent the place? Even a small rent would be better than planting yourself and finding things at the end of the harvest worse than nothing. Such is the demoralized condition of the Negroes in Liberty that until half of them die of starvation they will not realize the necessity of earning their bread in the sweat of their brows. Would Audley like to extend his white colony to Maybank? If some of the outbuildings had been spared, something might be done there with white labor; for the climate is so healthy, and the advantages of the salt water so great. . . .

How did the Negroes appear when you returned this time? Do they still seem to retain any of their former attachment? At this time the "Black and Tan" Convention is holding its sessions in this city. One of the papers calls them the "Bones-and-Banjo" Convention. A black Negro occupies the chair, and white and black are sprinkled alternately through the house. These are the men to frame a new constitution for the state! I think the sooner the Radicals run their race the better. . . .

My white servants seem quite cheerful and contented in my service, and if they will only remain so, I shall be satisfied. My young German house girl requires constant supervision, but she is so pleasant-tempered and respectful that I hope to make something out of her. She is too new a broom for me to know yet; it is common for all of them to run well for a month. . . .

Your affectionate daughter,
Mary S. Mallard. . . .

Mrs. Mary S. Mallard to Mrs. Mary Jones
New Orleans,
Thursday, December 26th, 1867

My dearest Mother, . . .

Yesterday was as mild as summer, and if it were not for the general financial gloom resting upon the city, I suppose it would be a "merry" Christmas. . . . There seems to be a general apprehension that there will be serious trouble with the Negroes in the country, many of whom are roaming around like Indians. Having made nothing, they are living upon the cattle, and it is thought they will soon make inroads upon the scantily filled barns of the planters. I fear there will be a like condition of things in Liberty, and I am so anxious for you to come away as soon as possible. . . .

Your affectionate daughter,
Mary S. Mallard. . . .

Mrs. Mary Jones to Mrs. Mary S. Mallard
Savannah,

Saturday, January 18th, 1868

Thus far, my darling child, am I spared on my way to you. The closing up of my life at home has been very painful. I am here with our ever kind and dear friends Dr. and Mrs. Axson, and expect to leave in the evening train of Monday the 20th via

Macon, Columbus, Mobile. I trust God for a safe and prosperous journey. You will know when I ought to arrive, and I know Robert will meet me at the depot. Your friends here all send warmest love. Kiss my dear little children for Grandmother. And with best love for Robert and yourself,

Ever your own affectionate mother,
Mary Jones.

I thought it best to attend to the box of pictures, and have shipped that and two trunks of my own from No. 3. Mr. Fleming thought I had best pay for them at the other end of the road, and said he had no doubt if Robert would say they were private papers of a minister and ask it, they would grant a reduction. They weigh heavily, and I will pay for them when I come.

   I have engaged a slab, and leave an inscription to be placed upon it. Wish I could have consulted you all, but I could not leave your father's grave uncared for, and have done the best I could.

Ever your mother,
Mary Jones.

Mary Jones did not see the end of Reconstruction. After her move to New Orleans to be with her daughter, she lived for fifteen more months. She died on April 23, 1869.

———————

Frances Butler Leigh

Frances Butler Leigh returned to Philadelphia in July of 1866. She expected to return to her home in Georgia later in the year, but her father put off the return while he repaired the house on Butler's Island. Impatient, Frances decided to return in March and went directly to St. Simon's. Later she regretted her decision because the building had not been finished.

   In the following months, she became depressed about the new "radical" governments and especially the willingness of the North to allow Negroes to vote. Stump speeches from the North were encouraging freedmen "to ride in the street cars with white ladies if you please." The result had been "two serious negro riots." She foresaw more trouble ahead.

   My return to the South in 1867 was much later than I had expected it would be when I left the previous summer, but my father was repairing the house on Butler's Island, and put off my coming, hoping to have things more comfortable for me. When, however, March came, and it was still unfinished, I determined to wait no longer, but if necessary to go direct to St. Simon's, and not to Butler's Island at all. . . .

   I thought things would be better this year, but notwithstanding my Northern luxuries, I found it much harder to get along. My father, finding it impossible to manage the rice plantation on Butler's Island and the cotton one here, gladly agreed to the Misses D——'s offer to plant on shares, they undertaking the management here, which allowed him to devote all his time to the other place. The consequence is that 'the crop,' being the only thing thought of, every able-bodied man, woman, and child is engaged on it, and I find my household staff reduced to two. . . . So I cook, and my maid does the housework, and as it has rained hard for three days and the kitchen roof is half off, I cook in the dining-room or parlour. Fortunately, my provisions are so limited that I have not much to cook; for five days my food has consisted of hard pilot biscuits, grits cooked in different ways, oysters, and twice, as a great treat, ham and eggs. I brought a box of preserves from the North with me, but half of them upset, and the rest were spoilt.

One window is entirely without a sash, so I have to keep the shutters closed all the time, and over the other I have pasted three pieces of paper where panes should be. My bed stood under a hole in the roof, through which the rain came, and I think if it rains much more there will not be a dry spot left in the house. However, as I would not wait at the North till the house on Butler's Island was finished, I have no one to blame for my present sufferings but myself, and when I get some servants and food from there, I shall be better off.

The people seem to me working fairly well, but Major D——, used only to Northern labour, is in despair, and says they don't do more than half a day's work, and that he has often to go from house to house to drive them out to work, and then has to sit under a tree in the field to see they don't run away.

A Mr. G—— from New York has bought Canon's Point, and is going to the greatest expense to stock it with mules and farming implements of all sorts, insisting upon it that we Southerners don't know how to manage our own places or negroes, and he will show us, but I think he will find out his mistake. My father reported the negroes on Butler's Island as working very well, although requiring constant supervision. That they should be working well is a favourable sign of their improved steadiness, for, as last year's crop is not yet sold, no division has been possible. So they have begun a second year, not having yet been paid for the first, and meanwhile they are allowed to draw what food, clothing, and money they want, all of which I fear will make trouble when the day of settlement comes, but it is pleasant to see how completely they trust us.

On both places the work is done on the old system, by task. We tried working by the day, indeed I think we were obliged to do so by the agent of the Freedmen's Bureau, to whom all our contracts had to be submitted, but we found it did not answer at all, the negroes themselves begging to be allowed to go back to the old task system. One man indignantly asked Major D—— what the use of being free was, if he had to work harder than when he was a slave. To which Major D——, exasperated by their laziness, replied that they would find being free meant harder work than they had ever done before, or starvation.

In all other ways the work went on just as it did in the old times. The force, of about three hundred, was divided into gangs, each working under a head man—the old negro drivers, who are now called captains, out of compliment to the changed times. These men make a return of the work each night, and it is very amusing to hear them say, as each man's name is called, 'He done him work;' 'He done half him task;' or 'Aint sh'um' (have not seen him). They often did overwork when urged, and were of course credited for the same on the books. To make them do odd jobs was hopeless, as I found when I got some hands from Butler's Island, and tried to make them clear up the grounds about the house, cut the undergrowth and make a garden, &c. Unless I stayed on the spot all the time, the instant I disappeared they disappeared as well. . . .

I spent my birthday at the South, and my maid telling the people that it was my birthday, they came up in the evening to 'shout for me.' A negro must dance and sing, and as their religion, which is very strict in such matters, forbids secular danc-ing, they take it out in religious exercise, call it 'shouting,' and explained to me that the difference between the two was, that in their religious dancing they did not 'lift the heel.' All day they were bringing me little presents of honey, eggs, flowers, &c., and in the evening about fifty of them, of all sizes and ages and of both sexes, headed by old Uncle John, the preacher, collected in front of the house to 'shout.' First they lit two huge fires of blazing pine logs, around which they began to move with a slow shuffling step, singing a hymn beginning 'I wants to climb up Jacob's ladder.' Get-ting warmed up by degrees, they went faster and faster, shouting louder and louder, until they looked like a parcel of mad fiends. The children, finding themselves kicked over in the general *melee,* formed a circle on their own account, and went round like small catherine wheels.

When, after nearly an hour's performance, I went down to thank them, and to stop them—for it was getting dreadful, and I thought some of them would have fits—I found it no easy matter to do so, they were so excited. . . . Both Major D—— and Mr. G—— spoke of this afterwards, saying 'How fond your father is of the people.' 'Yes,' said I, 'this is a [close personal] relationship you Northern people can't understand, and will soon destroy.'

I remained on St. Simon's Island this summer until the end of July, enjoying every moment of my time. . . .

—————

Most of the time Frances Butler Leigh ignored political events in the South. Occasionally in-formation would be received, but it had little to do with life on her Georgia plantation. However, a letter that she wrote in the summer of 1867 reminded her of the difficulties that she had forgotten.

St. Simon's Island:
June 23, 1867.

Dearest S——, We are, I am afraid, going to have terrible trouble by-and-by with the negroes, and I see nothing but gloomy prospects for us ahead. The unlimited power that the war has put into the hands of the present Government at Washington seems to have turned the heads of the party now in office, and they don't know where to stop. The whole South is settled and quiet, and the people too ruined and crushed to do anything against the Government, even if they felt so inclined, and all are returning to their former peaceful pursuits, trying to rebuild their fortunes, and thinking of nothing else. Yet the treatment we receive from the Government becomes more and more severe every day, the last act being to divide the whole South into five military districts, putting each under the command of a United States General, doing away with all civil courts and law. Even D——, who you know is a Northern republican, says it is most unjustifiable, not being in any way authorised by the existing state of things, which he confesses he finds very different from what he expected before he came. If they would frankly say they intend to keep us down, it would be fairer than making a pretence of readmitting us to equal rights, and then trumping up stories of violence to give a show of justice to treating us as the conquered foes of the most despotic Government on earth, and by exciting the negroes to every kind of insolent lawlessness, to goad the people into acts of rebellion and resistance.

The other day in Charleston, which is under the command of that respectable creature General S——, they had a firemen's parade, and took the occasion to hoist a United States flag, to which this modern Gesler insisted on everyone raising his cap as he passed underneath. And by a hundred other such petty tyrannies are the people, bruised and sore, being roused to desperation; and had this been done directly after the war it would have been bad enough, but it was done the other day, three years after the close of the war.

The true reason is the desire and intention of the Government to control the elections of the South, which under the constitution of the country they could not legally do. So they have determined to make an excuse for setting aside the laws, and in order to accomplish this more fully, each commander in his separate district has issued an order declaring that unless a man can take an oath that he had not voluntarily borne arms against the United States Government, nor in any way aided or abetted the rebellion, he cannot vote. This simply disqualifies every white man at the South from voting, disfranchising the whole white population, while the negroes are allowed to vote *en masse*.

This is particularly unjust, as the question of negro voting was introduced and passed in Congress as an amendment to the constitution, but in order to become a law a majority of two-thirds of the State Legislatures must ratify it, and so to them it was submitted, and rejected by all the Northern States with two exceptions, where the number of negro voters would be so small as to be harmless. Our Legislatures are not allowed to meet, but this law, which the North has rejected, is to be forced upon us, whose very heart it pierces and prosperity it kills. Meanwhile, in order to prepare the negroes to vote properly, stump speakers from the North are going all through the South, holding political meetings for the negroes, saying things like this to them: 'My friends, you will have your rights, won't you?' ('Yes,' from the negroes.) 'Shall I not go back to Massachusetts and tell your brothers there that you are going to ride in the street cars with white ladies if you please?' ('Yes, yes,' from the crowd.) 'That if you pay your money to go to the theatre you will sit where you please, in the best boxes if you like?' ('Yes,' and applause.) This I copy verbatim from a speech made at Richmond the other day, since which there have been two serious negro riots there, and the General commanding had to call out the military to suppress them.

These men are making a tour through the South, speaking in the same way to the negroes everywhere. Do you wonder we are frightened? I have been so forcibly struck lately while reading Baker's 'Travels in Africa,' and some of Du Chaillu's lectures, at finding how exactly the same characteristics show themselves among the negroes there, in their own native country, where no outside influences have ever affected them, as with ours here. Forced to work, they improve and are useful; left to themselves they become idle and useless, and never improve. Hard ethnological facts for the abolitionists to swallow, but facts nevertheless.

It seems foolish to fill my letter to you with such matters, but all this comes home to us with such vital force that it is hard to write, or speak, or think of anything else, and the one subject that Southerners discuss whenever they meet is, 'What is to become of us?'

Affectionately yours,
F——

I left the South for the North late in July after a severe attack of fever brought on by my own imprudence. . . .

———

The southern white response to Reconstruction was a grudging acceptance of its terms and a reluctance to participate in the process. A few were willing to cooperate with the new process but, for the vast majority of whites, their greatest fears had come to pass—the former slaves had become free and were now voting and would soon be holding political office. It was more than they could stand. Southern whites were stunned and now waited for decisions from the North.

The response of southern blacks was considerably different. For the first time in their lives, it was possible to get an education, to earn their own money, and to run their own lives. Reconstruction was a time of hope and progress, and many made the most of the opportunity.

◇ **CHAPTER 7** ◇

RADICAL RECONSTRUCTION AS SEEN BY NORTHERN AND SOUTHERN BLACKS

". . . we know not but that the assassin may await our coming, as marked for his vengeance."

—JOSEPH RAINEY

John Lynch

John Lynch, a former slave and later a modest success in the photography business, began to be active in Mississippi politics. He was able to read and write and soon was chosen for political office. He helped build the Republican party in Mississippi and rose rapidly into leadership positions.

The first election held in Mississippi under the Reconstruction Acts took place in 1867, when delegates to a constitutional convention were elected to frame a new constitution. The Democrats decided to adopt what they declared to be a policy of "masterly inactivity"—that is, to refrain from taking any part in the election and allowing the same to go by default. The result was that the Republicans had a large majority of the delegates, only a few counties having elected Democratic delegates. The only reason that there were any Democrats in the convention at all was that the party was not unanimous in the adoption of, and adherence to, the policy of "masterly inactivity." The Democratic party in a few counties in the state rejected the advice and repudiated the action of the state convention of their party on this point. The result was that a few very able men were elected to the convention as Democrats. . . .

135

Although a minor at that time, I took an active part in the local politics of my county. A Republican club had been organized at Natchez of which I was an active member, and which had weekly meetings. I was frequently called upon to address the club. When the state constitution was submitted to a popular vote for ratification or rejection, I took an active part in the county campaign in advocacy of its ratification. In this election the Democratic party pursued a course that was just the opposite of that pursued by them in the election of delegates to the Constitutional Convention. They decided that it was no longer unwise and dangerous for white men to take part in an election in which colored men were allowed to participate. This was due largely to the fact that the work of the convention had been far different from and much better than they had anticipated.

The newly framed constitution was, as a whole, such an excellent document that, in all probability, it would have been ratified without serious opposition but for the fact that there was an unfortunate, unwise, and unnecessary clause in it which practically disfranchised those who had held office under the Constitution and laws of the United States or of the state and who had taken an oath to support and defend the Constitution of the United States and had afterwards supported the cause of the Confederacy. This clause caused very bitter and intense opposition to the ratification of the constitution. When the election was over it was found that the constitution had been rejected by a small majority. . . .

─────────

There was no further effort to have Mississippi readmitted to the Union until after the election of 1868. The main issue in that election's campaign was the congressional Reconstruction policy. Republicans received a clear mandate, winning both the presidency and Congress. Reconstruction would continue, and the policy would be enforced.

One of the first acts of Congress after the presidential election of 1868 was one authorizing the president to resubmit Mississippi's rejected constitution to a popular vote. The same act authorized the president to submit to a separate vote such clause or clauses of said constitution as in his judgment might be particularly objectionable or obnoxious to any considerable number of the people of the state. It was not and could not be denied that the constitution as a whole was a most admirable document. The Democrats had no serious objections to the ratification of it if the clause disfranchising most of their leaders were eliminated. When it became known that this clause would be submitted to a separate vote and that the Republican organization would not insist upon its retention, no serious opposition to the ratification of the constitution was anticipated and none was made.

The time fixed for holding the election was November 1869. In the meantime, the state was to be under military control. General Adelbert Ames was made military governor, with power to fill by appointment every civil office in the state. Shortly after General Ames took charge as military governor, the Republican club at Natchez agreed upon a slate to be submitted to the military governor for his favorable consideration, the names upon said slate being the choice of the Republican organization of the county for county and city officials. Among the names thus agreed upon was that of the Reverend H. P. Jacobs for justice of the peace. It was then decided to send a member of the club to Jackson, the state capital, to present the slate to the governor in person and to answer questions that might be asked or give any information that might be desired about any of the persons whose names appeared on the slate. It fell to my lot to be chosen for that purpose, the necessary funds being raised by the club to pay my expenses to Jackson and return. I accepted the mission contingent upon the necessary leave of absence being granted by my employer to enable me to make the trip.

Natchez, at that time, was not connected with Jackson by railroad. The only way to reach Jackson from Natchez at that time, other than over land, was by steamer from Natchez to Vicksburg or New Orleans and by rail from Vicksburg or New Orleans to Jackson. The trip, therefore, would necessarily consume the greater part of a whole week. My employer not only granted me the leave of absence for that purpose, but stated that he would remain in the city and carry on the business during my absence. He was what was known as a Northern man, having come there after the occupation of the place by the federal troops. While he took no part in politics, I was satisfied that his sympathies were with the Republicans. I then proceeded on my mission.

When I arrived at the building occupied by the governor and sent up my card, I had to wait only a few minutes before I was admitted to his office. The governor received me cordially and treated me with marked courtesy and the most respectful consideration. He gave close attention while I presented as forcibly as I could the merits and qualifications of the different persons whose names appeared on the slate that I placed in his hands. When I concluded my remarks, the governor's only reply was that he would give the matter his early and careful consideration.

When the appointments were announced a few weeks later, the names of very few of those on the slate that I had presented were among them. My own name had been substituted for Jacobs for the office of justice of the peace. To me this was a source of much embarrassment. I not only had no ambition in that direction, but was not aware that my name was under consideration or had been suggested or thought of for that or any other office. Besides, I was apprehensive that Jacobs and some of his friends might suspect and accuse me of having been false to the trust that had been reposed in me, at least so far as the office of justice of the peace was concerned. I was strongly inclined to the opinion at first that the only way in which I could disabuse their minds of that erroneous impression was to decline the appointment. But I found out upon inquiry that in no event would Jacobs receive the appointment. I was also reliably informed that I had not been recommended or suggested by any one, but that the governor's action was the result of the favorable impression I had made upon him when I presented the slate referred to. For this, of course, I was in no way responsible. In fact, the impression that my brief talk made upon the governor with reference to my own fitness and qualifications was just what the club hoped I would be able to accomplish with reference to the slate as a whole. That it so happened that I was the personal beneficiary of the favorable impression that my brief talk made upon the governor may have been in one respect fortunate, but it was one for which neither the governor nor the one by whom the favorable impression was made could be justly censured. After consulting with a few personal friends and local party leaders, I decided to accept the appointment, although in consequence of my youth and inexperience I had serious doubts of my ability to discharge the duties of the office which, at that time, was one of considerable importance.

Then the bond question loomed up, which was one of the greatest obstacles in my way, although the amount was only two thousand dollars. How and in what way to give that bond was the grave and important problem I had to solve. It was the first time in the history of the state that a colored man had been commissioned to fill such an office. No one was eligible as a bondsman who was not an owner of real estate. There were very few colored men at that time who were thus eligible, and it was out of the question to expect any white property owner to sign the bond of a colored man at that time. But there were two colored men who were willing to sign the bond for one thousand dollars each who were found by the authorities to be qualified and eligible for that purpose. They were William McCary and David Singleton. The bond having been duly made according to law, I took the oath of office and entered upon the discharge of my duties as a justice of the peace in April 1869, which position I held until the thirty-first of December of the same year when I resigned to accept a seat in the lower branch of the state legislature to which I had been elected the preceding November. When I entered upon the discharge of my duties as a justice of the peace, the only comment that was made by the local Democratic paper of the town was in these words, "We are now beginning to reap the ravishing fruits of reconstruction."

Peter Randolph

Peter Randolph held no public office but was important in the efforts of the Freedmen's Bureau to help blacks in Virginia during radical Reconstruction. As a minister and a Virginian by birth, he stressed the ideas of education and money so important to the new freedmen. In his own words, "Give them education and money, and many of the unpleasant phases that now exist relative to the Negro would be unknown." He continued to work in Virginia until 1870.

Doubtless my readers will be pleased to hear something about the first political meeting I attended after the war, in Richmond. There was much excitement about this time, for the smell of powder was still in the air. A meeting was called by the Union people—including, of course, the colored—to consider plans for a new constitution. The big meeting was in the capitol, the late seat of the head of the confederacy. This was sacred ground made hallowed because of the distinguished Virginians and statesmen who had stood there. It was a thing unknown for a colored man to stand in those halls and on those steps to mingle his voice with the great men of the past.

He was known to tread upon those sacred precincts, only as a slave and servant, and never as a man advocating the rights of man. I took my place at the head of the big steps with the white Union men. My colored friends thought I was running a great risk by making myself so conspicuous when it was known that I came from Boston. I must confess that I did feel a little weak in the knees, for I did not know at what time a stray bullet might come my way, and rebuke me for daring to occupy a position that no other colored man had assumed. Finally I was called upon to address the assembly. I need not say there was silence, for all eyes were turned toward me, and they were anxious to hear what the colored man had to say.

I began my remarks, by saying that I was a Virginian by birth, and only a son of Massachusetts by adoption; that I had to leave Virginia to obtain and enjoy my freedom, and I had returned for the purpose of helping to build up my native state, so that she might form an important link in the great bond of Union. When the whites heard I was born in Virginia they seemed more anxious to hear me. I continued further by saying, that what we the colored people wanted, was money and education, so that we could own railroads and steamboats. And that when we came in possession of these we would have the white people to ride beside us and not behind us. When the meeting was over several of the local whites congratulated me, and offered to treat me with cigars, and so forth, but I politely declined. . . .

During the time Pierpont was governor of Virginia, a report came from Chester County, that the Negroes in that vicinity were in a state of insurrection, and that they were about to rise up and kill all the white people in that section. I was acquainted with the governor through my letter of introduction from Governor Andrew.

As there was considerable talk about this uprising, Mr. Pierpont requested my views on the subject. I informed him that I was in a position to know, if there was anything of the kind, but did not believe that there was a word of truth in the report; but that it was rather a pretext gotten up on the part of the whites to murder the colored people. The governor paid no attention to the rumor, by sending militia, and there was no riot. A few colored men were out hunting rab[b]its, and the whites cried, "Negro uprising."

This is a good illustration of many reported uprisings among the colored people of the South. Usually these reports originated among the white and not the colored people. This is one of the sham tricks of the South, to get up a Negro riot, call out the militia or the citizens in arms to butcher the blacks, for the purpose of keeping them in their places, as they say.

Of course there are good white people in the South, who took no part in these cruel outrages against the colored people. But they are to be criticized because they do not condemn them.

Every community is held responsible that permits one class of its citizens to outrage another class with impunity.

Hundreds of colored people in the South, since emancipation, have been whipped to death, lynched, and burned alive, until the question is asked, and asked rightfully, "Is the South civilized?"

What Thomas Jefferson said about slavery, so I repeat in substance, relative to the persecution of my people: "I tremble for my country when I think that God is just."

While speaking on this subject of southern outrages, permit me to say this also: that I believe much responsibility rests on the North in regard to this whole matter. The North should not be content as long as one man is oppressed, and his rights disregarded. If she is inclined to be negligent in this matter, let her remember the two hundred thousand colored soldiers who died in the defense of the Union, and the multitudes of white soldiers who were saved from death-traps, and starvation, by the hands of the poor slave.

The covenant that General B. F. Butler made with himself when he walked among so many dead and brave black soldiers, should be the sentiment of the whole North; never to forget them, or be untrue. . . .

During my stay with the church I had several of my white friends from Boston, Mass., to visit me, and see the nature of the work I was doing. It may not be out of the way here for me to mention a few names in this connection. The first is that of Mr. John Lovett, of the firm of James Lovett & Company. Mr. Lovett was much impressed with the congregation; but he had never looked upon such an assembly as he faced in my church. The congregation to him seemed to have the appearance of Joseph's coat, conspicuous for its many colors.

He afterward inquired about this peculiar composition of the audience, and wanted to know if white people were accustomed to attend regularly at the church. I took the opportunity to inform him that the people whom he supposed to be white were not white, but colored, according to the status of the South. "Why," said he, "they are as white as I am." I admitted the truth of his statement, but further explained by saying, that the condition of the colored child usually followed its mother, regardless of the white parentage; that is to say, if the mother was considered colored, the child was considered the same, though the father was white.

This same gentleman was much amused with a little incident that happened while he was present. I had in the pulpit with me a brother minister, who was overcome by the heat and labor of the day, and was inclined to fall in the arms of sweet sleep. At intervals, during my discourse, I would put my hand on this brother and endeavor to arouse him. This seems to have made such an impression on my friend Mr. Lovett, that years afterward, he would joke me about it, and relate the same to his friends.

Mr. Isaac Fenno, who was always thoughtful and kind to me, assisted me in my work among the freedmen, also visited Richmond during my stay. On the occasion of his visit I happened to preach in the Old African, or better known now, as the First Baptist Church. He was in the audience, but I did not know it until I was through my discourse. When I spied him in the congregation I made haste, like Zacheus, to come down and shake him by the hand, for I was more than truly glad to see him there, knowing as I did, the deep interest he had in my people. The hand-shake he gave me that morning was valuable as well as warm and sympathetic, for there was left from it a ten-dollar print in my hand. Such hand-shakes were not unwelcome in those days.

Mr. William B. Spooner, of whom I have spoken before, also made a visit, and because of his special interest and relation to the work among the freedmen, made a good report. Messrs. Walden and Haskell, the well-known tanners of Salem, must also be mentioned as among those who visited Richmond and inspected the nature of the work we were doing.

These gentlemen I have spoken of had more than a personal curiosity in the work I was doing, for they had aided me financially in prosecuting the same; and the visits made fully satisfied them as to the merits and faithfulness of the work.

Frederick Douglass

Frederick Douglass saw a great opportunity that should not be missed—an opportunity to establish "one law, one government, one administration of justice, one condition to the exercise of the elective franchise, for men of all races and colors." Reconstruction could put an end to anarchy and violence in the South and lay the basis for a fairer America. Douglass demanded justice for all when Congress met in Washington, D.C., in December 1866. His article "Reconstruction" was published in the December issue of the **Atlantic Monthly.**

The assembling of the Second Session of the Thirty-ninth Congress [December 1866] may very properly be made the occasion of a few earnest words on the already much-worn topic of reconstruction.

Seldom has any legislative body been the subject of a solicitude more intense, or of aspirations more sincere and ardent. There are the best of reasons for this profound interest. Questions of vast moment, left undecided by the last session of Congress, must be manfully grappled with by this. No political skirmishing will avail. The occasion demands statesmanship. . . .

If time was at first needed, Congress has now had time. All the requisite materials from which to form an intelligent judgment are now before it. Whether its members look at the origin, the progress, the termination of the war, or at the mockery of a peace now existing, they will find only one unbroken chain of argument in favor of a radical policy of reconstruction. For the omissions of the last session, some excuses may be allowed. A treacherous President stood in the way; and it can be easily seen how reluctant good men might be to admit an apostasy which involved so much of baseness and ingratitude. It was natural that they should seek to save him by bending to him even when he leaned to the side of error. But all is changed now. Congress knows now that it must go on without his aid, and even against his machinations. The advantage of the present session over the last is immense. Where that investigated, this has the facts. Where that walked by faith, this may walk by sight. Where that halted, this must go forward, and where that failed, this must succeed, giving the country whole measures where that gave us half-measures, merely as a means of saving the elections in a few doubtful districts. That Congress saw what was right, but distrusted the enlightenment of the loyal masses; but what was forborne in distrust of the people must now be done with a full knowledge that the people expect and require it. The members go to Washington fresh from the inspiring presence of the people. In every considerable public meeting, and in almost every conceivable way, whether at court-house, school-house, or cross-roads, in doors and out, the subject has been discussed, and the people have emphatically pronounced in favor of a radical policy. Listening to the doctrines of expediency and compromise with pity, impatience, and disgust, they have everywhere broken into demonstrations of the wildest enthusiasm when a brave word has been spoken in favor of equal rights and impartial suffrage. Radicalism, so far from being odious, is now the popular passport to power. The men most bitterly charged with it go to Congress with the largest majorities, while the timid and doubtful are sent by lean majorities, or else left at home. The strange controversy between the President and Congress, at one time so threatening, is disposed of by the people. The high reconstructive powers which he so confidently, ostentatiously, and haughtily claimed, have been disallowed, denounced, and utterly repudiated; while those claimed by Congress have been confirmed. . . .

Without attempting to settle here the metaphysical and somewhat theological question (about which so much has already been said and written), whether once in the Union means always in the Union,—agreeably to the formula, once in grace always in grace,—it is obvious to common sense that the rebellious States stand to-day, in point of law, precisely where they stood when, exhausted, beaten, conquered, they fell powerless at the feet of Federal authority. Their State governments were overthrown, and the lives and property of the leaders of the Rebellion were forfeited. In reconstructing the institutions of these shattered and overthrown States, Congress should begin with a clean slate, and make clean work of it. Let there be no hesitation. It would be a cowardly deference to a defeated and treacherous President, if any account were made of the illegitimate, one-sided, sham governments hurried into existence for a malign purpose in the absence of Congress. These pretended governments, which were never submitted to the people, and from participation in which four millions of the loyal people were excluded by Presidential order, should now be treated according to their true character, as shams and impositions and supplanted by true and legitimate governments, in the formation of which loyal men, black and white, shall participate.

It is not, however, within the scope of this paper to point out the precise steps to be taken, and the means to be employed. The people are less concerned about these than the grand end to be attained. They demand such a reconstruction as shall put an end to the present anarchical state of things in the late rebellious States,—where frightful murders and wholesale massacres are perpetrated in the very presence of Federal soldiers. This horrible business they require shall cease. They want a reconstruction such as will protect loyal men, black and white, in their persons and property; such a one as will cause Northern industry, Northern capital, and Northern civilization to flow into the South, and make a man from New England as much at home in Carolina as elsewhere in the Republic. No Chinese wall can now be tolerated. The South must be opened to the light of law and liberty, and this session Congress is relied upon to accomplish this important work.

The plain, common-sense way of doing this work, as intimated at the beginning, is simply to establish in the South one law, one government, one administration of justice, one condition to the exercise of the elective franchise, for men of all races and colors alike. This great measure is sought as earnestly by loyal white men as by loyal blacks, and is needed alike by both. Let sound political prescience but take the place of an unreasoning prejudice, and this will be done.

Men denounce the Negro for his prominence in this discussion; but it is no fault of his that in peace as in war, that in conquering Rebel armies as in reconstructing the rebellious States, the right of the Negro is the true solution of our national troubles. The stern logic of events, which goes directly to the point, disdaining all concern for the color or features of men, has determined the interests of the country as identical with and inseparable from those of the Negro.

The policy that emancipated and armed the Negro—now seen to have been wise and proper by the dullest—was not certainly more sternly demanded than is now the policy of enfranchisement. If with the Negro was success in war, and without him failure, so in peace it will be found that the nation must fall or flourish with the Negro.

Fortunately, the Constitution of the United States knows no distinction between citizens on account of color. Neither does it know any difference between a citizen of a State and a citizen of the United States. Citizenship evidently includes all the rights of citizens, whether State or national. If the Constitution knows none, it is clearly no part of the duty of a Republican Congress now to institute one. The mistake of the last session was the attempt to do this very thing, by a renunciation of its power to secure political rights to any class of citizens, with the obvious purpose to allow the rebellious States to disfranchise, if they should see fit, their colored citizens. This unfortunate blunder must now be retrieved, and the emasculated citizenship given to the Negro supplanted by that contemplated in the Constitution of the United States, which declares that the citizens of each State shall enjoy all the rights and immunities of citizens of the several States,—so that a legal voter in any State shall be a legal voter in all the States.

Hiram Revels

During the Forty-First and Forty-Second Congresses—1869–1873—a number of black Americans served at the national level. Hiram Revels of Mississippi was a senator from 1870 to 1871. Six others, including Robert DeLarge, Robert Elliott, and Joseph Rainey—all from South Carolina—and Josiah Walls of Florida, served from 1871 to 1873. Each felt the burden and the opportunity of representing millions of former slaves. They became active in the debates over civil rights, amnesty, public education, and enforcing the Fourteenth Amendment.

Hiram Revels, a northern black who went to Mississippi in 1865 as presiding elder in the AME church, delivered an impressive prayer at the convening of the Mississippi legislature in 1870 and subsequently was chosen to fill an unexpired term in the U.S. Senate from

February 27, 1870, until March 3, 1871. On May 17, 1870, Revels explained his position on amnesty for those Southerners disqualified for office by the Fourteenth Amendment. It was a moderate position.

Mr. President, I did not intend to take any part in this discussion. It was not my desire to do so. I do not rise now for the purpose of doing so, but merely to explain my position and that of the State which I in part represent, in regard to the question of general amnesty. I have been referred to by quite a number of honorable Senators who have already addressed the Senate on this subject, and at last I have been called upon by one to define my position and that of my State.

First allow me to speak of my own position, and then I will speak of that of the Republican party in the State that I represent.

I am in favor of removing the disabilities of those upon whom they are imposed in the South just as fast as they give evidence of having become loyal and of being loyal. If you can find one man in the South who gives evidence that he is a loyal man, and gives that evidence in the fact that he has ceased to denounce the laws of Congress as unconstitutional, has ceased to oppose them, and respects them and favors the carrying of them out, I am in favor of removing his disabilities; and if you can find one hundred men that the same is true of I am in favor of removing their disabilities. If you can find a whole State that that is true of I am in favor of removing the disabilities of all its people.

Now, my position is fully understood. Often I receive petitions from citizens of my State asking Congress to remove their disabilities; and how much I regret that it is not in our power to take that class of persons and put them by themselves and remove the disabilities of all of them at once. I would be glad to see this done, but we can only do it by the process adopted by Congress.

In regard to the State of Mississippi I have this to say: the Republican party, now dominant there, pledged itself to universal amnesty. That was in their platform; the speakers pledged themselves to it; and the Legislature redeemed that pledge by unanimously adopting a resolution asking Congress to remove the political disabilities of all the citizens of Mississippi, which resolution they placed in my hands, and made it my duty to present here, and which I have presented.

Now, I can say more, I believe, for the State of Mississippi than I can say for any of the other lately insurrectionary States. I do not know of one State that is altogether as well reconstructed as Mississippi is. We have reports from a great many other States of lawlessness and of violence, and from parts of States we have well-authenticated reports to this effect; but while this is the case, do you hear one report of any more lawlessness or violence in the State of Mississippi? No; the people now I believe are getting along as quietly, pleasantly, harmoniously, and prosperously as the people are in any of the formerly free States. I think this is the case. I do not think my statement exaggerates anything at all. Now, sir, I hope that I am understood. I am in favor of amnesty in Mississippi. We pledged ourselves to it. The State is for it.

Almost eight months later, on February 6, 1871, in his last speech before the end of his term as senator, Revels opposed an effort to prohibit blacks and whites from attending the same schools, arguing that Congress should do nothing that would increase the prejudices of whites against colored citizens.

Mr. President, I rise to express a few thoughts on this subject. It is not often that I ask the attention of the Senate on any subject, but this is one on which I feel it to be my duty to make a few brief remarks.

In regard to the wishes of the colored people of this city I will simply say that the trustees of colored schools and some of the most intelligent colored men of this place have said to me that they would have before asked for a bill abolishing the separate colored schools and putting all children on an equality in the common schools if they had thought they could obtain it. They feared they could not; and this is the only reason why they did not ask for it before.

I find that the prejudice in this country to color is very great, and I sometimes fear that it is on the increase. For example, let me remark that it matters not how colored people act, it matters not how well they behave themselves, how well they deport themselves, how intelligent they may be, how refined they may be—for there are some colored persons who are persons of refinement; this must be admitted—the prejudice against them is equally as great as it is against the most low and degraded colored man you can find in the streets of this city or in any other place.

This, Mr. President, I do seriously regret. And is this prejudice right? Have the colored people done anything to justify the prejudice against them that does exist in the hearts of so many white persons, and generally of one great political party in this country? Have they done anything to justify it? No, sir. Can any reason be given why this prejudice should be fostered in so many hearts against them, simply because they are not white? I make these remarks in all kindness, and from no bitterness of feeling at all. . . .

Mr. President, let me here remark that if this amendment is rejected, so that the schools will be left open for all children to be entered into them, irrespective of race, color, or previous condition, I do not believe the colored people will act imprudently. I know that in one or two of the late insurrectionary States the Legislatures passed laws establishing mixed schools, and the colored people did not hurriedly shove their children into those schools; they were very slow about it. In some localities where there was but little prejudice or opposition to it they entered them immediately; in others they did not do so. I do not believe that it is in the colored people to act rashly and unwisely in a matter of this kind.

But, sir, let me say that it is the wish of the colored people of this District, and of the colored people over this land, that this Congress shall not do anything which will increase that prejudice which is now fearfully great against them. If this amendment be adopted you will encourage that prejudice; you will increase that prejudice; and, perhaps, after the encouragement thus given, the next step may be to ask Congress to prevent them from riding in the street cars, or something like that. I repeat, let no encouragement be given to a prejudice against those who have done nothing to justify it, who are poor and perfectly innocent, as innocent as infants. Let nothing be done to encourage that prejudice. I say the adoption of this amendment will do so.

Mr. President, I desire to say here that the white race has no better friend than I. The southern people know this. It is known over the length and breadth of this land. I am true to my own race. I wish to see all done that can be done for their encouragement, to assist them in acquiring property, in becoming intelligent, enlightened, useful, valuable citizens. I wish to see this much done for them, and I believe God makes it the duty of this nation to do this much for them; but, at the same time, I would not have anything done which would harm the white race.

Sir, during the canvass in the State of Mississippi I traveled into different parts of that State, and this is the doctrine that I everywhere uttered: that while I was in favor of building up the colored race I was not in favor of tearing down the white race. Sir, the white race need not be harmed in order to build up the colored race. The colored race can be built up and assisted, as I before remarked, in acquiring property, in becoming intelligent, valuable, useful citizens, without one hair upon the head of any white man being harmed. . . .

Mr. President, I have nothing more to say. What I have said I have said in kindness; and I hope it will be received in that spirit.

———

Robert Elliott

During the years from 1871 to 1873, four black congressmen spoke out on issues of importance to their constituents. Disturbed by the lack of concern for black Americans and by the continuing unwillingness of Congress to pass legislation protecting the civil rights of blacks, these congressmen blamed prominent southern whites for the escalating violence and feared that the success of amnesty was a sign of the end of Reconstruction. Joseph Rainey of South Carolina protested against the growing number of murders of blacks in the South. Robert DeLarge of South Carolina spoke of the need for additional measures to enforce the Fourteenth Amendment. His colleague, Josiah Walls of Florida, backed the National Education Fund Bill, which was designed to provide additional money for black public school education.

On March 14, 1871, Robert Elliott of South Carolina vigorously opposed the removal of legal and political disabilities of white Southerners.

I believe, Sir, that I have been noted in the State from which I come as one entertaining liberal views upon this very question; but, sir, at a time like this, when I turn my eyes to the South and see the loyal men of that section of the country suffering at the hands of the very men whom it is proposed to-day by this Forty-Second Congress of the United States to relieve of their political disabilities, I must here and now enter my solemn protest against any such proposition.

Sir, it is nothing but an attempt to pay a premium for disloyalty and treason at the expense of loyalty. I am not surprised that the gentleman from Kentucky should introduce such a proposition here. It was due to the class of men that it is proposed to relieve that such a proposition should come from the gentleman from Kentucky and gentlemen upon that side of the House. I can appreciate the feeling of sympathy that the gentleman from Kentucky entertains for these men in the South who are to-day prohibited from holding Federal offices. They are his allies. They are his compatriots. They are to-day disfranchised simply because they rush madly into rebellion against this, the best government that exists under heaven . . .

The gentleman from Illinois [Mr. FARNSWORTH] took occasion, in his argument on Friday last, to compare the condition of the man who is to-day disfranchised and the man who is allowed to hold office in the South. He drew a parallel between the disfranchised old man and his servant, or slave, who to-day holds office or may do so. He tells you that you should take into consideration the condition of this poor old man who, because he simply happened to join the rebellion after having taken an oath to support the Constitution of the Government of the United States is prohibited from holding office, while his slave is allowed to hold office under the State and the United States governments. Ay, sir, the reason of this difference between the political status of the two is simply this: that while this old man, with whom the gentleman from Illinois sympathizes in his heart, was rebellious against the Government which had fostered and sustained and protected him, his slave was loyal to that Government, loyal to its army, and loved its flag, which the man who had been reared under it, who had been fostered and protected by it, had learned only to despise. The difference is this: that while that "poor old man," of whom the gentleman speaks so sympathizingly, would only curse the Government, would only ill-treat and murder its loyal adherents, the slave was the friend of that government, and the protector and defender of whose who were endeavoring to uphold it. . . .

I ask this House, I ask gentlemen on this side especially, whether they are willing to join hands with those who propose to-day to relieve these men of their disabilities? Are they willing to tell the loyal men of the South, whose only offense is that they have been true to the Government, that they have sustained Congress in its just and lawful acts, that they have maintained the authority of Congress; are gentlemen willing to tell these loyal men that Congress is not disposed to protect them, but, on the contrary, is willing at their expense to pay a premium for disloyalty?

Sir, I speak not to-day on behalf of the colored loyalists of the South alone. I wish it to be distinctly understood that I represent here a constituency composed of men whose complexions are like those of gentlemen around me as well as men whose complexions are similar to my own. I represent a constituency as loyal as the constituency of any other gentleman upon this floor. Those men appeal to you to-day to do justice to them. They ask you to protect them by legislation, instead of placing them under the heel of those men who have ruled in the South with an iron hand since the reconstruction acts were passed. Sir, I come here backed up by a majority as large probably as that of any gentleman on this floor; I come here representing a Republican district; but unless this Congress will aid those loyal men of the South, unless, instead of passing propositions of this kind, it will turn its attention, and that speedily, to the protection of property and life in the South, the Republican party in this House cannot expect the support of those whom I represent.

———————

Joseph Rainey

Several weeks later, on April 1, Joseph Rainey of South Carolina expressed his anxiety over the growing violence against blacks in the South.

Mr. Speaker, in approaching the subject now under consideration I do so with a deep sense of its magnitude and importance, and in full recognition of the fact that a remedy is needed to meet the evil now existing in most of the southern States, but especially in that one which I have the honor to represent in part, the State of South Carolina. The enormity of the crimes constantly perpetrated there finds no parallel in the history of this Republic in her very darkest days. . . .

I need not, Mr. Speaker, recite here the murderous deeds committed both in North and South Carolina. I could touch the feelings of this House by the story of widows and orphans now wandering amid the ravines of the rural counties of my native State seeking protection and maintenance from others who are yet unable, on account of their own poverty, to grant them aid. I could dwell upon the sorrows of poor women, with their helpless infants, cast upon the world, homeless and destitute, deprived of their natural protectors by the red hand of the midnight assassin. I could appeal to you, members upon this floor, as husbands and fathers, to picture to yourselves the desolation of your own happy firesides should you be suddenly snatched away from your loved ones. Think of gray-haired men, whose fourscore years are almost numbered, the venerated heads of peaceful households, without warning murdered for political opinion's sake. . . .

It has been asserted that protection for the colored people only has been demanded; and in this there is a certain degree of truth, because they are noted for their steadfastness to the Union and the cause of liberty as guaranteed by the Constitution. But, on the other hand, this protection is equally desired for those loyal whites, some to the manner born, others who, in the exercise of their natural rights as American citizens, have seen fit to remove thither from other sections of the States, and who are now undergoing persecution simply on account of their activity in caring out Union principles and loyal sentiments in the South. Their efforts have contributed largely to further reconstruction and the restoration of the southern States to the old fellowship of the Federal compact. It is indeed hard that their reward for their well-meant earnestness should be that of being violently treated, and even forced to flee from the homes of their choice. It will be a foul stain upon the escutcheon of our land if such atrocities be tamely suffered longer to continue. . . .

In conclusion, sir, I would say that it is in no spirit of bitterness against the southern people that I have spoken to-day. There are many among them for whom I entertain a profound regard, having known them in former and brighter days of their history. I have always felt a pride in the prestige of my native State, noted as she has been for her noble sons, with their lofty intellect or tried statesmanship. But it is not possible for me to speak in quiet and studied words of those unworthy her ancient and honorable name, who at this very day are doing all they can do to deface her fair records of the past and bring the old State into disrepute.

I can say for my people that we ardently desire peace for ourselves and for the whole nation. Come what will, we are fully determined to stand by the Republican party and the Government. As to our fate, "we are not wood, we are not stone," but men, with feelings and sensibilities like other men whose skin is of a lighter hue.

When myself and colleagues shall leave these Halls and turn our footsteps toward our southern homes we know not but that the assassin may await our coming, as marked for his vengeance. Should this befall, we would bid Congress and our country to remember that 'twas—

"Bloody treason flourish'd over us."

Be it as it may, we have resolved to be loyal and firm, "and if we perish, we perish!" I earnestly hope the [civil rights] bill will pass.

———————

A year later, on May 13, 1872, both Rainey and Elliott strenuously objected to the constant parliamentary maneuvers that blocked the civil rights bill, whereas the amnesty bill sailed through with no resistance. Rainey made his point with considerable earnestness.

M̲r. Speaker, there is no member on this floor who hails with greater satisfaction and gratification than myself a bill of this description, having for its avowed purpose the removal of those disabilities imposed by the fourteenth article of the amendments to the Constitution of the United States upon those lately in rebellion. There are many who are under these disabilities for whom I entertain the highest respect and esteem. I regretted that their course of action in the past made it necessary for Congress to impose on them any disabilities whatever. It is not the disposition of my constituency that these disabilities should longer be retained on them. We are desirous, sir, of being magnanimous; it may be that we are so to a fault; nevertheless, we have open and frank hearts toward those who were our former oppressors and taskmasters. We foster no enmity now, and we desire to foster none for their acts in the past to us, nor to the Government we love so well. But while we are willing to accord them their enfranchisement, and here to-day give our votes that they may be amnestied; while we declare our hearts open and free from any vindictive feelings toward them, we would say to those gentlemen on the other side, and also to those on this side who are representing more directly the sentiment and wishes of our disfranchised fellow citizens, that there is another class of citizens in this country who have certain dear rights and immunities which they would like you, sirs, to remember and respect.

The Republican members of this House will give their votes for the passage of this amnesty bill. The majority of them are also in favor of civil rights, which my people, the colored people, are desirous of having. We are in earnest about this matter. We are earnest in our support of the Government. We were earnest in the hour of the nation's perils and dangers; and now, in our country's comparative peace and tranquility, we are in earnest for our rights. We now invoke you, gentlemen, to show the same magnanimity and kindly feeling toward us—a race long oppressed; and in demonstration of this humane and just feeling give, I implore you, give support to the civil rights bill, which we have been asking at your hands, lo! these many days.

You will observe that when a bill is introduced for the purpose of removing political disabilities, no parliamentary maneuverings are resorted to by the Republicans to impede the passage of such a bill.

I want the House further to understand, and especially the gentlemen on the other side, that this apparent indifference and reticence on our part is not from any want of the knowledge of parliamentary tactics by which legislation is often retarded, and salutary measures hindered, but it is because we are disposed to facilitate and assist the furtherance of those measures we believe equitable and just to our fellow-man; thus doing unto others as we would they should do unto us. Now, in respect to the action of the Democrats, I regret very much to say that whenever a bill comes up here which is designed to relieve and benefit the outraged and oppressed negro population of this country, those whom I may strictly call my constituency, their apparent eagerness to defeat such desirable measures is perceptible on every hand, and is known to all. No vigilance or efforts were spared on their part to defeat the civil rights bill whenever it came up in its regular order. I hope, in the future, gentlemen, you will deal with us justly and generously as we now propose to deal with the late rebels. I hope you will assist us in securing our civil rights. I need not say to you that we fought for the maintenance of this Government while those who are about to be amnestied fought to destroy it. I thank the House for this courtesy.

Robert Elliott

A few minutes later Robert Elliott made similar remarks on the need for fairness and submitted a resolution calling on the Judiciary Committee to release the civil rights bill.

I do not want this resolution acted upon until the bill of the gentleman from Massachusetts [Mr. BUTLER] has passed. I desire simply, Mr. Speaker, to state my reasons why I introduce the resolution now.

I know full well that I have fallen under the ban of opprobrium, and that certain gentlemen in this House, have attempted to class me among those who are immodest, because on a former occasion I declined to give my vote for amnesty, while at the same time other citizens of the United States were deprived of their rights under the Government. I acted as I did in that regard not because I had any feeling against those who were laboring under political disabilities, but because I desired that the magnanimous action of the Government on behalf of those who were untrue to the Government in the past should go hand in hand with the righteousness of the Government in protecting its own citizens.

To-day, sir, when this bill for the removal of political disabilities has been presented here again, I intend to vote for the measure. But I desire at the same time to test the sincerity of those who claim that they are patriotic in this matter. I wish to see whether the gentlemen who claim that they desire the removal of the political disabilities of those who labor under them, and who sit upon the other side of the House, really mean what they say; for they know as well as I do that no bill for the removal of political disabilities can pass the Senate until this House shall have acted upon the bill for the protection of all citizens in their civil rights. If, therefore, they desire that the men who labor under political disabilities shall have amnesty, they will not filibuster, as they have been doing, but will allow the majority of the House—which has the right under all parliamentary rules to decide upon such questions—to act upon the civil rights bill, and let both bills go before the Senate for the sanction of that body. And I feel assured if the civil rights bill should pass the House along with the amnesty bill, both of them will become the law before Congress shall have adjourned.

That is the reason why I submitted the resolution at this stage of the proceedings, and I hope it will be adopted.

Joseph Rainey

On the last day of the session, March 3, 1873, tempers flared over the complaint of Congressman Acker of Pennsylvania that he had been treated unfairly by the Speaker. Rainey and his colleagues were unmoved by his complaint.

Mr. NIBLACK, of Indiana. One word further. While I am glad that the gentleman from Pennsylvania [Mr. ACKER] has had this opportunity to make his explanation, I wish to state that I distinctly remember that during the last session of Congress he did have an opportunity to offer his measure for the granting of a general amnesty.

Mr. CROCKER. I must ask that better order be preserved by members. If there is anything to be said by any one that in any way involves the official character of the Speaker of this House, we ought all to be able to hear and understand it.

Mr. RAINEY. Allow me to say, Mr. Speaker, that the gentleman from Pennsylvania [Mr. ACKER] was treated by the Speaker about as fairly during the last session as were the colored members of this House, the Republicans, and the rest of the Democrats.

We had a bill here for the relief of about four million people from the effects of the prejudices and the oppression that have for so long existed against them in this country, and which have been so continually fostered against them. Time and time again did we try to bring that bill before the House for its action, and the gentleman from Pennsylvania and many others on his side of the House refused to allow a vote of the House upon it, although it represented the true sentiment of the Republican members of this body.

And now, because a few men who had raised their traitorous hands against this Government have not had all their political disabilities removed, he gets up here to-day and undertakes to censure this House and the Speaker because he says he was not allowed to have passed a bill for their general amnesty. Sir, I say that if there are any people in this country who have a right to find fault, it is the class to which I belong, because that gentleman and his political friends would not allow the civil rights bill to be acted upon by this House. I say we should be generous to all, not simply to a few. I am sorry to know that the gentleman did not have more magnanimity than simply to desire to obtain something for the benefit of the few. I am sorry his heart was not large enough to embrace the down-trodden and oppressed people of this country, but that he rather desired to select the few for his generosity and allow the rest to go uncared for.

I think the sentiments the gentleman has uttered here to-day will not be indorsed by the people of the country. I hope the people will not believe there were any arbitrary rulings of the Speaker that prevented any measure from being properly brought before the House. No man has been refused by Congress the removal of his political disabilities who has been deserving of it and made application for it. Many of them have refused to have it, have said they would never ask for it. Yet their friends are continually urging that their disabilities should be entirely removed. Yet when a measure is brought forward for the benefit of the class to which I belong, a class that have always been ready to stand up for the country and its rights, and for the rights of all, who in the past have shown their liberality as they will ever be willing to do in the future—when their rights are sought to be enforced, they are denied equal justice, and by those who ask it for their friends in such liberal measure.

Black Soldiers

Additional information about the lives of blacks during radical Reconstruction can be gained from letters, petitions, and affidavits written in these years. Unlike Lynch, Randolph, and Douglass, these men and women leave us little information about their daily lives. Still, their efforts to find lost sons, to decide who should have custody of a child when the parents are not living together, or to gain a bounty for years of service in the army add to our knowledge about the black experience during these years.

349: Two Louisiana Black Corporals to the Secretary of War
Ship Island Miss Janary 31st 1867

Kind Sir I want to tell you Some thing of my afairs, I was Enlisted On the 15th Day of August 1864 I was Received Under (Capt) Horace Kimball I was Draft for One Years but I am kept Almost 3 Three Years and I am about to be Muster out Without any Bounty not onley that their has been men has been Enlisted the Same the as me [h]as and Now is gone home their is men out of Conpany H and Conpany I of the 10th both Companys I Ask my (Capt) if I would get any Bounty He said that He did not know if We would or not

So theirfore if he did not know I though[t] that I would write to you all to Say and find out Sectary Sir my family is out Dore but I hope that you will if you please to fix So that I will get that what is for me I Se[r]ves the U.S (A) all This time then to be turned out without any bounty Captain Jesse Lettis of the 10th USCA (Hy) Co F told me that He did Not Know if We would get any Bounty i have no space to live after Serving the US.A. Almost 3 Three Years then to put me out with[out] anything I am Sorry to know that. Sectary Kind Sir I am not Insulting Sir I am jist tring to tell you my afiars I have about 30 men of the Condishtion as me Enlisted the time I did and on the Sane terms for one year.

We was mustered in by 1st (Lt) McCalester at that time wich now He is now (Capt) of Company B of the 10th He was the man that Mustere us in the Army ot the U.S. kind Sir I would Acquent you befor now but I did not know as much about as I know now.

Sectary Sir I think that I aught to been muster out about 17 Seventeen Month ago accordingly to my Enlisement if you plase to let me know something about that —.

Yours Respectfully Servants
Philip Barrow
Anthony Dwayton

—————

350: Affidavit of the Mother of a Deceased Kentucky Black Soldier
Louisville, Ky., July 30th 1867.

Mary Fields (colored) being duly sworn, states that she is the mother of Frank Walker (deceased) late Private Co "F" 28 U.S.C. Troops, and that she sold her claim for arrears of Pay and Bounty due her son Frank Walker, to J. H. H. Woodward Claim Agent at Louisville Ky. in January 1867, for the sum of one Hundred and fifty (150) Dollars, and that it was her understanding that if when the claim was allowed by the

2ᵈ Auditor of the Treasury, it amounted to more than the sume above mentioned, She was to have all over that amount, except such amount as Mr Woodward was by law entitled to receive as fees for collecting the same, and that neither Mr Woodward or his Clerk explained to her that she would not receive any more than one hundred and fifty (150) dollars, if more than that sum was allowed by the 2d Auditor. She further states that she has been informed that her certificate was No 282,408 and for $359 10/100, and that Mr Woodward has been paid the same.

She further states that neither Mr Woodward or his clerk explained to her that she was selling her claim, and she was not aware of the contents of the paper she had signed, until a short time after the transaction had been conducted, when she was formed by Mr A. A. Burkholder claim agent, that she had sold all interest in said claim.

She further states that she has been married to her present husband about ten (10) years, but that he is not the father of Frank Walker, who was the son of her first husband.

Mary X Fields
her mark

───────────

351: Discharged North Carolina Black Soldier to the Freedmen's Bureau
Claim Agent at Baltimore, Maryland
East Newmarket Dorchester Co Md [December 1870]

Dear Sir   I Receved yore kind leter Concerning my Discharge in 1861 the manspation had not taken place but I was in the prtection By the youion Troops an Sat free by Presadence Lincon at the manspation I think in 1863 if I mis Stake not   Sir I was a volentery Sirlder in 1862 inlested under Capt Crass incruting oficer in Newbren NC Craveing Co an I never has Receve Eny Bounty yeat   Nether eny Back pay Sir all tho I had the promoust of bounty an all so back pay But my Lord and Savor Jesus Christ is Witness to day who knows All Things and Shall judge the world at the Last day knows I have not Receve a cent of Bounty Nether back pay   I was Born in the year 1846 July the 4   A volen terry Sirlder A Slave up an Tell the manspation   my Regament paper was to put in a frame an Set it up in a house an tell all the Batles that I had been in   I Enlested for three years Sooner   Discharge   that was in case if the war Should End in Side of three years the 35 US Should be Discharge   My Discharge was Stole in the city of Charleston S.C.   if you wish to kno the commanding all I will send them to you Sir and every private Sirlder   I come out the army in the year of 1865 the 22 of June

I was a Slave all of my life Tell the year of 1863   if you Wish to Know my Commanding Oficers an the mames of the private I will sen The names all To you if you wish Sir my   Discharg paper I Loss it at Charleston SC   Some [one] Stole it Soon after I was discharge in abote at the Walf S.C.   Sir I cant mot write very well an I lives so agreat wais [ways] of [off] from eny one that can wrigh So I have to try an do it my self   if you wish for me to come an State this to you at Baltimore I will Come   sir will remain yore true obt

Charles Jones

360: Affidavit of a Discharged Kentucky Black Soldier
Louisville. Ky. Jan. 2nd 1867

Abraham Riley (Colord) beeing duly sworn says, I live at Legrange Oldham County Ky. Two weeks ago I was discharged from the Army and returned to Legrange where I lived previous to going into the army. Three men named, James Fitzgerrald, William Wells, and William Hite (white) met me and asked me what I came back there for, saying that no "Damned Blue Coat Nigger" should live there, that either I or they must leave the place, and gave me three hours to get out of town. They said that none of Abe Lincolns free niggers could stay there and that I must go into a free state. They said that they would burn my house and drive my family away. I have not left Legrange, but am afraid that these men will come and drive me off.

Abraham X Riley
his mark

361: Freedmen's Bureau Agent at Christiansburg, Virginia
to the Freedmen's Bureau Superintendent of the 8th District of Virginia
Christiansburg Mont'y Co. Va. February 14th 1867.

Major—I have the honor to make the following Special report of the persecution by the civil Authorities of two returned Colored Soldiers, Thomas and Othello Fraction, late of the 40th US Colored Inft These Boys were formerly the Slaves of Robert T. Preston of this county (a Rebel Colonel) and on account of their enlisting in the U.S. Service, met with the displeasure of the Said Preston; who threatened to Shoot them, Should they ever again return to his premises. Thomas on being advised of the threatening language used by Mr Preston; wrote him a letter, Stating in Substance, that in case of their return, they would not quietly Submit to be fired upon, but would be prepared to defend themselves—although they did not Suppose he would carry the threat into execution. February 1866, having received a Furlough to visit their Homes, they proceeded to the premises of Mr Preston, where their Parents still resided—But were not long on the place, before a Servant had reported to them, that they had better leave at once, as Mr Preston had been apprized of their presence, and had armed himself to do them bodily harm. On hearing this, they thought best immediately to leave the premises; and having Strapped on their Knap-sacks, Started from the Cabin. A Short distance from the House Mr Preston overtook them, and raised his Pistol to fire, taking deliberate Aim; but the Cap Snapped, and the Pistol was not discharged. Then commenced a Series of Skirmishing, the colored men firing back, while Mr Preston received assistance from his friends. The Boy Thomas on receiving a wound at the hand of Mr Preston or one of his party, became disabled—and both of the Boys were Soon Secured. They were then incarcerated in Salem Jail, for attempting the life of Mr Preston, and remained in confinement three months, until released by order of Genl. Terry, Com'dg Dept. of Va. The full particulars of this case, I presume are on file at Dept. Hd. Quarters. Lieut Hiram L Hunt Stationed at Salem, Roanoke County Va, informs me that he investigated this case, and transmitted a Statement of all the proceedings to Richmond—and further he feels fully pursuaded that the Boys only acted in Self-defence; having been fol-lowed up and fired upon by Mr. Preston, when leaving his premises. He also thinks with his experience of the case, that they cannot get justice awarded them in Mont-gomery County.

Since their discharge from the Army, they have been living in the vicinity of Mr Preston's; but have never ventured upon his property, or molested him in any way, but tried to avoid meeting him as much as possible. On Wednesday the 6th inst, while working (one building a Log House for his Family—the other in the field) they were arrested by the Sheriff of this county, on a Bench warrant issued by Judge Fulton, Some four months Since, for the offence herein stated; and brought to Christian[s]burg for examination before a Magistrate. The case instead of being ex-amined at once, was postponed until the following Saturday—and the Boys incar-cerated in the county jail. On Saturday for Some trivial cause it was postponed until Wednesday of the present week— On Wednesday postponed again until Saturday; and thus three months may again elapse without a trial, while their Families are Suf-fering, and their Employers deprived of their labor. I would further State that one of the principle witnesses for the Boys is Somewhere in Richmond—another is in Salem, but neither of these have been Summoned to appear at the examination be-fore the Magistrate, although their testimony goes to prove, that the Boys simply acted in Self defence. Bail has also been offered by responsible parties, for their ap-pearances at any time, but rejected by the Magistrate, who appears affraid to take ac-tion in the case, lest he might offend "Col" Preston, who is a prominent Man of the county, and who, I understand is very anxious to have the Boys convicted and Sent to the Penitentiary.

Awaiting your instructions I remain Very Respectfully Your Ob't Servant
C S Schaeffer

[Endorsement] Bureau. R.F.&A.L. Hd. Qurs. Supt. 8 Dist, Dept Potomac, Wytheville Va., Feby 16th 1867. Respectfully referred to Bvt. Brig. Genl O Brown A.A.A. Genl, for instructions, The proceedings of the civil authorities in this case, es-pecially in View of the former incarceration and investigation, and the release of the parties, appear from the within Statement of Bvt. Capt. C. S. Schaeffer, Asst. Supt. to

be Very unjust and oppressive, The case has the appearance of being a revengeful and malicious prosecution, and the chances of Justice at the hands of the civil authorities appear to be Very Slight.—J H Remington Capt. & Bvt, Maj, V, R, C Supt 8th Dist.

<hr>

366: Mississippi Blacks to the Commander of the Department of the Gulf
Yazoo City [Miss.] January 20 1867

D' Sir by Request I Send you the Proceeding of [this] Place the Law in regard to the freedman is that they all have to have a written contract judge jones mayor of this place is enforcing of the Law   He says they have no right to rent a house nor land nor reside in town with[out] a white man to stand fer thim   he makes all men pay Two Dollars for Licience and he will not give Licence without a written contract both women and men have to submit or go in Jail

His Debuty is taking the people all the time   men that is traverling is stoped and put in jail or Forced to contract   if this is the Law of the United States we will submit but if it is not we are willing to take our musket and surve three years Longer or [have] more liberty. We the undersigner Looke to you fer Protiction and hope you will give it   you can write to any whit man of this place and he can testify to same

Yours Respictfully
Sined by twelve 12 Men
Please to complies With the colard Freedman at Yazoo City, Miss

<hr>

367: Petition of Kentucky Former Black Soldiers to the U.S. Congress
[Kentucky, July 1867]

MEMORIAL.
TO THE HONORABLE SENATE AND HOUSE
∽ OF REPRESENTATIVES, OF THE UNITED ∽
STATES OF AMERICA, IN CONGRESS
ASSEMBLED — COME GREETING:

The undersigned, citizens (colored) of the United States of America, respectfully present this our petition, to humbly ask your Honorable Assembly to grant us the right of Suffrage.

Your petitioners beg leave to say that they are residents of the State of Kentucky, by whose laws they are denied the right to testify in Court, &c. And they would further say, that many crimes have been committed upon them during the last year, for which they have failed to obtain redress. Colored men have been frequently murdered in cold blood by white citizens, and as we have not the right to testify against them, the criminals go unpunished.

They further beg to say that they are now and always have been loyal to the United States, and this *unquestioned* Loyalty subjects them to the malevolence of the friends of the "Lost Cause." It is objected by the opposers of Republicanism that we Negroes are too ignorant to prudently exercise the great boon of freedom. Gov. Clark, in his message to the Legislature of Kentucky in 1837, said that one-third of the adult white population were unable to write their names; ignorance was not considered a bar to the ballot in their case. It is believed that men vote their political convictions, not their intellectual acquirements. We are poor, but not paupers. In addition to all other tax, we pay tax on the following property, much of which has been acquired since freedom came to us: Fayette County, $91,800; Bourbon, $17,275; Boyle, $35,450; Jessamine, $8,500; Franklin, $53,730; and so in proportion through the entire State.

It is feared by friends and boastfully claimed by opponents, that if enfranchised, the negro would vote against the party that saved the Government. It is answered that many of your petitioners were *Soldiers;* they think they fought on the right side; *they* see no reason to change sides and vote against the *Liberty* for which they *fought.* It is believed by your petitioners that their enfranchisement will arrest the cruel spirit of robbery, arson and murder in Kentucky, as it most evidently has done in more Southern States.

Hoping that this our humble petition may be kindly received, and our prayer granted, we will ever pray, &c.

[170 signatures]

———

Both northern and southern blacks agreed that a successful Reconstruction depended upon the continuing support of the Republican party. It was an opportunity not to be wasted. Unfortunately, there was considerable violence due to the resistance of southern whites. This had to be dealt with vigorously, but the only permanent answer was to give the right to vote to all freedmen and then protect them in the exercise of that right. The Republican party was urged to stay the course until full equality was achieved.

Two other groups, carpetbaggers (northern whites in the South) and scalawags (southern whites in the South), also agreed that the Republican party had to continue its active support of Reconstruction. No change in the present policies was possible until a strong Republican party had been built in the south and blacks and whites in the South were free from intimidation and violence. A good start had been made, but much remained to be done. How long it would take was impossible to tell, but without such Republican support Reconstruction would quickly fail. Then all of the Republican efforts would have been in vain.

CHAPTER 8

CARPETBAGGERS AND SCALAWAGS

". . . the day, in Yazoo, was won by the Republicans, without the loss of life."

—ALBERT MORGAN

Marshall Twitchell

Marshall Twitchell remained in the South after completing his time as a Freedmen's Bureau officer. Marrying a southern woman and becoming business manager of his father-in-law's land, Twitchell quickly became an important leader in his parish and in Louisiana. However, his willingness to cooperate with the new Reconstruction acts, to work with freedmen, and to join the Republican party and run for political office began to cause serious problems for him. Soon he faced social ostracism and then, when that failed, threats of assassination. The future that had looked so hopeful for this intelligent and energetic carpetbagger now became less promising.

Our first year's crop was poor, although better than any around us. Mr. Coleman was discouraged and, not being able to meet his obligations, seemed to be inclined to give up everything. Mrs. Coleman said to me one day, "You Yankees are said to be awful cute; seems to me you might take Mr. Coleman's business and straighten it out." I replied that if I was given absolute control and they would all do as I directed, it could be done. Everything was at once placed in my hands. My plan was to get rid of some land which he [Coleman] did not need. By a little management which they thought extremely shrewd, I in one week succeeded in making the sale, putting us financially above water again. After this time I bought and sold without hardly ever consulting anyone. As a sample of my purchases I bought 400 acres of land for $1,500 and leased it for a portion of the crops, my portion of which for

159

the first year paid for the land. My success seemed to give everybody a desire to deal with me; consequently, all the opportunities for making money in the country were put in my way.

My first year's planting was during the government of the state before Reconstruction. I was appointed road overseer. At my last road working, when I dismissed the hands for the year, I informed them that they (the colored men) would be allowed to vote and that when that time came, they would be in great danger from two extreme parties. One party would put them back in slavery if they could; the other would crowd them forward into position so much faster than their education and experience in affairs of government would justify that the injury would be nearly as great.

The following summer, under the Reconstruction Act, registrars were appointed by General Sheridan and sent up from New Orleans to register the voters of the parish, black and white, and hold an election for a member to a constitutional convention. The supervisors of registration sent up were not lacking educational qualifications, but with the exception of the chairman, they reflected no credit upon the appointing power nor honored in any way their positions.

The chairman soon made himself acquainted with me and at the same time with the character of his associates, who could not be brought to look upon the registering of negroes as anything serious or important, taking anything for a name which their love for fun and the negroes' ignorance might give them. In looking over the roll after it was completed, I found that they had registered one [freedman] as Alexander the Great and another as Jeremiah the Prophet. It was so late that the only remedy I could apply was to have the "the" stricken out from each name. The negroes all presented themselves for registration; the white people also generally registered.

———————

Twitchell had not been interested in public office. However, he was acceptable to many whites as well as to "colored" men. He became very active in the Constitutional Convention in March of 1868 and soon found that his views on race and education were very different than those of the whites who had elected him.

As the time for the election approached, there seemed to be a general feeling of doubt in the minds of black and white about the kind of man who should be selected to represent the parish. It was finally decided by the white people that to at once put at rest the question of their loyalty, they would vote for me, with the idea that the authorities would be perfectly satisfied and that as I had married and was living there, the best interests of the country would be my interests as well as theirs, while very naturally the colored men all desired to vote for me. I was nominated by J. H. Scheen, a prominent merchant of Sparta, there being no objection to my nomination in the mass meeting. I was two weeks in making up my mind, after the committee waited on me, that I would accept the nomination, and it was only from the representations that I was the only man in the parish upon whom all the different elements would unite that I accepted. The nomination was accepted with a prepared schoolboy speech which I presume gratified my hearers most when they discovered that I was through.

A young man, the editor of the parish paper and a rejected lover of Adele's, came out as my opponent, saying that he thought I ought not to have all the good things; but he received only a few votes.

Raised in the state of Vermont where political excitement never runs high, of democratic parentage, I was at the time of my election perfectly independent. The question did not occur to me that it was in the least necessary for me to be a partisan, and had the question been asked whether I was a Democrat or Republican, I could not have answered.

The unreconciled Confederate element generally abstained from taking any prominent part in the election of delegates to the constitutional convention; consequently, the meeting of the convention showed its composition to be old Unionists, ex-Federal soldiers, and negroes of all complexions, from the bright octoroon to the full-blooded negro. With the exception of a few of the last class, all were very well fitted for their position. The Unionists were especially rich in men of experience, education, and ability. The ex-Federal soldiers with their Northern ideas of government were a very necessary balance between the two factions.

As one of the youngest men of the convention, I took an active part only upon the question that the school moneys of the state should be expended for the education of the children and that the system heretofore practised, of allowing the parents to deduct the school allowance from their taxes and then educate their children or not, should be done away with. I was very much surprised when I returned home to find that this act had made me very unpopular with the white people, who rightly looked upon it as a distinctly Northern idea.

After about one hundred days, the convention adopted the constitution, March 7, 1868, and provided for its being committed to the people [for ratification] on the 17th and 18th days of April following. Immediately after the adoption of the constitution by the convention, the Republicans met and nominated officers. I represented Bienville in the nominating convention, my first party action, taken for the reason that I found all elements there friendly to the Union and all accepting the results of the war.

Twitchell decided to run for parish judge despite opposition in his family. No other person had the confidence of the unionists and freedmen. At the election, the Ku Klux Klan became active against black Republicans. Twitchell became involved in racial politics, which began to be dangerous.

After [my] returning to the parish, the Republican candidates for parish officers were nominated. I took the head of the ticket as parish judge; Edward

W. Dewees, another ex-Federal, [was nominated] as representative to the legislature; [the nominees for] clerk, recorder, sheriff, justices of the peace, and constables [were] all Union men. On account of Northern birth, army record, and Southern marriage, I could better control the different elements of the party than anyone else and was consequently given the entire election management with an absoluteness never allowed in the Northern states, for which my army experience fitted me.

My wife's people used every argument possible to have me withdraw from the campaign. While I had no particular taste for the responsibilities and work of the leadership which was thrust upon me, upon canvassing the matter, I found that my withdrawal would break up the party. The colored people wanted a Northern man for their leader. The Unionists would obey no other Northern man in the parish.

I was informed by Judge Head a friend of mine and the most influential man in the other party, that they would contest the election and that they expected to be able to defeat our entire ticket. As the campaign advanced I learned from different sources, enough to satisfy me, that the contest would be so close that success would be gained only by the hardest work, closest attention, and best of management. In looking back I do not know how our management could have been better.

The week before the election I visited different portions of the parish, speaking to large crowds every day. My meetings were held at places ten or fifteen miles apart. I made the trip on an old mule, too slow to be of much use in the field, which used to vary the monotony of the journey by occasionally falling on its knees. When my feet and the mule's nose struck the ground, it would immediately rise and go on again as though nothing had happened.

During this political campaign the Ku Klux organization appeared with its murders and outrages. Moses Langhorne, a prominent colored man, was murdered in his house by masked men, his head cut from his body and taken away. Asa Shehea, a bright young mulatto who was acting as my political messenger, disappeared. It was reported that his hands and feet were tied, and then he was dropped into Lake Bistineau. These murders, with various whippings of prominent colored men in different portions of the parish, had such effect that upon the first day of the election I discovered the success of our ticket was extremely doubtful. The great fight was made against me, as the leader of the Republican party in the parish, and Dewees, we being the only ones who could influence the negro vote. Dewees was much the weakest one on the ticket.

The Democrats had nominated against me, largely through my secret influence, their most popular man, but one whom I knew was ineligible. The adoption of the constitution and the election of a Republican governor would result in preventing the issuing of commissions to any candidates who were under disability; the votes for such a candidate would be declared blank.

During the night of the first day [of the election], I sent a messenger to Dewees at Sparta, telling him my fears and instructing him to trade off votes for me wherever he could gain for himself. I vigorously pursued the same policy at Ringgold. The result was that the entire ticket was elected by a small majority, excepting

Dewees and myself. We quickly secured enough evidence of illegal votes to secure Dewees' election, and he went on to New Orleans to secure his seat in the legislature and file evidence of Head's ineligibility. Head was the acting parish judge at the time of the election, a just officer, a good man, and as I had no particular desire for the position, I took no steps to hurry him out. I felt that it would be quite as well for all concerned that he should learn for himself that he could not qualify for the office; that his election was a nullity; that under the constitution just adopted, the governor would fill the place by appointment, [and] that his competitor would be the appointee.

A few weeks after the election, [the Democratic] party committee returned from a visit to New Orleans and informed the people that they had lost all of the offices which they might have held; that their candidate for parish judge was ineligible and that I would be appointed in his place; that the legislature was strongly Republican and Dewees would get his seat. There was much abuse of their party leaders, who by their outrages had gained for the parish a bad reputation and then had not been successful, while our undisguised friendship and activity for each other had taught them that Dewees and I had no disagreement about the election, and my apparent desire to prevent the nomination of a competitor who was beaten was well known to all.

Smarting from the stings of conscience for murders committed, wounded in pride for being outwitted, they determined to terrorize, murder, or drive out the Republican leaders. Union men, having been humbled during the Confederacy, they did not think would require extreme measures. . . .

Twitchell's growing prominence resulted in efforts by southern white opponents of Reconstruction to ostracize him and, when this failed, to kill him. Alerted to these dangers, Twitchell managed to avoid them, but he was always aware of the danger of assassination.

About this time an attempt was made to socially ostracize me and, by sending anonymous letters to my wife, to create trouble between us. This last act had just the opposite effect from the one desired. The social customs and amusements of the country were so disagreeable to me that to be relieved of any part of them was a positive pleasure. Upon our first appearance at church after this plan had been decided upon, the minister aimed his whole discourse at my wife for having married one from outside of her people. I found the sermon so rich in political material that I commenced taking notes. This was soon observed and in some manner the speaker's attention was called to it, causing him to stop short in an address which to me was very interesting and amusing. Owing to the social standing of my wife's family, the ostracism gradually fizzled out.

As milder methods did not affect me, the public was prepared by the customary stories (sometimes that I was killed and at others that I would be) for my assassination.

I learned of all their stories, as they much preferred that I should be frightened out of the parish; for if they could satisfy the Republicans that their leaders were cowards, that party would soon fall to pieces.

About midsummer I received letters from Dewees to the effect that he could not sufficiently prove some outrages which were committed on the day of the election near Arcadia (twenty-five miles from where I lived), and if I could not get the testimony, he would lose his seat.

The taking of my life would be considered a very small matter in the minds of the Democrats if it prevented this testimony from reaching the city. I started from home at midnight and reached Freedmansville early in the morning, much to the surprise of the scared negroes who flocked out to see me. I ordered one to rub down and feed Wicked Bill; then taking the witnesses into a house, I took their testimony by virtue of my position as justice of the peace, which I had long held. In the afternoon I rode into Sparta on my way home, stopped, and by my remarks and actions indicated that I intended to stay all night in town.

My appearance here, coming in an opposite direction from my home, was of course a surprise. I knew the chivalry well enough to know that after dark they would receive reinforcements from different localities and from the grocery, and that I would then be in great danger. Just about dark I brought my horse up to the crowded steps of the store and remarked that it was so comfortable I thought I had better ride on to Rabun's (a Union family eight miles from Sparta) for the night. Their displeased looks were their only reply. I walked my horse out of the village and then for eight miles took that rapid gallop which only the mustang can long endure. Just before bedtime I reached Rabun's, took tea, and immediately started for home, eleven miles distant. At midnight my journey was ended, with my object accomplished. I had ridden fifty miles, much of the distance during the night, taken three affidavits, and created any amount of excitement in the past twenty-four hours.

Between Rabun's and Ringgold the road runs through a brushy swamp, where it was supposed I must pass in the morning. That road was carefully picketed, and so certain were they that I would be killed they sent a dispatch from the nearest telegraph station that Captain Twitchell had been in Sparta the day before and left for home late in the evening; his horse had reached home with blood upon the saddle but without the rider, and it was feared that the captain had been assassinated by some of his personal enemies. In a few days I had the pleasure of reading my own obituary, written in the customary "all virtue and no faults" style, in the New Orleans *Republican*.

Towards night the next day, individuals both black and white commenced calling. To the surprise of all, chagrin of some, and pleasure of others, they were able to see the man all thought dead. The supposed inconsolable widow was in the highest spirits, which naturally followed the hours of depression while I was absent on my dangerous trip. No one seemed to have the courage to ask if I had been away from home. My father-in-law's people did not know that I had been gone; the few negroes who were aware of the fact promptly replied that they did not know I had been away.

Fifteen miles from Sparta there was a strong Union settlement known as the Jones neighborhood. These people, during the war, gave much trouble to the

Confederacy, under the leadership of Tom Jones, one of those noble old Unionists who for three years endured the persecutions of the Rebels for a government which immediately ignored and neglected him as soon as it came to power. Jones had been our candidate for state senator. During my stop in Sparta I had so much to say about the Jones settlement and gave them so much apocryphal information about old Tom Jones that all were impressed with the idea that that was where I had been. Upon this false scent they commenced trying to find out where I had been, while I slipped away to New Orleans with my testimony before my visit to Freedsmanville, with its object, was discovered. The presentation of the testimony confirmed my friend Dewees in his seat; and when I had qualified before the secretary of state as parish judge in place of Head, who had been disqualified, I started for home.

Leaving the steamboat at Coushatta, I hired a mule for my twenty-five-mile ride, relying for my safety upon being in the country before I was expected. It did not occur to me then that the Knights of the White Camellia in Coushatta would receive their orders to dispose of me when I landed. The little delay which was necessary to procure a mule was sufficient for them to get ahead of me and picket the road at a point in the wood twenty miles from my house. Just before reaching this wood, a road turned to the left, making a circuit of six miles [before] returning to the main road. Busy with my thoughts, I did not notice until it was too late to turn back that the mule had taken the left-hand road, thereby, as I afterwards learned, saving my life. Two years later one of these pickets became a warm friend and supporter of mine and informed me that they waited so long for me at that point that they saw it would be too late for them to overtake me before I was out of the jurisdiction of their lodge, so no further attempt was made that day.

I made formal demand upon Head for my office as parish judge. The demand was refused and the case fixed for trial before Judge Lewis in chambers at Minden. This place was twenty miles north of my home, with no public conveyance. I had made arrangements to start on horseback at midnight but was taken violently ill (an unusual thing for me) with an attack of bilious colic, and not being any better at daybreak, my wife sent a note to my lawyer requesting him to go on with the case, as I could not be there. The courier, mounted upon my horse, was soon on his way with the letter. While passing through a swamp, the man was stopped by a picket who inquired where Captain Twitchell was and why he was not going to Minden, saying to the colored man, "I came near shooting you off from that horse, which I know is Captain Twitchell's and I almost wish I had. It would have served you right for working for such a man."

My political success and many evasions of assassination incurred the bitterness of my enemies at the same time that it brought to my support the elements which always follow success.

———————

In the next few years Twitchell became a skilled political leader for the Republican party in Louisiana. This required considerable personal courage because there were rumors about his possible assassination.

In the fall came the exciting presidential election of 1868. The Republicans of the parish of Bienville were completely cowed and frightened. I was compelled to advise them to stay at home and make no attempt to vote, as I knew the lives of many of them would certainly be sacrificed if they did. I rode to Ringgold the day of the election, walked up to the ballot box, and voted an open ticket for Grant. That I was determined to vote was well known by the onlookers, who parted as if by some prearranged plan, leaving me space to walk for thirty feet through a mob of my political enemies. I did not hear a word spoken from the time I appeared until I left. I reached home in a few hours, much to the joy of my wife and mother-in-law; although the latter was an intense Democrat, it pleased her that they were not able to frighten me out of voting. Those familiar only with Northern election methods might criticize my advice to Republicans, thinking that others might have voted undisturbed as I did. I knew they could not, and although I would risk my own life, I did not think it right for me to sacrifice the lives of my friends. The parish, which had gone Republican by 150-vote majority in April, cast but one Republican vote in November; 950 votes were suppressed. . . .

In the fall of this year [1870] I was elected to the state Senate from the senatorial district comprising the parishes of De Soto, Sabine, and Natchitoches, receiving nearly two-thirds of the 5,427 votes cast. Every parish gave a Republican majority. There was but little attempt at improper control of the voters. This was the last fair expression of the popular will which the district has ever known.

It had long been the desire of that portion of the country in which I lived that a new parish should be created out of portions of De Soto, Natchitoches, Bienville, and Bossier parishes. Legislative members had been elected upon that issue but had never been able to carry their point. It was well understood that I was favorable to the project. The largely Democratic northern portion of Natchitoches was strongly in favor of the new parish. Their committee waited upon me and an agreement was made: that I should make no speeches in that part of the country, for which they would give me the entire Democratic vote. [After the election,] I had a careful examination of the ballots made and found that they had given me thirteen votes. I immediately called on the chairman of the [Democratic] committee, showed him the figures, and informed him that I should be careful about ever again trading with those who would not or could not deliver the article traded. The desire for this trade was not on account of my ability as a speaker, nor do I think the Democrats favorable to the new parish feared my defeat; but the Southern Democratic party could no more then, than now, survive having the truth told to its voters.

On the first Monday in January [1871] I took my seat in the Louisiana Senate and at once commenced work pertaining to the parish of Red River. I soon discovered that the representatives from the parishes which would lose territory by the new bill were opposed to it for no other reason than that it made their parishes smaller. No attempt was made to answer the plea of inconvenience to the citizens under the present law; no claim [was made] against the justice and needs of the new law.

After becoming satisfied that I could not accomplish the passage of the act in an open manner, I resorted to the following ruse: The bill had passed the Senate and was in the House. Securing the services of a lawyer who was on good terms with the opponents of the bill in the House, I gave him an amendment which he represented to the House was one that would cause me to amend it again when it reached the Senate. It would then again have to go to the House, and in that way they would get the advantage of not having openly opposed the bill. The amendment was adopted and the bill came to the Senate, and three of the House members came in to see what I would do with the amendment. I called up the bill and moved that the Senate concur in the amendment. It was done and the Senate adjourned. The House members, surprised at the quickness with which the bill was disposed of and not understanding just what was its disposal, asked what I had done with the amendment. I told them that it was concurred in and the bill was passed, and to their surprise I informed them that I had written the amendment myself but presumed the lawyer did not tell them so. From this time on, Republicans of the 22nd district rarely differed in their views of questions before the legislature. . . .

There was a need for public schools for blacks and whites, but few people in Louisiana wanted these schools to be integrated. It was also difficult to get financial support for these schools. Twitchell's commitment was so strong that he built a schoolhouse on his property and employed his sister to run the school.

Immediately following the organization of the parish government, I took steps for the establishment of the public schools. I had received the hearty cooperation and assistance of all the people up to this time, but no one seemed desirous of assisting or having anything to do with the schools if the "niggers" could attend. I very soon discovered that this was a matter so serious that the schools must be given up entirely to the white children or that I must almost absolutely take charge of the matter and upon my own shoulders carry the responsibility of establishing schools which the colored children could attend. There was every reason that the schools should be open to the colored children. They were in a degraded state on account of their ignorance and were very desirous of attending. The school fund, which was raised by poll tax, was largely taken from the colored men on account of the black population being very much in excess of the white in the Red River valley. The only reason against their education was that the white people disliked to see the negro educated, a dislike which came entirely from the old system of slavery. After some delays in ineffectual attempts to satisfy the white people, I built a schoolhouse on Starlight and employed my sister Helen, one of the best of New England's teachers, to commence the school. I hoped by this course to sufficiently break down the prejudice against teaching colored schools so that I would be able to hire competent teachers.

The law required that the public schools should be open to all the children of the state, without regard to race or color. To enforce the law in my section meant the closing of the schools or a continuous rebellion. I opened two schools in each ward in the parish. The people were informed that one school was for the white children and the other for the colored. The separation was made by common consent and, at that time, much to the advantage of both races.

I then heard the general talk was that the negroes would soon tire of learning, and lack of scholars would close the colored schools. Every month the attendance increased, and then came the repeated rumors that the colored schools were to be broken up and the [school]houses burned by the wild young men of the neighborhood. I waited as long as I thought prudent and then notified the people that the day the colored school in any neighborhood was broken up, that day I would withdraw the money from the white school in that district. People well understood that I made no idle threats, and all trouble in reference to the schools was at an end until Democratic government took possession of the state, when one of their first acts was to destroy the colored schoolhouse at Starlight.

With the organization of the government, the parish entered upon an era of prosperity unequalled in Louisiana, if not in the whole South. For the first time since the war, the laborer felt a degree of confidence that he would get the profits of his labor; consequently, the landowners had no difficulty in making improvements which it had been impossible for them to accomplish with dissatisfied labor. Old fields were taken in and new ones opened, cabins built and repaired. So great was the improvement that the passenger on the deck of the steamboat could quickly discern when he entered the parish of Red River. The town of Coushatta was built at Coushatta Point, courthouse and jail erected, and in three years, from a simple steamboat landing, Coushatta had become the third town in size and importance on the Red River.

In two or three instances the Southern desperado made his appearance but was so quickly disposed of that the parish soon gained a reputation for law and order equalled only by its prosperity. I did not notice at that time that it was the carpetbaggers of the parish who always suppressed these bullies, but my after familiarity with the people gave me the reason. The Southerner raised among them had a certain fear for the half-drunk desperado loaded with revolvers and bowie knives. The carpetbagger had a contempt for him and naturally, when he first overstepped the bounds of law, was ready to seize him.

Albert Morgan

In early 1867, Albert Morgan, former officer in the Union army and carpetbagger from Wisconsin and now a planter in Mississippi, took his first steps into politics. He hoped that allowing freedmen to vote would protect their interests as well as those of like-minded southern whites.

Registration for all persons qualified to vote had been completed, and there was to be an election for delegates to the Constitutional Convention. Morgan was urged to be a candidate and reluctantly consented. He believed that blacks deserved a delegate who represented their interests. His ticket included a freedman and an ex-Union officer. It was formed on the last day before the election began. The opposing ticket had been in the field for several weeks.

Morgan had to campaign in an increasingly hostile environment. Success depended on getting out the black vote. He would get little help in doing so from the whites in Yazoo. In fact, it would become dangerous.

As our decision was not arrived at until the day before the election was to commence, and we could do nothing without tickets, it was apparent that an election was likely to be held in three precincts of the county before we could get "before the people." Besides, on examining our exchequer, we found there was not enough cash on hand with which to pay for printing the tickets. At one of the newspaper offices they flatly refused to print them for us without the cash in advance. But we succeeded at last, by promising "not to tell," in getting a rather poverty-stricken "devil" to guarantee to have a part of the five thousand we wished "struck off" ready "'gin night come on," to start with, and arrangements were soon made for forwarding the balance as our necessities might require.

Captain Clark got possession of a small lot and entered on his part of the work of the campaign, during the first day of the election. But it was night before I got my supply, and was started off on horseback to travel twenty-seven miles to the place where the election for the following day, on my part of the line, was to be held. . . .

It had been "sun up" an hour before I got off. The ride was about fourteen miles. But I was at the polling-place before the voters began to arrive. Inquiring of the officers of election the supposed cause of their tardiness, I found that none could account for it. There had been only about one-fourth, or possibly one-third, of the registered voters of the precinct at the polling-place the day before who had voted, they said, and what struck me as more unaccountable still, was their assurance that "none of the whites were voting." Several of Captain Bullfinch's people had accompanied me, and after reflecting a few moments, I asked them for their opinion of the cause.

"Dey is afeer'd, Kunnel, de colud people is, an' da doan know yo' is y'here with dem. 'Sides, de white folks don' 'low'd dar aint g'wain ter be no 'lection, no how."

"Ah! ha! that's it, eh!"

"Yes, sah, Mars Kunnel, dat's jes de way h'it ar', kase I done heerd um say down ter Benton, ter Mars Leedam's sto' how dey g'wain fur ter keep all day niggars frum votin' on da own 'count, kase dey wouldn't vote no how. 'Twan't no 'lection, dey 'low'd."

"Well," said I, calling him by name, "you go one way to some of your old fellow-servants;" and then to another one, "you go another, and tell them all to come here, I wish to see them."

In a moment they were off, on a fast trot, and I started out myself, following a blind path to see what I might be able to do in the way of helping to find the "lost" suffragans of Yazoo. I had proceeded about a mile, when, looking across a large open field, I saw what appeared to be a freedman, standing on the brow of a little hill. "Now," I said to myself, "I'll call this man, and see if I can't enlist him in the search." Waving my hat toward him, in token of my wish to have him come to me, he started as if to do so, but in a very halting manner. Then I alighted, hitched my horse and advanced to meet him. As we approached, I could see that he was in great fear about something, and I spoke up in a kindly voice:

"Uncle, why are you not at the election?"

The change in his manner reminded me of Uncle Isam, as he replied:

"Doan know, marsa."

"Have you registered?"

"Yes, marsa; done got my paper."

"Where is it?"

"Low'd—Beez yo' de gen'leman whar gi'e it to me?"

"No, my name is Morgan."

At this, the change in his manner still further reminded me of Uncle Isam, especially as he came close up.

"Beez yo' de Colonel Morgan, whar lib yan in de 'Azoo City?"

"Yes."

Wull, I d'clar'! Dey done 'low'd yo' is dead wid de col'ra. Bress de Good Marsta, do, yo' ain't. 'Low'd yo' might be de Kunnel when I done seed ye a coming yan, kase we done heerd frum one ouah feller-servants yo' cloze by Benton. Mighty likely yo' mount a come dis y'here way."

But there were other surprises in store for me; for, seeing his free and changed manner, several freedmen, who had remained hidden just over the hill from whence be had come, and entirely out of view until now, showed themselves. First, only their heads, as though peering at us, and now their bodies, standing. We walked up to them, when I found quite a large number, still lying upon the ground beyond the hill in a clump of trees.

These "outposts," becoming satisfied that I was, in fact, the person they had all heard so much about, but "nebber seed t'wel yit," shouted to those over the hill to come and join us, which they very promptly did. From their number I chose out several, whom I sent off after more, and the rest of us started for the polling-place. One of the number had a gun, a bird gun, which I requested him to take back home, assuring him that the Government at Washington was holding this election. At all events, there would be no need of such weapons at the polls, and he most cheerfully complied.

While on my way back to the polling-place, these poor people could not do enough for me, it seemed. They unhitched my horse, held my stirrup, and waited on me with as much deference, respect, and devotion, as if in their souls they felt that I was their deliverer.

I also gathered from them, as we walked along to the polling-place, among other things, that they had been told by their masters that there would be no election, and as if to prove the truth of this assertion, their masters had themselves remained at home. Some of these freedmen said they had heard threats made to the effect that if they went to the polling-places they would be killed. But, without previous concert, they had started to go, and falling in with each other on their several ways, they had become quite a numerous company by the time they reached the field where I found them. Here they had halted to talk the subject over, and had resolved to send one of their number on to the polling-place to "sarch for de troof." This was the man whom I first spied. Among their number was a preacher, who had recently attended conference, where he had been told of the proposed election, and how it would be conducted.

Arriving at the place of voting we found several freedmen there who had been "warned" by the two whom I had sent out and quite a goodly number besides. My opponent had captured some of these, however, and secured their votes for himself. On my arrival there in the morning, he appeared as much at a loss to understand why the people generally had not turned out to vote as any one else. Nor had he made any effort to find out—at least none such as I was making—and when the crowd which came with me arrived, of course he set out to capture them from me.

Mounting a wagon standing near the cross-roads grocery, he began his efforts in that direction by a speech, which he opened thus:

"Fellow-citizens and my colored friends." Then addressing himself altogether to the freedmen he informed them that he had no quarrel with "the white gentlemen present;" that he had been in the Federal army and was a Yankee the same as his opponent; that his opponent was a gentleman and all that, but he was a very young man, and without experience in public affairs, while, as they could all see, *he* was a man well advanced in years. He also informed them that he had outranked me in the army, and that he was the regular "Republican candidate;" his ticket was the only Republican ticket in the field. Then he reminded them that Mr. Lincoln, whose proclamation had made them all free, was a Republican; also of their duty to stand by the party that made them free, and then announced the platform on which the Republican—the "great Republican party"—stood, upon which he should stand "until death." It favored free speech, free men, free schools; it favored the right of the colored men to vote, the opening of the courts to them, and that they should receive fair wages; that whipping, branding and hunting them with hounds, and all that sort of thing should stop; that colored people should be allowed to own land and their wives and daughters like other people, or words to that effect. He concluded his remarks by informing the "colored friends" that the colored man on our ticket was a blacksmith, without property or education—could scarcely read or write, if he could do either at all, and that he could not be of any service in the convention more than to vote.

During the delivery of this speech there had been but slight manifestations of approval or sympathy from the freed people. They had remained almost as impassive as clay. When he ceased I got up on the wagon and replied briefly, in substance as follows:

"Fellow citizens: My platform is much the same as General Greenleaf's. I have never voted any other than the Republican ticket, and am a Republican." Then I explained that I could not see any difference in the tickets in point of "regularity," as we had all nominated ourselves, so to speak; that the difference between the General and myself was very great, yet very simple. I wished to see *all* men have and enjoy the *right* to vote, to hold office, be equals in the eye of the law. I wished to see free schools for all, courts and highways for all, fair wages for all, and lands for all who would work and earn them. "I wish to see you *all,* you, your wives and your daughters, living so above just reproach and so protected by the laws that no white, black, or other kind of man or woman either will dare to interfere with your enjoyment of each other's company." And, as to the colored man on our ticket, I explained that we had striven very hard to induce a native white man to stand, but had not succeeded in finding any who would; that we had done the next best thing we could think of, and put a freedman in the place. We would have been glad to have had but one "Yankee" on the ticket. Could we have got a native to stand then we would have had a ticket made up from all classes, and could have gone forward like a band of brethren in the work of reconstructing the State. I declared that I did not seek the office for myself, but for a principle; one which they might not all readily comprehend at first, but I hoped and believed they would eventually do so.

There could not have been more than a half dozen white men present, but I had addressed my remarks to them as much as to the colored people.

From the moment I began the interest of the freed people in my speech was apparent to all, and that interest continued to increase until they voiced their approval somewhat as follows:

"Dat's de talk, gen'lemens; yo' 'heah me. Dar! I tole ye hit wor' de Kunnel from de fust. Can't fool me. Now yo's a tellin' de troof," etc.

Seeing my success, my opponent undertook to entice them to his support by offering to treat. But he signally failed in that also. The few white men present looked on with the supremest indifference, if not contempt.

At the polling-place the next day there were a great many whites and two or three hundred freedmen. Having heard of the failure of their plan to "fool the darkies," they were now bent on coaxing, buying or intimidating them at the polls, and the "pulling and hauling" process began early in the day. Failing to coax or to buy them from voting, later in the day they began to threaten the freedmen.

The lists of names of all who had registered were in the hands of the judges, who caused the name of each one to be checked off at the moment of casting the ballot, so that it was impossible to prevent their old masters from knowing the fact that such a one had voted. Therefore, all who would vote subjected themselves to such vengeance as their old masters might choose to inflict.

During the day there was some speech-making by the late rebels, by my opponent, and by myself. The crowd was listening to me, when an old white man, who had elbowed his way until he was close up in front, inquired:

"What yo all g'wain ter do with our niggers, now you all done stole um f'om we all?"

"Make men of them," I replied.

"Men, hell!"

"Yes, men; we're not in favor of opposing any honest effort in that direction, at all events."

"Well, how ye g'wain ter make men outen of um?"

"Build school-houses and educate them."

"Edecate niggers! Yo' mount ez well try ter larn a mool ter read an' write, ez ter try ter larn a nigger."

"Well, we propose to make the trial."

"Yo' all 'low ye can larn a nigger ter read an' write?"

"Yes."

"Yo' lic! d——-n yo'!" ...

⸻

The voting on the Constitutional Convention was a victory for Morgan, but it led Democrats to increased violence. Southern whites were not willing to let go of their power. Elected to the Constitutional Convention, Morgan encountered great hostility and threats to his personal safety.

After the polls closed, and I was riding toward the polling-place of the next day, it being not yet dark, a shot, fired from near the roadside, passed whizzing by, so close to my head that I distinctly felt the force of the bullet. But it was not billeted with my name. . . .

When the ballots were all counted it was found that the question, "Convention or no convention," was decided in the affirmative, by a vote of more than eighteen hundred "for," to only three "against." The three votes "against" convention had probably been cast in obedience to a feature of the "plan" of the "anti-Yankee" element, which may appear further on in this narrative. It was also found that the "Morgan ticket" was elected by a vote of quite fifteen hundred, to less than four hundred for the "Yankee's ticket," as my opponent[']s ticket came to be called. The result staggered the natives.

They had hoped to succeed in their plan of deceiving the negroes as to the importance of their votes upon that question by staying away from the polls themselves. When they discovered that they had failed, they deluded themselves into the belief that they could, by making fair promises to "our nigros," persuade them to have faith in their sincerity. And they showed their utter ignorance of the character of the *free* negro, by trying to bribe him not to vote, when the other two means had failed; and they added to their duplicity, treachery and ignorance, still another quality, viz., brutality, when at last they resorted to intimidation to accomplish their purpose. . . .

⸻

On January 7, 1868, the new legislature, composed of freedmen, southern whites, and northern whites, convened in Jackson, the capital. Morgan's trip to Jackson began his four-year service in the state senate. However, the road to Jackson was full of danger.

On the morning of my departure I waited at the post-office in the company of the postmaster and other friends, black and white—negroes and Yankees all—until the stage drove up. When it came, I took my seat along with other passengers, male and female, some of whom were natives and some drummers for

Northern mercantile houses. The white women appeared not to know me. The native white men did, and to my cheerful salutation, "Good-morning, all—room for me?" they scowled and barely nodded. But the drummers returned my salutation cheerily and one of them "hitched along," making room for me to sit down. But I was not to be allowed to go in peace; for, espying me as I got up into the stage, a handful of white urchins began halloaing, "O'oophie!" "O'oophie!" "polecat!" The drummers seemed not to know what this meant nor to whom, if to any one it was directed; and one of them inquired of me about it.

But at that moment there appeared a dozen or more loungers near the corner, some of them full-grown men, others half-grown, who approached the stage door, and, making horrid grimaces, ejaculated: "Halloa, polecat!" "Whar ye goin', polecat! g'wain ter de nigger convention?" "Ha! ha! ha! He! he! he!" "Well, good-bye, Morgan. Take good car' yo'self. Haw! haw! haw!" Then the driver having got his mail on board, cracked his whip, and away we sped on our journey of twenty-six miles to the railway station. But from the moment the boys began to shout, "O'oophie," the "white ladies" showed signs of uneasiness. One of them coughed, while the white native "gentlemen" fiercely scowled. When the loungers appeared at the stage-door, and joined in the outcry, these native "gentlemen" smiled approvingly upon them. By the time we were off, above the crack of the driver's whip and the rumbling of the stage, arose the shouts of this rabble, "O'oophie!" "polecat!" "Morgan!" "O'oophie!" until we were out of hearing of them. Of course I was relieved of the necessity of answering the drummer's inquiry. He had already joined the rabble, and during our ride together, which was as far as the next station, Benton, where he left us for the purpose of introducing his firm to the merchants of that "berg," as he informed us, he was the most offensive in his speech and manner of the whole company. All the drummers "cut" me at once, and my ride was anything but a pleasant one.

At Benton there were similar cries after me as at Yazoo City, when we started; also at Deasonville, the next station, and at the railway depot. On entering the car my identity was made known to other delegates on board, who were *en route* from counties in the northern part of the State by these very cries; for nearly all of them had passed through a similar experience. In fact none of us were spared now that we were on board of the train, but were marked for all manner of jest, scorn, or violent abuse, according to the temper and gifts of our fellow-passengers, some of whom were *en route* to the capital to "see the fun." Very naturally these "outcasts" came together and formed a group by ourselves; for, all the world over, "misery loves company."

The scope of this narrative will not admit of any reference to my experiences during this period outside the limits of Yazoo County, nor during my term of four years in the State Senate afterward. . . .

———————

Deeply committed to the work, Morgan campaigned for the ratification of the Fourteenth Amendment. Finally there was a Republican party in Yazoo. There was also a vote on ratifying the new Mississippi constitution. It did not pass the first time.

T hat general election in Mississippi, when all the people participated for the first time, will long be remembered in Yazoo.

The Governor and all State and county officers, with rare exceptions, were opposed to any "reconstruction" of the State, and zealous supporters of their own "plan," which was founded upon the idea that, as the State had failed, by rebellion, to take itself out of the Union, the only act necessary to entitle the people to share in the government of the whole country, was the surrender of their arms.

True, this people had sent men to a representative body so called, which upon the demand of Andrew Johnson, in order to "disarm the adversary," as that President put it, had resolved that, "The institution of slavery *having been* destroyed in the State of Mississippi neither slavery," &c., "shall hereafter *exist.*"

By whom was that institution destroyed! By the "sovereign State?" No, never. By the "sovereign people" of the State? No, never. What did they mean by such an ordinance?

They did *not* mean to surrender by their own act their *legal* claim to be reimbursed from the national treasury to the full extent of the market value of the slaves emancipated by the will of the nation; they did not mean to estop their successors from resolving that, after all, slavery *had not* been destroyed. They did mean to dodge the question, and they did it. They justified their tergiversation on the ground of "present duress." Thus they thought, felt and acted *then.*

This new constitution dodged nothing. Under its provisions the negro was a man, and all men were to be equal in their right to life, liberty and the pursuit of happiness. Recognizing the institution of concubinage prevailing in the State as more demoralizing to the family and more destructive of manhood and womanhood than even that slavery which had been "destroyed," this new constitution declared that:

> *"All persons who have not been married, but who are now living together, cohabiting as man and wife, shall be taken and held for all purposes in law as married, and their children, whether born before or after the ratification of this constitution, shall be legitimate, and the legislature may by law punish adultery and concubinage."* **(Sec. 22, Art. 12.)**

Recognizing in the diverse elements composing the body politic, and the illiteracy and low civilization of the community those dangerous germs that without restraint might, in a night, under favorable conditions, overspread the State with bankruptcy and ruin, this constitution declared further that:

> *"The credit of the State shall not be pledged or loaned in aid of any person, association or corporation; nor shall the State hereafter become a stockholder in any corporation or association."* **(Sec. 5, Art. 12.)**

And

> *"The legislature shall not authorize any county, city or town to become a stockholder in or to loan its credit to any company, association or corporation, unless two-thirds of the qualified voters of such county, city or town at a special election, or regular election to be held therein, shall assent thereto."* **(Sec. 14, Art. 12.)**

And

"The legislature shall never authorize any lottery, nor shall the sale of lottery tickets be allowed, nor shall any lottery heretofore authorized, be permitted to be drawn or tickets therein to be sold."

Excepting these provisions, and the spirit of the Thirteenth and Fourteenth Amendments to the National Constitution, relating to slavery and the qualifications of a voter which entered into its fibre, this new constitution would have been accepted without a dissenting voice by the people of California, Iowa, Wisconsin, Ohio, Pennsylvania, Massachusetts, or Maine, as the equal of their own in the propriety and wisdom of its provisions. Yet, the people of Yazoo divided upon it so bitterly that one portion of the whites became savages in their efforts to defeat it, while another lent themselves to all manner of devices, by cajolery, by bribery, and by intimidation, to the same purpose.

Opposed to them were Charles, the General, five other Northerners, a handful of Unionists, the freed people — the Republican party of Yazoo.

As the laws forbade freed people to own or acquire lands, there was but one plantation in the "hill portion" of the county where the Republican party could hold meetings, and there were but two in the "swamp portion." All other places of meeting were upon the broad highway, in the little negro church we helped to build, the Yankee stronghold, secretly in the cabins of the freed people, upon forbidden premises, or by secret meetings upon premises, the consent to occupy which had been secretly given.

Of the Democrats, one party rode through the county as K. K. K.'s, threatening and endeavoring to *scare* the freed people from their right to vote. They did not dare to kill, because of the sterling qualities of the Freedman's Bureau agent. But freedmen were whipped and "bundled" out of their houses without warning and driven upon the highway.

On election day the "chairman" of the Democratic party and his numerous coadjutors fastened themselves upon Charles and the General, and assumed to be their "protectors" and "defenders" against calumny or personal violence, thinking by this means to arouse a suspicion in the minds of the freed people that, at the last moment, they had been either converted, bribed, or driven to join the side of "the people." And such reports were circulated far and near.

Merchants deliberately rolled out of their warehouses barrels of flour, huge sides of bacon, or pork, or tossed out pairs of shoes, boots, pants, coats, hats, dresses, nay, money, which was freely and openly tendered to the freed people, in consideration of their consent to be led to the polls by one of their former masters and there voted for what *they called* "the people's ticket." Lawyers, doctors, ministers, planters turned out personally and worked throughout the election as though they were working for life or for liberty.

Nay, more, fair women, old, and those of tender years, turned out and cooked food, went upon the street, and personally solicited by coaxing and by coddling black and white negroes, votes for this "people's ticket."

"The human hornet" [Henry Dixon] was omnipresent, irresistible, irrepressible.

Now on horseback, hunting for voters coming from the country, now running towards Charles or the General, as though he would ride them down to give "the chairman" or some one of his aids an opportunity to interfere for their protection, Henry Dixon was a host in himself.

So persistent were "the chairman" and his aids in their attentions to Charles and the General, so often did they have to "interfere" to "protect" them, so completely were they hemmed in and deprived of the power of locomotion by the crowd pressing about them, the day must have been lost but for the sagacity, courage, and fidelity of the freedmen themselves.

One of these, W. H. Foote, was as active, zealous, and effective for the Republicans as Dixon was for the Democrats. He went everywhere—into the most violent and blood-thirsty crowds of whites—with head erect, brave words of cheer for friends, and only defiance for enemies. He was a "new-comer," and little known.

His audacity shocked the "whites" as the sudden appearance of some unexpected and invincible force upon the battlefield will shock a grand army about to clutch a great victory. Planters, merchants, doctors, lawyers, all who did not know him, said:

"Why! look at that nigro; who is he? He has the audacity of a white man! Where is he from?"

Before they had time to rally, Foote would have accomplished his business—retaken some hapless freedman captured by the Democrats, inspired him to fidelity just as he was ready to surrender, and would be gone to some other quarter of the town on similar duty.

Hearing that a large body—about four hundred voters—on their way in to vote, had been halted by Dixon and others of his party, just over the brow of Peak Tenariffe, he procured a horse, rode out to the place, and, when met by Dixon with a threat that if he interfered they would shoot him, he replied: "Shoot and be d—d!" Then, turning to the freedmen, he cried out, "Men, this is our day. The new constitution is for our freedom as well as that of our former masters. If ye reject it, ye reject liberty. Follow me!" They all obeyed.

Dixon and his party had told these freedmen that Captain Morgan, the General and all the other Yankees "done sold out and left the country" that very morning, and, if they went to town there would be bloodshed, because the white people never would submit to be governed by their slaves. Surprised and overwhelmed by the audacity of Foote, nearly the whole party had deposited their ballots before "the enemy" could recover. Then there would have been bloodshed but for the cool head and brave heart of Charles.

Learning of what had been done, the party that had held him prisoner for above three hours broke, and joining their comrades from other points were about to break the "line," as the long file of Republican voters which Foote had rescued, was called. Being released, and divining the cause, Charles pursued them, and arrived upon the ground just in time to place himself between the angry and now half-crazed whites and Foote and a handful of freedmen, who, armed mostly with sticks, were "stanin' thar groun'," and, "talkin' back" to the whites in a manner most exasperating—to them. Seeing Charles' movement, several of the "guard" who had done but little else during the election but to keep near him and the General, and certain other very solid freedmen, gathered close in around him, literally making a shield for him of their bodies.

But his cool, calm, unimpassioned words—he had purposely left his pistol at home that day—stilled the storm after a brief spell. The whites put up their pistols. Foote and one or two of his party put up theirs. The sticks went back into service as canes, and, so, through similar trials, hair-breadth escapes, and exhibitions of sagacity, fidelity, and courage, the election passed and the day, in Yazoo, was won for the Republicans, without the loss of life.

The continuing hostility toward northern whites and the prejudice toward freedmen never ceased to amaze Morgan. Often these feelings came out in relaxed social gatherings where people felt free to express their innermost thoughts.

At that first *general* election in Yazoo I was not present, and the facts here given relative to it are faithfully set down as they were detailed to me subsequently over and over again by both the General and Charles, scores of the freedmen, and others, Republicans and Democrats.

There were several counties in the State without active capable Republican leadership.

Yazoo had more than her share, so I had been detailed for service in the State-at-large. There is one county in the north of Mississippi where at the time of which I write the blacks outnumbered the whites two to one, and where there was a strong "Union element" before the war. In the course of my canvass it was announced that Judge Loring and myself would visit the county seat of that county on a certain date "for the purpose of addressing the people upon the issues of the day"—our new constitution.

Arriving there on the day appointed we were surprised to find that, although public announcement of the meeting had been duly made, there was no one present nor any sign of preparation for the speaking.

After supper, guided by a genial host, we were seated on the ample gallery surrounding the low story-and-a-half hotel on three sides, enjoying our cigars just as the moon lifting herself above the grove of China trees which surrounded the courthouse, deepened by contrast the mystic shadows that hung like a pall over the dense forest of cypress and gum which covered the lowlands between us and the Mississippi River. The notes of the mocking-bird reached our ears from the valley below. The soft and gentle air was odorous with the fragrance of sweet flowers. Our journey with horses had been long, our supper excellent and our cigars were luxurious. One after another the neighbors and townspeople dropped in—for the Yankees had come—took seats upon the porch, its long steps, in chairs upon the ground in front, upon benches scattered about, or, lay down upon the warm earth; all chatting about their goods, their crops, their horses, their neighbors, or politics. Nearly all were smoking like ourselves. There was no drunkenness nor any liquor drinking. Below us lay their homes and firesides.

They had heard there was to be a speaking there that day. "Oh! yes; but it was their busy season and they had not 'low'd to go nohow." "Why were none of the colored people out?" the judge inquired of the principal lawyer of the place.

"Well, our people didn't think it was best."

In the course of a discussion between one of the physicians of the place, a person of undoubted skill and much learning in his profession, I drew out the acknowledgment that, after all, it was not so much the "disfranchising clauses" of the new constitution that "our people" objected to as another clause, viz: Section 22, of Article XII, relating to concubinage; for, while hotly replying to some criticisms I had advanced upon the nature of the canvass inaugurated by the leaders of the party opposed to the ratification of the new constitution, that popular physician exclaimed:

"Why, sir, that so-called constitution elevates every nigro wench in this State to the equality of ouah own daughters. The monstrous thing! Look at it faw a moment! Ever since Washington's time—and he understood it—the world wide fame of the fair ladies of the South faw beauty, faw refinement, and faw chastity has been ouah proudest boast. This vile thing you call a constitution robs us of that too."

"My good sir, how do you make that out?"

"Possibly you all are ignorant of the effects of the work you've been doing down there at Jackson. But that only illustrates another objection ou' people have to anything you all may do. Such work ought never to be entrusted to strangers, faw the very good and sufficient reason that they can't be expected to know the peculiarities of the people to be affected by it. Everybody who has resided in the South long enough to get acquainted with ou' people and thar ways must know that the nigro women have always stood between ouah daughters and the superabundant sexual energy of ouah hot-blooded youth. And, by G—d, sir, youah so-called constitution tears down the restrictions that the fo'sight of ouah statesmen faw mo' than a century has placed upon the nigro race in ouah country. And, if you all ratify it and it is fo'ced on the people of the State, all the d—n nigro wenches in the country will believe they're just as good as the finest lady in the land; and they'll think themselves too good faw thar place, and ouah young men'll be driven back upon the white ladies, and we'll have prostitution like you all have it in the North, and as it is known in other countries. I tell you, sir, it'll raise h—l generally 'twixt ouah young men, and the nigros, too. The end of it all will sho'ly be the degradation of ouah own ladies to the level of ouah wenches—the brutes!"

During this speech neither the speaker nor any of his auditors appeared to be in jest. On the contrary they were all in sober earnest, and while it was being delivered that *philosopher* was the center of interest. Full twenty of his neighbors and fellow-townsmen heard this argument thus presented, and not a voice was raised in disapproval, or to modify in the slightest degree the force of the only inference to be drawn from it in its bearing upon the character of the women of the State, no less than the men.

Hardly were we comfortably in bed when we heard a knocking at the door, so faint at first that we did not know what it was. The Judge sprang out and opened it while I stood ready for defence. A young freedman crept in, trembling so from fear we could ill make out anything he said. At last, by putting this and that together, we learned that the freed people who had heard of the meeting would have a[t]tended only the "white gentlemens" sent word that there would be "a fight" in town that day.

There had never been a Republican meeting in the county, nor yet a school for colored children, and we afterward learned that fully half of the colored population did not know they were free.

I ought to add here, in justice to the women of the South and to myself no less, that I could not then have been brought to utter in support of any cause such reasoning as that physician advanced against our new constitution. Even now when the cause of truth, seeking to promote human liberty and happiness by meeting out simple justice to the negroes of the South, imperiously demands that I shall sacrifice my own pride, my own feelings and my own "interests" upon its holy altar, I have brought the incident forward and given it a place here only because it illustrates better than any other I might give, the utter absence of *prejudice against color* on the part of the *native* whites of Mississippi. . . .

Charles Hays

During 1865 and 1866, Charles Hays, plantation owner and former officer in the Confederate army, began to lose confidence in the Democratic party. It seemed unable to respond in any reasonable manner to the challenges of Reconstruction. Its only position was resistance, and Hays felt that this would not be successful. He believed that Alabama should rejoin the Union, that blacks deserved fair treatment, and that because the war was over, political parties should offer a platform for the future. Hays decided that the Republican party was the only viable choice. This decision led him into politics, where his consistent support of the Reconstruction acts made him the object of vicious attacks. To his fellow white Southerners, he had become a hated scalawag.

It seems inconsistent at best that a Black Belt planter who had worked more than a hundred slaves and fought for the Confederacy would switch to the Republicans. But Hays fundamentally accepted the new order envisioned by congressional Republicans. That fact distanced him greatly from most of his fellow whites, who in the words of one Freedman's Bureau official considered "the Negro as a connecting link between the white man and Baboon." Hays's empathy for the freedmen was apparent. He would speak of what was "right and just" and the cause of the "oppressed" and "downtrodden." While he considered social equality unfeasible, he considered the extension of political and economic opportunities to the freedmen a fundamental goal, necessary and in his mind morally correct.

As he had watched events play out in 1866–67, Hays had grown increasingly disillusioned with the Democrats. He regretted the state legislature's rejection of the Fourteenth Amendment. He later recalled despairingly "the reign of an Andrew Johnson governor" (Robert Patton) and a rebellious "Andrew Johnson General Assembly" that had refused to ratify the amendment. He also realized that Southern resistance would only prolong the period of limbo outside the Union and risked the establishment of more radical and punitive terms for reentry. Alabama had been out of the Union seven years, and acceptance of real change promised the state's return. But nothing less than acceptance would work, and the Democratic power structure either did not comprehend or refused to accept that reality.

Undoubtedly Hays came to his decision after much anxiety, introspection, and doubt. But the decision had been made by the time of that hot August day [1866] in Eutaw. He thanked the Republicans for their confidence and promised faithful service. The Republican party had found an unlikely spokesman. So had the freedmen. Confused and destitute, searching for dignity and equitable treatment, the former slaves would look to Charles Hays for direction.

Hays assumed a prominent role in local Republican politics during the summer and fall of 1867. As a leading member of the local Union League, he helped mobilize Greene County blacks in the months before the constitutional convention referendum. He delivered speeches and rallied blacks to Republicanism. At Clinton, a small Greene County community, Hays was especially effective. He reported in September that following the oratory there, "we used them up . . . badly." Conservatives in Greene County mounted some opposition initially but then totally capitulated. A group representing the county Democratic party visited Hays at his home on September 17. An understanding was reached; Hays agreed not to deliver any more speeches, and the Conservatives promised not to oppose the local nominees to the constitutional convention. With obvious satisfaction, Hays wrote fellow Republican Charles W. Pierce the next day, "I look upon the canvass as closed in Greene" and explained that the Republican nominees could "run around the track without opposition." What this meant for the Republican party was obvious. And there were benefits for Hays: he was in the enviable position of facing no opposition in his bid as a congressional convention delegate.

Pierce, a Union veteran and native of New York, served as the ranking officer at the subdistrict Freedmen's Bureau headquarters in nearby Demopolis. Hays advised him to disband any black military organizations in the interest of peace, but he also asked that troops be sent to Eutaw on election day in case of disorder. In the meantime the voter registration continued. As the October election neared, Pierce wrote Hays, "Without exception so far as I can learn all will vote the Republican ticket . . . whose platform and principles they fully endorse." Blacks attended rallies and even delivered speeches, but these activities did not fully prepare Greene County whites for what they witnessed during the first week of October: former slaves casting ballots at the polls in Eutaw.

A large majority of Alabama blacks, and whites in fewer numbers, approved the constitutional convention. Since the Democrats did not offer any candidates, all of the elected delegates were Republicans. Hays and four others were elected from the Twenty-second District (Greene and Hale counties). Alabamians had registered and held a referendum quicker than any other state. The constitutional convention, scheduled to meet the next month in Montgomery, offered the earliest test for the Republican-inspired democratic experiment. . . .

———————

Hays was a member of the state Constitutional Convention, which met from November 5 to December 6, 1867. He was concerned about disfranchising southern whites who had not voted in the constitutional referendum earlier in the year. It did not make sense to alienate a whole class of southern whites who could be supporters under different circumstances. He tried to avoid partisanship while advancing the interests of Alabama and its black citizens. Soon, however, Hays would be attacked for his "desertion" of the southern white class.

Hays took no part in the debate . . . Yet, he clearly objected to political punishment. Enfranchising blacks, but arbitrarily denying a class of whites the vote, he believed fundamentally wrong. Hays also feared the political fallout from such a move. Proscription would embitter native citizens whom the young Republican party desperately needed to attract. His position, given his Southern and Confederate background, was reasonable and to be expected. He was one of twenty-two delegates to vote with the Conservative Rump to sustain Semple's attempt to head off disfranchisement. Of the numerous Northern newspaper correspondents covering the first constitutional convention, one, a *New York Herald* reporter, connected Hays to "a small band of moderate and rational delegates." . . .

On December 5 the convention voted 67 to 9 in favor of accepting the constitution. Almost one-fourth of the delegates were absent or abstained, and, several days later, thirteen white delegates, eight of whom had voted against the document, signed a public letter of protest. Among them were Semple, Speed, and other moderate delegates with whom Hays was in agreement.

Hays had generally opposed partisanship . . . Yet he recognized the inherent improvements offered by the document. Besides, he expected the disabling provisions to be repealed (a clause allowing the legislature to remove the voting restrictions was incorporated into the constitution). Nothing could be done unless state government was legitimated and Alabama readmitted to the Union. Despite his reservations, Hays signed the constitution.

Ratification of the constitution still remained to be accomplished. Although opposition to the convention had been limited, opposition to the document itself was overwhelming. The ratification campaign stimulated the revival of the Democratic-Conservative party in Alabama. Acting largely on the advice of former governor Lewis Parsons, the State Democratic Executive Committee pursued a policy of "active non-participation." As expected, whites registered with no intention of voting for or against the constitution, hoping to deny the mandatory majority needed for ratification by boycotting the election.

The convention had formed a Republican caucus and nominated a state ticket just before recessing. William H. Smith, a Randolph County Unionist, received the gubernatorial nomination. At the caucus and in the weeks ahead, other Republicans announced for various offices. Hays's inactivity at the convention could have been construed as stemming from a personal disillusionment with politics, the Republican party, or both. Nothing could have been further from the truth. He was eager to pursue a political career, and declared for the Twenty-second District (Greene and Pickens counties) seat in the state senate in December.

The peculiar circumstances of the campaign—he had no opposition and the election would not stand if the constitution failed—dictated Hays's strategy. He impressed on the freedmen that voting for the constitution was in their interest, reiterating the themes of Union and the Republican party using reason, promises, and oratorical flourishes (quoting Shakespeare and the Bible). Hays rallied blacks to his candidacy by articulating Republican guarantees of citizenship and opportunity. A rueful opponent later conceded that Hays "made the black man believe he was their special friend," and another estimated that "he could go out there and blow a horn" and rally 2,500 black voters. A phalanx-like coalition had begun to take form.

Overall, between February 1 and February 5, 1868, almost 71,000 Alabamians voted for ratification. But a majority of registered voters did not participate in the election, apparently defeating the constitution. Gen. George G. Meade, who had replaced Pope as Third District commander, suggested to President Johnson that the convention reassemble and draft a more acceptable document. Meade's suggestion went unheeded. Because of the situation in Alabama, congressional Republicans framed the Fourth Reconstruction Act. The measure, which became law without President Johnson's signature on March 11, 1868, stipulated that only a majority of the votes actually cast in a constitutional referendum was necessary for ratification. Applied ex post facto, the last of the Reconstruction Acts validated the February election and provided for absolute Republican hegemony in Alabama.

The organization of a state government awaited the convening of the legislature in July. With readmission certain, political debate crystallized. Whites generally equated Republicanism with black equality, disenfranchisement, the recent enemy, and imposed authority. The constitution, considered by many to have been fairly defeated, provided another source of alienation. A large white majority considered themselves victims of an illegal government bent on degrading whites and elevating blacks. Republicans assailed the opposition as treasonous and backward-looking. The unprecedented circumstances made for extreme partisanship. As one Alabama Republican observed, "Whigs and Democrats used to abuse each other very fiercely in speeches and newspapers but such things scarcely ever affected our social relations." Party affiliation took on added dimensions in Reconstruction Alabama. Elaborating, he explained, "I notice what I never noticed before, that the estimate of a man is more controlled by his politics than by anything else."

Perhaps no Republican in Alabama during the next decade would understand that statement better than Charles Hays. As a Republican, he fell immediately into disrepute among white Greene Countians. The family's high standing made his alleged apostasy more shocking. The Hays name became one of reproach. Invoking the esteemed memory of George Hays, an observer regretted "the fall of the son." In the hill counties of Alabama, where Unionists had thrived and often became

Republicans after the war, political toleration existed. But in the Black Belt heartland there was very little of that among the white population. White society in the county where Hays had been raised and claimed friends rejected him. The extent of the personal ostracism is uncertain, but evidence suggests that few hid their antipathy. As Hays himself stated, any white in the Black Belt "in favor of the policy of Congress and of the Reconstruction Acts is regarded as an enemy of the country."

Hays quickly became the object of scurrilous and hyperbolic attacks. An indictment of his conduct, taking the form of a public letter to the *Tuscaloosa Independent Monitor,* appeared as the constitutional convention closed. Its author, signing himself, "I know em," believed that Hays's recent Republican conversion could best be understood in the context of his past. Of "low Celtic origin," Hays had inherited land (ill-got) and slaves (whom he abused). Hays's detractor dismissed his Civil War service in opportunistic terms, claiming that Hays had lingered at home before capitalizing on his brother-in-law's officer status and gaining a position analogous to a "camp-follower." Even so, vanity required that he stick "a star on each shoulder" and style himself "major." Calculation and self-interest continued to guide him after the war, continued the critic. Hays's attraction to Republicanism was transparent. A combination of necessity (Hays needed blacks to work his lands) and an inflated sense of his own importance (though he could not be elected "overseer of a neighborhood road") explained his apostasy.

Hays became accustomed to such attacks. Rarely did he reply. An abiding belief in the correctness of his position provided him with a measure of personal peace. In 1867, two years removed from the war, as the South finally began to move toward regaining its former place in the Union, Hays was confident about his course. He faulted Johnson. The president had opposed the Civil Rights Bill, the Fourteenth Amendment, and the First Military Reconstruction Act on the grounds they represented an unconstitutional federal usurpation of power. Behind that rationalization was a not-so-muted attempt to establish the freedmen as second-class citizens. Hays blamed Democrats for not recognizing that "the past is gone." The "past" that he spoke of was less a finite period of time than a mindset. His willingness to accept the freedmen's new standing, combined with his fellow whites' unwillingness, formed the crux of an irresolvable disagreement. . . .

———————

Hays and Senator William Warner campaigned in Alabama in the fall of 1868. There was constant heckling and threats of violence. A bitter and uncompromising foe of the Republican party, Edward Randolph, founder of the local chapter of the Klan, organized opposition to the speeches by these two men.

On October 28, at about noon, the Greene County senator [Hays] began his speech in a second-floor courthouse room. Two or three hundred freedmen and about twenty or thirty whites, including Randolph, were in the audience. Hays quickly got to the point: a vote for Ulysses Grant was a vote for peace. Casting a ballot for the Seymour-Blair ticket risked a resumption of the sectional conflict. It required little provocation on Hays's part to upset some obviously intoxicated whites, who began taunting him and making it almost impossible for him to continue. The situation soon worsened, and when a pistol shot rang out from downstairs, chaos reigned temporarily. Following the return of order, Warner was asked to speak, but he declined out of deference to Hays, and the meeting broke up. Randolph gloated in his account (complete with illustrations) of the retreat of the "so-called white men." Warner and Hays concluded their eventful swing through the Black Belt several days later, just before the election.

Grant ran well in all sections of the country and easily defeated Horatio Seymour. He carried nine of the eleven former Confederate states. His defeat in Georgia and Louisiana was directly attributed to the crimes of nightriders. In Alabama, where twelve companies of infantry supervised the election, Grant received 76,414 votes to Seymour's 72,477.

The Union general triumphed in Alabama because of his strong showing in the Black Belt. In counties like Greene, where freedmen far outnumbered whites, Grant received three times as many votes as Seymour. Hays was partly responsible for the large black turnout. Aware of the senator's contribution, editor John G. Stokes of the *Montgomery Alabama State Journal* praised Hays for working "untiringly and with zeal" and for epitomizing those "who have stood out against the storms of obloquy and abuse."

Several days later, in early November, the state legislature met in Montgomery. Returning to the theme of economic development, Governor Smith stated in his opening remarks that "capitalists abroad are anxiously seeking information respecting the latent resources of Alabama." Surveys of the Coosa, Cahaba, and Black Warrior rivers were badly needed, and Smith urged that they be undertaken. Hays listened in agreement. Yet he was more interested in Smith's comments about the recent political violence. The governor called attention to a pattern of disturbances. Without mentioning the Ku Klux Klan, Smith asked that a committee be formed to investigate the situation.

In part, Smith was reacting to the shocking murder of M. T. Crossland. Several days earlier the Tuscaloosa County Republican senator and two companions had been ambushed not far outside of Tuscaloosa, and Crossland was killed by a shotgun blast. Although various theories were advanced concerning his death, the most logical assumed he had been murdered because of his Republican loyalties.

Hays stayed extremely busy during the two-month session, introducing and steering through legislative channels measures both local and state in design. Due to his efforts the period of collecting taxes in Greene was extended. More important, Hays authored a bill providing for the strict observance of a constitutional article earmarking one-fifth of annual state revenues for education. As a member of the Internal Improvements Committee, Hays backed the governor's development plans, applauding the approval of the Coosa River survey plan and regretting the defeat of the Cahaba River plan. Anxious that the projected Black Warrior study go forward, Hays drafted a congressional memorial requesting federal funds.

Consideration of a common carrier bill pointed to Hays's deepening commitment to colorblind principles of fairness. Laws guaranteeing equal access to public accommodations were passed by several Republican-controlled Southern legislatures. Early attempts to do so in Alabama failed. During the first session a measure establishing integrated accommodations on steamboats, railroads, and other public conveyances had passed the house but had stalled in the senate. A similar proposal now suffered the same fate. That was not Hays's fault. On December 16, in an unrecorded "long speech," Hays futilely promoted the common carrier bill.

Bringing to justice political outlaws concerned Hays even more. The subject of enforcement legislation gained wide attention. The Joint Committee on Outrages (formed at Smith's request soon after the legislature met) submitted its conclusions following the Thanksgiving recess. Committee members had taken testimony establishing the existence of an active and conspiratorial white brotherhood. The committee proposed three statutes. Prospects of passing some enforcement legislation had improved since the failure of the Ku Klux Klan Bill during the first session. Gubernatorial pressure, recent presidential election violence, the Crossland murder, and the committee findings contributed to a sense of urgency.

For several days, in late November and early December, the subject totally dominated discussion. Democratic reaction was predictable and sometimes innovative. The *Montgomery Advertiser* ridiculed "imaginary Ku Klux Klans," and the *Mail* warned facetiously of "these strange and dreaded creatures that carry their heads under their arms" and "live in the crevices of the rocks." The legislature enacted two laws. One established severe penalties for masked outlaws, absolved anyone of fault who killed these disguised criminals, and threatened law enforcement officials with punishment for failing to pursue such offenders diligently. A second statute leveled a $5,000 fine on citizens in counties where mobs or disguised outlaws committed political murders; surviving relatives would receive the money. Governor Smith signed both before the legislature broke up on the last day of the year.

Hays felt such coercion was necessary. Certainly his recent experiences while campaigning indicated the need for protection. And profoundly affecting him was the murder of M. T. Crossland. The Tuscaloosa County senator's death was more than a distant crime to condemn in the abstract. Hays and Crossland had been friends. Taking the execution-style fate of Crossland for what it was—a political assassination—Hays denounced the perpetrators. Hays initially impressed those he met as genial. A better acquaintanceship with him revealed a certain volatility. As an observer commented, the Crossland murder was "well-calculated to rouse Senator Hays's venom." Hays had drafted a resolution denouncing the "cold-blooded" murder and the "organized band of assassins." Later, as a congressman, he would shift his focus to the entire South and demand enforcement legislation. For the present the theater was Alabama.

By the end of 1868 Hays had resolved a personal dilemma. He had originally left the Democratic party because Conservatives seemed wedded to the past and oblivious of the war's mandate. Little had changed since he made that decision. His former party remained pledged to white supremacy, and—equally offensive to Hays—unresigned to the authority of the federal government. Hays considered the Seymour-Blair platform an uncompromising manifesto that only rebels, not loyal citizens, could embrace. Yet the extremism of some Radicals had caused him to vacillate briefly. But the course of men such as Datus Coon and Isaac Sibley was ultimately less upsetting to Hays than that of the unrepentant and unreconstructed Conservatives. And Hays could work inside the Republican party to temper certain elements. He hoped to exert a moderating influence. When *Eutaw Whig and Observer* editor Joseph Taylor accused Hays of inciting unrest among the freedmen, Hays replied, "I defy him to point to a single act of mine since I have been in public office which was extreme, vindictive, or bitter." The Republican pointed out that he had counseled peace and opposed measures that threatened tranquility. In the same public letter Hays pointed to his love for Alabama. His words had little effect. The incongruity of Hays's personal background and his recently adopted political loyalties continued to confound and anger whites. Hays's enemies invariably attributed his Republicanism to self-aggrandizement and opportunism. They were not completely wrong. Hays was neither selfless nor disingenuous. He had already turned his attention to higher office.

James Alcorn

James Alcorn, a cotton planter, former Confederate general, and member of the Whig party for many years, accepted the necessity for change in the postwar South. The greatest change was the freedom of the former slaves. He believed that this could best be managed by a new political party patterned after the old Whig party. It could negotiate between the Democratic and Republican parties and find reasonable ground for compromise. Alcorn wanted to avoid a polarized party system with a southern white party and a southern black party controlled by Northerners.

His efforts over the next few years to create a Whig-like party were in vain. Finally, in the early months of 1869, Alcorn began to talk like a Republican. He favored the building of railroads, a public school system, and equality at the ballot box. It was clear that his political future would be as a Republican, although his enemies had another word for his politics—scalawag.

B̶y the beginning of August, 1869, without waiting for endorsement by the state organization, or possibly with its tacit backing, Alcorn was openly campaigning for the national Republican party, although not expressly for the governorship. He was also active in creating a faction that would have the support of the national party and would be loyal to him. He warned against "Conservative Republicans" who were ready to betray the party to the Democrats and negate the results of reconstruction, and spoke of rejecting the advances of a group which included J. L. Wofford, one of the founders of the party in Mississippi. This group, he hinted, had been responsible for the defeat of the previous year.

On September 29 he was nominated by acclaim at the Republican state convention to be its gubernatorial candidate, a nomination which took place in the presence of General Ames, the commander of the military district including Mississippi.

In his acceptance speech Alcorn acknowledged that his convictions had placed him for twenty-five years in opposition to the majority of the people of his state, but he stressed that above all else he wanted to work to promote the common good. He felt his nomination commissioned him to make a generous offer of alliance from the Negroes to the whites. He denounced the hypocrisy of the opposition Democratic party which claimed it wanted the cooperation of the colored people but at the same time declared null and void the Reconstruction acts which gave them their rights. The Democrats, he charged, were responsible for the separation of the political parties on the basis of race, and he tried to show the fairness of the demands of the Negroes. At his insistence the demand for universal suffrage was linked with that for general amnesty. . . .

Alcorn's decision to run made a favorable impression in the state. One contemporary's reaction was that his nomination "was a surprise to everyone and a very gratifying one to many. He [Alcorn] had lived in Mississippi since early manhood, had accumulated a large estate, was a man of great ability, and one of the best speakers on the hustings in the State." He added that Alcorn was "an imperious, fearless man, who could not be cajoled nor bought nor intimidated." An "Old Whig" wrote the *Weekly Delta* that he did not like either party, but admired Alcorn because he was a gentleman of strong character, great eloquence, and lofty courage, concerned with the interests and institutions of the South. He ended by saying that, "Since I must choose between two *men* and there is only *one* in the race, I am for Alcorn."

Alcorn gave his opening speech at Hernando and began an energetic campaign, reminiscent of his prewar career. The executive committee of the Republican party published a schedule which called for him to deliver a speech in a different town throughout Northern and Central Mississippi every day from October 11 to November 16. . . .

Color was added to the campaign by an element of personal danger, for the Ku Klux Klan was active in the state, contributing to an undercurrent of widespread lawlessness. J. F. H. Claiborne, among others including Alcorn's wife, tried to persuade him not to run, believing that he "would fall a martyr under a cloud that would cover [him] in [his] grave." Adelbert Ames attempted, against his wishes, to use soldiers to protect him.

Even his audiences sometimes felt the danger. While addressing a group in Ripley, he had an altercation with a local political leader whom he called a liar. Expecting violence, the audience scrambled out through the door and windows while Alcorn called after them not to leave, that his opponent was "a drunken cowardly vagabond." He won over an audience in Aberdeen by coolly drawing a six-shooter out of his satchel when he heard the click of pistols near the rostrum, and challenging any would-be assailant to stand up and face him. At Winona "several of the more desperate whites" wanted to kill Alcorn with a rifle while he was speaking from the railroad depot platform to a large crowd composed mostly of demonstrative Negroes, but "conservative Democrats" prevented them from carrying out their plan. . . .

. . . Alcorn won by an overwhelming majority, and carried with him a large majority in both houses of the state legislature. Grant had the constitution of 1868 resubmitted to the voters, with the proscriptive clauses against ex-rebels and rebel sympathizers listed separately. The electorate ratified the constitution and rejected the clauses. Alcorn began his term of office with a Republican legislature and a new constitution. . . .

―――――――――

As he assumed the office of governor, Alcorn gave a speech that expressed his Whiggish ideas but that angered many whites who had supported the war. His words, "secession, I have ever denounced as a fatal fallacy," hardly expressed the views of most Mississippians. And his message that taxes would rise was equally offensive.

  Flanked by his official family and bolstered by a sense of political power, Alcorn early in his inaugural speech voiced a viewpoint few Southerners shared and many detested to the point of violence. In voting for secession, he declared, he had sacrificed conviction. "Secession, I have ever denounced as a fatal fallacy. In casting my lot with my own people in the late war, I sought not justification behind logical subtleties." He repeated his belief that he had been liable for punishment as a rebel, and after expressing his pleasure at "bowing out" military rule, he spoke, with reference to the national government, of "a magnificent mercy never shown before by a government since established authority first dealt with rebellion after the fierce fashion of 'a short shrive and a long rope.'"

  He seemed aware that rebellion cannot be justified unless it is accompanied by reasonable hope of success or caused by extreme provocation. Since his position before the war had been that such provocation did not exist, and he had realized that the rebellion would fail, his position, and parenthetically that of the South, had been unjustifiable. He was one of the few Southerners on whom the reality of the preceding events had made an impression, and he may have hoped to shock recalcitrant Mississippians into an appreciation of the situation.

  And this situation involved deep changes with which the new civilian government would have to cope. Alcorn tried to make the people aware of these changes by pointing out how the duties of the state had increased. It must now consider the welfare of individuals rather than just the heads of a few favored "families." He warned that, because of this concern for a wider group, taxation would be much greater. However, the application of these taxes would tend to enrich the state, particularly through the promotion of industrial colleges and public schools because of the principle "that the highest production of wealth follows the combination of muscle and intelligence." In the interest of economy he was not in favor of large expenditures on public works, and he planned to inactivate the militia. As an inducement to keep the peace, he warned that he would call out the militia if an outbreak of lawlessness made it necessary, and this in turn could result in heavier taxation.

  He advocated equality at the ballot-box, in the jury box, and in the distribution of public offices to colored persons and to poor whites. Then he softened this equalitarian stand by adding: "Wealth, intelligence, social position have always [been], as I trust they ever shall be, great power in the state."

  In order to promote the "material interests" of the state he felt taxation should not bear too heavily on industry, there should be no increase in the public debt, and the productive powers of the state should be developed. He contrasted the more practical accomplishments of the North, such as construction of canals, harbors, and railroads, with the intellectual abstractions of the South and told his listeners that Southerners "must abandon their political theorizing for the wiser statesmanship which devotes itself, in the first place, to the fosterage of material interests.". . .

Alcorn remained the persistent Whig in matters of reform and taxation. His message appealed to the wealthier planters and to those who saw the need for industrial change. It resulted in financial prosperity in Mississippi that compared favorably with other reconstructed states in the South.

. . . He urged public education for the children of the poor whites as well as the colored people, and spoke approvingly of the newly inaugurated system of free labor. Both of these developments would aid the industrialization of the state; but the overtones of equality at the lower levels of society which they carried must have sounded disquieting to poor white ears. Such reforms had greater appeal to the upper classes who would be indirectly benefited by them, and to the Negroes who were looking to him for leadership. For the former, he also promised not to increase the public debt, and he hoped for public improvements with Federal aid. In the old Whig idiom he spoke of his love of the Union, "of [his] heart swelling to the dimensions of the patriotism of Henry Clay." . . .

The problems with which Alcorn had to deal were similar to those faced by the governors of the other reconstructed southern states, and dominant among the issues was that of finance. As he had warned in his inaugural speech, the government for the many was a more expensive enterprise than it had been before the war. The auditor's books showed that he started his administration with a public debt of $1,177,339.46. He had to meet the increased expense of an expanded court system and executive department, of the inauguration of a public education system, and of repairs to the lunatic asylum, the state capitol, and the executive mansion. . . .

During the first year of Alcorn's administration operating expenses jumped about $500,000 over those of 1869, and the state debt by the end of the year had risen about $600,000. But Alcorn argued that these figures compared favorably with the administration of 1861: "When the exceptional demands incident to the wreck of war are considered, when the fact is considered that the duties of the State Government of 1870 are not only fuller, but that they apply in that fuller degree to double the number of people, I insist that the cost of the State Government, whatever may be the fact as to its absolute economy, was relatively, very decidedly less in 1870 than it was in 1861."

Attorney General Morris turned his defense of the administration's financial operations into an attack on its principal critics, the Democrats. He believed the state's financial condition compared favorably with that of the prewar administration of the men who now criticized it: "The Government of the United States committed to the hands of these same men and their associates large donations of money and lands for educational purposes, for internal improvements, &c. nearly all of which they squandered and stole—a very small percentage of which was ever appropriated to the objects designed by the Government in the donation."

A congressional investigating committee found the increase in rate of taxation in Mississippi to pay for these increased expenses far less than in some northern states where no serious complaints were made. During the entire Reconstruction period Mississippi financed its state governmental activities almost entirely through taxation, starting with a nearly empty treasury and with what, under the circumstances, was a considerable debt. . . .

In the area of civil rights, Alcorn took a strong position for separate but equal facilities. On such matters he was very conservative. He would not be easily influenced by black Republican leadership.

With regard to railroad legislation, Alcorn's administration was also able to show a comparatively good record. Like most Southerners attempting to get their states to emulate the North's industrial growth, Alcorn believed in the power of railroads as a sort of magical growth-and-prosperity stimulant for the areas through which they would go. But while many of his southern fellow governors outdid each other in extending the hospitality of their states to railroad promoters, he was wary of granting them too much power. In a message to the state senate in 1870 he recommended that the job of inspecting railroads be added to the duties of the board of public works. He also wanted the board to be able to regulate connections between railroads, and to have the right to inspect and, if necessary, condemn railroad structures. . . .

One of the most vulnerable parts of Alcorn's administration was its attitude on civil rights. After his inauguration the remaining sections of the Black Codes of 1865–66 were quickly repealed. The codes were statutes passed in southern states dealing with the social and economic conditions of the freed slaves. The various laws were attempts to adapt the restraints of slavery to the Negroes' new status. In June, 1870, an act rescinding the last section closed with a declaration that it was its intention to remove from the record all laws which in any way discriminated between citizens of the state on the basis of race. Also in 1870 a commission appointed by Alcorn codified the state laws incorporating the same prohibition against discrimination.

To all this Alcorn no doubt gave his approval, but Negro leaders wanted to go further and eliminate discrimination in transportation facilities, although at this time only three or four states in the Union had passed laws specifically prohibiting such segregation. In a general railroad bill passed by the legislature in late June, these leaders succeeded in having a clause inserted which would make it a penal offense to compel any person to occupy any particular car or section of a car. Although

Alcorn based his veto on other undesirable features in the bill, he also objected to this section on the grounds that the apparent meaning of the clause was inconsistent with a later section which declared the bill was not to mean that any railroad company might not provide "separate cars for ladies and gentlemen and separate cars for smoking." According to his reasoning, this left the decision for placing passengers to the discretion of the brakeman or conductor.

In a message to the senate, a few weeks later he asked that this bill be amended to have the railroad companies furnish "equal accommodations for the two races, the white race to be assigned to the one and the colored to the other." This amendment was voted down, 4 to 15. Then two Negro senators, Robert Gleed and William Gray, succeeded in getting enough reluctant white Republican votes to pass a law against discrimination on any type of public transportation. In an attempt to avert such legislation, Alcorn had the presidents of the railroads in Mississippi meet the Negro members of the legislature at the executive mansion and offer to provide them with equal but separate facilities. Alcorn is supposed to have lectured them on their refusal and to have warned them that their demands could not be enforced without bloodshed. What actually happened was that although the law passed, it was ignored in practice, and Negroes continued to accept segregated travel facilities. Jason Niles also supported this portion of Alcorn's objection to the general railroad bill, and later tried to get the antisegregation bill tabled. . . .

Alcorn's annual message of 1871 devoted considerable space to optimistic comments on the social conditions of the state. . . .

On the whole, the optimistic tone of Alcorn's message could be justified, since to all appearances his administration had gotten off to a good start during its first year. He had taken effective steps to improve the state's financial condition and could show considerable success in preventing speculation in state bonds. He was actively trying to encourage agriculture and industry. No major scandals marred his administration, and if there were flaws in the optimistic picture he drew, they appeared susceptible of mending. As chief executive of his state, Alcorn attacked the numerous problems by bringing into play those same characteristics which had enabled him to rise to a position of esteem and wealth in the frontier country of Coahoma County—a high code of personal ethics, shrewdness in his dealings, a puritanical dedication to hard work, and extraordinary energy. Apparently responding to the drive of that energy, Mississippi seemed to be moving back into its place as a regularly functioning state within the framework of the Union. Alcorn's practical approach, influenced by his persistent Federalist-Whig viewpoint, appeared to show that the past could be successfully invoked to meet the changes of the present.

In the fall of 1871 the Republican party in Mississippi maintained control of the legislature but with a smaller majority. The campaign had been tough, and Alcorn, considering it a victory, decided to resign as governor and take the position of senator from Mississippi, to which he had been appointed by the legislature in 1870. The term began in March 1871,

and he arrived in time for the opening of the second session of the Forty-Second Congress in
December 1871.

His first speech was on December 21, and it concerned the Amnesty Bill, which proposed
to restore the right to hold office to all but a few former Confederates still excluded by the
Fourteenth Amendment. It was a matter that he felt deeply about.

It is in no party sense that I appeal to the Senate to pass this bill. I appeal to them in a sense of justice to the people of my State; I appeal to them as one here representing Mississippi in part, whose disabilities this nation had the magnanimity to remove; and I now declare in this place that if the removal of my liabilities had depended upon my petition to this Congress, they would have still existed, for I would not have petitioned Congress to remove them. Subdued, conquered as the South was, while she lay bleeding at the feet of the nation, while she lies to-day prostrate and powerless for anything except simply the restoration of her civil society and her civil government, I would have left it to the nation to decide what should be done with me, and I would have asked no higher, no better, no other fate than that which was common to the people among whom I lived.

But the Congress of the United States removed my disabilities. I felt grateful for it. There are others in the South, equally sensitive with myself, who feel that they should have some consideration from the Government, and who, after you have liberated four thousand men who you may say came forward early in the work of reconstruction to apply for the removal of their disabilities, are entitled to some consideration at least. I am here to speak it for them; and I am not one who feels that I received my position here because others are excluded from holding it. No, sir; I would not hold an office in the State or in the nation if I believed that I obtained that office by reason of some constitutional exclusion resting upon others. Before there were disabilities, before the fourteenth amendment was passed, after the first reconstruction, I was chosen to a seat in the Senate of the United States. When the Legislature of the State of Mississippi was full of ex-rebels; when the Governor of the State was an ex-major general of the confederate States army; when the speaker of the house was an ex-confederate general; when the president of the senate was a man who had been a gallant colonel in the southern war; when the State senate and house were full of returned soldiers, my name, without solicitation upon my part, was brought forward, and after a contest for a few days I was elected over all my opposers. I then was indorsed by that class of our people.

The gentleman elected with me and myself were rejected here; we were not admitted; but of this I did not complain, for I was one who had no complaint to utter. I felt that the Government of the United States should control the question of reconstruction; and instead of inviting us to that political banquet, I should have been glad if they had conducted the affair of reconstruction in their own way, holding the South at the same time with a firm hand, so that the law should be enforced and the rights of citizens protected. But, sir, we were invited to come and participate in a political struggle, and this necessarily brought forward all the recollections of the past.

When we come, as I shall take occasion to do at some future time, to pass in review the whole question of reconstruction, I propose to show that all the responsibility of this agitation does not rest with the southern people. . . .

Once more, then, I say, if we are to have this bill, let it be now. I do not now insist upon extending it further than it goes; but I state here that at all times and upon all occasions whenever a proposition comes up to remove the disabilities of the people who were engaged in the rebellion I cannot do less than vote for it, and I will vote for it. . . .

By the spring of 1872 many senators were unwilling to extend the Ku Klux Klan act. Believing that it was no longer necessary they felt that the South should be left to take care of its political problems. On May 21 Alcorn made a speech ending with a plea that Mississippi be allowed to administer its own justice without federal interference.

Now, Mr. President, for three hundred miles on the Mississippi front in the State of Mississippi there has not been a case of Ku Klux violence established or even charged since the year 1868 within my knowledge. In all that vast rich delta that is now scarce of labor, susceptible of the production of a bale of cotton to an acre, where capital seeks to obtain labor, they are sending out their emissaries, as I have said, and agents every year to bring labor there; and I undertake to say there is not a plantation there that has the amount of labor it could use. In all those river counties for three hundred miles not a man holds an office unless he holds it at the will of the colored people, and a majority of the offices, I will say two thirds of the offices, are in truth and in fact held by the colored people. Is it possible that the courts cannot administer justice to the colored people in a society like this? Is it possible that the county in which I live, where the colored population is seventy-six per cent. of the whole; in the county below me, where it is eighty per cent.; in the county below that, where it is eighty-three per cent.; and in the county below that, where it is ninety per cent. of the whole, justice cannot be administered to the colored people when we have a thorough Republican, a true man, an excellent lawyer, a man of unspotted reputation, to preside as judge, and a northern man, who is a citizen of Mississippi in full accord with the Republican party, and in the full confidence of the colored people, as prosecuting attorney?

I undertake to say that justice is administered there, and that there is no complaint in all that district of country that justice is not administered; that colored men sit upon juries, and it is frequently the case that the jury is entirely composed of colored men. Colored men are overseers of the roads. A colored man is the sheriff of Issaquena county, appointed by myself . . . A colored man is elected sheriff of Adams county; a colored man is elected sheriff of Jefferson county, and colored men are officers in several other counties in the State of Mississippi; and yet it is said justice cannot be administered there, when every judge who sits upon the bench is a

Republican, appointed by a Republican Governor and confirmed by a Republican senate.

I repel the charge that justice is not administered in Mississippi. I assert that the Governor of Mississippi when he delivered his message to the Legislature in January, and declared that the condition of Mississippi was peace, told the truth; that when he wrote to me on the 15th of May, the present month, declaring that the condition of Mississippi to-day was peace, that peace reigns throughout her borders, the Governor, who is a northern man, but who is a citizen of Mississippi interested in our society, identified with us, a part of us, a man whom we all respect, and who is entitled to our respect, told the truth.

I stated the fact that I did not think there was any necessity for the suspension of the writ of *habeas corpus,* that the condition of Mississippi to-day was one of repose, that if Congress would allow the people there to do something toward going forward in the reconstruction of the State and not attempt to do everything by legislation, allow time to do its work, and the effect of this new order of things to adjust itself, everything would be in Mississippi as we would desire it, and that this intervention and this violent legislation that is calculated to disturb the repose of the State and engender hostilities between the races in the State is an intervention that no man who is interested in the peace and prosperity of this country, either North or South, would desire to see. . . .

The accomplishments of the Reconstruction governments, despite consistent opposition by southern whites, were remarkable in the few years of their existence. Suffrage was granted to black males. Property qualifications for holding office and for voting were eliminated. For the first time, a free public school system was set up throughout the South. Railroads and industry were expanded, and modern legal codes were also established.

In order to pay for these changes, money had to be raised. This meant that taxes and state debts needed to be substantially raised. The largest portion of these debts involved railroad bonds issued to support the necessary construction. Expenditures also included schools, roads, jails, and other public works. During the years of Reconstruction the average state budget doubled in size.

There was also corruption in various southern state legislatures, most notably South Carolina and Louisiana. Some legislators took advantage of the opportunity and voted themselves substantial raises. Others overcharged the state government for services and goods—printing, road or bridge repairs, or materials used in building schools or public buildings. However, corruption had existed in the South before the radical governments and existed in the North during the same years. It was not unique to the Republican governments of the South during Reconstruction.

Thus, radical Reconstruction can be considered both a success and a failure. It began the process of modernizing the South and added three important amendments to the Constitution—the Thirteenth, which freed the slaves; the Fourteenth, which gave black men and black women civil rights and equal protection under the laws; and the Fifteenth, which gave the vote to black males. But radical Reconstruction cost money and involved considerable corruption. To many Northerners it was the best that could be done. To Southerners it was extreme and unnecessary and should be ended as soon as possible. During the years of radical Reconstruction, counter Reconstruction began. It would end in the election of Rutherford B. Hayes to the presidency in 1876 and the removal of federal troops from the South in 1877.

PART III

❧ COUNTER ❧

RECONSTRUCTION

By the early 1870s the Republican party had been in power for more than a decade. It had won the war and put in place a Reconstruction policy that disfranchised many southern whites and elevated the freedmen to office and the ballot. This policy continued to receive support by most Northerners for several more years. As late as 1870 and 1871, enforcement acts were passed to punish those who opposed Reconstruction measures. The Republican party appeared to be united behind this policy despite the continuing resistance by most southern whites.

However, as stories of corruption within the Grant administration and in the governments in the South began to surface, a split opened up in the Republican party. Men like Lyman Trumbull and Carl Schurz, unhappy with the president and his policies, objected to the new enforcement acts as unwarranted and dangerous. Other mainline Republicans argued the opposite: that there was no real alternative—the rights of American citizens had to be protected at all costs. This resulted in the formation of the Liberal Republican party, which supported the Democratic party candidate for president in 1872, Horace Greeley. This ill-fated effort led to a lopsided victory for a second term for President Grant and a humiliating defeat for Greeley; the electoral vote was 286–62.

Thus, as the new year began, it appeared that the election of Grant meant a continuing commitment to Reconstruction. However, it soon became clear that federal protection for black rights and northern whites in the South was no longer certain. Southerners were determined to end any protection of black rights, whereas many Northerners, tiring of the process, began to see the governments in the South in a more negative light. Thus, the cry of Southerners to be left alone to solve "the race question" began to sound reasonable.

The reader will note a continuance of the three main themes during the years of counter Reconstruction. First, the physical destruction done during the war still echoed in the writings of many white Southerners. Second, the escalation of hostility to Reconstruction led many Southerners to organize in order to overthrow the carpetbagger-scalawag-black governments in the South. This resulted in many more acts of violence by white Southerners in order to regain political power. And third, southern resistance to the new freedoms given to the blacks was growing. These freedoms involved political and civil rights that blacks were unwilling to lose. Finally, an additional theme emerged in these later years. At first it was simply northern discontent with the slow progress of Reconstruction. Then it became widespread disillusionment with the entire effort and a desire to have it end. Many Northerners began to feel that Reconstruction was really a southern problem that only Southerners could solve. The cost had become too high, and the number of reports of corruption made many believe that it was no longer worth the effort. Unless this mood could be reversed, the end of Reconstruction was near. ∎

CHAPTER 9

SOUTHERN WHITES OPPOSED TO RADICAL RECONSTRUCTION TAKE CONTROL

". . . it is time for us to organize. We have been temporizing long enough."
—*Atlanta News*

Newspaper Editorials and Articles

By the fall of 1874 southern whites had become angered to the point of violent action. They could see little hope of regaining political control. The level of frustration with the Reconstruction governments was rapidly rising. Some of this could be seen in the renewed activity of the KKK and the White League, an organization dedicated to ending Reconstruction at any cost. At the same time, many southern whites who had been Republican shifted to the Democrat party. In 1874 there was a revolutionary effort in Louisiana and successful elections in Texas, Arkansas, and Alabama.

The reason for the successes was the new willingness of the South to use force. In Mississippi the motto was "peacefully if we can, forcibly if we must." The methods that were used included force, intimidation, social and business ostracism, the purchase of votes, the forming of "rifle clubs," and the termination of employment. These became effective methods of "discouraging" black voters. It took considerable courage to withstand this constant pressure and harassment. As the federal government became less willing to send in troops to protect the Reconstruction governments, conservative efforts to take control became more successful. Finally, with the election of 1876 and the victory of Rutherford B. Hayes, the southern whites again gained control of their governments.

It was especially difficult to find firsthand accounts by southern conservatives describing the process of regaining power in the South. Two continued to write—Frances Butler Leigh and George Browder—but William Gilmore Simms and Mary Jones were dead, and David

Harris stopped writing in his journal. (He died in 1875.) Thus, documents of those years such as newspaper articles and editorials were used to provide a way of understanding the thinking of southern white conservatives. The chapter closes with firsthand accounts by Frances Butler Leigh and George Browder.

On September 10, 1874, the **Atlanta News** *published the following editorial. It was virtually a declaration of war on northern radicals. The time for action had come.*

∞   "MEET BRUCE FORCE WITH BRUTE FORCE"   ∞

Let there be White Leagues formed in every town, village and hamlet of the South, and let us organize for the great struggle which seems inevitable. If the October elections which are to be held at the North are favorable to the radicals, the time will have arrived for us to prepare for the very worst. The radicalism of the republican party must be met by the radicalism of white men. We have no war to make against the United States Government, but against the republican party our hate must be unquenchable, our war interminable and merciless. Fast fleeting away is the day of wordy protests and idle appeals to the magnanimity of the republican party. By brute force they are endeavoring to force us into acquiescence to their hideous programme. We have submitted long enough to indignities, and it is time to meet brute-force with brute-force. Every Southern State should swarm with White Leagues, and we should stand ready to act the moment Grant signs the civil-rights bill. It will not do to wait till radicalism has fettered us to the car of social equality before we make an effort to resist it. The signing of the bill will be a declaration of war against the southern whites. It is our duty to ourselves, it is our duty to our children, it is our duty to the white race whose prowess subdued the wilderness of this continent, whose civilization filled it with cities and towns and villages, whose mind gave it power and grandeur, and whose labor imparted to it prosperity, and whose love made peace and happiness dwell within its homes, to take the gage of battle the moment it is thrown down. If the white democrats of the North are men, they will not stand idly by and see us borne down by northern radicals and half-barbarous negroes. But no matter what they may do, it is time for us to organize. We have been temporizing long enough. Let northern radicals understand that military supervision of southern elections and the civil-rights bill mean war, that war means bloodshed, and that we are terribly in earnest, and even they, fanatical as they are, may retrace their steps before it is too late.

———————

In nearby Alabama the following platform adopted by citizens of a majority white county was readopted by a large majority of conservative county conventions. The issue of race was uniting southern whites to use all available means to defend themselves.

∽ "PIKE COUNTY PLATFORM" ∽

Whereas the republican party of Alabama, for years past, has distinctly made and tendered to the people of this State an open, square issue of race; and

Whereas the tendencies of the doctrines, teaching and practices of said party, as more recently illustrated and evidenced by the passage of the United States Senate of what is known as the civil-rights bill, are to the effect that the negro, by reason of his emancipation, is elevated to, and ought of right to enjoy, social as well as political equality; and

Whereas the white people of the South have sedulously endeavored to prevent this issue of race, and in various ways sought to escape and avoid the said issue, well knowing the direful consequences that would follow it; and

Whereas the white people of the South have hitherto forborne, and hoped to escape the consequences thus hurled defiantly into their faces by the poor negroes, at the instance of the thieving crew known as carpet-baggers, and the more contemptible and infamous gang known as scalawags, who, in full view of this issue, have, for the sake of plunder, power, and spoils, sided with the aforesaid deluded negroes, regardless of the hateful and direful consequences to ensue from the passage of said odious civil-rights bill, which is the culmination of all radical diabolism.

Therefore, we respectfully suggest to our county convention for consideration the following resolutions:

Resolved, That we, the people of Troy beat, for the protection of our dearest and most sacred interests, our homes, our honor, the purity and integrity of our race, and to conserve the peace and tranquillity of the country, accept the issue of race thus defiantly tendered and forced upon us, notwithstanding our determination and repeated efforts to avoid it; and further

Resolved, That nothing is left to the white man's party but social ostracism of all those who act, sympathize or side with the negro party, or who support or advocate the odious, unjust, and unreasonable measure known as the civil rights bill; and that from henceforth we will hold all such persons as enemies of our race, and we will not in the future have intercourse with them in any of the social relations of life.

These are the sentiments of the democrats and conservatives of Pike County, with their fifteen hundred white majority.

———

A Republican statement about the election methods of the conservative white Southerners was made to a committee of the House of Representatives in the fall of 1874. Military groups were forming, and they were wearing "the usual gray uniforms."

∽ CONSERVATIVES USE RADICAL METHODS ∽

It was the advice of the democratic executive committee to the planters to furnish a list of the colored men in their employ who voted the colored ticket; and also all those who voted the democratic conservative ticket. In my opinion there is a determination here, on the part of the native white element, not to submit to republican principles and republican rule . . . Two weeks ago . . . Mr. Price on the Mobile and Girard Railroad . . . said, "You republicans were not fairly defeated. I know myself that on the train on which I was conductor on the day of the election, a great number of white men went from Georgia into your State and voted at three or four different places three or four different times on that day." If it had not been for the interference of the federal authorities in New Orleans, the republican administration would certainly have been overthrown in the State prior to the election. Military organizations were being effected in every part of this State. In my own town military organizations organized and applied to the governor for arms under the "militia law," and he refused to grant them. In Tuskegee and other places in the state arms were purchased by private subscriptions of citizens. Tuskegee is in Macon County. There were companies there numbering about sixty, fully armed and equipped, and there were white military organizations all over this State, because on the day the governor was inaugurated five or six different military organizations from different parts of the State were here armed and participating, and wearing the usual gray uniforms.

As the election grew near, many independent candidates tried to avoid the extremes of the two political parties. However, vigorous efforts were made to force them to return to the Democratic party. Often the language was biblical—"choose you this day whom ye will serve."

On October 14, 1874, the **Opelika Times** *(Alabama) published the following article, which was signed by an "Old Whig":*

○> WHIPPING INDEPENDENTS ○> INTO LINE

Can any man who sees the coming storm, and who, by blood or marriage, or adoption, feels the least possible interest in the future of our starved and cursed land, refuse to strike hands with his distressed fellow-citizens and join heart and soul in this their earnest endeavor to break the chains that are now being forged for our captivity? Is this hour of peril a time when any true man can hide from the draft made upon him by common suffering and a common threatened ruin? Is not the battle to be fought this fall one of common interest, and how dares any man either to go into the enemy's camp or seek to lay his burden upon the shoulders of another? . . . Is it not the time when the 80,000 white voters of Alabama should march as men with one banner and one voice? . . . Men, now, who walk out . . . between the two contending parties, begging quarters from friend and foe, are verily independents, (!) and deserve first to be shot down. Such independent men as these are seeking, through cowardly apprehensions, to make themselves the nucleus of the disaffected elements of the two parties, and thereby secure a position through cunning which they do not have the manliness to win upon principle. They are reaching out their arms to gather with one from the black fold and with the other the white. Perfectly independent; independent of race, color, and previous condition; independent of organization; independent of the history of consequences and results; independent of everything and everybody except office and the love of self. Rage scourge, devastate plague, ravage plague, ravage war, waste disease, and everybody sink if he swims . . .

The protege of radicalism, these independents, the spawn of corruption or poverty, or passion, or ignorance, come forth as leaders of the ignorant or deluded blacks, to attack and plunder for avarice, and defile and deflower for passion. There may be no God to avenge the South, but there is a devil to punish independents without priestly benediction, and Alabama will witness the ceremony . . .

Satan hath been in the democratic camp, and, taking these independents from guard-duty, led them up into the mountains and showed them the kingdoms of radicalism, his silver and gold, store-houses and bacon, and all these promised to give if they would fall down and worship him; and they worshiped him, throwing down the altars of their fathers and trampling them under their feet . . .

A square, brave, bold republican, such as was old Thad Stevens, we admire, and colored men admire him; but one who comes as a ravenous wolf under sheep's clothing even a negro and the devil must abhor. Such a man as Stevens, if taken in battle, would be entitled to the treatment of a soldier of war, but those independents who followed the Southern army, dressed up in confederate uniform, plundering and preying upon the remnant of subsistence left by the army, were not soldiers, although they wore the confederate regalia, and if taken by either army or citizens, would find no protection under either the laws of God or man . . .

Hard is life; but life cursed by passion, cursed by infidelity, cursed by ignorance and prejudice, by treason to race and country; cursed by ingratitude; yea cursed by the bite of radicalism, is a Gethsemane of crucifixion whose agony is left without a language . . . The rule of radicalism is the reign of Apollyon, Ashtaroth, Azriel, Baal, Belial, Beelzebub, Diabolus, Pluto, Pan, Satan, Zamiel, of black crook, and living, consuming devil. Independents minister at his altar . . .

All of the good . . . men of Alabama are for the white man's party. Outcasts, liberals, liars, hand-cuffers, and traitors to blood are for the negro party. Decide where you will place yourself in November.

In 1874 the Democrats won back the House of Representatives, transforming a 110-vote majority for the Republicans into a 60-vote majority for their party. Republicans still controlled the Senate, but it was clear that changes were coming.

The next year in Mississippi the **Aberdeen Examiner** *published an editorial on the impending political campaign of 1875:*

A REVOLUTION NOT
A POLITICAL CAMPAIGN

The republican journals of the North made a great mistake in regarding the present campaign in Mississippi in the light of a political contest. It is something more earnest and holy than that—it is, so far as the white people and land-owners are concerned, a battle for the control of their own domestic affairs; a struggle to regain a mastery that has been ruthlessly torn from them by selfish white schemers and adventurers, through the instrumentality of an ignorant horde of another race which has been as putty in their hands, molded to our detriment and ruin.

The present contest is rather a revolution than a political campaign—it is the rebellion, if you see fit to apply that term, of a down-trodden people against an absolutism imposed by their own hirelings, and by the grace of God we will cast it off next November, or cast off the willfully and maliciously ignorant tools who eat our bread, live in our houses, attend the schools that we support, come to us for aid and succor in their hour of need, and yet are deaf to our appeals when we entreat them to assist us in throwing off a galling yoke that has been borne until further endurance is but the basest of cowardice . . .

We favor a continuance of the canvass upon the broad and liberal basis that has heretofore characterized it; that is, we favor appealing to the negro by everything good and holy to forsake his idols and unite with us in ridding the State of a sway that we despise; but at the same time that we extend the olive-branch and plead for alliance and amity, we should not hesitate to use the great and all-powerful weapon that is in our control; we should not falter in the pledge to ourselves and our neighbors to discharge from our employ and our friendship forever, every laborer who persists in the diabolical war that has been waged against the white man and his interests ever since the negro has been a voter.

In Louisiana the race issue dwarfed all other issues. Not even politics or economics had as much appeal as the single issue of race. In 1874 three former Confederate officers published a newspaper called **The Caucasian,** *demanding that old party labels be forgotten and that the one issue be "white man vs black man." This resulted in the formation of the White League, dedicated to assassinating or intimidating officials, breaking up public meetings, and intimidating black voters. Many public officials resigned when faced with these threats rather than expose their families to this danger.*

The following excerpts are from (1) the constitution of the Crescent City White League and (2) the Louisiana White League platform:

⌘ THE WHITE LEAGUE ⌘

1. The object of this club is to assist in restoring an honest and intelligent government to the State of Louisiana; to drive incompetent and corrupt men from office; and by a union with all other good citizens, the better to maintain and defend the

constitution of the United States, with all laws made in pursuance thereof; and to maintain and protect and enforce our rights, and the rights of all citizens thereunder.

2. From the time that the right of suffrage was . . . accorded too hastily to a race in the infancy of freedom, we firmly resolved that it was our duty, and a wise expediency, to accept the policy of the reconstruction laws in their full scope. We endeavored at once to address ourselves to the intelligence of the negro, to explain to him that slavery having been forever abolished, he, as a citizen possessing all the rights of white citizens, had the same interests, and the same duties as the white men. . . . We invited him to our meetings, we called him to our platforms, we placed some of them upon our tickets. Election after election they turned a deaf ear to us; treated all our advances with distrust and suspicion; unhesitatingly followed the leadership of men whom they knew to be unworthy and dishonest, and, with scarcely an exception invariably voted like a body of trained soldiers obeying a word of command. We still hoped that time and experience would give them discretion. . . . We thought that a right which they owed to the white race would not be persistently used by them to accomplish the ruin of the white men. In this hope we have been most grievously disappointed . . . .

Any one who has been to their meetings, or overheard their private conversations, knows that they dream of the gradual exodus of the whites, which will leave Louisiana to their exclusive control, like another Hayti [Haiti]. The increasing spirit of caste founded on the most absurd inversion of the relations of race, shows itself in every form. Their incessant demands for offices from the State, city, and Federal Government, for which they are unfit, and to which they have no title other than the color of their skins; the development in their conventions of a spirit of proscription against white radicals and even against honorable republicans who fought in the northern armies for their liberation; their increasing arrogance, which seems to know no bounds; their increasing dishonesty, which they regard as statesmanly virtue; their contemptuous scorn of all the rights of the white man which they dare to trespass upon, all these signs warn us that the calamity which we had long apprehended is now imminent, and that we must prepare for all its consequences. Disregarding all minor questions of principle or policy, and having solely in view the maintenance of our hereditary civilization and Christianity menaced by a stupid Africanization, we appeal to the men of our race, of whatever language or nationality, to unite with us against that supreme danger. A league of the whites is the inevitable result of that formidable, oath-bound, and blindly obedient league of the blacks, which, under the command of the most cunning and unscrupulous negroes in the State, may at any moment plunge us into a war of races. . . . It is with some hope that a timely and proclaimed union of the whites as a race, and their efficient preparation for any emergency, may arrest the threatened horrors of a social war, and teach the blacks to beware of further insolence and aggression, that we call upon the men of our race to leave in abeyance all lesser considerations; to forget all differences of opinions and all race prejudices of the past, and with no object in view but the common good of both races, to unite with us in an earnest effort to re-establish a white man's government in the city and the State.

Several years earlier the **Planters Banner** *published an article on the KKK entitled "Spreading News of the Klan." In those years, the Klan received considerable attention and usually a positive press. Newspapers even announced Klan parades. It was said that ". . . only in rare exceptional cases, and these the most aggravated, that it undertook to punish."*

SPREADING NEWS OF THE KLAN

There is much excitement among the negroes and even some of the white folks, all over Attakapas, about the Ku-Kluxes that have lately appeared in this country. I am not superstitious, and will not tell you what I believe about these strange, ghostly appearances, but will give you some general items and rumors.

The negroes have entirely deserted one prairie in Attakapas since the election, having been run out by the Ku-Kluxes.

The negroes of Lafayette parish were lately nearly all of them preparing to leave, the K. K. K.'s having frightened them every night, and carried off a carpet-bagger from Illinois. One negro, a big-talking radical, somewhere in the parish of St. Martin, was lately carried off by these confederate ghosts, at night, and has never been heard of since.

A night traveler called at the negro quarters, somewhere in Attakapas, and asked for water. After he had drunk three blue buckets full of good cistern water, at which the negro was much astonished, he thanked the colored man and told him he was very thirsty, that he had travelled nearly a thousand miles in twenty-four hours, and that was the best drink of water he had since he was killed at the battle of Shiloh. The negro dropped the bucket, tumbled over two chairs and a table, escaped through a back window, and has not since been heard from. He was a radical negro.

White men on white horses have lately been seen sailing through the air at midnight at Pattersonville, Jeanerette, and at various places all over the southern part of this State.

If negroes attempt to run away from the K. K. K's, these spirits always follow them, and catch them, and no living man hears from them again.

The leader of this new order is said to be perfectly terrible. He is ten feet high and his horse is fifteen. He carries a lance and a shield like those of Goliath of the Philistines . . .

Attakapas,
May 20, 1868.
K. K. K.

By 1876 it was not uncommon for advertisements for labor to specify Democrats, not Republicans. Respectable people would not hire Republicans. The following were in the **Charleston Journal of Commerce** *on October 2, 3, and 5, 1876.*

Housekeepers can get their meats from "Democratic Headquarters," stalls Nos. 49, 50, 57, and 58, Lower Market. Also, Nos. 9 and 10, Upper Market. . . . It is not democratic money alone we want, but Wade Hampton and reform.

Daniel Cooper
Dederick Stokien
John Stokien

To our merchants, wharf-owners, and tradesmen generally:
   The Workingmen's Democratic Association are now prepared to furnish from 100 to 200 able bodied men for any kind of work. Apply at their hall, Queen street, near Meeting, from 9 to 12 m., 2 to 6, and 7 to 9 p.m.

A Card
   Until further notice I will receive applications from those seeking employment, on Mondays, Wednesdays, and Fridays; and orders from employes for straight-out democratic workingmen, on Tuesdays, Thursdays, and Saturdays. I am prepared to furnish democrats with democratic labor at reasonable wages, to any extent at a moment's notice. To employ republicans and starve democrats no longer pays. It is a crime, and will be held to strict accountability.

R. S. Tharin
75 Broad Street

Prior to the election in 1876 southern newspapers were filled with editorials that called for citizens to recognize the importance of ending Reconstruction. All citizens were urged to support "a white man's government."

∞ A WHITE MAN'S GOVERNMENT ∞
OR MILITARY RULE

The greatest excitement and enthusiasm pervade the ranks of the whites, and they are determined to redeem the State from her ignoble thrall at any cost and at any sacrifice.

   Troops have no terrors for them. They want troops; they want all the troops that can be sent to the State, for the true soldier deeply sympathizes with the cause of the oppressed white man everywhere, and they are determined to have either a white man's government or military rule.

In 1890 Hilary Herbert edited a book on Reconstruction entitled Why the Solid South? Or, Reconstruction and Its Results. Individuals from each of the southern states were asked "to write as impartially as possible, to understate rather than to overstate fact," about Reconstruction in their individual states. The purpose of the book was to convince northern businessmen to invest money in the South. It was dedicated to the businessmen of the North.

The following excerpt from Chapter 4, entitled "Reconstruction in South Carolina," written by John J. Hemphill, a businessman in South Carolina, illustrates some of the patterns that developed in the southern states during Reconstruction. It begins by describing great dissatisfaction among citizens in South Carolina.

The most peaceable citizens of the state felt that they were without a government to protect them; that in fact the government was inimical to them; that it protected and rewarded the criminals while it punished the innocent and law-abiding. Under such circumstances it is not to be wondered at that men would try to do something to protect themselves. . . .

The intelligent property owners of the state, having practically no influence on legislation, realizing the dreadful condition to which they were being reduced, and knowing that no redress could be had through any branch of the state government, organized in 1871, what was known as the Tax-payers' Convention. This body, as a whole, was thoroughly representative of the virtue, intelligence and property of the state. They discussed fully the condition of public affairs and issued an address to the public, in which they set forth the status of the public debt, the financial condition of the state, etc., and hoped in this way to bring to bear the honest sentiment of the country in favor of a change, and thus stay, in a measure, the hand by which they were being ruined. Their effort produced no appreciable results.

In 1874 another convention was held, in which again the dreadful state of affairs was plainly and fully made known, and an appeal issued to the country.

In addition, a large committee was appointed to proceed to Washington to lay before the President a full statement of the condition of our affairs, and to make known to him the position to which we had been reduced, and to invoke his aid toward providing some relief.

With some difficulty, a meagre sum was raised from the impoverished people to meet the expenses of this committee, but before they could reach the National Capital the state officials drew $2,500 of the money of these same tax-payers from the treasury, and sent several of their number to see the President and arrange that no heed should be given to the committee of citizens. So completely successful was their mission that when the committee of tax-payers arrived, the mind of the President was completely closed to their appeal and they were not even heard with patience. Thus again the efforts of the tax-payers proved utterly futile. . . .

During Moses' administration the pardoning of criminals became a simple matter of bargain and sale. Any convict who had strong friends or a long purse, was in no danger of having to serve out a sentence in the Penitentiary. So common and notorious did the pardoning of criminals become, that judges announced from the bench, their unwillingness to put the people to the expense and trouble of convicting criminals for the Governor to pardon. During his term of two years he issued 457 pardons. On October 31, 1874, there remained in the penitentiary only 168 convicts, and Moses pardoned 46 during the month of November following, which was the last month of his service as Governor.

In May, 1875, Governor Chamberlain declared in an interview with a correspondent of the Cincinnati *Commercial,* that when, at the end of Moses' administration, he entered on his duties as Governor, two hundred trial justices were holding office by executive appointment, who could neither read nor write the English language. . . .

As the term of Governor Moses was coming to a close the nominations for state officers were made. The regular Republicans nominated D. H. Chamberlain, for the governorship, who had been the Attorney-General during Scott's administration; and the bolting Republicans placed against him John T. Green, a native, a Republican and a Circuit Judge, and again the Democrats or Conservatives joined them and supported their candidate.

The administration of state affairs under Moses had become so intolerably rotten and corrupt that the reputable and honest people of the state were outraged beyond all expression, and even the more cautious participants in the schemes of plunder were frightened into a manifestation of opposition to such a course. The election showed over 12,000 more votes than had been cast at any time since 1868, and the majority of the regular Republican ticket was reduced to about one-third of the usual number.

Governor Chamberlain, quite in contrast with his predecessors, talked reform after his election as well as before it. In his inaugural address he exposed unmercifully the extravagance of expenditures under the former administrations and insisted that there must be a change. He pointed out among other extravagances that the expenses of the Legislature for six years for mileage, pay of members and employees, etc., had been $2,147,430.97 and for executive contingent expenses $376,832.74.

Some portions of the negro militia organized and armed by Governor Scott were still in existence and in January 1875 a serious affray occurred in Edgefield county between men of different races. The usual course before that in all such cases had been for the Governor to work up these troubles into insurrections and have some negroes killed and then appeal to the President for troops to suppress them. Governor Chamberlain took the wiser course of simply issuing his proclamation directing the militia and other military organizations to disarm and cease all military exercises. This was done and the trouble was allayed at once. It was the first instance since 1868 in which a reasonable and just policy had been adopted toward the white people of the state in such cases, and their astonishment and delight at receiving some kind consideration at the hands of their own state government was too marked to escape notice. The result fully justified the wisdom of the Governor's course. During the first sitting of the Legislature of 1874–75, the Governor had a long and severe contest with the baser elements of his own party. They endeavored to have the State Treasurer, who was a strong friend of the Governor, removed from office, but this was defeated by a combination between the Democrats and some of the Republican friends of the Governor. He vetoed during this session nineteen bills chiefly on the grounds of extravagance and profligacy, and in every one he was sustained by the same combination of political elements.

In the face of great and unrelenting opposition in his own party Governor Chamberlain, by the aid of the Democrats and some of his political allies in the Legislature, had been able to accomplish some marked and wholesome reforms in public expenditures, and for this he had won the warm praise of a number of the leading papers and many of the prominent conservative citizens of the State. His course had done much to allay race antagonism, had created a greater sense of security in the public mind and given the people some ground for the hope of better days in the future.

The support by southern states of Governor Chamberlain changed quickly because of the actions of the South Carolina legislature. The issue was the choice of judges. Two "corrupt" men were to be appointed to two of the most important posts in the state. This rallied conservatives to organize in order to take back their government. Hemphill continued:

These feelings were, however, entirely dissipated by one act of the Legislature of 1875, which set at defiance all the efforts at genuine reform in the state, and left no ground for any reasonable man to base a belief on that public affairs would ever permanently improve under the control of the party then in power.

Eight judges were to be chosen that session. It was well known that the Governor had expressed himself as being greatly interested in having selected men of ability and especially of personal integrity.

While he was temporarily absent the conspirators went into an election and chose for two of the most important posts in the state, F. J. Moses, Jr. and W. J. Whipper. Mr. Allen, the author of "Chamberlain's Administration in South Carolina," characterizes this action as "an offence against public honor and safety on the part of the legislative body more flagrant than any other which stained the era of reconstruction in South Carolina, and perhaps the most alarming legislative action in any Southern state."

On his return to Columbia and learning what had been accomplished by the Republicans of the General Assembly, the Governor declared, in a published interview, "This calamity is infinitely greater, in my judgment, than any which has yet fallen on this state, or, I might add, upon any part of the South."

A few days subsequent to this Governor Chamberlain in declining an invitation to the banquet of a New England Society said: "I cannot attend your supper to-night; but if there ever was an hour when the spirit of the Puritans, the spirit of undying, unconquerable enmity and defiance to wrong ought to animate their sons, it is this hour, here, in South Carolina. The civilization of the Puritan and the Cavalier, of the Roundhead and the Huguenot is in peril. Courage, determination, union, victory, must be our watchwords. The grim Puritans never quailed under threat or blow. Let their sons now imitate their example!"

The election of these men to two of the most important judicial positions in the state, in spite of all opposition, both inside and outside of the party in power, sent a thrill of horror through the entire commonwealth and aroused the people to an extent unprecedented for years.

Large meetings were held in nearly every county in the state, in which the firm determination was expressed that these men should never be permitted to enter as judges into the courts of justice. Fortunately the use of any forcible means was obviated by the refusal of the Governor to commission either Moses or Whipper upon legal grounds, which were afterwards, in another case, approved by the Supreme Court of the state. Whipper threatened to take his office by force, but was deterred from such a course by the prompt action of the Governor in issuing a proclamation, in which he declared that he would arrest him and every one aiding and abetting him as rioters and disturbers of the peace.

Governor Chamberlain, in a letter to President Grant, again characterizes these men chosen by his party as judges as follows: "Unless the entirely universal opinion of all who are familiar with his career is mistaken, he (Moses) is as infamous a character as ever in any age disgraced and prostituted public position. The character of W. J. Whipper, according to my belief and the belief of all good men in the state, so far as I am informed, differs from that of Moses only in the extent to which opportunity has allowed him to exhibit it. The election of these two men to judicial offices sends a thrill of horror through the state. It compels men of all parties who respect decency, virtue or civilization to utter their loudest protests against the outrage of their election."

The election to such places of these two men, not only wholly incompetent, but well known to be flagrantly dishonest and corrupt was the beginning of a change in the state.

At nearly every one of the mass meetings held in the different counties to protest against this action of the General Assembly, resolutions were adopted by the people, declaring that all hope of securing even a tolerable government under the dominant party had been dissipated and that the sole prospect of reform in public affairs lay in the reorganization of the Democratic party and its induction into power.

Governor Chamberlain quickly apprehended that this would be the result. In his first utterance for the public, after the Moses-Whipper affair, he said: "I look upon their election as a horrible disaster—a disaster equally great to the state and to the Republican party. The gravest consequences of all kinds will follow. One immediate effect will obviously be the reorganization of the Democratic party within the state as the only means left, in the judgment of its members, for opposing a solid and reliable front to this terrible *crevasse* of misgovernment and public debauchery. I could have wished, as a Republican, to have kept off such an issue."

He rightly appreciated the situation. The negroes seemed to be elated by this defiance of decency upon the part of their chosen Representatives in the legislature, and the whites were thoroughly aroused to a sense of the danger that confronted them. The negro militia in some portions of the state became greatly interested in parading and drilling, and the whites seeing this thought that it was prudent to be ready to take care of themselves and their families.

As a result of this condition of things there were several bloody encounters between the blacks and whites, in which a number of persons were killed and wounded.

These troubles, of course, did not conduce to a kindly feeling between the two races, and the sentiment that the intelligent tax-payers of the state must control public affairs or be ruined and driven from their homes continually grew and increased among the people.

For a time there was great difference of opinion among the leading men of the state as to whether it was wisest to try again the plan of compromising on a ticket with the opposition, or make a straight out Democratic nomination. The latter was finally decided upon. The other course had been tried for eight years and no appreciable benefit had been derived from it. And while the efforts of Governor Chamberlain in behalf of economy and decency had resulted in some temporary good, it had been made manifest that he was unable to control his own party.

In 1868 we had nominated for Governor an honorable and able citizen of the state; in 1870 we had joined in nominating an able carpet-bagger, whom the Republicans had before that placed on the bench; in 1872 we had, in conjunction with some Republicans, supported another carpet-bag Republican official who had some claims to honesty; and in 1874 we had again given our votes and influence to a native Republican of fair ability and character who had been named for Governor by the dissatisfied Republicans.

In all of these several instances we had also nominated and supported tickets for the Legislature and county offices made up partly of blacks and partly of whites. We had held conventions of the tax payers and appealed to the country, and had sent a delegation to the Capital of the Nation for the purpose of acquainting the President of the United States with the true condition of the state, and had protested in every possible way against such inhuman tyranny.

The issue became race supremacy. Now only whites could be elected to important positions. At last southern white conservatives believed that it was possible for an honest administration to be elected. To be certain of a successful election, the race issue was again stressed. Hemphill continued:

All these efforts had proven to be worse than worthless, and it had become manifest that the real question that confronted the people of the state was one of race supremacy.

The Republicans renominated Governor Chamberlain and the Democrats put in the field a full ticket of white men, with General Wade Hampton at the head of it. The campaign that followed was the most exciting ever known in the state, and resulted in the election of the Democratic ticket.

With the installation of these officers and the meeting of the General Assembly began the first honest and economical administration that the state had known since the beginning of reconstruction, and from that time to the present the affairs of the state have been managed with a regard for the people's welfare. The public schools and the institutions for higher education have been cared for and supported. The interest on the public debt has been paid, and instead of selling six per cent. bonds of the state at twenty-five or thirty cents on the dollar, the four-and-a-half per cent. bonds of the state are now bringing more than par. Instead of salaries costing $230,800, as in 1872, they were reduced to $106,200 in 1876. In place of paying $712,200 for legislative expenses as in 1871, this item was reduced to $42,000 in 1880. The public printing, which cost $450,000 in 1872, was reduced to $6,900 in 1878. The state, counties, towns and school districts have now no floating debt and all obligations are paid as they mature. Instead of profligacy we have honesty; instead of extravagance, economy; instead of uneasiness, we have contentment, and instead of rioting, peace.

The resources of the state are being greatly developed; the manufacturing enterprises are multiplying wonderfully, and the people are looking to the future for still greater development of its industries and resources.

All we ask is to be let alone, and that, surely, is not so great a request that it cannot or ought not be granted.

Jno. J. Hemphill.

Frances Butler Leigh

The last two accounts here are by Frances Butler Leigh and George Browder. Both had lived through the years of moderate and radical Reconstruction. Now they would witness the shift in power back to the white South. Each was strongly pro-southern in sentiment and anxious for the South to be freed of northern control. Soon they would be pleased.

Frances and James Leigh returned to England for the summer and then came back to the plantation in the fall of 1873. They had new plans for the replacement of freedmen with British workers. James Leigh, a minister, was interested in the plantations and wanted to make them successful. A church was built at nearby Darien. They continued to go north for the summer to avoid malaria. Frances had two children, Alice Dudly in 1874 and Pierce Butler in 1876. Pierce lived for only twenty-four hours. That tragedy plus falling prices finally convinced them to return to England for good.

In May of the same year [1873] I sailed for Europe, and in June was married. I remained in England until the autumn of 1873, when we returned to the United States. During the interval the accounts that reached us from the South were not satisfactory. The expenses, it is true, were cut down to nearly one-half what they had been before, and the negroes gave but little trouble, but one overseer turned out to be very incapable and entirely wanting in energy, making no fresh improvements and planting the same fields each year that had been under cultivation since the war, letting all the rest of the place grow into a complete wilderness. We also had a terrible loss during our absence in the destruction by fire of our mills and principal buildings. They were undoubtedly set on fire by one of the negroes to whom we had shown many and special favours, which had only had the effect of spoiling him to such an extent that he would not bear the slightest contradiction or fault found with his work. He had been reprimanded by the overseer and a dollar deducted from his wages for some neglect in his work, and this put him into such a passion that he refused to take his wages at all and went off, saying that it should cost us more than a dollar. This, and the fact that he was seen about the mill the morning of the fire, where he had no business to be, made us feel pretty sure that he was the incendiary, and although we never could prove it, it was a generally accepted idea that he was the man.

By this fire about fifteen thousand dollars worth of property was destroyed, including all our seed rice for the coming planting, and had it not been for the efforts of the Irishmen who were at work on the place, the dwelling-houses and other buildings would have gone too. The sight of a large fire seems to arouse the savage nature of the negroes; they shout and yell and dance about like fiends, and often become possessed by an incendiary mania which results in a series of fires. They never attempt to put it out, even if it is their own property burning.

Soon after this came the news that the teacher I had left on the Island to train and educate the people, not only intellectually but morally, had turned out very badly, and had led one of my nicest young servant girls astray, which, with the other disaster, so disheartened me as to make me feel unable to struggle any longer against the fate which seemed to frustrate all my efforts either to improve the property or the condition of the people, and I said I would do no more. My husband, however, took a more practical view of the matter, and decided that as we could not abandon the property altogether we must go on working it, so he telegraphed the agent to get estimates for a new mill and to buy seed, and in fact to go on, which he did, and in course of time a new mill was built and a fresh crop planted.

————

The Leigh family was optimistic about the possibility of British labor, but soon it was obvious that it would not work. This was a bitter and costly disappointment. The only answer was to continue with the freedmen.

In the autumn of 1873 we determined to return to America, and the agitation among the agricultural labourers in England being then at its height, I thought we might advantageously avail ourselves of the rage among them for emigration, to induce a few to go out to Butler's Island and take the place of our Irish labourers there. It seemed a capital plan, but I did not know then what poor stuff the English agricultural labourer is made of as a general rule. Eight agreed to go, and a contract was made with them for three years, by which we bound ourselves to send them back at the end of the time should they desire to come, and have in the meantime fulfilled their part of the agreement; the wages we agreed to give them were the highest given in the United States, and about three times higher than what they had received at home. As we intended to stop some little time at the North we shipped them direct to the South, where they arrived about a month before we did. On November 1 we followed, and I was most warmly greeted by all the negroes, who at once accepted my husband as 'massa.'

Our own people seemed pretty well settled, and Major D——said gave but little trouble, the greatest improvement being in their acceptance of their wages every Saturday night without the endless disputes and arguments in which they used formerly to indulge whenever they were paid. But there were still a great many idle worthless ones hanging about Darien, and when we arrived the wharf was crowded with as dirty and demoralised a looking lot of negroes as I ever saw, and these gave the town a bad name.

Our Englishmen we found settled in the old hospital building which I had assigned to them, and which had been unoccupied since the school had been broken up, with the exception of one room which the people still used as their church. Besides this there were three others, about twenty feet square, nicely ceiled and plastered, into which I had directed the Englishmen should be put, and in *one* of these we found them all, eight men sleeping, eating, and living in the same room, from preference. They had not made the least effort to make themselves decently comfortable, and were lying upon the floor like dogs, although Major D—— had advised them to put up some bedsteads, offering the carpenter of the party lumber for the purpose, and an old negro woman to make them some straw mattresses, giving them a week to get things straight before they began their work. Two of them fell ill soon after, and then we insisted upon their dividing, half the number using one sleeping room and the rest the other, keeping the third for a general living room, kitchen, &c. At first they seemed in good spirits and well satisfied, but nothing can describe their helplessness and want of adaptability to the new and different circumstances in which they found themselves. They were like so many troublesome children, and bothered me extremely by coming to the house the whole time to ask for something or other, until at last, one Saturday evening when they came to know if I would let them have a little coffee for Sunday, as they had forgotten to buy any, the shop being only half a mile distant across the river, I flatly refused, and said they must learn to take care of themselves. One was afterwards very ill, and I really thought he would die from want of heart, as from the first moment he was taken ill he made up his mind he should not recover, and I had to nurse him like a baby, giving him his medicine and food with my own hands, and finally when he was really well, only weak, we had to insist upon his getting up and trying to move about a little, or I think he would have spent the rest of his life in bed.

To make a long story short, they soon began to get troublesome and discontented, were constantly drunk, and shirked their work so abominably, that our negro foreman Sey begged that they might not be allowed to work in the same fields with his negroes, to whom they set so bad an example, by leaving before their day's work was finished, that they demoralised his gang completely, and made them grumble at being obliged to go on with their work after the 'white men' had left. So when the end of their second year came we were most thankful to pay their way back to England and get rid of them. All left except one, who after starting rather badly settled down and became a useful hard-working man, and is still with us as head ploughman, in which capacity he works for about eight months of the year, spending the other three or four on our deserted cotton place, as the unhealthiness of the rice plantation prevents his remaining there during the summer months. During this time he plants a good vegetable garden for himself, spends most of his time fishing, and is taken care of by an old negro woman, who he assured my husband worked harder and was worth more than any white woman he had ever seen. But I am afraid his experience had been unfortunate, for he was the only married man in the party we brought out, and his being the only one who did not wish to return made us suspect domestic troubles might have had something to do with his willingness to stay.

The Irish laborers proved to be the better workers. They enjoyed the work and showed initiative and an ability to survive. Surprisingly, Irish relations with the English were more difficult than with the blacks. The Irish and English had little love for each other.

We had for several years employed a gang of Irish labourers to do the banking and ditching on the Island, and although we made no agreement with them about returning in the spring when we dismissed them, they came down each succeeding autumn, taking the risk of either being engaged again by us or by some of our neighbours, and hitherto we had always been ready to do so. But the winter we first had our Englishmen we decided not to have the additional heavy expense of the Irishmen, and so told them we did not want them. The result was that they were very indignant with the Englishmen, whom they regarded as usurpers and interlopers, and whose heads they threatened to break in consequence.

Major D——, half in fun, said to them, 'Why, you shouldn't hate them; you all come from the same country.' To which Pat indignantly replied, 'The same country, is it? Ah, thin, jist you put them in the ditch along wid us, and ye'll soon see if it's the same country we come from.' A test they were quite safe in proposing, for the Englishmen certainly could not hold a spade to them, and after trying the latter in the ditch we were glad enough to engage our Irishmen again, which quite satisfied them, so that after that they got on very well with their 'fellow countrymen,' only occasionally indulging in a little Irish wit at their expense. They certainly were a very different lot of men, and while the Englishmen were endless in their complaints, wants, and need of assistance, the Irishmen turned into a big barn at the upper end of the plantation, got an old negro woman to cook for them, worked well and faithfully, were perfectly satisfied, and with the exception of occasionally meeting them going home from their work of an evening when I was walking, I never should have known they were on the place.

I must record one act to their honour, for which I shall ever feel grateful. Two years after the one of which I am now writing I was very ill on the plantation, and the white woman I had taken from the North as cook was lying dangerously ill at the same time, so that the management and direction of everything fell upon my nurse, an excellent Scotch-woman, who found some difficulty in providing for all the various wants of such a sick household. The Irishmen hearing her say one day that she did not know where she should get anything that I could eat, brought her down some game they had shot for themselves, and, being told that I liked it, every Monday morning regularly, for the rest of the winter, sent me in either hares, snipe, or ducks by one of the servants, without even waiting to be thanked, the game they shot being what they themselves depended upon for helping out their scanty larder.

I felt a little anxious at first about the effect such a new life and strange surroundings might have upon my husband, for although he had seen it before, it was a very different matter merely looking at it from a visitor's point of view, and returning to live there as owner, when all the differences between it and his life and home in England would be so apparent. However, I soon found that I need not be uneasy upon that score, as he at once became deeply interested in it, and set about learning all the details of the work and peculiarities of both place and people, which he mastered in a wonderfully short time, showing a quick appreciation of the faults and mistakes in the previous system of planting which he had followed since the war, and which he very soon tried on an entirely different plan. This was so successful that in a year the yield from the place was doubled and the whole plantation bore a different aspect, much to the astonishment of our neighbours, who could not understand how an Englishman, an English parson at that, who had never seen a rice field before in his life, should suddenly become such a good planter. The negroes, after trying what sort of stuff he was made of, became very devoted to him, and one of the old men, after informing my sister some little time afterwards how much they liked him and how much good he had done them all, wound up with 'Miss Fanny (me) made a good bargain dat time.'

My husband wrote a number of letters to England from the plantation during the time we remained there, which were published in a little village magazine for the amusement of the parishioners who knew him, and which I think I cannot do better than add to this account of mine, as they will show how everything at the South struck the fresh and unbiassed mind of a foreigner who had no traditions, no old associations, and no prejudices, unless indeed unfavourable ones, to influence him.

After having spent the summer at the North, we again returned to the plantation in November, taking with us this time an addition to the family in the shape of a little three-months-old baby, who was received most warmly by the negroes, and christened at once 'Little Missus,' many of them telling me, with grins of delight, how they remembered me 'just so big.' I very soon found that the arrival of 'young missus' had advanced me to the questionable position of 'old missus,' to which however I soon became reconciled when I found how tenderly 'Little Missus' was treated by all her devoted subjects. Oddly enough, the black faces never seemed to frighten her, and from the first she willingly went to the sable arms stretched out to take her. It was a pretty sight to see the black nurse, with her shining ebony face, surmounted by her bright-coloured turban, holding the little delicate white figure up among the branches of the orange trees to let her catch the golden fruit in her tiny hands; and the house was kept supplied almost the whole winter with eggs and chickens, brought as presents to 'Little Missus.'

———————

Frances Butler Leigh almost died in January of 1876. Her Negro maid and many freedmen helped pull her through the crisis. Sadly her old housekeeper was not so fortunate; she died soon after Leigh recovered.

Another summer at the North and back again to the South, from whence nothing but good reports had reached us of both harvest and people. Indeed our troubles of all sorts seemed to be at an end, at least such as arose from 're-construction.' It came in another shape, however, and in January 1876 I was taken very ill, and for five days lay at the point of death, during which time the anxiety and affection shown by my negroes was most profound, all work stopped, and the house was besieged day and night by anxious inquirers. My negro nurse lay on the floor outside my door all night, and the morning I was pronounced out of danger she rushed out, and throwing up her arms, exclaimed, 'My missus'll get well; my missus'll get well! I don't care what happens to me now.' And when at last I was able to get about once more, the expressions of thankfulness that greeted me on all sides were most touching. One woman, meeting me on the bank, flung herself full length on the ground, and catching me round the knees, exclaimed, 'Oh, tank de Lord, he spared my missus.' A man to whom something was owing for some chickens he had furnished to the house during my illness refused to take any money for them, saying when I wished to pay him, 'No, dey tell me de chickens was for my missus, and I'se so glad she's got well I don't want no money for dem.' My dear people!

Our poor old housekeeper, less fortunate than myself, did not recover, but died just as I was getting better, and in looking over her letters after her death, in order to find out where her friends lived, so as to let them know of her death, I found to my astonishment that she had been in terror of the negroes from the first, and had a perfect horror of them. Being so fond of them myself, and feeling such entire confidence in them as not even to lock the doors of the house at night, it never occurred to me that perhaps a New England woman, who had never seen more than half-a-dozen negroes together in her life, might be frightened at finding herself surrounded by two or three hundred, and it was only after her death that I found from the letters written to her by different friends at the North, in answer to hers, what her state of mind had been. There were such expressions as these: 'I don't wonder you are frightened and think you hear stealthy steps going about the house at night.' 'How horrible to be on the Island with all those dreadful blacks.' 'The idea of there being only you three white people on the Island with two hundred blacks!' &c. She had apparently forgotten, in making her statement, the eight Irish and six English labourers who were living on the Island, but still the negroes certainly did greatly outnumber the whites, and could easily have murdered us all had they been so inclined. But there was not the least danger then, whatever there might have been the first year or two after the war, and even at that time I never felt afraid, for had there been a general negro insurrection, although my own negroes would of course have joined it, there were at least a dozen, I am sure, who would have warned me to leave the place in time.

My sister paid me a visit this winter—her first to the South since the war, except in 1867, when she spent a month with us, but on St. Simon's Island, where she saw little or nothing of the negroes—and she was greatly struck with their whole condition and demeanour, in which she said she could not perceive that freedom had made any difference. In answer to this I could only say that if she had been at the South the first three years after the war, she would have seen a great change in their deportment, but that since that they had gradually been coming back to their senses and 'their manners.'

This winter we had the pleasure of seeing a very nice church started in Darien for the negroes. For three years my husband had been holding services for them regularly on the Island in a large unoccupied room which we had fitted as a chapel; but we found this hardly large enough to accommodate outsiders, and as many wished to attend who were not our own people, we thought Darien the best place for the church. While it was being built, service was held in a large barn or warehouse, which was kindly lent for the purpose by a coloured man of considerable property and good standing in the community, who although a staunch supporter of the Presbyterian Church himself, was liberal minded enough to lend a helping hand to his brethren of a different persuasion. . . .

George Browder

George Browder, a Methodist minister in Kentucky, took little interest in political affairs from 1870 to 1876. His health was poor, and at first he served as an assistant to the Allensville Circuit. He recovered enough to accept a full-time appointment to the Allensville Circuit and for two years was an active preacher. In early 1876 he again became interested in politics and the possible end of Reconstruction. He hoped that Samuel Tilden would be elected and troops withdrawn from the South. For some time he had been disillusioned with President Grant and Republican policies in the South.

March 4 [1876]—Papers are full of accounts of Genl Balknaps malfeasance in office. He is charged with high crimes and misdemeanors in *selling* the offices at his command and has been impeached in Congress. His wife is a party to the disgrace. Alas for our country. Crime runs riot. Men in High Places are corrupt.

November 7—This is Presidential Election day & millions of freemen are greatly concerned as to the result. I pray God to direct to the right result. I came home to vote—but the car caught fire at Russellville & we were delayed until the polls closed—so I missed the vote I was anxious to cast for my friend John W. Caldwell for Congress—& Samuel J. Tilden for President. News will be received with lively interest.

November 8—The news of Tildens election is flashing over the wires—& the country is alive with expectancy. Tildens majorities are immense in the states he has carried—but he may not carry the electoral college.

November 9—Everybody is talking about the election. Democrats are exultant & Republicans are down.—but the result is yet uncertain.

November 10—Up early & off to find Halls chapel on Morgantown circuit. At Russellville the people are jubilant over recent dispatches that Tilden has carried *all* the Southern states—besides Conn—N. York—N. Jersey—Del—& Md & Oregon & Ind—securing a large vote in the electoral college. I reached Wm Subletts in Warren County at night & was cordially welcomed. I heard guns firing through the night in commemoration of the Democratic successes.

November 11—Bro Sublett went with me 12 miles or more to Halls Chapel in time for meeting. I preached on the Invitation & Refusal—Lu[ke] 14.15–35 with considerable liberty & proceeded at once to hold Quarterly Conference. While we were at church—the heavy boom of cannon sounded—in attestation of the wild joy of the Warren County Democrats over the reported election Tilden & Hendricks. I hope they are not too soon.

November 13—Set out for home. I drove over as rough road as a buggie can well travel but Prince behaved well & I got through. I rested a little at Auburn & got to Russellville at or before sundown & stopped with Wilbur Browder. Found the town full of *painful* suspense on account of late dispatches that Republicans claim Louisiana—S. C. & Fla & Oregon giving Hayes a majority of *one* in the electoral college—while the Democrats claim that Tilden is beyond doubt elected on fair count. The whole country is excited & leading men are flocking to N. Orleans—to see a fair count of the vote. One more vote will elect Tilden.

November 14—After getting myself & my horse shod—I came home through a drizzling rain blowing full in my face—but my gum coat came in good place. I find my dear wife & children well—but perplexed about the presidential suspense. . . .

January 15 [1877]— . . . The paper to day confirms the reports that the Republican State government of Louisiana is about to break down & the Democrats are getting stronger in their position. It seems now that *all* the Southern States are Democratic & the prospect is that the People will be more harmonious & prosperous than for years—& it is to be hoped that the Presidential question will be settled without war. There has been much talk in the papers & in private circles about civil war—the Republicans declaring that Mr Tilden is not elected & Mr Hayes *shall* be inaugurated & the Democrats with equal earnestness asserting that Hayes is defeated & that Tilden shall be inaugurated. The condition of public affairs has been *very critical* & the popular mind so much excited & the proofs of fraud in the Returning Boards of La. S. C. & Fla. so glaring—that collisions were constantly expected & if once begun—no man could foresee the end. Gracious Lord save our country from war! . . .

February 17—The country is now excited over the news that the electoral commission of 8 Republicans & 7 Democrats—by a *strictly party vote*—have decided to rule out all the evidence of glaring fraud & swindle & have given the vote of Louisiana to Hayes & Wheeler. It is indeed humiliating to think that men occupying the honorable & responsible position of judges of the Supreme Court of the U.S. would consent to be cheats & party tricksters for political demagogues—as either the one or the other set of these men seem to have done. I fear for our country. . . .

———————

After years of planning and effort, southern whites finally regained political power in the South. The Democratic party was now the white man's party, the Republican party in the South was in disarray, and the North was abandoning its support of Reconstruction governments. It was a time of rejoicing for Southerners as they cast off the control of the hated radical Reconstruction governments. At last they felt vindicated as control passed into the hands of native southern whites.

The feelings of the carpetbaggers, scalawags, and blacks in the South were quite different. For them it became a time of despair, pain, and anger. All they had worked so long to gain was fast slipping away. Desperately they tried to stop the tide of counter Reconstruction. Slowly abandoned by the North and under constant harassment in the South, they could be successful only by a monumental effort, and time was running out.

CHAPTER 10

THE RESPONSES OF
TWO CARPETBAGGERS AND
TWO SCALAWAGS

". . . the time for action has arrived . . . It is a battle between law and lawlessness, between law-abiders and law-breakers."

—CHARLES HAYS

The ending of Reconstruction was a time of profound change and danger for those who supported Republican policies in the South. The growing reluctance of the North to continue support for the efforts of carpetbaggers and scalawags to remake the South meant physical danger and economic ruination. There was no middle ground. The federal government either acquiesced to the efforts of Democrats to keep freedmen in a subordinate position or supported the efforts of Republicans to guarantee equal treatment for blacks and support of the Thirteenth, Fourteenth, and Fifteenth Amendments. For those who stayed in the South, decisions would need to be made on a daily basis. It could be literally a matter of life or death.

Marshall Twitchell

Marshall Twitchell, carpetbagger from Vermont and state senator in Louisiana, was an important leader in the Republican party in Louisiana from 1871 to 1877. In those years he won the grudging respect and enduring hatred of many of his Democrat opponents. The deaths of his wife, a newborn son, and three sisters (all of natural causes) and the later murder of three family members—one brother and two brothers-in-law in the Coushatta Massacre—were bitter experiences for him. The latter events alerted the federal government to the need for two companies of troops, which were sent and presided over the election of 1874.

The Democrats won it by violence and intimidation, but Republicans were restored to office by the state returning board, which examined the election results and determined that there had been violence and fraud.

During the next year there were fewer acts of violence, although threats were made to murder the remaining males of Twitchell's family and to take possession of the executive branch of the government by revolutionary means. He took his mother and three orphan grandsons north for protection and returned to face a crisis in the legislature of Louisiana, which severely tested his courage and leadership skills.

On the first Monday in January, 1876, the legislature met for the memorable session in which the governor was impeached, tried, and acquitted all in one day. My habits of industry and temperance, in connection with the belief that I would not be frightened from doing my duty, together with my good physical endurance, which enabled me to remain in the Senate chamber without rest during the longest session, caused me to be elected chairman of the Republican caucus and manager of my party in the Senate. The session was one long, continuous struggle between the Democratic majority of the House and the Republican majority of the Senate. I consider this the most trying of all my public experience.

Many of the Republicans were discouraged and disgusted by the apparent willingness of the North to allow them—and the right—to be sacrificed that they might get rid of a troublesome object. The Democrats were encouraged by this action and were ready with money and promises to work upon any weak Republican whom they could reach. Many a time in the Republican caucus, to offset these influences, we were compelled to call attention to the many murders of our friends and comrades yet unpunished.

The hardest part of our work was to keep up the courage of weak senators so as to retain our majority in that body. I had served four years in the Senate. The Republican senators were, without exception, men with whom I was well acquainted, knowing all their peculiarities and their weaknesses. In true army style they were divided so that in protracted sessions, where the purpose was to tire us out, I could allow my party to go to their meals by reliefs, taking good care that no two weak ones should go by themselves. No one seemed to think, nor did I, that it was at all necessary for me to leave the chamber for either meals or rest.

I remember one day in which the struggle was so continuous, extending even into the morning hours, my mind was so occupied that I entirely forgot it was necessary for me to eat, and retired without having tasted food since my breakfast. In the morning at the restaurant I remarked that I was not feeling well. The waiter replied, "I noticed that you did not come to your dinner yesterday." It then occurred to me for the first time that I had forgotten to dine the day before. A good breakfast cured my sickness.

The crisis of the winter came when the House passed resolutions impeaching the governor. This movement had been carefully planned and the Democrats believed that success was certain. All bills required for the interest of the state which the two houses could agree upon had been passed. It was decided that immediately after the resolution had passed, the House should adjourn for three days (constitutional limit without consent of the Senate), and during these three days it was expected that the government would be overturned and enough Republican senators disposed of or changed so that when the Senate met for the trial, there would be a majority for his impeachment. Better than any other living man, I knew the danger of exposing the Republican senators to the machinations of the Democrats outside the Senate chamber and unsupported by each other's presence.

———————

Twitchell seized on the opportunity that presented itself when the House adjourned for three days. If the Senate could stay in session, it was possible to complete the entire impeachment process before the House reconvened. But first he had to convince the governor and other dignitaries to go forward immediately.

The House appointed me manager to appear before the Senate with their articles of impeachment, intending by this course to prevent the Senate from acting upon the articles immediately. On being informed of its action by a friend in the House, I called an executive session and then confidentially informed my Republican colleagues of what had taken place and that we must remain in session until the course which we should pursue had been decided.

Governor Kellogg with fifteen or twenty of the leading Republicans of the state were in a short time together in the lieutenant governor's private room to consult upon the question. The chief justice of the state was somewhat averse to any hasty or unjudicial proceedings, and when I entered the room, it seemed as though, with the single exception of ex-Governor Warmoth, all were in favor of proceeding slowly and with judicial fairness. As soon as it was possible for me to speak, I informed them that with the adjournment of the state Senate all vestige of Republican government in Louisiana would disappear, that I knew a Republican majority in the chamber would not be possible three days later if we adjourned with the governor suspended, that the trial must take place at once, without it was the intention of the party leaders to abandon the contest for Republican government in the state.

Someone remarked that the trial in such haste would be irregular. I replied that if assassination and revolution could be checked and right prevail with a slight judicial irregularity, I thought we had better have the irregularity. My opinion prevailed, and the doors of the Senate were immediately opened and the high court of impeachment formed.

Rules for the government of the court were immediately adopted, the secretary of the Senate instructed to notify the House, and a recess of thirty minutes taken to give the House managers time to appear before the Senate with their articles of impeachment. . . .

———————

Twitchell presented the articles of impeachment from the House and then presented evidence that the process was in fact contrary to law and should be dismissed. Because the House had not appointed a committee, it could not respond quickly to his strategy.

The Democrats, finding that their plan must be changed to meet our unexpected move, hastily appointed a management committee which appeared in the Senate and claimed recognition. It was known to all present that the House had appointed no committee before its adjournment, equally as well known that they had been adjourned for a number of hours, and that legally no committee could have been appointed.

Mr. Wiltz, a member of the House, afterwards lieutenant governor and governor, one of the pretended members of the committee, came into the Senate chamber and in a dictatorial style demanded that he should be heard. He commenced an exciting and revolutionary speech. I called for order and demanded that the gentleman who was disturbing the high court of impeachment of the State of Louisiana be removed that the proceedings of the court might be continued. The chief justice discovered at once that we did not intend to give the House any chance to recover from their mistake of not appointing a committee to prosecute the governor before it adjourned. He directed the sergeant at arms to remove the noisy gentleman who was disturbing the court.

Thus the last move of the Democratic House failed. After many hours of parliamentary struggle, my order was adopted, the governor acquitted, and the high court of impeachment adjourned, *sine die* [end of the allotted time]. . . .

———

By this time Twitchell, an important leader in Louisiana, was regularly criticized in the press with blatant falsehoods. It angered him, and he considered how best to respond.

During my early political life in Louisiana I had never taken any notice of the misrepresentations and falsehoods of the local press. The opinion of the public there, I found, was influenced by a man's actions and conduct, not by what the newspapers said, and it did not occur to me that these falsehoods could have any effect on Northern public opinions. I did not think that the North would so readily accept the story of the men who had so lately been in arms against the government and were then, in most cases, barroom loafers and gamblers, in preference to the statement of a man who for four years had fought to sustain the government and was earnestly attempting to support and perpetuate the principles of freedom, for which he had fought.

Absent in the army, I was not familiar with that class of our stay-at-home citizens who were willing that their neighbors' sons should be sacrificed upon the field of battle provided they could by some contract gain profit for themselves by the continuance of the war. These citizens were willing that the rights for which they did not fight, the principles of patriotism which their souls were too small to possess, and the ex-Federal soldier in the South for whom they had no care should all be sacrificed to increase their prospects for Southern trade.

Under the advice of old politicians, I made up my mind to take more notice of these newspaper attacks, and when the Democratic committee was appointed to investigate the charges against United States Senator West, I took occasion to explode an old libel which appeared in the New York *Herald*. From the New Orleans *Republican*:

> As the committee appointed by the Senate to inquire into the manner of Senator West's election never made a report, Senator Twitchell who was accused by the back biting New York *Herald* of having received a bribe for his vote on that occasion did not have an opportunity to properly vindicate himself. At the request and by the advice of some of his friends, the following correspondence is published:
>
> Senate Chamber,
> New Orleans,
> *March 6, 1876.*
> Senator Robertson, Chairman of Joint Committee to Investigate charges growing out of the election of Hon. J. R. West to the United States Senate:
>
> Sir—The New York *Herald* having charged that I received a bribe for my vote at the election of Hon. J. West to the United States Senate, I now request you to state whether, during the investigation of the joint committee, that charge against myself was sustained, or whether it was alleged by any witness, either directly or by implication, that I received any bribe or other corrupt consideration whatever for my vote on that occasion.
>
> Respectfully, your obedient servant,
> M. H. Twitchell.
>
> Senate Chamber,
> New Orleans,
> *March 6, 1876.*
> Hon. M. H. Twitchell, State Senator:
>
> Dear Sir—In reply to your note of this date making a request for information whether, during the investigation of the joint committee to investigate charges growing out of the election of Hon. J. R. West to the United States Senate, any charge was brought against yourself in connection with such election, or whether a charge made against you by the New York *Herald* was sustained or alluded to, I have the honor to state, most emphatically, that no witness who testified before the joint committee either charged or implied in any manner whatever, that you received any bribe or other corrupt consideration for your vote at the election of Hon. J. R. West, and to remain your obedient servant,
>
> W. A. Robertson,
> Chairman Joint Committee.

Because the fall elections were eight months away, Twitchell decided to go north to avoid the dangers of violence or possible assassination. Unfortunately for him, his enemies had already decided to get rid of him once and for all. He was not ready for the sudden attack.

Under the constitution and laws of the state, an election was to take place in November [1876] for members of the House, governor, lieutenant governor, one half of the other state officers, and one half of the Senate. The first Monday in January [1877] the old members of the Senate (a holdover body) would meet in the chamber, the old lieutenant governor presiding, and immediately proceed to complete the quorum of the Senate by swearing in new members; they would then recognize the House [and], meeting with it in joint session, the lieutenant governor presiding, receive the returns and declare the election of the governor, lieutenant governor, and other officers.

It required the addition of one member to the Senate to make it complete, for the transaction of business. The holdover senators were equally divided in politics, but the lieutenant governor, a Republican, made the Senate practically a Republican body. The death or inability to attend of a single Republican senator, however, might change the entire result of the election.

A Democratic majority in the old Senate might insist on swearing in Democratic members and setting aside for examination the credentials of Republican senators, keeping the Senate all the time Democratic, recognizing a Democratic body as the House, and declaring the Democratic candidates for governor and state officers elected.

At the last caucus of Republican senators [in March 1876, eight months before the election] I especially cautioned holdover senators to keep out of the canvass and all places of personal danger, explaining to them what might be the result if one of them was assassinated. It did not occur to me that I was at all in danger. I had become so prominent from the murder of my relatives two years before that I thought the Democrats would consider it wise for them not to again attract public attention to those old murders by another outrage in the same locality and family.

The Democratic leaders, through their happy faculty of making mistakes, listened to the fears of those who had been engaged in the slaughter of my family and decided that I should be the victim, thus quieting the assassins of the Red River districts by the murder of a man from whom they feared prosecution for their previous murders, getting rid of a troublesome Republican leader, and changing the political status of the Senate, and through that, the state.

Immediately after the adjournment of the legislature, I made business arrangements preparatory to spending the summer in the North, as I had fully determined to act myself upon the advice which I gave my colleagues, to be away from the dangers of the political campaign in Louisiana. I well knew that my presence there was of less importance to my political comrades than the chance of my absence would be when the Senate met the first Monday in January.

I reached Starlight the last of April, expecting in a few days to be able to return to the North. On the first of May, I stopped at Coushatta a number of hours later than was my usual custom, and noticing many leaders of the Democratic party coming into town from the country at an unusual time for them, I asked one if he was not a long distance from home for so late an hour. He replied that he had come to see if they couldn't pass a bill which they had been for a long time trying to get through. It did not occur to me at the time that the question whether I was to be shot or not was the bill under consideration.

On the morning of May 2, I started for Coushatta with Mr. King, the last of my Northern brothers-in-law and the one who had escaped assassination two years before on account of his serious illness at the time. As we stepped down to the river and took our places in the skiff, the negro ferryman urged me not to cross that morning, but I was so accustomed to negro timidity that I disregarded his advice and ordered him to pull for the Coushatta shore. Just as we were about to touch the bank I looked up from the paper which I was reading and saw a man standing behind a woodpile leveling his rifle at me. I called out, "Down in the boat," and the first shot went over us; then to the ferryman, "Pull back to the other shore." The next shot passed through the skiff and entered my left thigh. I immediately went over into the water, passing under the skiff, and caught hold of the lower edge with my hand, keeping the skiff much of the time between myself and the assassin, while all the time I was partially concealed under the boat and in the water. King, having a revolver, fired two shots at the assassin and was shot dead. One shot at him or me shot the ferryman in the hand.

The assassin was one of the coolest of the kind which the South ever produced; and as a marksman, he was an expert, using his repeating rifle and revolver with such rapidity and accuracy that notwithstanding the poor mark I gave him by the time I had reached the middle of the stream, he succeeded with his last rifle shot in shattering my remaining arm, and I floated on my back away from the skiff. He then fired two shots from his revolver, the last one striking my coat.

Apprehensive that more might follow and hit my body next, I told the ferryman to call out that I was dead. This he promptly did, the words being repeated by ladies on the shore, and the assassin coolly and leisurely mounted his horse and rode away.

The ferryman brought the skiff on the lower side of me, I threw my only uninjured limb on the edge of the boat, and the ferryman, with his unwounded arm, rolled me over into the skiff upon the body of King.

In a few moments I was moved from the skiff to a cabin by my friends. By my directions the commandant and surgeon of the army post were sent for. In a very short time they appeared. I said to Colonel Pennypacker, "I place myself under your protection and request the attendance of your surgeon."

Considering the fact that I had a wound in the back of my neck, a ball in my leg, and each arm shot twice through, I was but very little weakened, for the cold water of the river had so completely chilled me that it stopped the flow of blood which ordinarily would have taken place.

The colonel caused me to be moved at once into a house near his camp, where the next morning my [left] arm was amputated and buried at Starlight with the body of King. For twenty-eight days there was about an even contest for my life, between vitality with good nursing and my many wounds and the warm climate. So severe was the struggle that had I been addicted to the use of whisky, tobacco, or anything weakening to my system, the result would not have been long in doubt. With the exception of Colonel Pennypacker, commanding the camp, I was the only one who did not consider my case hopeless.

I was abundantly supplied by my many friends with wild meat, of which I stood in the greatest need; [I] was lying flat on my back, able to move but one foot, and yet my stomach digested more meat and blood-making food than it ever had before or since in the same length of time.

J. W. Harrison, formerly of the 7th Vermont, under the direction of my sister Helen, took charge of me so far as nursing and guarding the house was concerned. He soon learned of an overheard conversation between the assassin and some friend of his which took place the night after the shooting. The assassin said, "If I had shot the damn nigger, I should have got him, as he would have sunk before anyone could have reached him from the shore." This evidently referred to my being pulled into the boat by the ferryman. There was considerable dissatisfaction between the assassin and the society that employed him. He claimed his pay, and they contended that he had not completed his job.

My foresight in being removed to the camp instead of to my own house was very embarrassing to the assassins. Although in the edge of camp, Mr. Harrison knew the people too well to trust to that for my protection at night; consequently, some trusted friends of undoubted nerve and courage remained in hiding near the house with a Winchester rifle to intercept any prowler who might attempt to murder me. I lacked for nothing in the way of care and attention, although with but two exceptions all offers came from my Republican friends.

My attempted assassination was so purely political that my Democratic friends doubtless felt that their assistance would not be acceptable. I am certain that anything which they would have sent me to eat would have first been tried by the dog. . . .

For nearly a month I was encouraged to bear the discomforts of lying in one position by the hope that my right arm might be saved. I know not how long the surgeon had hopes of saving the arm, for I had no doubt of the favorable result until the flesh in the forearm began to decay and I saw them removing the maggots.

On the last day of May, late in the afternoon, the surgeon came into the room, lingering much longer than his custom, evidently dreading the disclosure he was about to make; finally he informed me that the arm could not be saved and that he would take it off in the morning.

I said very well and turned my face to the window, watching the sun as it disappeared behind the trees, reviewing my past life, and trying to imagine what would be my future in the world, without arms and all my near relatives in the grave, except one sister, a mother, and four little boys.

The picture looked so dark and discouraging that I fully made up my mind that life was not worth retaining longer. Sister Helen first recovered her courage and came to my bedside. I said to her, "The surgeon says my right arm must come off, and I do not see any use of living longer." She asked me if I had ever made any money with my hands, and then said, "There are plenty of hands in the world to do the work of heads which have the ability to direct." This gave me a new thought, and in a few moments I had my old-time courage again. The next morning the arm was skillfully amputated, and I started on the road to final recovery. . . .

One morning a delegation of colored ministers came, requesting the privilege of being allowed to look at me. The surgeon consented upon the condition that there should be no conversation, as he feared that any excitement would prove fatal. They filed into my room, ranged themselves by my bedside, and stood there with the tears rolling down their cheeks. After repeated questioning, one of them said, "Yes, the colored people are very much excited. We learned yesterday that Major Haney was to be appointed president of the school board as soon as your death, which is expected daily, occurs." Haney was notorious as a drunken gambler, intensely bitter against the colored schools.

My temper was thoroughly aroused at the thought that as soon as life had left my body, the first plan to be carried into effect was to be the checking of civilization by closing the colored schools. I resolved at once to defeat them as long as possible, and told the delegation to return to their people and say that I was going to recover. . . .

—————

Twitchell went back north to Indianapolis, Indiana, and then, upon the death of his sister, returned to his boyhood home in Vermont, where his mother still lived. She was overwhelmed by the sight of her armless son. However, he visited the Philadelphia Centennial, where he was fitted with "the best artificial arms in use," and she recovered her health and hope. Several months later, on October 26, Twitchell married Miss Henrietta Cushman Day, his sweetheart at Leland Seminary. Two months later he and his new wife left for the convening of the state legislature in New Orleans. He still had business to finish before severing forever his ties with Louisiana.

The last of December, I left the North with my wife for New Orleans, to be there for the meeting of the legislature the first Monday in January [1877]. The Republican leaders had been killed or driven out and the voters so intimidated that the Democrats had succeeded in getting into the ballot boxes a majority of votes. The only thing which stood in their way was the state returning board, which was created for just such an emergency. The constitution of the state made each house the sole judge of the qualifications of its members. It also provided that after a gubernatorial election the two houses should meet in joint session and declare the vote for governor. He then stepped forward and took the oath of office, then returned to the executive chamber and received a committee from the Senate and a committee from the House, and the government was complete.

The returning board, as required by law, threw out [the votes of] districts where the evidence was beyond question that there had been no fair election. The result of the election so declared by the returning board gave the electoral vote of the state to [Rutherford B.] Hayes; and by a larger majority Packard, the Republican nominee for governor, was elected with a Republican legislature. It was the tactics of the Democrats to dispute everything and declare that they had carried the election from the top to the bottom.

I knew that the first Monday in January the very existence of a Republican government in Louisiana would depend upon the nine holdover Republican senators being in their places in the Senate chamber, so that with the aid of the lieutenant governor presiding, the swearing in of new Democratic senators could be delayed until [enough other Republicans had arrived that] the nine holdover Republicans had a majority and a quorum.

I had calculated correctly that my train would reach New Orleans at ten a.m. of the day that the legislature met, but by some management of the Southern politicians and the railroads, the train was three hours late. I at once drove to the State House and found the Senate in session, a Republican senator talking against time, waiting for my arrival, when the swearing in of Republicans would commence by the Republican majority which we possessed in the casting vote of the lieutenant governor.

As I entered the chamber, senators crowded around me, the proceedings stopped, and a recess of five minutes declared. My comrades of the Senate, who had not seen me since the amputation of my arms, tried to greet me pleasantly, but the tears flowed. Senator White, now on the supreme bench, was one of the first Democratic senators to speak to me or to make the attempt; his emotions would not allow him to speak, and he returned to his own side of the chamber. The arrival of one man, or part of a man, changed the entire programme. . . .

With only a few months study in the law office of Judge Roberts, no experience in political management or legislative action, no experience as a merchant or planter, I had creditably filled offices and positions as member of the constitutional convention, justice of the peace, president of the parish school board, parish judge, United States commissioner, and member of the state Senate; while by the erection of mills, stores, and the purchasing of plantations, I had accumulated a fortune of at least $100,000. In two years this had all gone, and with it my only brother, my three sisters and their husbands, and both of my arms. A life of success, failure, and tragedy, all in seventeen years. . . .

Albert Morgan

Albert Morgan, a carpetbagger from Wisconsin and cotton planter, served at the Mississippi Constitutional Convention and for five years in the state legislature. On August 3, 1870, he married Carrie Highgate, a black schoolteacher from New York. They would have six children. In 1873 he ran for sheriff of Yazoo County and won. The incumbent refused to surrender his office and was killed in a battle outside the jail. For several months there was a conflict between Morgan and the whites who supported the former sheriff. Finally Morgan was installed and began to serve out his term of office.

In the fall of 1875 Mississippi conservatives decided to "carry the election peaceably if we can, forcibly if we must." Morgan had warning that there would be violence in Yazoo and that he would be in the middle of the action. He could not know that his days in Mississippi were numbered.

It was impossible for me not to see in all these preparations a settled purpose on the part of the irreconcilables to take possession of the government by force if necessary. And although it was my duty as captain of the ship to maintain a confident exterior, I knew that Major Gibbs was speaking the truth when he warned me . . . that such was not only their intention, but that they also believed in their ability to accomplish their purpose; for as the major, and others like him during that period, often declared, "we all hold the strings to Uncle Sam's money-bag, at Washington, now."

I visited the capital and stated to the Governor the facts I have here related, and was not at all surprised to learn from him that he was constantly in receipt of similar information from other Republican strongholds. The signs all pointed one way. There could be no mistaking them. I attended a caucus of the Republican members of the legislature, called to consider the situation, and made use of my knowledge of the plans and purposes of the enemy in behalf of a measure which the Governor had suggested for organizing and arming the militia of the State, so that in case of riot or insurrection, he would have the means with which to defend his own authority, and execute the laws. Two-thirds of the members of that caucus were personally known to me, and had been witnesses to my faithful services in behalf of the establishment of our free State government. Many of them were my warm, personal friends. They believed everything I said respecting the situation in Yazoo, and what was made known as to other localities. Yet nearly every colored member, who spoke upon the subject, opposed arming the militia. The two principal reasons assigned by them for opposition were:

First. It would tend to arouse race antagonisms.

Second. They had faith in General Grant, and believed that he would come to their aid should they be attacked.

Besides these, there were good, well-meaning colored members, who refused to believe that "ole marstah" would resort to violence to accomplish his political ends. There were a goodly number of old masters in the legislature, and they were all as gentle and harmless, outwardly, as cooing doves. It was not an unusual thing during that session to see these old masters and those good, trusting negroes, arm in arm, upon the public streets, exchanging courtesies in the committee rooms, at restaurants and at saloons, upon the most familiar terms.

Perfect peace reigned throughout Mississippi, and the warning voice of the governor, and others, found an echo only in the laughter, derision, or curses of the Barksdales, the Georges, the Singletons, Lamars *et als.*, who meekly, everywhere and at all times, declared that they never would consent to obtain power through such means as they were most foully and wickedly charged with preparing to use. But no sooner had the legislature adjourned, than affairs took on a different aspect. The gentle, cooing Democratic doves ruffled their feathers and cawed like hungry carrion crows. . . .

But the color-line movement made less rapid progress in Yazoo. At a numerously attended convention of the enemy the report of the committee on platform was amended by striking out the resolution favoring the Vicksburg "color line" policy. There was a bitter struggle, and the amendment was adopted by but one majority. Yet that majority was Mr. Fountain Barksdale, the same who had so gallantly fallen in line with "our nigros" and rescued my brother Charles on a certain occasion from a "murderer's cell" in that "common jail," and from that kuklux band. When I heard that, I was tempted to go straight to Mr. Barksdale, and resign my "dictatorship" in his favor. But, while that would have brought relief to me, and to my anxious wife, it would have been a betrayal of my party associates; desertion in the face of the enemy. It sprang from gratitude to him and my joy that, after all, my planting had taken deep root, and might continue to thrive even though I should be destroyed. It lasted for only a brief moment, and henceforward I saw only the martyr's crown.

The changed manner of the enemy throughout the State so alarmed Republicans that a hasty consultation was held at the capital and a committee dispatched to visit the President, lay all the facts before him, and learn what would be his course in the event of a general insurrection against the constituted authorities. Returning, this committee reported, and their words were passed from one to another of the local leaders, that the President had assured them of his full sympathy and had promised to protect our government and the right of Republicans to vote, to the utmost of his authority. But he had also said that the people of the North had grown tired of these appeals for help from the South. It would therefore be necessary that it should be clearly such a case as, under the Constitution, would justify his exercise of the Federal power in our behalf. To make such a case it must be made clearly to appear that the enemy were actually using force, not merely threatening to do so, and, that its application was so widespread and violent that the State authorities were powerless to control it.

This report was perfectly satisfactory to "we all" Republicans. There were few cowards in our ranks. Resting secure in "Grant's promise," for so the President's assurances were regarded, they prepared to meet the enemy, feeling that should they be killed, their death would not have been in vain.

In Yazoo, our party had never before been so united. The conduct of the irreconcilables after the death of Mr. Hilliard and especially that of those who had won victory at Vicksburg upon the color-line, had greatly alarmed the members of the A. M. E. Church, and they were now among my staunchest supporters. So far as I knew I was the unanimous choice of our party for re-election.

No Republican meetings had yet been held in the county preparatory to the approaching election, when all the county officials, members of the legislature, a State treasurer and members of Congress were to be chosen. So, as preliminary thereto a meeting of our county committee was called. At that meeting the preparations being made by the irreconcilables for carrying the election by force, were freely commented on by all. . . .

All knew of the organization of white independent military companies, and of the very extensive arming that had been going on. Some had seen whole boxes of Winchester rifles and shot-guns, brought into the county for distribution to these companies. Mr. James M. Dickson and Mr. Houston Burrus mentioned an effort made by the human hornet [Henry M. Dixon], by tumbling before them as they walked down Main street a pile of dry-goods boxes, to compel them to quit the sidewalk, and walk in the street, or fight. It was 1868 come again, but our party was stronger now than then. One of the members of that committee was an ex-confederate captain; another, our Senator, and the colored men upon it could read and write. All the important officers of the county were in the hands of our party. Ames was governor, Grant was still President, and we had his promise. . . .

Thus, harmony was interrupted by what Morgan called "a fraudulent communication" claiming that sixteen hundred army guns were in the hands of Negroes who were ready for a fight. It was signed by three Negroes who were never found. This provided the justification for the violence that followed.

I well knew the place where the irreconcilables met in "consultation." It was there a well-known leading church member, chairman of the white man's committee, made his memorable declaration: "The only way to get rid of Morgan is to kill him. We've tried coaxing and bribery. We've tried to drive him. Meanwhile his hold is growing stronger and stronger. He must be killed."

I had lately several times seen the human hornet coming from there, and once, just before the day of our meeting, we met and passed each other on the street. His face was so white and pale, his lips so clinched and livid, his gait so nervous and meteoric that I shall never forget the shock he gave me, nor the sulphuric odor in his trail. From that moment I believed that he had been chosen to kill me when the opportunity should arrive, and I also believed that the fraudulent correspondence was intended as a cover for the crime. It had already been published throughout the State and telegraphed North. On the day of the meeting, the pastor of the A. M. E. Church, of the church on the hill we helped to build, and other leading colored men, came to me with further evidence of the purpose of the enemy to attack our meeting that night, and many craved my consent for the Republicans to go armed. This I not only refused to give, but forbade them to do so, and I expressly advised them to carry their Bibles instead.

They saw as clearly as I that the storm was at hand, but they could not know as I did its extent and power. It was my duty to shield them and preserve the peace. At the same time, as a citizen and a candidate for re-election, it was my duty to attend the meeting and to make the speech.

"Why not postpone it?"

"Because that would have been a surrender, and would have encouraged the enemy to further aggressions. Besides, we had promise of aid from the Executive of the nation, upon the express condition that we went forward with our canvass, and were attacked with such violence as the State government would be powerless to suppress or control."

Similar meetings would be held in other parts of the State, about the same time. Our only escape from the issue was in a cowardly surrender.

"We all" Republicans in Yazoo would die if necessary for our cause.

Would the enemy attack us?

Morgan knew that he had been singled out as the most dangerous of the Republican leaders. His enemies meant to kill him, but he refused to back down.

I believed they would, in some manner, that night. But we had often before passed through similar trials by the exercise of patience, forbearance, and self-control. I believed I should be able to exercise those virtues on this occasion as fully as I had done so many times before. But would *all* the others? I had urged them to do so, as the only means of escape from actual violence. There had been many tests of their ability to do so. I believed that they would. There was some consolation for me in the fact that my wife and children were absent at our summer home at Holly Springs, and knew nothing of my peril.

On my way to the meeting the human hornet crossed my path, and there was the same sulphuric odor in his trail that I had the last time before observed. The hall was lighted by small tallow dips. Except upon the speaker's platform, where there was a lamp and several candles, the light was dim.

There were present our Senator, the ex-confederate captain, and several more "native white Republicans," perhaps a hundred colored men, the mass of whom were in the raised seats in front of the platform, and one of my deputies, an ex-confederate officer.

I had just commenced my speech when there filed into the hall, in regular order, as if by preconcert and arrangement, some seven or eight of the most substantial white men of the town, and took their seats all together immediately in front of me.

This recalled to my mind the recommendation of the Raymond *Gazette,* for a "committee of ten discreet, intelligent and reputable citizens" and so forth. Following this "committee" came the human hornet, Fritz Halder and others of the violent class, who lounged about inside the doorway. Almost from the first the former began interrupting me, and sometimes to dispute my statements. This was politely objected to by some one in the audience. But I suggested that they be allowed to ask questions, and I promised to try and answer. At this point the human hornet withdrew, and almost immediately returned, bringing with him a reckless, worthless colored man, whose property had been levied on by the delinquent tax collector, for unpaid taxes.

This colored man found his way to near the middle of the audience, and then began a bitter denunciation of me. He was requested to sit down, whereupon the human hornet rushed to his side, and while in the attitude of drawing his pistol, proclaimed the right of the fellow to go on, and his purpose to protect him in it. Even this did not disturb the Republicans in the audience, all of whom preserved a calm and orderly exterior, however great their indignation, and I felt so confident of their ability to maintain this attitude, that I was encouraged by it to persevere in the policy of submission to the insults and wrongs of the enemy, as Charles and the General had so successfully done in 1867 and 1868, particularly in their Sabbath-school.

I felt sure that it was all done to provoke some of us to resistance, when, as during the reign of the kuklux, they would seize upon it as a sufficient pretext for any violence they might choose to inflict. Therefore I proceeded in what I had to say with great caution. As a careful surgeon seeking among the vital organs of the human frame for some murderous bullet will exercise his greatest skill and caution to not cut them, and will take care lest he cause needless pain, I endeavored with all the skill and tenderness of which I was capable, to get hold of the heart-strings of the enemy without shocking them, and thus find my way to their intellects. But, as one walking from shore to shore upon a rope spanning Niagara's chasm must realize how slender indeed is the line between him and the river of death below, I could not help feeling that all our planting on that old stubbleground hung, as my life did, by a single thread, and so whenever there was an interruption, or the enemy appeared ruffled, I would cease speaking until the surface at least was calmed. Thus I hoped to pass safely through. But should I reach the other shore?

The result showed that I had miscalculated the extent of the enemy's trust in their majority in the House of Representatives at Washington.

I had not believed that they would dare to kill unless some sort of violent resistance to their methods was offered by some one. There was the weak point in my armor, and it was at that point they surprised me. For after the battle of *nerve* had proceeded for perhaps half an hour, certain of the "committee" appeared to get restless, the hornet became exasperated, and upon my mentioning the name of the chairman of our board of supervisors, he exclaimed in accents of fire: "He's a thief! He's a thief!"

Some person sitting at the right of the platform, and full twenty-five feet from the hornet, replied "Oh! no! no!" rapidly.

Instantly the hornet, with the rapidity of a meteor, and with pistol in hand rushed toward the person. Then there was a shot, and then a volley, all within an instant of time. The lights on that side of the hall went out; those upon the platform burned brightly.

There are those who refuse to believe in special providences.

What was this?

At that moment, as from the first, I believed that I stood for the best thought, the highest purpose and the noblest impulses of American freemen. I also believed that "committee," as a whole, together with the hornet, and the sleuth-hounds in attendance, at the same time stood as from the first they, too, had done, the loyal representatives of the same thought, purpose, and impulse, that had made an armed camp of the South in defence of secession, slavery, and miscegenation, and, when the former was overthrown and the camps disbanded, had pursued their main object, first in the guise of kuklux, later in disguise as National Republicans, and now, again, because Ohio and Massachusetts had gone Democratic, and they held the purse-strings at Washington, were once more openly in arms in defense of that object.

———————

It all happened so quickly. Morgan had not expected the violence. Suddenly shots were fired, and the lights went out.

I did not run. On the contrary, observing the violent movement of the hornet, I turned toward him and commanded peace. At that instant the first shot was fired, and before I could take two steps toward them, the volley. I stood, fronting them, in the full glare of the lights upon the platform, when that volley was fired, and the hornet and his aids were not more than twenty feet distant.

That volley was fired directly at me, and each bullet was aimed to kill.

What was it?

The end piece of the little plain, pine board table, at which I was standing when the first shot was fired, afterward contained three bullet holes. The window facing and wall at the back of the platform was "literally peppered" with bullet marks. The day following, when asked by his admiring associates, "why in h—l he allowed Morgan to escape," the hornet, puzzled and confused by his failure to kill me, declared:

"I stood just so"—describing his position at the front and right of the platform, which put him directly in my front as I turned and commanded the peace, and was not twenty feet distant from me—"and emptied every barrel of my two navics at the—"

He stood in the dim light, while I stood upon the platform in the bright light.

What was it? . . .

Did I shoot? Yes, twice; but while standing thus in the bright light upon the platform the light in which the hornet and his party were went out.

It was said that the enemy put out the lights. I am inclined to think, however, that the dim light of the few tallow dips upon that side of the hall was obscured by the dense smoke from the rapid discharge of the enemy's pistols. At all events, it became so dark there that I could see no one. Then it was that I got out of range of their pistols by way of the window at the back of the platform, to a ladder which reached from it over a narrow court to the roof of the hotel adjoining. This ladder gave way under me and I fell to the pavement, full twelve feet below. Shocked and dazed for a moment, I quickly recovered and climbed back into the hall. While doing so I heard the market-house bell striking. It was unlike the fire signal, or any other that I had ever heard upon it.

The hall was not yet entirely empty. Men were still hurrying from it by the rear stair-way, and Mr. Mitchell lay at full length upon the floor. I spoke to Dick (every one called him Dick), and it would seem that he recognized my voice, for he raised his eyes to mine.

It was a murderous bullet. Entering the neck from the rear, it ranged downward, touching the spine in its course. The pistol from which it was fired had been placed so close to the neck, that the flame from the powder ignited his coat-collar, and powder was burned into the skin.

It was said that at the moment the hornet started toward the man who had presumed to question his charge against Mr. Bedwell, Dick and Fritz Halder were seated together upon a dry-goods box. Afterward, as many still remember, Halder went from store front to store front along Main street, boasting, "I killed Dick Mitchell, I killed Dick Mitchell."

Mr. Foote was badly wounded in the side, but had made his escape. There were others wounded, but Dick was the only one killed. Our Senator and all the other white Republicans had left the hall. My deputy, Mr. Redding, remained in care of Dick. He at once informed me that the hornet and his party left the hall by the front way so soon as I escaped through the window. I had not been two minutes here when some colored men, who were searching for me, came and informed me that the main street was full of armed white men, and that they were searching for me. On the street at the rear of the hall were quite a large number of my colored friends who remained, to "die by you, Colonel." They were not armed; some few may have had pistols. But what could we do against that mob of whites, some of whom I could see, with guns in their hands, hurrying toward the market-house.

These friends of mine did not fail to comprehend the meaning of it all. They meant what they said. They would have followed me in an effort to arrest the hornet and his aids, but that I would not attempt to do.

Finding my way home, I had not been there five minutes when the house was thronged with colored friends, some of whom had stood by our little garrison in its darkest hours, and among them the pastor of that other church. All were anxious that I should make a stand and fight the mob. But to their prayers and entreaties I held firmly to my resolve, and advised them all to go home, go to bed, advise every colored man they could see or could get word to, to do the same, and, upon no pretext whatever to come to town.

"What yo' goin' to do, sheriff?"

"Stay right here in my own house."

"Day'll be y'here and kill yo' sure."

"Never mind me, you all go home, as I tell you."

"Never 'low to leave the Colonel that way—never! Die first!"

Then I reasoned with them, pointed out to them the folly of fighting those well-armed companies, and reminded them that every one of our white friends had vanished. After reason and persuasion failed, I commanded them. Then they departed; some cursing, some crying. The last one had but just disappeared through the back yard, when tramp tramp, tramp, sounded the tread of the hornet's company, upon the pavement, approaching my house. This was my castle.

———

For the next few days Morgan remained in hiding. Any action of his as sheriff would mean violence, and he wanted to avoid it. Also, he did not want to die.

Fortunately, only a few days before, I had purchased a fresh supply of cartridges for my Spencer rifle, and with this, and other weapons ready to hand (the very same we had armed our ancient stronghold with), I would be able to make at least a show of resistance. Now they were upon the gallery and banging against the door. My hostler, Frederick Harris, opened it and they entered.

"Whar's Colonel Mawgin?"

"Doa'n know, Mar's Dixon, 'deed I don't, Kunnel hav'n bin y'here senz de meetin' I 'low."

Evidently they believed him, for, after spying about upon the first floor a moment, they went away regularly as they came, tramp, tramp, tramp, keeping step for all the world just like a company of trained soldiers.

What was it?

Let Fred answer.

Scarcely had they departed when I heard his soft step upon the narrow stairway leading to my stronghold. In an instant his black face appeared, his eyes shining through his grateful tears like two stars, and his words, just above a whisper, low and solemn:

"Praise de Lord, Kunnel! Praise de Lord! I jes prayed an' prayed, an' He answered my prar, an' comed an' stood 'afo' me dar, an' put de words in my mouth, and done sent Dixon away."

But all night long I heard every little while the tramp of squads of men marching.

The next day, looking out from the window of my stronghold, I could see them. They were as well armed, and under as perfect discipline, apparently, as any troops of our late armies were. Including the cavalry company from the country, there were not less than three hundred armed white men in the town. Their weapons were Winchester rifles, needle-guns, double barrelled shot-guns and pistols.

There were no armed colored men anywhere that I could see, or hear of, and scarcely any at all to be seen upon the streets. This was a great relief to me, for it showed their faith in me, and took away the only pretext there was for the presence of armed whites, whose numbers, nevertheless, were constantly increasing. The enemy promptly caused a warrant to be issued, charging me with attempting to murder Dixon, placed it in the hands of the hornet and his aids, offered a large reward for me, dead or alive, visited the capital of the State, Holly Springs, and other points where I possibly might be found, in search of me, marched to the court-house and took possession of it and of my office—upon the ground that the sheriff was a fugitive from justice—assembled the board of aldermen of the town and caused an appropriation of a thousand dollars to be made for pay of the soldiers, established a cordon of pickets around the town, with instructions to allow no colored man without a pass to enter or depart from it, and by such, and various and sundry other means, usurped full and complete authority. Still "our nigros" refused to "rise." . . .

Trusting the President's "promise," I had remained in the town because, when the United States troops should come, it would be essential to the success of their mission that some semblance of lawful government remained. I believed that the presence of no more than two United States soldiers, with authority from the President to act for the preservation of peace, and for the protection of the lawful government, would be sufficient to cause the enemy to disperse to their hiding places, when I could once more resume the functions and duties of my office, Republicans might once more return to their homes, and we could proceed with our canvass. Once it was rumored about that the troops were coming. The effect of this rumor was enough to induce the hornet and his company to quit the court house, and abandon my office; but it was a false report. Immediately afterward the town resumed its "war-like appearance," and the enemy's methods were resumed with renewed vigor.

From my hiding place I could see the rows of bright, shining army-guns near the market-house, stacked, and with sentries on guard over them, precisely as I have so often seen them in our old army camps, and on our marches against the rebels, in those other war days.

I could also see armed bodies of mounted men riding out on their "scouting" expeditions to the country for the purpose of suppressing "nigro risings" that were "about to occur." These parties usually went "armed to the teeth," and carrying ropes at their saddles. . . .

─────────

The election of 1875 was easily won by the Democratic party in Mississippi. Morgan was still on the ballot, although he had been chased out of the county. The vote count was 4,044 for his opponent. Morgan received two votes, both cast by his bitterest enemy, "the hornet," who said that it would "not do to be too d—d unanimous."

That campaign in Yazoo has been called "the coronation of the Mississippi plan." So it was; for in twenty-six other counties of the State that year the enemy were less humane. In some of that number Republicans resisted by violence the aggressions of the enemy, and were massacred in crowds of ten, twenty, fifty, and, in one county, it was said quite one hundred were killed. But in Yazoo, instead of summoning the unarmed colored men against the disciplined and fully equipped ranks of the white league, the Republican leaders made their fight upon the picket-line, trusting to the reserves at the North to fill their places when they should be all killed, captured, or in retreat. Therefore, only leaders were killed in Yazoo, and only so many of them as was necessary to convince the Republicans that their opponents would kill if necessary, that they had the power to kill, and that there were none to forbid it, or to punish them for it afterward. Therefore the mass of the Republicans remained silent and passive. Ohio and Massachusetts had gone Democratic. Had I summoned a posse of colored men and resisted, of course there would have been a general massacre in Yazoo, too. That I would not do. . . .

By such means as I have here but faintly detailed Yazoo and Mississippi were "redeemed." . . .

─────────

Charles Hays

Charles Hays, a Republican scalawag in Alabama, was elected for four terms to the U.S. House of Representatives during Reconstruction. One of the most controversial figures in the South, he represented the Fourth District of Alabama from 1869 to 1877. During those years he took increasingly radical positions on issues of race. By 1873 he was willing to support a bill by Ben Butler that penalized those who denied equal access to public accommodations on the basis of race. Later he supported a sweeping Civil Rights Bill, inspired by Charles Sumner, that challenged the position of separate but equal in the South. Hays had shifted to a position supporting full civil rights for all blacks, a position that was an anathema to most white Alabamians. This shift became clear when, on January 31, 1874, Hays spoke on the need for passage of the Civil Rights Bill.

I am very well aware, sir, that in taking the step I do I shall receive the censure of those who sit and worship in the temples of a dead past, forgetful of the great events which have been indelibly recorded upon the pages of our country's history within the last decade. I am aware, sir, that the hate of the ignorant and the scorn of the untutored will be invoked against me. All these things are sources of profound regret; but they shall not deter me from the faithful discharge and sacred observance of a duty which God, reason, and conscience tell me is right.

Coming from the far South, being once the owner of a large number of slaves, thoroughly conversant with their history in the past and present, I feel that I have some idea of what should be accorded them now. Set free by the strong arm of Federal power, cut adrift upon the cold charities of an inhuman world in ignorance and penury that they did not bring upon themselves, struggling against adverse winds and storms of hate, in my opinion, sir, the colored race have set an example that fairly entitles them to the plaudit of "Well done, ye good and faithful servants."

The discussion of this question of "civil rights" has brought about a state of feeling in the South which is to be deplored. Fancies have taken the place of facts. Imagination has been called upon to paint pictures which reality could not do. Newspapers, politicians, demagogues, and inciters of sectional hate have preached to the white masses of the South that Congress was upon the verge of enacting a law enforcing "social equality" and blotting out the lines between knowledge and ignorance. You and I know better. . . .

The appeal is made that such an undying antipathy exists between the races as will render this law dangerous to be passed. I believe no such twaddle. Thousands of the most intelligent men of the South were born and raised upon the old plantations. Childhood's earlier days were passed listening to the lullaby song of the negro nurse, and budding manhood found them surrounded by slave association. Was there prejudice then? Was cry against "social equality" raised then? Never, sir; but now that they are free and receiving the enlightenments of education, for the first time the fact is discovered that the negro, who molded our fortunes, built our railroads, erected our palatial mansions, and toiled for our bread, is a curse upon the face of the earth, and not entitled to the protection of society.

Sir, for one, as a southern man, I feel a debt of gratitude to them. I remember that when the tocsin of war called southern men to the field of battle; when our whole country, from Virginia to Texas, was populated by none other than women and children, and when "insurrection" and "revolt" could have butchered those that were near and dear to us, the poor negro toiled on and toiled well; protected our defenseless homes, and fed our destitute widows and starving children. In that hour of bondage and slavery they proved true to me and mine, and now that it lies in my power to pay the debt, the instincts of honor tell me to do it willingly and cheerfully, "as best becomes a man."

No possible harm can come to the white man by the passage of this law. Get upon the cars to-morrow morning and start South; take your seat in the finest palace-car, and you will find southern women traveling and sitting side by side with colored women as nurses and servants. Is objection raised to this? Not at all. Does any one feel debased by the negro there? Not at all. Why then should the case be changed when that negro buys a first-class ticket and travels alone? Have not southern men associated with them for ages? Has any great conflict arisen heretofore? If "social equality" has been practised it has been voluntary.

Sir, this talk about "social equality" will not bear the scrutiny of reason and common sense. It is the cry of the old-time office-holder and cod-fish aristocrat, who uses the negro now as he once did the poor white man—to make capital of. Who brought about this state of affairs? When the thirteenth amendment was offered to the South was it accepted? No, sir; the very men who to-day are deluding the people by the specious cry of "social equality" caused the South to reject that proposition. Andrew Johnson and his providential provisional governors dictated the policy of the South. That move failed. Then came the fourteenth amendment, and, last of all, the fifteenth amendment. If, then, any one is responsible for the present state of affairs it is the southren democracy themselves, who would not listen to reason, but rushed blindly on in the wonted paths of prejudice and hate.

This new issue is upon us and must be met. There is no ground for retreat. The past is gone, and the present is upon us. True-hearted patriots cannot swerve from the path, but, guided by the logic of events, must cheerfully accord to our colored fellow-citizens every right that belongs to a "freeman," and every privilege that is guaranteed them by the Constitution of the country. "The world moves;" and a vindication of our course will come as sure as the waters flow or the stars shine.

———

It was clear that Hays was becoming more radical in his politics, and he was busy introducing bills and securing funds for Alabama. He enjoyed the challenges of his third term in Congress.

Hays was more active during the first session of the Forty-third Congress than at any past or future period. He introduced twenty-five bills, three sets of resolutions, and thirteen petitions. Days after the session had opened in December 1873 he asked the House to compensate Alabamians for the cotton that

Treasury agents had illegally confiscated after the war. Hays also introduced a bill that would have provided reimbursement for the burning of the University of Alabama by federal troops during the war. On January 13 he took the floor again. He had come to an appreciation of the navy during several years of committee service, and efforts to subtract funds from a naval appropriations bill caused him to protest. Noting that European rivals were busily adding to their strength, Hays maintained that the United States could not "stand idly by, hugging the elusive phantom that arbitration . . . and compromises can always avert war and strife." He argued that naval strength was vitally important and warned against the dangers of false economy, charging that more rather than less money was needed. Hays made a passing reference to the situation in Santo Domingo. The congressman obviously supported the administration's controversial attempts to annex that island. To him, it was clear "that little gem of an island . . . sooner or later must be ours."

Less than a week later Hays rose in behalf of education. On the same day, January 19, he introduced two bills that would increase the number of public schools in the South. The first required the federal government to grant Alabama all the undisposed public lands in the state for the benefit of the Free Public School Fund. More grandiosely, the other measure called for federal underwriting of public schools throughout the former Confederacy. Neither emerged from the Committee on Education and Labor. . . .

Other matters were beyond debate. When some Republicans doubted the wisdom of a color-blind society and the ideological underpinnings of Reconstruction, Hays reaffirmed his commitment to fundamental justice. Justifying the extension of the Ku Klux Klan Act, he had paraphrased the Declaration of Independence, reminding colleagues that "all men are born free and equal." The congressman advocated civil rights legislation and spoke of "the sacred and inalienable rights of liberty." Hays had recently eulogized Thomas J. Speer in Congress. He praised the Republican House member from Georgia for his personal qualities and paid his respects to the deceased congressman's family. Less conventionally, Hays noted the unpopular but brave political stand Speer had assumed. Hays compared him to a solitary rock in the ocean withstanding storms and waves. Hays's words for Speer applied equally to himself:—each man had "embraced the humanizing cause of equal rights and exact justice for all men." Hays had become a Radical by 1874. As has been pointed out, the meaning of that term had changed. Early in Reconstruction, Radicals favored political equality for blacks and the proscription of some white Southerners. By the early 1870s black participation in politics was a reality and political penalties against whites had been removed. The term "Radical" had taken on a new connotation. It referred to Republicans who favored something approaching real equality for the freedmen and also a continued federal presence in the South. Authorship of the Hays-Hawley letter would confirm Hays's Radical credentials. . . .

The elections of 1874 were critical to the future of the Republican party in the South. Few states still remained under Republican control. In only four was complete control in Republican hands—Arkansas, Louisiana, Mississippi, and South Carolina. Democrats had already regained control in Alabama as well as Tennessee, Georgia, and Virginia. Violence was escalating. Hays received news that confirmed his fears—conditions were worsening in his Fourth District. But this did not deter him from running for reelection.

Hays had decided to seek a fourth term. He was a young man—only forty in 1874—and he still allowed himself to speculate about a Senate seat. Also, from a political standpoint, as he realized, his retirement would be tantamount to surrendering the Fourth District to the Democrats. There were other considerations. Living in Washington did not prevent him from overseeing what lands he had left between sessions. Queen [his wife] enjoyed the amenities of the city. . . . There was no compelling reason to return to Alabama and every reason to stay in Washington. Under the circumstances Hays made known his intention to seek a fourth term.

Hays had moved with purpose toward political office and its rewards. Once he secured a seat in Congress, he beat back Democratic opposition with that same determination. He was less accustomed to challenges from Republicans. Yet Alexander Curtis, a Perry County freedman, now openly sought the nomination. His efforts failed, however, and Curtis endorsed Hays when the incumbent congressman was renominated on July 29 at Uniontown in Perry County. In an otherwise unremarkable acceptance speech, Hays included a warning, stating that order must be maintained in the Fourth District and troops might be necessary.

His words proved tragically prophetic. On August 1 a Fourth District Republican, Walter P. Billings, was shot as he rode home after addressing a Republican audience at a Sumter County rally. Billings had moved from Missouri to Alabama the previous year and opened a law office in Livingston. According to the *Meridian Mercury* (in nearby Mississippi), he was a "mischief-making carpetbagger." His murder gained statewide attention and a familiar debate followed. Republican charges of Democratic complicity were met by denials.

Hays became involved when the *Mercury* accused him of agreeing to meet with Republican governor Lewis to plan retaliation. Hays had known Billings, but not well. The congressman had received a letter of introduction from him the previous March in Washington. Later that spring, Billings had written Hays several follow-up letters regarding the civil rights question. Rebutting the *Mercury* in a public letter, Hays mentioned meeting Billings at Uniontown for "the first and last time." He denied any plot with Governor Lewis. Some Democrats claimed that on the day of his death Billings had boasted of having $10,000 in campaign money on his person. It followed, according to rationale, that his assailants had wanted to rob him. Hays countered that Billings had not been robbed and it "would be mockery to doubt . . . that he was murdered because he was an [*sic*] Republican."

Hays was in Montgomery on August 20 when Alabama Republicans held their state convention. The killing of Billings—though the most spectacular murder— was by no means an isolated example of Republican mistreatment. Discussion of political terrorism dominated the proceedings. A hastily formed Committee on Outrages weighed evidence, concluded that a critical situation existed, and recommended that Governor Lewis appoint a commission to conduct an investigation.

More immediate action was taken in secret caucus: Hays, Congressman Alexander White, and Senator Spencer were designated to travel to Washington and request military protection from the president. At the convention, Hays had placed the name of incumbent governor David Lewis in nomination to succeed himself. Lewis was nominated by acclamation.

Democrats met the next month in Montgomery. George Smith Houston, a Limestone County Unionist, received the gubernatorial nomination. More important was the party platform. In Alabama, as elsewhere in 1874, the so-called "white-liners" dictated party strategy. The accommodationist-minded Southern New Departurists had been repudiated. Past Democratic efforts to attract blacks now yielded to the interest of energizing Alabama whites through racial appeals. Men like John Forsyth, editor of the *Mobile Register,* accentuated the differences rather than the similarities between the Republican and Democratic parties. Alabama Democrats unabashedly raised their platform on "the preservation of white civilization."

In the meantime, Hays and the other designated Republicans met with President Grant. The chief executive was at his Long Branch, New Jersey, retreat when the Republicans reached the city. Attorney General George H. Williams first listened to their pleas, which he described as "very threatening and full of trouble." He briefed the executive at Long Branch on September 2. Several days later, the Alabama delegation, joined by several Republicans from South Carolina and Louisiana, visited Grant there. Little of what was said is known. Much can be surmised. Appealing to the administration was a tried and tested strategy of Southern Republicans. Yet Grant's response had often been more capricious than consistent. He had recently refused to help struggling Republican regimes in Arkansas, Mississippi, and Texas. In spite of what happened in the past, he did not hesitate now. He empowered the attorney general and secretary of war to ready soldiers for election day.

What Hays said to Grant at Long Branch, though not documented, may be assumed. That he was incensed is certain. Several days earlier the Alabama congressman had been wired news of the murder of another Fourth District Republican, Thomas Ivey, a mail agent on the Chattanooga Mobile Railroad who had campaigned for Hays in the past. On the afternoon of August 29, a band of whites stopped the train on which he was riding in Sumter County, and shot and killed the freedman. Less than a month had passed since Billings's death. Hays undoubtedly used strong language at Long Branch. He spoke in the same terms several days later to Joseph B. Hawley.

———

The Hays-Hawley letter, as it was called, was a lengthy letter (five thousand words) written by Hays describing in detail murders, atrocities, violence, and repressions in Alabama. Written in graphic detail and published by Hawley, it sparked a national debate.

Hawley was one of the country's better known congressmen. The Connecticut politician had recently presided over the Republican National Convention of 1872. Hawley also edited the well established *Hartford Daily Courant.* As fellow Republicans in the Forty-third Congress, Hays and Hawley knew each other, but apparently not well. On the evening of September 6, somewhere in the city, Hawley overheard Hays privately discussing the violence directed at Alabama Republicans. The editor-congressman listened to Hays's rendition with empathy and indignation. Maintaining that such conditions begged to be exposed and rectified, he asked the Alabamian to reduce his comments to writing and permit their publication. Hays consented without hesitation. Hawley followed up the next day, September 7, with a formal written request. He referred to the previous evening's "informal narration of late occurrences." Would the congressman provide "the substance of what you have told me?" Such was the beginning of a collaboration that caused a nationwide controversy.

Hays began at once. The words came easily. He underlined some for emphasis and struck out others, and the length of the letter increased. Drawing upon newspapers, telegraphic dispatches, correspondence, and his general knowledge, the congressman completed his work within days. Hawley read and approved the narrative and, after forwarding the lengthy letter to the *Courant,* went hunting.

The shocking exposé was spread across the front page of the *Hartford Courant* on September 15. A devastating picture of Fourth District conditions began with a survey of Sumter County. Hays summarized the shootings of Walter Billings and Thomas Ivey. In Hays's estimation, Billings had been killed because he was a "Yankee" and a "Republican." Hays referred readers to Billings's widow for further details of the "revolting murder." He also recounted how a local citizen who had attributed the Republican's death to politics was severely beaten by several whites and ordered to "keep his mouth shut about that d—d Yankee, Billings." Ivey was likewise executed because he was a "meddlesome" Republican and a "nigger." Without imparting any blame (but the implication was clear), Hays also mentioned the recent murders of five Sumter County freedmen in one night. He attributed the carnage in that county generally to "a murderous band of Democrats."

Affairs were not dramatically better in Hale County. Hays recounted that John Stokes, former editor of the *Montgomery Alabama State Journal,* had delivered a speech at the county seat of Greensboro on July 20. That night two pistol-carrying whites visited Stokes in his hotel room and warned the Republican against speaking in Greensboro again. On another occasion masked men had sought out Jonathan Bliss, a delegate to the Republican state convention. The freedman fled moments before they arrived. As of yet, Bliss had not returned to Hale [County].

Incidents elsewhere in the Fourth District indicated a similar pattern of brutal political repression. Joseph Speed, the former state superintendent of public instruction, was one of the few white Republicans in Perry County. Hays claimed that a crowd mobbed Speed in Marion. Republicans in Choctaw and Marengo, also in the Fourth District, lived constantly in danger. A rumor that freedmen were preparing to wage race war had recently precipitated tragedy in Choctaw. Whites organized, conducted a search, and, failing to find the nonexistent private army, killed ten blacks and wounded thirteen others returning from church. In Marengo County, William Lipscomb, a white man, was found shot to death in the road. Hays let his Northern readers draw their own conclusions concerning the death of the "earnest Republican."

Unrest prevailed in Choctaw, Hale, Marengo, Perry, and Sumter counties, but Republican mistreatment was worst in Pickens County. "This is a county in West Alabama," Hays began, "where the white men publicly boast that no white man ever cast a Republican vote and lived through the year." Hays described Pickens as an inbred bastion of white supremacy. Landowners still worked blacks as slaves on "secluded plantations" in a region "untouched by the civilizing influences of railroads and rivers." Rarely did notice of outrages escape Pickens, but Hays offered two exceptions. A group of whites had lynched four blacks in mid August. At about the same time a raft bearing the decomposing bodies of two freedmen and one white man was discovered floating down the nearby Tombigbee River. Around the necks of the two black men were placards reading, "to Mobile, with the compliments of Pickens County."

Republicans outside the Fourth District also suffered. Three southeastern counties—Coffee, Macon, and Russell—and Madison in the north provided the settings for more political terrorism. In less detail, Hays outlined trouble there. The letter, carrying over from the *Courant's* front page (and including accounts that Hays lifted verbatim from newspapers), was about 5,000 words in length.

Descriptions of Democratic-inspired terrorism were standard fare in large northern and Midwestern Republican newspapers. A highly partisan and national newspaper press, divided into Democratic and Republican camps, had long disputed the political violence in the South. Republicans used the accounts to justify enforcement legislation and troops during elections. Democrats argued that the reports were manufactured for self-serving political reasons and pejoratively referred to the "outrage mill." The debate was beyond resolution. Even so, the imprimatur of a congressman lent a legitimacy that other so-called "outrage" accounts from the South lacked.

Neither Hays nor Hawley could have predicted the uproarious reaction that ensued. The correspondence quickly became known as the "Hays-Hawley letter" and created a furor among America's highly partisan newspapers. The collaborative effort eventually drew comment from major dailies in every section of the nation. If not "copied through the country," as the *Indianapolis Sentinel* insisted, or "read from a hundred stumps, like the Declaration of Independence," as a *Cincinnati Commercial* journalist remarked, the letter was spread far from Connecticut. Commenting that "the entire nation stood aghast," the *New York Tribune* reasoned that "one of the vexed questions of the day" concerns "whether Alabama is really under a rule of terror." . . .

———————

The response of the Democratic press was immediate and vehement. Hays's motives, his evidence, and his veracity were challenged. It was a nationwide story that called attention to conditions in the South, particularly in Alabama and its Fourth District. The debate did not subside for some time. Meanwhile Hays had to win reelection; the main issue was civil rights and Negro equality.

In the Black Belt, unlike the Tennessee Valley or the piney woods of southern Alabama, Reconstruction politics had always been absolutely predicated on race. Since 1867 blacks had voted Republican. With few exceptions, whites had cast Democratic ballots. Without changing the political agenda in the Fourth District, the "white-line" emphasis on race sharpened the focus. Some previously apathetic Fourth District whites might vote, but generally Hays stood to lose little support that he did not automatically forfeit as a Republican.

In Montgomery, when the Democrats held their state convention in September, Fourth District Democrats had caucused and nominated James Jones as the congressional challenger. The forty-two-year-old Marengo County citizen had attended Princeton University and studied law at the University of Virginia. After serving the Confederacy, Jones returned to Demopolis and was practicing law with Francis Strother Lyon when he agreed to challenge Hays.

Whereas fellow Democrats Gideon Harris and William Smith had failed to unseat Hays, Jones had some hope of succeeding. Hays had provided him some leverage by both speaking and voting in favor of the Civil Rights Bill. Jones rarely failed to make the direct connection between Hays and the controversial measure. Although Jones did not denounce blacks in the savage manner of a later school of demagogues, he made it clear that the present social distance between the races should not narrow. The Democrat presented the cause of Caucasian superiority at Linden in Marengo County on August 11. To maintain otherwise, he stated, was to dispute the historical record. "We will never submit to social equality," Jones concluded. He advanced the same theme at Jemison in Chilton County on August 29. A warm reception was assured in a county where Democrats had earlier passed a resolution condemning "any man, or set of men, who attempt to force upon us the 'Civil Rights bill,' Social Equality, and amalgamation of races."

Associating Hays with "black equality" formed only part of the stratagem. Jones regularly referred to irregularities surrounding the distribution of federal supplies to flood victims and charged Hays with political profiteering. Sometimes undeserving parties had claimed the pork [part of the federal supplies]. Foes now derisively referred to Hays as "Side-Meat Charley." A Hale County Democrat wrote an acquaintance in September that the rations were "being distributed in Greensboro and other favorable voting places." He accused Hays of bribery. "What stuff are the American people made," he continued, "that they can quietly allow this proceedings . . . under the flimsy veil of humanity." The Hays-Hawley letter provided Jones more anti-Republican material. He incorporated into his standard remarks a bitter critique and read, depending on where he spoke, appropriate sections of the celebrated letter. Jones left an Autauga County rally early in October with "the mendacious 'Side-Meat' Charley impaled upon infamy's high pinnacle." . . .

Hays did not begin campaigning until October. As was his practice, he traveled with other Republicans. Samuel Reid, former editor of the *Montgomery Advertiser* and a belated Republican convert; Anthony Dillard, chancellor of the Western District; and Alexander Curtis, a Perry County freedman, often composed the entourage. Recent violence and Hays's notoriety demanded unprecedented security: a U.S. marshal usually accompanied the Republican. U.S. soldiers, who took up posts in various Black Belt towns, provided further protection.

Hays, Reid, and several others filled a date in Marion on October 13. Hays spoke first, defending his much-publicized letter, and if "Old Perry" was correct, the other speeches were anticlimactic. "When I say [Hays] more than surprised his audience by the ability and power with which he gave an account of his stewardship and of the issue between the Republican and Democratic parties," the Perry County resident assured, "I give him but a faint expression to the general feeling of admiration and enthusiasm with which his remarks were received by thousands of his old constituency." If the observer lacked objectivity, he correctly pointed to Hays's continued bedrock support among blacks. The Republican caravan crossed into Greensboro and Hale County the next day where another large crowd of freedmen congregated. Hays answered Democratic objections to troops in a speech described as a "vigorous vindication." The scenario was the same in Tuscaloosa on October 16. Freedmen assembled, a crude speaker's platform was erected, and four to five hours of Republican oratory followed. The next day, in Eutaw, the congressman again justified the presence of soldiers and defended the Hays-Hawley letter. Republicans congregated a week before election day in Livingston. As always, Hays spoke of equality and opportunity. He also mentioned federal troops and of maintaining the peace and informed his audience that in view of recent crimes, President Grant had promised to establish a permanent garrison in Sumter County.

The Democrats mounted a strong campaign with the active support of most of the local newspapers. Hays's critics focused on the "slanders" and "lies" in his famous letter to Hawley. Hays was savagely vilified at every stop of his campaign.

A merciless Democratic press challenged and ridiculed Hays as he carried his campaign forward. In Marion, Hays received what must have been a mixed reception. "This pistol-carrier and whiskey-drinker," began E. C. Heidt of the *Marion Commonwealth,* "boasts of having written the 'Hawley letter,' and declared that he stood ready to write another of the same character." With Ryland Randolph, by then editor of the *Tuscaloosa Blade,* Hays's differences were long-standing. After Hays spoke in Tuscaloosa, Randolph ridiculed the "champion liar and remorseless slanderer" who would be more at home in the devil's kingdom or a penitentiary than in Congress.

Although Hays drew close scrutiny, attention remained focused on civil rights. Custom, if not law, had traditionally separated the races, and James Jones warned through election day of Republican efforts to alter that natural arrangement. E. C. Heidt put the question in practical terms for readers of the *Marion Commonwealth.* Voting the Republican ticket was tantamount to endorsing mixing with former slaves in theaters, hotels, hacks, streetcars, steamboats, the University of Alabama, and the recently founded Agricultural and Mechanical College at Auburn. When Hays spent the night at a black's home, the *Birmingham Independent* reported he was "ready not only to preach but to practice social equality." That such appeals raised racial consciousness in the Black Belt is certain. Even so, unrestrained opposition also stoked

Republican sentiment in the predominantly black counties. The political implications in a district where there were three times as many blacks as whites were obvious. In fact, editors like Benjamin Herr of the *Livingston Journal* had warned against the pitfalls of totally writing off the black vote. Corresponding with Robert McKee, editor of the *Selma Southern Argus,* Herr maintained that "a race alignment will involve serious consequences to the 'black counties.'"

Hays easily won reelection on November 3. An appreciably increased turnout of white voters did not offset the unprecedented number of blacks who voted Republican in the Fourth District. Hays received 23,813 votes to Jones's 18,438. The methodology was familiar to Democrats: the incumbent carried every black county except Choctaw and Pickens (where freedmen constituted a bare majority). In one black county (Perry) Hays claimed only sixty-nine fewer votes than Jones combined in Bibb, Choctaw, and Fayette counties.

But the Black Belt was one of the few areas where Alabama Republicans ran well. The Democratic party dominated elsewhere, gaining control of the legislature, six of eight congressional seats, and the governorship. George Smith Houston received 107,118 votes to Lewis's 93,934. The civil rights issue had provoked more white participation than any other Reconstruction question. Intimidation and possible fraud also contributed to the verdict. On election day, in Eufaula and Mobile, fatalities resulted when whites fired on black voters. Economic coercion also had an effect. What remained, for a combination of reasons, was the fact of Democratic redemption in Alabama. That was not lost on Hays.

There was more bad news from a Republican standpoint. Democratic candidates triumphed almost everywhere nationally and turned a 110-seat House deficit into a 60-seat majority. . . . Only in Louisiana, Mississippi, Florida, and South Carolina did Republicans cling to power. What Hays had always feared, that the Republican party in the South would not survive its infancy, was closer to reality than ever before. Returning to Congress provided him little solace. He realized the prospect of a Republican renaissance was bleak.

———————

Despite growing pessimism, Hays again spoke out in defense of his earlier words and actions. The House was considering the passage of a bill to ensure fair elections in the South when the Select Committee on Alabama Affairs released a report on the allegations set forth in the Hays-Hawley letter. The Republican majority corroborated most of the charges, but two Democrats signed a minority report denying all evidence of violence and accusing federal troops of interfering in the election of 1874. This brought Hays to his feet for the last major speech of his congressional career.

M̶r. Speaker, in view of the fact that the minority of the committee appointed to investigate affairs in the State of Alabama has seen fit to rehash a number of the falsehoods, which the democratic press of the South published concerning my letter on "outrages" to General Hawley, of Connecticut, I deem it proper on this occasion to claim a few minutes' attention from the House to vindicate myself for the course I saw proper to pursue in order to protect the republicans of my State from personal violence and intimidation at the late election. . . .

It is very easy, Mr. Speaker, for the minority of this committee who have gone to Alabama to come back with a whitewashed report of the doings of their Ku-Klux political brothers in that crime-ridden country.

They tell us Alabama has the same peace and quiet within her borders that Georgia has, that Mississippi has. I am free to admit it, sir; and that peace is the peace that the wolf gives to the lamb, or the assassin to his victim. It is, sir, as the gentleman from Michigan [Mr. CONGER] is wont to remark, "the peace of the grave."

The colored men, who compose the body of the republican party, have been made "peaceful" by the shot-gun of the raiding white-leaguer, the bowie-knife of the southern desperado, or the whip-lash of an ex-slave master.

Sir, it is in evidence in the testimony taken before your Alabama investigating committee that witnesses were afraid to be examined before that committee for fear that they too might be made "peaceful" after they had retired from the investigating room.

I do not desire to claim the attention of this House in arguing as to the truth or falsity of the charges of intimidation, violence, and murder in Alabama.

The book of testimony that is at the command of every member on this floor most fully sustains every specification made, and the committee say in substance that the atrocities committed in Alabama are such as have only been "witnessed heretofore in savage warfare."

It remains to be seen if in America, this boasted land of liberty and freedom, an American citizen has the right to utter such sentiments as he may see fit not in derogation of the Constitution of our country.

If the republican party allows this session of Congress to end without throwing some protecting aegis over the shoulders of republicans in Southern States, our doom is sealed; liberty of speech will be throttled, and maintenance of liberty in that country will be "among the things that were." If you have no helping hand to offer the republicans of the South in their struggle against the desperate and reckless attempts of the White League democracy to destroy the Government, you may as well sound the funeral knell of liberty and independence in that country. We do not want to suspend the *habeas corpus* writ to intimidate voters; we do not want soldiers to overawe white men; but what we do want is a fair chance to express ourselves at the ballot-box for the men of our choice. . . .

Mr. Speaker, some people arraign me for being a republican, and point at me as one of those who followed the confederate flag until it was furled in disaster and defeat. I have no apology to make to such men. I did follow it and wanted it to succeed. But it did not succeed, and when it failed I was one of those who proposed to remain quietly and peaceably at home upon my plantation and vote for whatever I thought best for the people of my State and my country.

Sir, I was forced into the position that I have taken here to-night. I was forced into the position I occupy upon this floor. The very moment that I said to the people of my country that I proposed to be a republican and that I proposed to obey the honorable edicts of those who had fought and carried the flag of the Union through the land I was denounced, (and let me say just here that they freed as many slaves of mine as they did of any other man in my country or upon this floor). I have followed the fortunes of the republican party because I believed it was right, and because I believed that such a course would bring us peace, happiness, and prosperity. Upon those who charge me with being the maligner of my people I hurl back the imputation, and trust to posterity for that vindication which should be dear to every honorable man in the land.

Now, sir, the question has come to this: whether we shall have another revolution or whether we shall abide by the decision of the majority of the people of this nation! The question has resolved itself into this: Is this a "government of the people, for the people, and by the people," or is it a government of a country which proposes to control all votes of the people by intimidation and violence? . . .

But, Mr. Speaker, I will say no more on this; but before I conclude let me say to my friends that the time for action has arrived—the supreme test has come. It is a battle between law and lawlessness, between law-abiders and law-breakers.

It may seem idle to tell you, but unless something is done to avert the coming storm the waves of a new revolution, terrible in its magnitude, bitter in its hatred, and disastrous in its results, will be upon you.

In conclusion, as for the maledictions which the democratic leaders and party press deem proper to bestow upon me for my faithful discharge of duty to my country and my State, I shall endure them in silence and peace, and trust to that spirit of justice which sooner or later must come to vindicate my record from the aspersions which have been so foully cast upon it.

———

During his last two years in Congress Hays had severe personal problems that made it difficult for him to be an effective legislator. He lost most of his considerable wealth and was constantly beset by creditors. Also Hays was dogged by an allegation that he had appointed to West Point a man who was not a resident of the Fourth District. This led to an investigation by a House subcommittee that finally exonerated him, but it was an embarrassing affair.

During those same years the Republican party in Alabama fell on hard times. The Democratic legislature redrew several congressional districts, gerrymandering the Fourth and Sixth Districts and making them largely white and Democratic. This made it impossible for Hays to win a fifth term. Also, in 1876 the Constitutional Convention controlled by Democrats provided for economic retrenchment and legislative apportionment. Finally, blacks had to cast ballots in their home districts where there was no protection, rather than in county seats where troops could protect them.

Hays did not participate in the 1876 contest. Alabama Republicans superficially smoothed over differences, but they failed to offer strong opposition. George Smith Houston defeated the Republican gubernatorial nominee by 40,000 votes in August. Samuel Tilden easily carried Alabama in November, and the Demo-crats claimed seven of the eight congressional seats. In the Sixth District, where Hays sat out the election, the Republicans did not even offer congressional opposition.

The victor in the presidential election would remain uncertain for several months. Although Tilden claimed more electoral votes than Hayes, the returns from Florida, South Carolina, and Louisiana were disputed. An Electoral Commis-sion established soon after Congress convened in November would make a final determination.

In early November Hays returned to Washington as a congressman for the last time. He did not take the floor and continued his absentee pattern during the three-month lame-duck session. Attention was focused on the Electoral Commission. On March 2, 1876, Rutherford Hayes was certified the victor.

In one of his last official acts, on the final day of the Forty-fourth Congress, Hays wrote the president. The letter, dated March 3, coincided with the day of Hayes's private inauguration at the White House. He recommended the appointment of James L. Alcorn to the cabinet. The Mississippi Republican's Senate term was expir-ing. Hays had consistently recommended extending office to native Southern whites. By now he realized something else. Patronage was about all the Republican party could claim in the South. Eight years of service in the House of Representa-tives concluded for Charles Hays on March 3, 1877, when the Forty-fourth Congress adjourned.

James Alcorn

In the last years of Reconstruction, James Alcorn became an important Republican leader. He was a hard worker and an eloquent spokesman for the South.

A prominent part of Alcorn's senatorial activity was his continuous ef-fort to project the image of a moderate and reasonable Southerner. In a speech on behalf of a supplementary civil rights bill on May 22, 1874, he reminded his listen-ers that he had belonged to the slaveholding class and had been a Rebel, but that he was now an advocate of civil rights. Mississippi already had a more stringent civil rights law than the one under consideration, but his Negro constituents were anx-ious that the rest of the country receive similar benefits. He denied that equality be-fore the law would be degrading to the white race because it would bring about social equality. He reasoned that "Society exists and is governed by its own laws. They are unwritten, but they are none the less determinedly maintained." That the de-graded race could be brought to a level with the most exalted "is true as far as law can make it so." As so many Southerners would do after him, he denied that the South was prejudiced against the Negro, claiming that he himself had been nursed as a baby and raised by a colored nurse who was still a member of his family and was

held in great affection. While he advocated nondiscrimination in theaters and hotels, he reiterated his belief in separate schools and claimed that the Negroes in Mississippi "who control the state" believed in it also.

The action of the southern people in resisting reconstruction, he asserted, was
not due to prejudice "but to an inherent pride of soul. They believed that the action
of the government was intended to insult and degrade them." He lashed out at "in-
triguing whites" who promised the Negro civil rights "and rob him at the same time."
The only way for peace in the South was for the southern whites to give the Negro
these rights so as to remove from the demagogue his power over him.

Following Alcorn's defeat in 1873 he became much more vocal as a spokesman for
the South, and he attacked the Ames government and radicals in general in Mississippi whenever an opportunity presented itself. He did it to the extent that during
one debate Senator Cameron of Pennsylvania objected as a matter of "good taste"
to Southern senators constantly bringing up local matters, and he noted that no one
was more apt to do it than the senator from Mississippi.

Alcorn also showed a great knack for turning almost any subject under debate
into a plea for the South. When an appropriation for the Centennial Exhibition at
Philadelphia was being discussed, he announced he would vote against it because
such an affair should represent the people and be supported by the wealthy, not by
a tax on the "toiling millions." The rich would enjoy it, but the poor of the South
would not be able to participate, and he then elaborated on the theme of southern
poverty. . . .

Throughout his term in the Senate, Alcorn was a very articulate member and a
hard worker. He reported out many of the bills referred to the Committee on Mines
and Mining although he was not chairman, and admitted that he had had to study
hard to familiarize himself with the subject. He kept his select committee on levees
working during congressional recesses, and apologized to his constituents in 1873
when his work on the committee investigating the Louisiana election kept him from
attending Senate sessions. . . .

While Alcorn worked hard in Washington, supporting his party and the Southern
viewpoint, his opponents at home made their attempt to plant the Republican party
firmly on Mississippi soil. Ames began his gubernatorial term in a conciliatory manner with a plea in his inaugural address for economy, and for tolerance and understanding between the races; but by midsummer he was in trouble. The corrupt
Republican regime in Vicksburg was overthrown by force, and Ames, after refusing
to act on his own because he felt he had no means within his power to suppress such
disturbances, appealed to Grant for Federal troops. Grant did not respond because,
according to Ames, he was trying to get Democratic support for a third term. Things
quieted down, but on August 25, his superintendent of education, Cardozo, was arrested and charged with fraud, and Ames wrote of the incident as "an illustration of
the character of the material we have to work with." Grant finally agreed to send him
troops if necessary, and forwarded assurances of support through Benjamin Butler,
his father-in-law.

In 1875 the pattern repeated itself, only more violently. The legislature started
impeachment proceedings against Ames's lieutenant governor for taking a bribe in

connection with a pardon; violence broke out among Negro members of his party; and the "white liners" began a wide-scale program of intimidation looking toward the fall election. Ames was frustrated in his attempts to form a militia, and his letters began to reflect more and more his disgust at the "barbarous spirit" of the whites and the cowardice of the Negroes. Early in September he asked once more for troops, and when Grant again failed to respond, he began organizing a Negro militia. . . .

Alcorn had lost all hope of building a permanent Republican party in Mississippi. He was uncomfortable with the heavy reliance on the black vote and believed that "no state can be maintained under carpetbag rule." There was little left for him to do in Mississippi.

In spite of the fact that popular opinion focused opposition to Ames around Alcorn and the *Pilot* [the Jackson newspaper that was critical of Alcorn] linked him with it, he took no active part in the political affairs of his state during this period, except for the incident at Friar's Point. P.B.S. Pinchback, Negro Senator from Louisiana, sent him an inquiry concerning this affair, and he replied with a letter giving his reasons for his opposition to Brown, as well as his views on the election campaign of 1875 and the Republican party in Mississippi:

> In the canvass of this year I have said not a word. I could not support the party in Miss while it was the mere mouthpiece of Ames. I could not support the democrats—and so I held my peace. . . . Ames has pretty well wound up the Republican Party in this state. The democrats have shown great political sagacity, they supported Ames two years since that he might drive every decent white man in the state out of the party, they have succeeded admirably—it is now a settled question that no state can be maintained under carpet-bag rule.

He added that with good government Mississippi could have been kept in the Republican ranks, but he expected the party now to lose control of the state house of representatives. He closed with a brief summary of his political position: "I am a republican now as in the past, have done all I could to save Mississippi from democratic rule, have spent six years of my life in the cause. All my labor is lost."

As the situation continued to deteriorate, Butler made another appeal to Grant, which resulted in the latter's famous opinion that the country was "tired of the annual autumnal outbreaks in the South." However, a representative from the Attorney General's office, George K. Chase, was sent to Mississippi, and he met with Ames and Democratic party leaders Ethelbert Barksdale and J. Z. George. As a compromise Ames agreed to disarm his Negro militia in return for a promise of a fair election, and the Attorney General promised to send troops if the agreement was not kept. Acts of violence continued to occur, which Barksdale and George vigorously denied. They managed to keep the situation in status quo until the eve of the election, when Ames found the troops too far away and their orders too ambiguous to be of any help. He bitterly described Grant's order placing soldiers at his disposal as "a sham, and the election a fraud." The Democratic party gained complete control of the state through the election of its members to local offices and the legislature, leaving Ames isolated in the governor's mansion.

This method of overthrowing Republican carpetbag rule became known as the "Mississippi plan," a program of intimidation and violence kept just short of what would provoke federal intervention. It was aided in Mississippi by the Grant administration which had begun during 1875 to withdraw its support of Ames by disregarding his requests concerning patronage. This action made the administration's attitude so evident that the Republican state convention refused to endorse it, although the executive committee did do so before it went to Washington in an unsuccessful attempt to have Pease and two other Ames opponents removed from Federal office. But Ames put his finger on the underlying reason for his predicament and failure when he wrote his wife: "I am fighting for the Negro; and to the whole country a white man is better than a 'Nigger.'" . . .

The demoralized Mississippi Republican party met in state convention on March 31, as Morton's resolution was being passed by the Senate, and Ames was resigning his office. Defeat produced a surface conciliation, and the leaders of both factions were included in the state's delegation to the national presidential convention. The delegates at large named were Alcorn, Bruce, Powers, and Ames. The state convention adopted a resolution thanking Morton for his efforts on behalf of Southern Republicans, but did not instruct the delegates. Alcorn attended the national convention at Cincinnati and was named to the Republican congressional committee. One reporter in describing the Mississippi delegation at the convention noticed Alcorn and Ames seated in the same row, with Bruce, the chairman of the delegation, no doubt uneasily occupying the seat between them.

As an indication of how superficial the conciliation had been, the Mississippi delegation scattered its votes among the contenders in varying patterns until the seventh and last ballot, when it joined the movement toward Hayes. It is impossible to ascertain how Alcorn voted, but it is difficult to imagine him casting a ballot for Conkling, Morton, or James G. Blaine. Blanche Ames, writing to her husband at the convention, expressed surprise at Hayes's nomination, but added that "at least Alcorn's man was beaten." The most likely possibility seems to have been Benjamin H. Bristow, who was a native Kentuckian.

Regardless of whom he had supported, Alcorn continued to be an active Republican. On July 15, 1876, he gave a long speech at the Friar's Point courthouse in which he reviewed again the prewar and post-Appomattox blunders of the South, and blamed them all on the leadership provided by the Democratic party. He cited Rutherford B. Hayes's conciliatory letter and promised that if the South would support the Republican party new issues would arise to take the place of war, race, and reconstruction. Political parties would again be like the Whigs and Democrats of earlier times. In September the Memphis *Daily Appeal* interviewed him and found that he expected Mississippi to go Democratic that fall. He also said that he had refused the solicitations of "influential leading Republicans" to be candidate for governor. Carpetbaggers had ruined the Republican party in Mississippi, infesting it with thieves and rascals, and it was his desire to see them kicked out and the party placed in the hands of honest, honorable men.

Nevertheless he continued to campaign in Mississippi for Hayes, speaking at one meeting on the same platform with a Judge Stafford who three years before had been an Ames supporter. The Democrat against whom they were both debating was an Alcorn opponent of twenty-years' standing, Albert Gallatin Brown. Alcorn was also still enough of a regular Republican to vote against his old friend and comrade-in-arms at the Friar's Point riot, James R. Chalmers, whose political affiliations at that time were, and continued to be, highly ambiguous.

———————

Alcorn still had hopes of continuing his political career but not as a senator from Mississippi. His best chance was a cabinet appointment in the new Republican administration. Rutherford Hayes, searching for a Southerner to put into his cabinet, appeared to be seriously considering Alcorn.

It may be that Alcorn still hoped to obtain, through a favor to himself, some recognition by the party of white Southern Republicans. The appointment of Robert Alcorn [a cousin] in June, 1876, to be receiver of public monies at Jackson was a suggestion of rising administration regard. Just before the national convention [James] Alcorn wrote Amelia: "In the Herald of 22n you will observe . . . speculation for V [Vice] Presidency. Its speculation on my name is idle. I could not reach it, if I could would not have it." Three days later Charles Nordhoff of the New York *Tribune* wrote Ohio Governor Hayes that Grant had informed "Southern men" he would like to see either Alcorn or George W. McCrary of Iowa nominated for the Vice-Presidency. While the speculation on Alcorn's name was, as he so clearly saw, ephemeral, it indicates that he had established himself as a representative of the white Southern Republican wing, a proper recipient of favors to that group.

This is apparent later that year when after his nomination and apparent election, Hayes began to consider appointments to his cabinet. In line with his desire to include a Southerner, he specifically considered Alcorn, and received numerous letters from constituents in Ohio as well as the border states and the South urging his appointment. One such letter suggested Alcorn for Secretary of the Navy, and Lynch, who claimed that he, too, interceded for Alcorn, later wrote that Alcorn wanted to be Postmaster General.

However, according to recent research, a meeting of Southerners was held at Alcorn's home in Washington early in February, 1877, to promote the candidacy of a Southern Democrat, David M. Key, to be Postmaster General. At some point Hayes decided not to encourage the conservative white Southern wing of the party, and Alcorn may have felt this was the best way left to promote the interests of his region. In any event, he had already disengaged himself from state politics, and now he was withdrawing from partisan national politics also.

While Hayes was trying to make up his mind concerning southern representation in his cabinet, Congress faced a far more serious matter, that of the challenge by the Democrats of the validity of Hayes's election. Nor were all Republicans in Congress, where the issue would have to be decided, ready to support the President-elect. Some feared he might be under the influence of the reform wing of the party, and Southern Republican congressmen were concerned that his reconciliation policy in the South might mean lack of support for them.

In December one of Hayes's friends in Washington expressed uneasiness because "no one seems to know how Alcorn of Mississippi stands." Early in January, just before the Electoral Commission plan was presented to Congress, Alcorn made his position known to Hayes, and when he did so it was with an emphatic statement of support. He declared that it was his belief that Hayes had been honestly elected, that Samuel Tilden could not have carried Louisiana in an honest election, and that Mississippi should not be counted for either side since the Democrats were in "armed occupation" and the election had been a fraud and a farce.

It has not been possible to ascertain whether or not he had reason to believe he was still being considered for a position in Hayes's cabinet when he made this statement. On September 17, 1876, in an interview with a reporter from the Memphis *Daily Appeal* he had expressed concern that if Tilden were elected by a slim majority "we may have a revolution in which the stability of our form of government will become involved." Even if the possibility of political reward were still present, a factor which may have inspired his silence in December, Alcorn's realistic appraisal of the situation in the South and a sincere concern with the preservation of his country's institutions no doubt also prompted him to take this stand.

In the Senate he translated his views into a course of moderation. Consistently supporting Grant's position, Alcorn voted for the establishment of the Electoral Commission, in opposition to Democrats who feared Republican domination of it and Republicans who felt it would compromise the validity of Hayes's claim. He also spoke on behalf of the commission and helped defeat hampering amendments which would have empowered it to go behind the findings in each state and would have permitted it to sit "with open doors." As the findings of the commission on the election in each state under investigation were presented, Alcorn voted with the majority to accept them. His position during these two crucial months as Congress struggled to resolve the election dispute did not waver, although at one point during the period he learned that he was no longer being considered for a cabinet post. This meant the end of his political career since the Democratic Mississippi legislature had already selected Lamar to succeed him as Senator.

After casting the last of his votes on behalf of the findings of the Electoral Commission and witnessing the peaceful inauguration of Hayes, he returned to Coahoma County and retirement from state and national politics. His political career had been buried in the collapse of the Republican party in Mississippi and at the age of sixty-one he had no desire for new adventures of that nature, even had he been able to overcome his deep dislike of the Democrats. The hopes with which he had gone to Washington had failed to materialize. He obtained only sporadic backing from the Grant administration in spite of the support which he gave it; he received none when he needed it most; and the Hayes administration appeared even more unpromising. He had brought home no Federal money for the Delta, and seemingly he made little lasting impression with his speeches on behalf of the South.

At home he had been unable to lead his organization to victory over Ames in 1873, and in 1875, as Ames headed for certain defeat, he refused to assume the leadership of the opposition. Men and events had moved along in time further than Alcorn realized, thus destroying the rapport between him and other white Republican leaders. While Alcorn thought in terms of a neo-Whig party, ex-Whigs, such as Simrall, Peyton, and the Yergers became indistinguishable from latter-day native and Northern Republicans, such as Powers, McKee, Pease, Wells, Musgrove, and Vasser. Alcorn was unable to adapt to this new era the Whig political framework from the past within which he had hoped to build his organization. Whiggery, the only viable political opposition to the Democrats which had ever existed in the state, could not be revived, and with the failure of the Republican party political impoverishment settled over Mississippi.

———————

Reconstruction was over for the two carpetbaggers and two scalawags. Marshall Twitchell and Albert Morgan returned to the North to put their lives back in order. Neither returned a wealthy man. Twitchell had little money and two artificial arms, and Morgan had lost all that he had earned in his ten years in the South. For Charles Hays and James Alcorn, it was also painful. Hays was virtually bankrupt with no political future. Alcorn had considerable wealth in his plantations but no prospects in politics.

The responses of these men had been to resist the efforts to reverse Reconstruction, but they had been to no avail. Now they returned to their private lives trying to understand what had happened to them and to begin life anew. It was not an easy task.

A similar story can be read in the responses of northern and southern blacks to the events of counter Reconstruction. They, too, had high hopes for a bright future in the postwar South. But as Reconstruction came to an end, each had to deal with the painful reality that their hopes would not be realized.

CHAPTER 11

THE RESPONSES OF NORTHERN AND SOUTHERN BLACKS TO THE POLICIES OF COUNTER RECONSTRUCTION

". . . there was a complete and radical change in the situation . . . like a clap of thunder from a clear sky."

—JOHN LYNCH

John Lynch

John Lynch, black Republican congressman from Mississippi, served two terms during Reconstruction, 1873–1877. His major effort was to support the passage of the Federal Election Bill, which was to enforce law and order efforts in the South, and to stamp out the Ku Klux Klan. However, he was stunned by the election of 1874, which reversed Republican efforts in the South and in Mississippi. He could not understand how this had happened.

After the presidential election of 1872, none could be found who questioned the wisdom or practicability of the congressional plan of reconstruction or looked for its overthrow, change, or modification. After that election the situation was accepted and acquiesced in by everyone in perfect good faith. No one could be found in any party of either race who was bold or reckless enough to express the opinion that the congressional plan of reconstruction was a mistake or that Negro suffrage was a failure. On the contrary, it was admitted by all and denied by none that the wisdom of both had been fully tested and clearly vindicated. . . .

Notwithstanding the general acceptance of this plan after the presidential election of 1872, we find that, in the fall of 1874, there was a complete and radical change in the situation. It was sudden and unexpected. It came, as it were, in the twinkling of an eye. It was like a clap of thunder from a clear sky. It was the state and congressional elections of that year.

In the elections of 1872 nearly every state in the Union went Republican. In the state and congressional elections of 1874 the result was the reverse of what it was two years before—nearly every state going Democratic. Democrats were surprised and Republicans were dumbfounded. Such a result had not been expected, looked for, predicted, or anticipated by anyone. Even the state of Massachusetts, the birthplace of abolitionism—the cradle of American liberty—elected a Democratic governor. The Democrats had a majority in the national House of Representatives that was about equal to that which the Republicans elected two years before. . . .

It was the state and congressional elections of 1874 which proved to be the death of the Republican party at the South. The party at that section might have survived even such a crushing blow as this but for subsequent unfortunate events . . . . Under these conditions its survival was impossible. If the state and congressional elections of 1874 had been a repetition of those of 1872, or if they had resulted in a Republican victory at all, Republican success in the presidential election of 1876 would have been a reasonably assured fact. By that time the party at the South would have included in its membership from forty to fifty percent of the white men of their respective states, and as a result thereof, it would have been strong enough to stand on its own feet and maintain its own independent existence regardless of reverses which the parent organization might have sustained in other sections. But at that time the party in that section was in its infancy. It was young, weak, and comparatively helpless. It still needed the fostering care and protecting hand of the paternal source of its existence. . . .

. . . after the state and congressional elections of 1874 the situation was materially changed. The liberal and conservative element of the Democracy was relegated to the rear and the radical element came to the front and assumed charge. Subsequent to 1872 and prior to 1875 race proscription and social ostracism had been completely abandoned. A Southern white man could become a Republican without being socially ostracized. Such a man was no longer looked upon as a traitor to his section, an enemy to his people, or false to his race. He no longer forfeited the respect, confidence, goodwill, and favorable opinion of his friends and neighbors. . . . But after the state and congressional elections of 1874, there was a complete change of front. The new order of things was then set aside and the abandoned methods of a few years back were reviewed, reinaugurated, and readopted. . . .

———————

In 1875 Lynch ran for reelection. Democrats were bold, outspoken, and defiant. It was to be the fight of his life.

This was a sad and serious disappointment to the colored men who were just about to realize the hope and expectation of a permanent political combination and union between themselves and the better element of the whites, which would have resulted in good, honest, capable, and efficient local government and in the establishment and maintenance of peace, goodwill, friendly, cordial, and amicable relations between the two races. But this hope, politically at least, had now been destroyed and these expectations had been shattered and scattered to the four winds. For the colored men the outlook was dark and anything but encouraging. . . .

My own renomination for Congress from the Sixth, or Natchez, District was a foregone conclusion, since I had no opposition in my own party, but I realized the painful fact that a nomination this time was not equivalent to an election. Still, I felt that it was my duty to make the fight, let the result be what it may.

If congressmen had been elected in 1874, the state would have returned five Republicans and one Democrat as was done in 1872. But in 1875 the prospect was not so bright and the indications were not so favorable. The Democrats nominated for treasurer Hon. William L. Hemingway of Carroll County. He was an able man and had been quite prominent as a party leader in his section of the state. The defiant attitude assumed, the aggressive position taken, and the bold declaration contained in the platform upon which he was nominated were accepted by the Republicans as notice that the Democrats intended to carry the election—"peaceably" and "fairly"—but of course to carry it just the same.

The Republicans nominated Hon. George M. Buchanan of Marshall County upon a platform which strongly endorsed the national and state administrations. Mr. Buchanan was a strong and popular man. He had been a brave and gallant Confederate soldier. He had been for several years sheriff and Tax Collector of his county. He was known, therefore, to be especially fitted for the office of state treasurer. As sheriff and Tax Collector of Marshall County, one of the wealthiest counties in the state, he had handled and disbursed many thousands of dollars, every dollar of which had been faithfully accounted for. His honesty, integrity, ability, fitness, and capacity no one questioned, but everyone unhesitatingly admitted.

The administration of Governor Ames was one of the best the state had ever had. The judiciary was quite equal to that which had been appointed by Governor Alcorn. The public revenues had been promptly collected and honestly accounted for. There had not only been no increase in the rate of taxation, but, on the contrary, there had been a material reduction. Notwithstanding these things, the Democrats, with the radical element in charge of the party machinery, determined to seize possession of the state government *vie et armis* [by force of arms], not because it was at all necessary for any reason or from any point of view, but simply because conditions at that time seemed to indicate that it could be safely and easily done.

After the nominations had all been made, the campaign was opened in dead earnest. Nearly all Democratic clubs in the state were converted into armed military companies. Funds with which to purchase arms were believed to have been contributed by the national Democratic organization. Nearly every Republican meeting was attended by one or more of those clubs or companies, the members of which were distinguished by red shirts indicative of blood, the attendance being for the purpose, of course, of keeping the peace and preserving order. To enable the Democrats to carry the state, a Republican majority of between twenty and thirty

thousand had to be overcome. This could be done only by the adoption and enforcement of questionable methods. It was a case in which the end justified the
means and the means had to be supplied.

The Republican vote consisted of about ninety-five percent of the colored men
and about twenty-five percent of the white men. The other seventy-five percent of
the whites, or most of them, formerly constituted a part of the flower of the Confederate army. They were not only tried and experienced soldiers, but they were
fully armed and equipped for the work before them. Some of the colored Republicans had been Union soldiers, but they were neither organized nor armed. In such
a contest, therefore, they and their white allies were entirely at the mercy of their
political adversaries.

Governor Ames soon took in the situation. He saw he could not depend upon the
white members of the state militia to obey his orders and support him in his efforts
to uphold the majesty of the law and to protect the law-abiding citizens in the enjoyment of life, liberty, and property. To use the colored members of the militia for
such a purpose would be adding fuel to the flames. Nothing, therefore, remained
for him to do but to call on the national administration for military aid in his efforts
to crush out domestic violence and enforce the laws of the state, which was done,
but . . . was not granted.

When the polls closed on the day of election, the Democrats, of course, had carried the state by a large majority, the same party having secured a heavy majority in
both branches of the legislature. Of the six members of Congress, I was the only one
of the regular Republican candidates that pulled through and that by a greatly
reduced majority. In the Second, or Holly Springs, District, G. Wiley Wells ran as
an Independent Republican against A. R. Howe, the sitting member and regular
Republican candidate for reelection. The Democrats supported Wells, who was
elected.

The delegation therefore consisted of four Democrats, one Republican, and one
Independent Republican. While the delegation would have consisted of five straight
Republicans and one Democrat had the election been held in 1874; still, since the
Democrats had such a large majority in the House, the political complexion of the
Mississippi delegation was not important. My election, it was afterwards developed,
was due in all probability to a miscalculation on the part of some of the Democratic
managers. Their purpose was to have a solid delegation, counting Wells as one of
that number, since his election would be due to the support of that party.

But in my district the plan miscarried. In one of the counties there were two
conflicting reports as to what the Democratic majority was. According to one report
it was 250. According to the other it was 500. The report giving 250 was no doubt the
correct one, but the other no doubt would have been accepted had it been believed
at the time to be necessary to insure the election of the Democratic candidate. To
overcome the majority in that district was more difficult than that of any of the
others. While their candidate, Colonel Roderick Seal, was a popular man, yet it was
well known that I would poll a solid Republican vote, or such of it as would be allowed to vote, and some Democratic votes in addition. Fortunately for me, there was
a split in the party in my own county, Adams, for county officers, which resulted in

bringing out a very heavy vote. This split also made the count very slow, covering a period of several days. My name was on both tickets. The election took place on Tuesday, but the count was not finished until the following Friday evening. Hence the result for member of Congress in that county could not be definitely ascertained until that time.

The Democratic managers at the state capital were anxious to know as soon as possible what the Republican majority in Adams County would be for congressman; hence, on Wednesday evening the editor of the local Democratic paper received a telegram from the Secretary of the Democratic state committee, requesting to be informed, immediately, about what the Republican majority would be in Adams County for congressman. The editor read the telegram to me and asked what, in my opinion, would be my majority in the county. My reply was that I did not think it would exceed 1200. In that opinion he concurred, hence his reply was in these words: "Lynch's majority in Adams will not exceed 1200."

Upon receipt of this telegram the majority of 250 instead of 500 was deemed sufficient from the county heretofore referred to. If the Republican majority in Adams would not exceed 1200, the success of the Democratic congressional candidate by a small but safe majority was assured on the face of the returns. Since Adams was the last county to be reported, no change could thereafter be made. When the count was finally finished in Adams, it was found that I had a majority of over 1800. This gave me a majority in the district of a little over 200 on the face of the returns.

The disappointment and chagrin on the part of the Democratic managers can better be imagined than described. But the agreeable surprise to the Republicans was at least equal to the disappointment and chagrin on the part of the Democrats. The defeated Democratic candidate threatened to make a contest for the seat on the ground of violence and fraud, but this was so ridiculous and absurd that the managers and leaders of his own party would not allow him to carry the threat into execution.

━━━━━

During the next year Lynch made two important speeches to the House of Representatives. On June 15, 1876, he tried to correct misconceptions about carpetbaggers by a fellow congressman and warned of the dangers of using force to deprive blacks of their right to vote and hold office.

In speaking of carpet-baggers—of that class of men who came to the State for no other purpose than to fill their pockets—my colleague seems to have entirely forgotten that his own party did not only set the example for the colored people to follow in this respect, but the hostility of his party toward the colored voters was such that it was made incumbent upon them to accept the best material that it was possible for them to get. Is it strange, then, that they put some of that class of men in office? But let me explain what I mean when I say the democratic party set the example for the colored people to follow in this respect.

The gentleman ought to be aware of the fact that that very class of men have been taken up by the democratic party and elevated to power and position whenever they would consent to serve that party. I have witnessed with sorrow and regret that the very class of men whom the democratic party would denounce, repudiate, and condemn in one election would be taken up by them at the very next election and eulogized to the skies, although they were carpet-baggers, provided they would join their party.

Does my colleague desire me to make an illustration? I will not do it by referring to my own State. I will not be so uncharitable as to do that, but I will take a case from another southern State, and refresh his memory in that particular. He will perhaps remember that there never was a carpet-bagger in the South that was more universally denounced, repudiated, and condemned by the democratic party than was Ex-Governor Warmoth, of the State of Louisiana. They said so many bad things about him, accused him of so many bad things, that I among others was induced to believe that at least some of them were true. But yet when that gentleman decided to join the democracy, or rather decided to affiliate with them at that election, I was surprised to find that the party that had denounced, repudiated, and condemned him had opened wide its doors for his reception. They did not only receive him immediately into their ranks but they regarded him as one of their most notable and trusted leaders, one of the shining lights of their party, and they were ready to honor him with the highest office in the gift of the people of the State. It is believed that when the important announcement was made that Warmoth intended to affiliate with the democracy they had a grand jollification meeting in honor of that important event, and the chief mogul of the party, I imagine, took the young political convert by the right hand and exclaimed solemnly in these words. "Warmoth, we have regarded you as a bad man; we have accused you of being a corrupt man, a dishonest man, a public plunderer of our people; but we now confess that there is only one sin of which we considered you guilty: affiliation with the republican party. But as you have left that organization it makes no difference with us *now* how much you may have stolen, how much you may have plundered us, how much you may have corrupted the morals of our people. These *little* sins will be charged against you no more forever. [Laughter.] Enter thou into the joys of the democracy, for as you have been found faithful over a few things we will now make you ruler over many." [Renewed laughter.] That is in brief the history of the democratic party in the Southern States on the carpet-bag question, in consequence of which I think it comes with very bad grace from the leaders of that party to complain of carpet-bag rule at the South. . . .

Now, sir, let me admonish gentlemen on this floor from other sections, let me admonish the democrats from the North, and I would appeal especially to my honorable friend from New York [Mr. Cox] who so gracefully occupies the chair in the absence of the honorable Speaker—a gentleman for whom I have the highest regard, because I look upon him as a man of moderate views except on some questions, [Laughter.] let me say to him, as a leader of his party, and a creditable one, too, at that; let me say to others from the North who are leaders of the democratic party, to put your power, put your votes, put your organization upon record against mob law and violence, and try to gain the colored vote by honest means, by argument, persuasion, and reason. When you succeed in gaining the colored vote by those means no one will regret it. I will not regret it, but I will rejoice to see the day come when men will be enabled to vote as they please without personal risk to themselves by doing so. I trust that the northern democrats will try and get our southern brethren to come up to the standard that you keep at the North, to tolerate differences of opinion, and try and educate them up to the necessity of allowing men to vote how they please and for what party they please. When you do that we shall have peace and good-will at the South. But under existing circumstances that cannot be done. No government can be sustained and upheld by the public sentiment of a people when one portion of the country is controlled and governed by a band of men organized into an army for the purpose of intimidating men who do not belong to the party they are identified with.

Now I appeal to the public sentiment of the country to crush out mobocracy at the South; to vindicate freedom of speech, freedom of opinion, freedom of the press, and the purity of the ballot-box.

That is what I am in favor of, and I trust the gentlemen from the North will see the necessity of this course. Otherwise you will lay the foundation for the dissolution of this Republic.

Mr. Chairman, I could say more if I had more time, for this is a subject that I could speak upon for hours. It is a subject that my honorable colleague knows I am as deeply interested in as he is, and while I take pleasure in saying that a large number of the white democrats in my State did not countenance the violence resorted to for the purpose of overcoming the republican party, yet it is an unfortunate fact that that party could not have been wiped out of existence as it has been by any other means than by violence and intimidation.

Two months later, on August 12, 1876, Lynch spoke at length about Reconstruction, the color line, and violence. The earlier remarks of Congressman Lamar, one of Lynch's most energetic opponents, were the reason for this speech.

Now, sir, let me say something with regard to the policy of reconstruction. It will be remembered by those who heard the speech of my colleague [Mr. Lamar] that he made the remark that the reconstruction policy of the Government was the foundation of all of the political evils at the South; that that was the foundation of the color-line in politics, because the reconstruction policy of the Government enfranchised the colored men and disfranchised the white men; and that therefore there was a gulf between the two races, and that was the cause of the race struggles of the South and all the evils of which we complain. Before answering that argument let us see what are the logical deductions to be drawn from it. If it be true, as he asserted, that the enfranchisement of the colored men at the South was the cause of all of our troubles there, it seems to me that we can draw no other deduction from that argument (if there is anything in it) than that the only effec-tual remedy is to remove the cause; that you cannot remove it unless you disfran-chise them and remand them back to their former condition. That seems to me to be the logical deduction to be drawn from the argument, though he did not say so, and I do not wish to be understood as placing him in the attitude of advocating that proposition. I am merely stating what seems to me the only conclusion to be arrived at as the logical result of the argument.

Let us inquire whether there is anything in that view of the case. I take issue with my honorable colleague in that respect, and will endeavor to show by referring to my own State that he is entirely mistaken. Why, sir, my colleague seems to have for-gotten that in the State of Mississippi we have never had any serious troubles be-tween the two races since the re-admission of that State into the Union until the latter part of 1874 and during the campaign of 1875. Until then we never had any serious troubles whatever. The two races got along well together and never had any serious difficulty of any kind, the democratic party sometimes putting colored men on their own ticket. If then, the enfranchisement of the colored men was the cause of all the troubles in the South, is it not remarkably strange that it took the demo-cratic party from five to eight years to find it out? Is it not remarkably strange that we could get along so well together for five to eight years without finding out that the incorporation of the colored element into the body-politic was the cause of our difficulties? No, sir; I will tell you what was the cause. The democratic victories at the North in 1874 so encouraged and exasperated the lawless and turbulent elements at the South as to give them the entire control of the party machinery in the demo-cratic party. That was the cause of it. . . .

In referring to this question of the prevalence of violence and the drawing [of] the color line in politics, I am willing for one to give my colleague credit for every-thing that he says on that point. I am willing to give him credit for sincerity in dep-recating the drawing of the color line and the inauguration of brute force and violence. The only thing upon which I take issue with him in that respect is this: He believes, honestly, no doubt, that in giving utterance to conservative sentiments here and elsewhere, in deprecating the drawing of the color line and the inauguration of violence, he represents the controlling element in the ranks of the democratic party in Mississippi. I believe (and I presume he will give me credit for honesty and sin-cerity in this opinion) that he does not.

I am willing to admit, as I said upon a former occasion, that there are in the State of Mississippi numbers of white men who are not identified with the republican party and whom I believe to be honestly opposed to these violent measures and to drawing the color line in politics. I may be pardoned for mentioning the names of one or two of these gentlemen, because their names are somewhat national; they are known to the country. I will mention for instance the present speaker of the house of representatives of Mississippi, Hon. H. M. Street. I will also mention Hon. J. W. C. Watson, of Marshall, the editor of the paper that opposed the impeachment of the governor upon party grounds; General A. M. West, of the same town; ex-Governor Charles Clarke, and ex-Governor and ex-United States Senator Albert G. Brown, of Hinds. These men, I believe, are honestly opposed to this policy of violence and the drawing of the line in politics. I have always believed that my colleague [Mr. Lamar] was one of that number; I am willing to give him credit for it; but when he asserts that in his conservative utterances he reflects the sentiments of the controlling element of his party, I take issue with him. His position cannot be substantiated, for it is not correct.

It is sometimes said that these violent measures are sometimes necessary to get rid of bad government, heavy taxes, and dishonest officials. I have asserted on this floor more than once that this cannot be truthfully said of Mississippi. I did not make groundless assertions and empty declarations, but presented facts and figures to substantiate what I said. Not one of my democratic colleagues has denied or can deny my position on this question. In that State there was no occasion whatever for the inauguration of violent measures on the ground that bad, incompetent, or dishonest men had control of the government. . . .

In conclusion let me warn the House and the country, not with any feeling of malice, not with any feeling of hatred, for I have none, that if you expect to preserve the constitutional liberties of the people as well as to uphold the perpetuity of republican institutions you must see to it that lawlessness is crushed out at the South. I say to the northern democrats, you must see to it, with my honorable friend from New York, [Mr. LORD,] that your party stands upon the platform which that gentleman made in the resolutions introduced here yesterday to crush out mob law and violence at the South, whether proceeding from political friends or from political enemies. If the democratic party has a legitimate majority in the State of Mississippi or any other State, it is entitled to the vote of that State and ought to have it. If the republican party has a legitimate majority in that State or in any other State, it is entitled to the vote of that State and ought to have it. This is what honest men of all parties ought to be willing to say. And now, sir, I am satisfied that the people of this great Republic, realizing the necessities of the situation, will see to it that this grand and glorious Union of ours must, shall, and will be preserved. [Applause.]

As a result of the revolution of 1875 the Democratic party was now in control of Mississippi. The Democrats quickly changed the boundaries of the congressional districts of the state, making five Democratic and one Republican district "certain." The Republican district that took in every county on the Mississippi River was called the "shoestring district." Lynch was urged to run for reelection against James Chalmers.

General James R. Chalmers, of Fort Pillow fame, was agreed upon to make the fight in the "shoestring district." They realized the fact that, to overcome the Republican majority in that district, it was necessary to have a leader who had neither conscience nor scruples and who would inaugurate, encourage, and countenance and approve any and all methods and schemes that would be found to be necessary to accomplish the desired purpose, however questionable, despicable, vicious, or criminal they might be, the shedding of innocent blood not excepted.

Chalmers had demonstrated at the Fort Pillow massacre that he was the man for the occasion, hence he was selected. Mr. Lamar and his friends felt and believed that this was a grave political blunder but, under the circumstances, all they could do was to hold their peace and wait for future developments.

The radicals were in control of the party organization and therefore declared the party policy, which the conservatives could not afford to openly antagonize. The radicals held that conditions at that time did not make it necessary for them to concede anything to the Republicans or show them any consideration whatever. The Democrats not only had complete control of the state government, but were reasonably sure of success at the approaching presidential and congressional elections. They were, therefore, masters of the situation. Their acts, however questionable, would not and could not be made a subject of inquiry or investigation by anyone, because the party to which they belonged and which would be the beneficiary of their acts and deeds would control the machinery through which such an inquiry or investigation would be made, if at all. They therefore had nothing to fear. On the contrary they felt, and not without reason, that every restraint had been removed and that they were at liberty to do whatever was believed to be necessary to accomplish the purpose desired. Why, then, show favors or grant concessions? The fact that the Republicans had a large majority in the "shoestring district" made no material difference. What was true of that district was equally true of the state. That is, the Republican majority in the state was nearly, if not quite, as large as it was in that district, and yet they had captured the state.

Since that had been done, why not, through the same methods, complete the work and take everything? "No," they declared, "we concede nothing. We want and must have everything in sight, the 'shoestring district' included; hence Chalmers *must* be returned elected. He is just as much entitled to a seat in Congress as any of the others, because it is impossible to so apportion the state into congressional districts as to make five Democratic districts out of six without resorting to extraneous methods to secure their election. The same methods that we shall be obliged to adopt in the 'shoestring district' will have to be adopted in the other five, the only difference being that in the 'shoestring district' we shall have to supply them upon a larger scale, since we shall have a much larger majority to overcome, but the methods will be the same. Then why not take all?"

The conservatives could not deny that the radicals had reason and logic on their side as matters then stood, but in applying them, they were, in the opinion of the conservatives, making a grave political mistake. The conservatives not only admit the truth of every assertion. The concessions advocated and advised by the conservatives were believed by them to be expedient, judicious, and wise from a party standpoint. The "shoestring district" was the one in which I lived. In the formation of that district the members of the legislature no doubt believed that I would be the candidate of the Republicans since I was at that time a member of Congress. Although the fact was developed before the nomination was made that the Democrats had decided to carry the district at any cost, I felt it was my duty to make the fight for the Republicans if they desired to have me do so.

It was the opinion of the party leaders that I was the strongest and most available man in the district to make the race; hence I had no opposition for the Republican nomination. When the district convention met at Vicksburg, my name was placed in nomination in a very able and eloquent speech delivered by Captain Thomas W. Hunt, a brave and gallant ex-Confederate soldier. I made an active and aggressive canvass of the district, which covered a period of more than two months, although at several points I did this at a very great personal risk. This was especially true at Friar's Point, Port Gibson, Fayette, and Woodville.

At Friar's Point, which was said to be the home of Chalmers, it came to my knowledge that an organized plan had been perfected to create a disturbance at the meeting that I was to address, which would result in breaking it up with possible bloodshed and rioting, which I am sure was true, for I could not fail to see unmistakable evidences of it when walking the streets of the town. It so happened that Friar's Point was also the home of Senator Alcorn who, when this was brought to his notice, took the necessary steps to prevent it and succeeded in doing so. To make sure his plans should not miscarry, the senator not only attended the meeting, but acted as its presiding officer. The result was a peaceable and orderly meeting which I addressed without serious interference or interruption.

At the other places I was fortunate enough to have personal friends among the Democrats who used their influence to preserve the public peace and maintain order, in which they were successful, at least to the extent of preventing riotous outbreaks, but they could not at every point prevent the breaking up of the meeting. At Fayette, for instance, the armed Democratic club took possession of the place where the meeting was to be held, the Republicans standing in the rear. When I ascended the platform and attempted to speak, my voice was drowned by the noise, yells, and groans of the crowd. After a fruitless effort of about an hour in this direction, the attempt to deliver an address was abandoned. This, however, was harmless and innocent amusement, in comparison with the riot and bloodshed which had been contemplated and which no doubt would have been carried out but for the admonition and advice of wiser heads.

Before the campaign was over, I could see just what was contemplated being done. It was not possible to inaugurate violence enough to prevent the polling of a Republican majority in the district. In any event, the decision had been made that Chalmers must be returned elected. What they might fail to accomplish through intimidation and violence must be accomplished in some other way, and it was done. Of the votes polled, there was a Republican majority of about 10,000. According to the *official* returns, however, there was a Democratic majority of about 4,600. This was only one of a large number of instances that contributed to Mr. Tilden's immense popular majority for president. While Mr. Tilden did not reach the presidency, the Democrats had a large majority in the House of Representatives. I contested the pretended election of Chalmers but the House Committee on Elections, of which John R. Harris of Virginia was Chairman, would not even take up the case for consideration. It was a case that could not bear the light of day. The best thing to do with it, therefore, was to suppress it and thus allow nothing to be said about it or done with it in the House. . . .

Despite his disappointment at not being elected for a third term, Lynch continued to speak out. He vigorously opposed the creation of an electoral commission to pass on the Hayes-Tilden election results.

When the bill creating this commission came before the House, I spoke and voted against it, chiefly for two reasons. In the first place, I believed it was a bad and dangerous precedent to subject the presidency of the United States to a game or scheme of luck or chance as was contemplated by the bill then under consideration. Either Hayes or Tilden had been elected and the result should be ascertained and declared according to the forms of law. In the second place, I had a suspicion that it was the outgrowth of an understanding or agreement which would result in the abandonment of Southern Republicans by the national administration.

Mr. Lamar, for instance, did not hesitate to declare that it was more important that the South should have local self-government than that the president should be a Democrat. In other words, what Southern Democrats wanted was to be let alone— that the national administration should keep hands off and allow them to manage their own affairs in their own way, even if that way should result in a virtual nullification, in part at least, of the war amendments to the federal Constitution.

I had a suspicion that this concession had been granted upon condition that the Southern Democratic leaders in Congress would consent to the creation of the proposed commission and to the ratification of this decision whatever it might be. To such a bargain I did not care to be even an innocent party. My suspicions were strengthened by the fact that the principal opposition among Democrats to the creation of the commission and the ratification of its decision came from Northern Democrats. Southern Democrats, with a few notable exceptions, not only favored the creation of the commission and the ratification of this decision, but even the fiery Waterson was induced to hold his peace and to give expression to his righteous indignation through the medium of a silent vote. That my suspicions were well founded, subsequent events more than demonstrated. I took the position that Mr. Hayes had been duly and legally elected, at least according to the forms of law and in the manner prescribed by the Constitution and that he should, therefore, be duly inaugurated and inducted into office even if it should be necessary for the then president, Grant, as commander-in-chief of the army and navy, to use the military force of the government for that purpose. I contended that having been thus duly and legally elected, the title to the office should not be subjected to chance or luck and that the incoming president should not be bound by any ante-inauguration pledges, promises, or agreements which, in the opinion of some, would have a tendency to put a cloud upon his title to the office. But the bill was passed and the commission was duly appointed. . . .

———

On March 1, 1877, two days before the end of his term in office, Lynch delivered his final speech. He directed the House's attention to the frauds perpetrated in Mississippi in the recent elections. In great detail he painted a picture of an election "beyond the bounds of reason, decency, and propriety."

Mr. Speaker, I do not rise for the purpose of making a partisan speech. I recognize the fact that we are still in the midst of an important crisis, in consequence of which it behooves every lover of his country to put patriotism above party. It is not my purpose to speak with regard to the manner in which the late election was conducted in Louisiana, except in an incidental way. My main purpose is to call public attention to some of the grave irregularities that were committed in the State which I have the honor in part to represent upon this floor. It is hardly necessary for me to say that this is to me anything else but a pleasant duty. Every consideration of love of home, of section and people, would necessarily cause me to be anxious to throw the mantle of charity over the faults and shortcomings of that people, rather than expose them to the public gaze. I confess that my inclination is in this direction. But when the offenses of a people or a portion of them are sufficiently grave to bring reproach upon our institutions and demoralize society, then their concealment will be more in the nature of a crime than a charitable act. It is in obedience, therefore, to a sense of public duty that I shall lay before the country some of the causes that produced what is called by some, the great political revolution, in the State of Mississippi. But I shall not do this because the electoral votes of that State have been cast for the candidate of the democratic party. However anxious we may be that the man of our choice should be successful, yet I hold that it is the duty of every true American citizen to cordially and cheerfully acquiesce in the will of the people when legally and fairly ascertained according to the forms of law, whether it be in accordance with our wishes or not. I presume there are none who will deny that the perpetuity of our system of Government depends upon the sacredness and security of the ballot-box, and that whenever our elective system ceases to be pure and sacred, then the foundation-stone of our governmental system will have been destroyed and the final dissolution of the Government, possibly through a bloody revolution, will be but a question of time.

Mr. Speaker, I have not the slightest hesitation in asserting that if elections such as the one held in Mississippi in November last are to be accepted by the people of this country as a legal and valid expression of the will of the people of a State, then indeed our elective system will have come to be a convenient medium for giving legal effect to the most outrageous frauds that were ever committed in the conduct of elections. The frauds that were committed upon the ballot-box in that State at the last election in the interest of the democratic party, to say nothing of terrorism and violence, were carried so far and were made so general in their application that they have not, in my judgment, a parallel in the history of a State in this Union.

Mr. Speaker, these frauds were carried so far beyond the bounds of reason, decency, and propriety that no man who has the slightest regard for his reputation, who believes in maintaining and upholding our governmental system, can for a moment defend them, countenance them, or indorse them. . . .

After extensive remarks on specific violations in four counties—Adams, Clairborne, Jefferson, and Washington—he concluded with a solemn warning.

If the present lawlessness is allowed to continue; if mob law is allowed to take the place of civil law; if fraud is accepted as the popular method of carrying elections, and violence as the legitimate plan of controlling public opinion, then the decay of that section will necessarily follow. In this connection I will make a quotation from the minority report of Senators BAYARD and McDONALD, who, as members of a Senate committee, investigated the Mississippi election of 1875, which I cordially indorse:

> Having thus stated the limitations upon the power of Congress, which a respect for the Constitution of our Government and to the decisions of its highest judicial tribunal has dictated, we cannot refrain from an expression of our abhorrence and hearty reprobation of every act of lawless and so often brutal interference with the rights of citizenship which were related by witnesses in our presence.
>
> Prosperity and happiness can never thrive in a community where such scenes of violence can be enacted without condign punishment. By a law higher than man's the "wages of sin is death," and it will be vain for the people of Mississippi to look for the advancement of their State to that position in the ranks of wealth, influence and reputation which those who love her would desire to see her occupy, until the spirit of law shall be strengthened and assert itself over the "dangerous classes," who have brought disrepute upon her good name.

Frederick Douglass

Frederick Douglass continued his passionate defense of blacks in the South. Radical Reconstruction was under attack, but his position never wavered—support for the Republican party and its policies in the South. Only the Republican party could be trusted with the rights of blacks so recently gained. On June 13, 1872, his article "Protection of the Ballot" was published in the **New National Era.**

∽ PROTECTION OF THE BALLOT ∽

Leading Democratic journals are much exercised because of the disposition of Congress to protect the citizens of the United States in their exercise of the elective franchise. Protection by the General Government has been made necessary to the safety of black voters in the Southern States because the Democratic party (now merging into the Liberal Republican party) have considered it their right to murder and intimidate . . . . by attempting to deprive citizens of the exercise of the elective franchise. It is not used to make men vote either this way or that way, but to protect them in voting in whatever way they may choose. What wrong is there in this? Who is in any way injured? Protection of voters means that Republicans shall not be allowed to use force or unlawful means to drive Democrats from the polls, nor shall Democrats be allowed unlawfully to drive Republicans away.

This is pronounced by the *Patriot* of this city a "daring scheme of usurpation," endangering the very foundations of civil liberty. Any one not blinded by party passion and Negro hate can readily see how foolish and false is the position taken by the *Patriot.* Of what value is this Government if it does not protect its citizens in the exercise of those rights which distinguish it from tyrannical and monarchical governments. It is easy to understand from the opposition made by Democrats and Liberal Republicans to all measures for real protection of voters in what condition we may expect to find ourselves should that combination succeed in obtaining control of the Government. All their opposition to the enforcement act, the Ku Klux bill, and the civil rights bill goes to show that success for them means a strong effort to subjugate the Negro. . . .

Several years later, on August 25, 1874, as conditions in the South significantly worsened, Douglass wrote to a friend of his growing frustration.

To Hon. Gerrit Smith
Washington, D.C.
August 25, 1874.
My dear Sir:

. . . Trouble and violence are now running riot in the Southern States, and the papers represent my race as the aggressors. I cannot believe it. During all the late rebellion the Negroes of the South were left on the plantations with old men, children and defenceless women, and no act of wrong was done by them to the feeblest. It is not reasonable to suppose that these Negroes have now become the demons of wrath and fury they are now painted. I am glad to know that you still believe in us and are ready to help us in the way of Education which after all is our best protection. For want of knowledge we are killed all the day long. I do not know that I shall be able to reside in Washington in case of a change in the administration. The wave of violence now sweeping over the South in that case would be likely to come here also. I shall however continue to toil and trust, and counsel my people to do the same. . . .

Always truly yours,
Frederick Douglass

The following year, on February 26, 1875, in a speech to New Hampshire Republicans, Douglass continued to support with great eloquence the Republican Reconstruction policies

in the South. The speech was recorded by a reporter for the Concord, New Hampshire,
Daily Monitor.

. . . It was said that we Republicans had violated the constitution in using the strong arm of the federal government in repressing lawlessness in the South. But those who said this, without the least scruple had used the same means for the spread and maintenance of slavery. A Democratic President sent soldiers into Boston to drag back into the hell of slavery that noble fugitive, Anthony Burns, who was free, first by nature, and second by his own heroism. No Democratic politician or paper had any protest to make to such use of federal troops. After instancing the heroic exploits of Capt. John Brown, he said: While slavery was the base line, it was considered perfectly constitutional for the military power to be used to hand John Brown over to the hangman. But now when Gen. Grant sends gallant Phil Sheridan to New Orleans (cheers) to repress Southern violence, they called it unconstitu-tional—worse than that—"Centralization." (Laughter.) If however, the American people could stand centralization for slavery, they could stand centralization for lib-erty. I have no fear of centralization while the ballot is in the hands of the American people. That would keep everything within constitutional limits.

Another charge against the Republican party is that they have a bill pending in the Senate, to establish social equality. What is social equality? In what does it con-sist? Where does it begin and where does it end? He confessed he hardly knew. He knew what social inequality was, and had known it for a good while. They had a great deal of it where he came from. A great deal of the social, but no equality. I never heard of any Democrat denouncing the social relations of the South while slavery existed. Now there was such a thing as social inequality there. If you don't be-lieve it, take two facts. Two hundred years ago the Mayflower brought to Plymouth a company of white persons, and the same year a Dutch galliot [ship] landed at Jamestown a company of colored persons. There were no intermediate races then. During all the time since we had had slavery, and social inequality. Out of that social inequality there had come a million and a half of intermediates. (Laughter and applause.) Now he never heard of any objection to social equality while that was go-ing on. It was all right, perfectly proper. That was social inequality. I am not here to find fault with this. I accept the inevitable. It places me in a position where I can speak impartially, at any rate. (Loud laughter and applause.) I hardly know which is which, or which is the other. He then pointed out in a terse manner in what social equality did or did not consist, and said all that the colored race demanded was a guarantee of civil rights, and social equality would then take care of itself. What they asked was only civil equality. He set forth the improbabilities that the colored people, from their very nature, would be changed from that docile and sub-missive attitude which they maintained during the absence of their masters at the war, into the wolves and tigers which they are represented to be by some of the white people of the South, and the probabilities that their masters, inflamed by their resentment that their former human chattels were now American citizens, and in some instances holding offices, were purposely defaming the character of the negro, in order thereby to reduce the colored people as nearly as possible to a state of slavery.

Now, I ask you my friends, to protect these men. Not with guns. There is a better way than that. I do not ask you to shoulder your muskets and to go down South. You can protect them, if you like, by your moral influence, by the power exerted by your ballots,—for every Democratic victory costs the warm, dripping blood of my people, while every victory of the Republican party helps to protect them in their little homes. When you vote for the Republican party, you are doing something not merely for New Hampshire, but for the whole Union; your vote either stanches the quick running blood of the persecuted negro, or it opens new wounds in his body to bleed afresh.

Thirty years ago, when I appealed to you for the American slave, your sympathies were kindled, your moral indignation aroused, and your voice went forth, and slavery fell. I come to ask for the same sympathy now, but with additional claims. When the cloud of battle lowered upon the country, and threatened to overwhelm us with defeat and disaster, Abraham Lincoln called upon the negro to advance; and they came 200,000 strong, to the defence of the flag. Not only because our cause is just, but because we did this, I am emboldened to ask you that the liberty which you gave us in your justice and magnanimity, you will now defend and protect, and maintain to the end. Stand by us. I believe you will. I know you will. I feel it in my bones. I was at Lancaster last night. The people were there. I was at Manchester two nights ago. The people were there. I am at Concord to-night, and the people are here. (Loud cheers.) We have watered your soil with our tears, drenched it with our blood, and tilled it with our hard hands, and fought for your country, and we only ask to be treated as American citizens; to be treated as well as those who fought against you. Don't punish your friends and reward your enemies; don't lavish all your love upon those who sought to cut the throat of the republic, but reserve a little for those who tried to save it to the extent of their ability. (Loud and prolonged applause.) . . .

———

The next year, on March 13, 1876, Douglass met with a number of blacks to honor P. B. S. Pinchback, a black Louisiana Republican whose election had been nullified by the U.S. Senate. Despite that action, Douglass counseled support of the Republican party.

. . . The Republican party is still the party of justice and freedom. It is, relatively, the black man's party. Compare them in this wise, the one is heaven and the other is hell. For one, I shall stand by the party of Sumner and Lincoln. If justice and protection is not obtained here I do not look for it elsewhere. The logic which would make us quit a roof with seven small holes in it in exchange for the open field and the pitiless storm is not the logic for me. Some talk about dividing our votes between the two parties has come to my notice of late. It has not made much impression upon me.

If We Do This We May Expect to Fall;

for between two stools—you know the rest. It is argued that such a course would deprive the Democratic party of all motive for keeping up its crusade against us. Granting that such would be the case, it equally follows that it would deprive the Republican party of all motive for a vigilant and determined effort to protect us in our rights. I make these remarks because the Democratic press seems willing enough to seize every occasion to destroy the colored man's confidence in the Republican party, at the same time that its own party is doing its utmost to reduce us again to something akin to the hateful condition of bondage from which we have been so recently delivered.

I am not a very sensitive man, but I already feel here in Washington the baneful effects of Democratic ascendancy in one branch of the National Legislature, and I ask colored men to consider what would be the state of things if that party had all the branches of the Government in its hands. I am not among those who think the American people are now going to put this Government back into the hands of the party of rebellion and slavery: nor do I despair of the ultimate peace and freedom of my race. But one thing I know, and that is, there is no middle ground for us. We must either have all the rights of American citizens or we must be exterminated, for we never can again be slaves. Nor can we cease to trouble the American people while any right enjoyed by others is denied or withheld from us. . . .

In the summer of 1876 the Republican party's convention to nominate a president and vice president met in Cincinnati, Ohio. At the end of the day, Douglass stepped up to the speaker's platform and spoke on the issue dearest to him — preserving the rights of the freedmen. He was constantly interrupted with cheers and applause. It was a speech that came from the heart.

Mr. Chairman and Gentlemen of the National Convention: Allow me to express my deep, my heartfelt gratitude to you for the warm, cordial invitation you have extended to me to make my appearance on this platform at this time. The work to which you have called me is somewhat new; it is the first time in my life that I have ever had the pleasure of looking the Republican Party squarely in the face (applause and laughter), and I must say, and I hope you will acquit me of everything like a disposition to flatter, that you are pretty good looking men. (Laughter and applause.) But I will not detain you here by any attempt at a speech. You have had speeches, eloquent speeches, glorious speeches, wise speeches, patriotic speeches, speeches in respect of the importance of managing correctly your currency, speeches in defense of purity of administration, and speeches in respect of the great principles for which you struggled, and for which the race to which I belong struggled on the battle-field and poured out their blood. (Cheers.)

The thing, however, in which I feel the deepest interest, and the thing in which I believe this country feels the deepest interest is that the principles involved in the contest which carried your sons and brothers to the battle-field, which draped our Northern churches with the weeds of mourning and filled our towns and our cities with mere stumps of men, armless, legless, maimed, and mutilated—the thing for which you poured out your blood and piled a debt for after-coming generations higher than a mountain of gold to weigh down the necks of your children and your children's children—I say those principles involved in that tremendous contest are to be dearer to the American people in the great political struggle now upon them than any other principles we have. (Applause and cheers.)

∞ FURTHER PROTECTION ∞ DEMANDED.

You have emancipated us. I thank you for it. You have enfranchised us, and I thank you for it. But what is your emancipation—what is your enfranchisement? What does it all amount to, if the black man, after having been made free by the letter of your law, is unable to exercise that freedom; and after having been freed from the slaveholders' lash he is to be subject to the slaveholder's shotgun? (Cheers.) Oh, you freed us; you emancipated us; I thank you for it; but under what circumstances did you emancipate us? Under what circumstances have we obtained our freedom? Sir, our case is the most extraordinary case of any people ever emancipated on the globe. I sometimes wonder that we still exist as a people in this country; that we have not all been swept out of existence, and nothing left to show that we had ever existed. Look at it! When the Israelites were emancipated, they were told to go and borrow of their neighbors—borrow their corn, borrow their jewels—load themselves down with the means of subsistence after they should go free in the land which the Lord God gave them. When the Russian serfs had their chains broken and were given their liberty, the Government of Russia—aye, the despotic Government of Russia—gave to these poor emancipated serfs a few acres of land on which they could live and earn their bread; but when you turned us loose, you gave us none. You turned us loose to the sky, to the storm, to the whirlwind, and, worst of all, you turned us loose to the wrath of our infuriated masters. (Applause.)

The question now is, do you mean to make good the promises in your Constitution? Talk not to me of finance. Talk not of mere reform in your administration. (Applause.) I believe there is honesty in the American people—honesty in the men whom you elect—wisdom in the men to manage those affairs; but tell me, if your hearts be as my heart, that the liberty which you have asserted for the black man in this country shall be maintained! (Applause.) You say, some of you, that you can get along without the vote of the black man of the South. Yes, that may be possible, but I doubt it. At any rate we, in order to secure our protection hereafter, feel the need, in the candidate whom you will place before the country, of the assurance that the black man shall walk to the ballot-box in safety, even if we have to bring a bayonet behind us. (Applause.) And I have these feelings—without bringing forth either of the gentlemen named here—that the Government of the United States and the moral feeling of this country will surround the black voter as by a wall of fire, and instead of electing your President without the black vote you may count in the number of your victorious Republican States, five or six at least of the old master States of the South. (Cheers.) . . .

Joseph Rainey

During the Forty-Third Congress three black congressmen and one black senator continued their efforts to secure "equal rights and equal political privileges for all." Arguing for a deeper commitment to civil rights protection, they believed that the interests of both blacks and whites were the same. No longer was the United States white man's land. The challenge was for the two races to work together to achieve progress, education, and civilization in the South and across the country.

On December 19, 1873, Joseph Rainey entered the debate on the Civil Rights Bill. Referring to promises made by some white Republicans in the last session, he asked that these promises be honored and that the bill be passed as soon as possible.

Mr. Speaker, I did not expect to participate in this debate at this early period; and I would have preferred to wait until I should have had a full exposition of the opinions entertained by the other side of the House. I know, sir, that gentlemen on the other side have professed a great deal of friendship for the race to which I belong; and in the last presidential election they pledged themselves that they would accord to the negroes of this country all the rights that were given to other citizens. I am somewhat surprised to perceive that on this occasion, when the demand is made upon Congress by the people to guarantee those rights to a race heretofore oppressed, we should find gentlemen on the other side taking another view of the case from that which they professed in the past. The gentleman from Kentucky [Mr. BECK] has taken a legal view of this question, and he is undoubtedly capable of taking that view. I am not a lawyer, and consequently I cannot take a legal view of this matter, or perhaps I cannot view it through the same optics that he does. I view it in the light of the Constitution—in the light of the amendments that have been made to that Constitution; I view it in the light of humanity; I view it in the light of the progress and civilization which are now rapidly marching over this country. We, sirs, would not ask of this Congress as a people that they should legislate for us specifically as a class if we could only have those rights which this bill is designed to give us accorded us without this enactment. I can very well understand the opposition to this measure by gentlemen on the other side of the House, and especially of those who come from the South. They have a feeling against the negro in this country that I suppose will never die out. They have an antipathy against that race of people, because of their loyalty to this Government, and because at the very time when they were needed to show their manhood and valor they came forward in defense of the flag of the country and assisted in crushing out the rebellion. They, sir, would not give to the colored man the right to vote or the right to enjoy any of those immunities which are enjoyed by other citizens, if it had a tendency to make him feel his manhood and elevate him above the ordinary way of life. So long as he makes himself content with ordinary gifts, why it is all well; but when he aspires to be a man, when he seeks to have the rights accorded him that other citizens of the country enjoy, then he is asking too much, and such gentlemen as the gentleman from Kentucky are not willing to grant it. . . .

Now, gentlemen, let me say the negro is not asking social equality. We do not ask it of you, we do not ask of the gentleman from Kentucky that the two races should intermarry one with the other. God knows we are perfectly content. I can say for myself that I am contented to be what I am so long as I have my rights; I am contented to marry one of my own complexion, and do not seek intercourse with any other race, because I believe that the race of people I represent, to the extent of the opportunities which they have had, and considering how recently they have escaped from the oppression and wrongs committed upon them, are just as virtuous and hold just as many high characteristics as any class in the country. I think the statistics will prove that there is as much virtue among the negroes as among the whites. Sir, we are not seeking to be put on a footing of social equality. I prefer to choose my own associates, and all my colleagues here and the whole race I belong to prefer to make that choice. We do not ask the passage of any law forcing us upon anybody who does not want to receive us. But we do want a law enacted that we may be recognized like other men in the country. Why is it that colored members of Congress cannot enjoy the same immunities that are accorded to white members? Why cannot we stop at hotels here without meeting objection? Why cannot we go into restaurants without being insulted? We are here enacting laws for the country and casting votes upon important questions; we have been sent here by the suffrages of the people, and why cannot we enjoy the same benefits that are accorded to our white colleagues on this floor? . . .

I say to you, gentlemen, that you are making a mistake. Public opinion is aroused on this question. I tell you that the negro will never rest until he gets his rights. We ask them because we know it is proper, not because we want to deprive any other class of the rights and immunities they enjoy, but because they are granted to us by the law of the land. Why this discrimination against us when we enter public conveyances or places of public amusement? Why is a discrimination made against us in the churches; and why in the cemeteries when we go to pay that last debt of nature that brings us all upon a level?

Gentlemen, I say to you this discrimination must cease. We are determined to fight this question; we believe the Constitution gives us this right. All of the fifteen amendments made to the Constitution run down in one single line of protecting the rights of the citizens of this country. One after another of those amendments give these rights to citizens; step by step these rights are secured to them. And now we say to you that if you will not obey the Constitution, then the power is given by that Constitution for the enactment of such a law as will have a tendency to enforce the provisions thereof. . . .

Richard Cain

Several weeks later Congressman Richard Cain of South Carolina argued that the proposed Civil Rights Bill would simply put the black man on the same footing with white men. To those who argued that blacks were already treated equally, he provided evidence to the contrary.

Sir, the gentleman [Mr. VANCE.] states that in the State of North Carolina the colored people enjoy all their rights as far as the highways are concerned; that in the hotels, and in the railroad cars, and in the various public places of resort, they have all the rights and all the immunities accorded to any other class of citizens of the United States. Now, it may not have come under his observation, but it has under mine, that such really is not the case; and the reason why I know and feel it more than he does is because my face is painted black and his is painted white. We who have the color—I may say the objectionable color—know and feel all this. A few days ago, in passing from South Carolina to this city, I entered a place of public resort where hungry men are fed, but I did not dare—I could not without trouble—sit down to the table. I could not sit down at Wilmington or at Weldon without entering into a contest, which I did not desire to do. My colleague, the gentleman who so eloquently spoke on this subject the other day [Mr. ELLIOTT.] a few months ago entered a restaurant at Wilmington and sat down to be served, and while there a gentleman stepped up to him and said, "You cannot eat here." All the other gentlemen upon the railroad as passengers were eating there; he had only twenty minutes, and was compelled to leave the restaurant or have a fight for it. He showed fight, however, and got his dinner; but he has never been back there since. Coming here last week I felt we did not desire to draw revolvers and present the bold front of warriors, and therefore we ordered our dinners to be brought into the cars, but even there we found the existence of this feeling; for although we had paid a dollar apiece for our meals, to be brought by the servants into the cars, still there was objection on the part of the railroad people to our eating our meals in the cars, because they said we were putting on airs. They refused us in the restaurant, and then did not desire that we should eat our meals in the cars, although we paid for them. Yet this was in the noble State of North Carolina.

Mr. Speaker, the colored men of the South do not want the adoption of any force measure. No; they do not want anything by force. All they ask is that you will give them, by statutory enactment under the fundamental law, the right to enjoy precisely the same privileges accorded to every other class of citizens. . . .

════════

Two weeks later, on January 24, 1874, Cain again defended the place of blacks in the South, arguing that it was time to settle this racial question "for all time."

The gentleman wishes that we should prepare ourselves to go to Africa, or to the West Indies, or somewhere else. I want to enunciate this doctrine upon this floor—you have brought us here, and here we are going to stay. [Applause.] We are not going one foot or one inch from this land. Our mothers and our fathers and our grandfathers and great-grandfathers have died here. Here we have sweated. Here we have toiled. Here we have made this country great and rich by our labor and toil. It is mean in you now to want to drive us away, after having taken all our toil for two hundred years. Just think of the magnitude of these gentlemen's hearts. After having taken all our toil for two hundred years; after having sold our wives and children like so many cattle in the shambles; after having reared the throne of great king cotton on our labors; after we have made their rice-fields wave with luxuriant harvests while they were fighting against the Government and keeping us in bondage—now we are free they want us to go away. Shame on you! [Applause.]

Now, Mr. Speaker, we are not going away. We are going to stay here. We propose to stay here and work out this problem. We believe that God Almighty has made of one blood all the nations upon the face of the earth. We believe we are made just like white men are. [Laughter.] Look: I stretch out my arms. See; I have two of them, as you have. Look at your ears; I have two of them. I have two eyes, two nostrils, one mouth, two feet. I stand erect like you. I am clothed with humanity like you. I think, I reason, I talk, I express my views, as you do. Is there any difference between us? No so far as our manhood is concerned, unless it be in this: that our opinions differ, and mine are a little higher up than yours. [Laughter.]

The gentleman states that this idea of all men being created equal is a fallacy, announced some years ago by Thomas Jefferson, that old fool-hardy man, who announced so many ideas that have been woven into the woof of the nation, who announced so many foolish things that have made this nation strong, and great, and powerful. Sir, if he was in error, I accept the error with pleasure. If he was a foolish man, I would to God that North Carolina had been baptized in that foolishness about two hundred years ago. [Great laughter.]

The gentleman also states that if you pass this bill your power over the South will pass away; that the power of the republican party in the South will pass away. Sir, let me tell the gentleman that behind this bill are nine hundred thousand voters; that, like the warriors of the tribe of Benjamin, every one of them is left-handed and can "sling a stone at a hair's breadth;" that each will come up stronger and mightier and more infused with power than ever before when you pass this bill giving them their rights, as other men have them. They will come up as never before to the support of the republican party, and they will make the South a source of joy and gladness.

The gentleman also talks about the colored people deteriorating. Sir, who tills your lands now? Who plants your corn? Who raises your cotton? I have been in the South during the last ten years. I have traveled over the Southern States, and have seen who did this work. Going along I saw the white men do the smoking, chewing tobacco, riding horses, playing cards, spending money, while the colored men are tilling the soil, and bringing the cotton, rice, and other products to market.

Sir, I do not believe the gentleman from North Carolina wants us to go to Africa; I do not believe it. It was a slip of the tongue; he does not mean that the black people should leave North Carolina; not a bit of it. If they did you would see such an exodus of white people from that State as you never saw before, for they would follow them wherever they might go. [Laughter.]

Sir, we feel that we are part and parcel of this great nation; and as such, as I said before, we propose to stay here and solve this problem of whether the black race and the white race can live together in this country. I make the statement that I regard it as essential to their welfare and interests that they should live together in this country. Why not? I can see no reason why not, if they contribute their quota to the advancement of progress and civilization. Sir, the mechanics of the South are almost altogether colored people. The carpenters, the machinists, the engineers—nearly all the mechanics in the Southern States are colored people. Why can we not stay here and work out this problem?

I ask Congress to pass this bill for the reason that it would settle this question, once and forever. The gentleman says that he does not desire that the colored people shall be crowded into the schools of the white people. Well, I do not think that they would be harmed by it; some few of them might be. But experience has taught us that it is not true that great harm will come from any such measure. I think, therefore, that if we pass this bill we will be doing a great act of justice, we will settle for all time the question of the rights of all people. And until that question is settled there cannot be that peace and harmony in the country that is necessary to its success.

The gentleman says the colored people and the white people are living together now in North Carolina in amicable relations. I am glad for that admission, for he rounded off all that he had said before by that last sentence. He said that the two races could not live together, and yet at the close of his speech he says that the whites and blacks are now living in North Carolina in amicable relations. Sir, if they are so living now, why not hereafter? Will peace and good order be destroyed because all are to have their rights? Sir, I do not think so.

I close with this thought: I believe the time is coming when the Congress of the United States, when the whole nation, will recognize the importance of the passage of this bill in order to settle this question once and forever. I regard the interests of the black man in this country as identical with the interests of the white man. I would have that set forth so clearly and unmistakably that there should be no antagonism between the races, no friction that should destroy their peace and prosperity. I believe Almighty God has placed both races on this broad theater of activity, where thoughts and opinions are freely expressed, where we may grasp every idea of manhood, where we may take hold of every truth and develop every art and science that can advance the prosperity of the nation. I believe God designed us to live here together on this continent, and in no other place, to develop this great idea that all men are the children of one Father. We are here to work out the grand experiment of the homogeneity of nations, the grand outburst of the greatness of humanity, by the development in us of the rights that belong to us, and the performance of the duties that we owe each other.

Our interests are bound up in this country. Here we intend to stay and work out the problem of progress and education and civilization. I say to the gentleman from North Carolina, [Mr. ROBBINS,] and to the gentleman from Virginia, [Mr. HARRIS,] and to the gentleman from New York, [Mr. cox,] who discussed civil rights the other day, and to gentlemen from the other States, that we are going to remain in this country side by side with the white race. We desire to share in your prosperity and to stand by you in adversity. In advancing the progress of the nation we will take our part; and if the country should again be involved in the devastation of war, we will do our part in the struggle. We propose to identify ourselves with this nation, which has done more than any other on earth to illustrate the great idea that all races of men may dwell together in harmony, working out together the problem of advancement and civilization and liberty.

Mr. Speaker, we will drive the buzzard away; we will scare the crow back to North Carolina. We will take the eagle as the emblem of liberty; we will take that honored flag which has been borne through the heat of a thousand battles. Under its folds Anglo-Saxon and Africo-American can together work out a common destiny, until universal liberty, as announced by this nation, shall be known throughout the world.

James Rapier

On June 9, 1874, Congressman James Rapier made arguments similar to those of his black colleagues, urging that after seven years of debating, it was time to pass the Civil Rights Bill.

Mr. Speaker . . . I must confess it is somewhat embarrassing for a colored man to urge the passage of this bill, because if he exhibit an earnestness in the matter and express a desire for its immediate passage, straight-way he is charged with a desire for social equality, as explained by the demagogue and understood by the ignorant white man. But then it is just as embarrassing for him not to do so, for, if he remain silent while the struggle is being carried on around, and for him, he is liable to be charged with a want of interest in a matter that concerns him more than any one else, which is enough to make his friends desert his cause. So in steering away from Scylla I may run upon Charybdis. But the anomalous, and I may add the supremely ridiculous, position of the negro at this time, in this country, compel[s] me to say something. Here his condition is without a comparison, parallel alone to itself. Just think that the law recognizes my right upon this floor as a law-maker, but that there is no law to secure to me any accommodations whatever while traveling here to discharge my duties as a Representative of a large and wealthy constituency. Here I am the peer of the proudest, but on a steamboat or car I am not equal to the most degraded. Is not this most anomalous and ridiculous? . . .

Let me cite a case. Not many months ago Mr. Cardoza, treasurer of the State of South Carolina, was on his way home from the West. His route lay through Atlanta. There he made request for a sleeping-berth. Not only was he refused this, but was denied a seat in a first-class carriage, and the parties went so far as to threaten to take his life because he insisted upon his rights as a traveler. He was compelled, a most elegant and accomplished gentleman, to take a seat in a dirty smoking-car, along with the traveling rabble, or else be left, to the detriment of his public duties.

I affirm, without the fear of contradiction, that any white ex-convict (I care not what may have been his crime, nor whether the hair on the shaven side of his head has had time to grow out or not) may start with me to-day to Montgomery, that all the way down he will be treated as a gentleman, while I will be treated as the convict. He will be allowed a berth in a sleeping-car with all its comforts, while I will be forced into a dirty, rough box with the drunkards, apple-sellers, railroad hands, and next to any dead that may be in transit, regardless of how far decomposition may have progressed. Sentinels are placed at the doors of the better coaches, with positive instructions to keep persons of color out; and I must do them the justice to say that they guard these sacred portals with a vigilance that would have done credit to the flaming swords at the gates of Eden. Tender, pure, intelligent young ladies are forced to travel in this way if they are guilty of the crime of color, the only unpardonable sin known in our Christian and Bible lands, where sinning against the Holy Ghost (whatever that may be) sinks into insignificance when compared with the sin of color. If from any cause we are compelled to lay over, the best bed in the hotel is his if he can pay for it, while I am invariably turned away, hungry and cold, to stand around the railway station until the departure of the next train, it matters not how long, thereby endangering my health, while my life and property are at the mercy of any highwayman who may wish to murder and rob me.

And I state without the fear of being gainsaid . . . that there is not an inn between Washington and Montgomery, a distance of more than a thousand miles, that will accommodate me to a bed or meal. Now, then, is there a man upon this floor who is so heartless, whose breast is so void of the better feelings, as to say that this brutal custom needs no regulation? I hold that it does and that Congress is the body to regulate it. . . .

————————

At the end of his address, Rapier argued that as a man and a citizen, he could not accept less than equal treatment.

Mr. Speaker, nothing short of a complete acknowledgment of my manhood will satisfy me. I have no compromises to make, and shall unwillingly accept any. If I were to say that I would be content with less than any other member upon this floor I would forfeit whatever respect any one here might entertain for me, and would thereby furnish the best possible evidence that I do not and cannot appreciate the rights of a freeman. Just what I am charged with by my political enemies. I cannot willingly accept anything less than my full measure of rights as a man, because I am unwilling to present myself as a candidate for the brand of inferiority, which will be as plain and lasting as the mark of Cain. If I am to be thus branded, the country must do it against my solemn protest. . . .

After all, this question resolves itself to this: either I am a man or I am not a man.

If one, I am entitled to all the rights, privileges, and immunities common to any other class in this country; if not a man, I have no right to vote, no right to a seat here; if no right to vote, then 20 per cent of the members on this floor have no right here, but, on the contrary, hold their seats *in violation of law.* If the negro has no right to vote, then one-eighth of your Senate consists of members who have no shadow of a claim to the places they occupy; and if no right to a vote, a half-dozen governors in the South figure as usurpers. . . .

I ask for the passage of the civil-rights bill before we shall adjourn. We ask it as a measure of justice to those people who have been true to the nation and to the party in power. We ask it at the hands of President Grant and the republican party. We ask it too, sir, as a matter of sound public policy in the interest of the republican party and the country. To say that the intelligent colored people are not desiring this measure is, sir, I repeat, adding insult to injury. We ask it: we are not in a position to demand it. We plead for it respectfully, but in no uncertain voice, and confidently look for its early passage.

Blanche K. Bruce

Blanche K. Bruce became the second black man to serve as a senator from Mississippi. He was selected by the Mississippi legislature for a six-year term on February 4, 1874, and assumed the position thirteen months later on March 5, 1875. Bruce was the only black senator for the next six years. For several months he kept a low profile. However, on March 31, a resolution to investigate the Mississippi election of 1875 reached the floor of the Senate. Having observed firsthand the fraud and violence of this election, Bruce rose to his feet to speak in favor of the creation of a five-man committee to investigate the election. He firmly believed that this would lead to a reversal of the election results. His speech may have tipped the balance. The measure passed.

M r. President, I had hoped that no occasion would arise to make it necessary for me again to claim the attention of the Senate until at least I had acquired a larger acquaintance with its methods of business and a fuller experience in public affairs; but silence at this time would be infidelity to my senatorial trust and unjust to both the people and the State I have the honor in part to represent.

The conduct of the late election in Mississippi affected not merely the fortunes of partisans—as the same were necessarily involved in the defeat or success of the respective parties to the contest—but put in question and jeopardy the sacred rights of the citizen; and the investigation contemplated in the pending resolution has for its object not the determination of the question whether the offices shall be held and the public affairs of that State be administered by democrats or republicans, but the higher and more important end, the protection in all their purity and significance of the political rights of the people and the free institutions of the country. I believe the action sought is within the legitimate province of the Senate . . .

The truth of the allegations relative to fraud and violence is strongly suggested by the very success claimed by the democracy. In 1873 the republicans carried the State by 20,000 majority; in November last the opposition claimed to have carried it by 30,000; thus a democratic gain of more than 50,000. Now, by what miraculous or extraordinary interposition was this brought about? I can conceive that a large State like New York, where free speech and free press operate upon intelligent masses— a State full of railroads, telegraphs, and newspapers—on the occasion of a great national contest, might furnish an illustration of such a thorough and general change in the political views of the people; but such a change of front is unnatural and highly improbable in a State like my own, with few railroads, and a widely scattered and sparse population. Under the most active and friendly canvass the voting masses could not have been so rapidly and thoroughly reached as to have rendered this result probable.

There was nothing in the character of the issues nor in the method of the canvass that would produce such an overwhelming revolution in the sentiments of the colored voters of the State as is implied in this pretended democratic success. The republicans—nineteen twentieths of whom are colored—were not brought, through the press or public discussions, in contact with democratic influences to such an extent as would operate a change in their political convictions, and there was nothing in democratic sentiments nor in the proscriptive and violent temper of their leaders to justify such a change of political relations. . . .

The evidence in hand and accessible will show beyond peradventure that in many parts of the State corrupt and violent influences were brought to bear upon the registrars of voters, thus materially affecting the character of the voting or poll lists; upon the inspectors of election, prejudicially and unfairly thereby changing the number of votes cast; and, finally, threats and violence were practiced directly upon the masses of voters in such measure and strength as to produce grave apprehensions for their personal safety, and as to deter them from the exercise of their political franchises.

Lawless outbreaks have not been confined to any particular section of the country, but have prevailed in nearly every State at some period in its history. But the violence complained of and exhibited in Mississippi and other Southern States, pending a political canvass, is exceptional and peculiar. It is not the blow that the beggared miner strikes that he may give bread to his children, nor the stroke of the bondsman that he may win liberty for himself, nor the mad turbulence of the ignorant masses when their passions have been stirred by the appeals of the demagogue; but it is an attack by an aggressive, intelligent, white political organization upon inoffensive, law-abiding fellow-citizens; a violent method for political supremacy, that seeks not the protection of the rights of the aggressors, but the destruction of the rights of the party assailed. Violence so unprovoked, inspired by such motives, and looking to such ends, is a spectacle not only discreditable to the country, but dangerous to the integrity of our free institutions. . . .

———————

Despite the continuing attacks upon the record of the freedmen during radical Reconstruction, Bruce believed that considerable progress had been made. The state debt and taxes had been reduced, and the judicial record compared favorably with previous tribunals under conservative white control. The evidence of success was in his eyes "creditable and hopeful."

A notable feature of the outrages alleged is that they have referred almost exclusively to the colored citizens of the State. Why is the colored voter to be proscribed? Why direct the attack upon him? While the methods of violence, resorted to for political purposes in the South, are foreign to the genius of our institutions as applied to citizens generally—and so much is conceded by even the opposition—yet they seem to think we are an exceptional class and citizens, rather by sufferance than right; and when pressed to account for their bitterness and proscription toward us they, with more or less boldness, allege incompetent and bad government as their justification before the public opinion of the country. Now, I declare that neither political incapacity nor venality are qualities of the masses of colored citizens. The emancipation of the colored race during the late civil strife was an expression alike of the magnanimity and needs of the nation; and the subsequent and early subtraction of millions of industrial values from the resources of the insurrectionary States and the presence of many thousand additional brave hearts and strong hands around the flag of the country vindicated the justice and wisdom of the measure.

The close of the war found four millions of freedmen, without homes or property, charged with the duty of self-support and with the oversight of their personal freedom, yet without civil and political rights! The problem presented by this condition of things was one of the gravest that has ever been submitted to the American people. Shall these liberated millions of a separate race, while retaining personal liberty, be deprived of political rights? The practical sense of the American people definitely settled this delicate and difficult question, and the demand for a more pronounced loyal element in the work of reconstruction in the lately rebellious States furnished an opportunity for the recognition of the political rights of the race, both in the interest of justice and good government.

The history of my race since enfranchisement, considered in connection with the difficulties that have environed us, will exhibit hopeful progress and attest that we have been neither ungrateful for the civil and political privileges received nor wanting in appreciation of the correspondingly weighty obligations imposed upon us. . . .

. . . we began our political career under the disadvantages of the inexperience in public affairs that generations of enforced bondage had entailed upon our race. We suffered also from the vicious leadership of some of the men whom our necessities forced us temporarily to accept. Consider further that the States of the South, where we were supposed to control by our majorities, were in an impoverished and semi-revolutionary condition—society demoralized, the industries of the country prostrated, the people sore, morbid, and sometimes turbulent, and no healthy controlling public opinion either existent or possible—consider all these conditions, and it will be seen that we began our political novitiate and formed the organic and statutory laws under great embarrassments.

Despite the difficulties and drawbacks suggested, the constitutions formed under colored majorities, whatever their defects may be, were improvements on the instruments they were designed to supersede; and the statutes framed, though necessarily defective because of the crude and varying social and industrial conditions upon which they were based, were more in harmony with the spirit of the age and the genius of our free institutions than the obsolete laws that they supplanted. Nor is there just or any sufficient grounds upon which to charge an oppressive administration of the laws.

The State debt proper is less than a half million dollars and the State taxes are light. Nor can complaint be reasonably made of the judiciary. The records of the supreme judicial tribunal of the State will show, in 1859–'60, 266 decisions in cases of appeal from the lower courts, of which 169 were affirmed and 97 reversed. In 1872–'73 the records show 328 decisions rendered in cases of appeal from below, of which 221 were affirmed and 107 reversed; and in 1876, of appeals from chancellors, appointed by Governor Ames, up to date, 41 decisions have been rendered, of which 33 were affirmed and 8 reversed. This exhibit, whether of legislation or administration, shows there has been no adequate provocation to revolution and no justification for violence in Mississippi. That we should have made mistakes, under the circumstances, in measures of both legislation and administration, was natural, and that we have had any success is both creditable and hopeful. . . .

———————

Bruce's plea was not for new laws; rather it was for enforcement of those laws already on the books. After such enforcement was carried out, he was hopeful for the future of the South.

We simply demand the practical recognition of the rights given us in the Constitution and laws, and ask from our white fellow-citizens only the consideration and fairness that we so willingly extend to them. Let them generally realize and concede that citizenship imports to us what it does to them, no more and no less, and impress the colored people that a party defeat does not imperil their political franchise. Let them cease their attempts to coerce our political co-operation, and invite and secure it by a policy so fair and just as to commend itself to our judgment, and resort to no motive or measure to control us that self-respect would preclude their applying to themselves. When we can entertain opinions and select party affiliations without proscription, and cast our ballots as other citizens and without jeopardy to person or privilege, we can safely afford to be governed by the considerations that ordinarily determine the political action of American citizens. But we must be guaranteed in the unproscribed exercise of our honest convictions and be absolutely, from within or without, protected in the use of our ballot before we can either wisely or safely divide our vote. In union, not division, is strength, so long as White League proscription renders division of our vote impracticable by making a difference of opinion opprobrious and an antagonism in politics a crime. On the other hand, if we should, from considerations of fear, yield to the shot-gun policy of our opponents, the White League might win a temporary success, but the ultimate

result would be disastrous to both races, for they would first become aggressively turbulent, and we, as a class, would become servile, unreliable, and worthless. . . .

I have confidence, not only in my country and her institutions, but in the endurance, capacity, and destiny of my people. We will, as opportunity offers and ability serves, seek our places, sometimes in the field of letters, arts, sciences, and the
professions. More frequently mechanical pursuits will attract and elicit our efforts;
more still of my people will find employment and livelihood as the cultivators of the
soil. The bulk of this people—by surroundings, habits, adaptation, and choice—will
continue to find their homes in the South, and constitute the masses of its yeomanry.
We will there probably, of our own volition and more abundantly than in the past,
produce the great staples that will contribute to the basis of foreign exchange, aid
in giving the nation a balance of trade, and minister to the wants and comfort and
build up the prosperity of the whole land. Whatever our ultimate position in the
composite civilization of the Republic and whatever varying fortunes attend our career, we will not forget our instincts for freedom nor our love of country. Guided and
guarded by a beneficent Providence, and living under the genial influence of liberal
institutions, we have no apprehensions that we shall fail from the land from attrition
with other races, or ignobly disappear from either the politics or industries of the
country.

Mr. President, allow me here to say that, although many of us are uneducated in
the schools, we are informed and advised as to our duties to the Government, our
State, and ourselves. Without class prejudice or animosities, with obedience to authority as the lesson and love of peace and order as the passion of our lives, with
scrupulous respect for the rights of others, and with the hopefulness of political
youth, we are determined that the great Government that gave us liberty, and rendered its gift valuable by giving us the ballot, shall not find us wanting in a sufficient
response to any demand that humanity or patriotism may make upon us; and we ask
such action as will not only protect us in the enjoyment of our constitutional rights,
but will preserve the integrity of our republican institutions.

Joseph Rainey

*During the last days of the Forty-Fourth Congress, Congressman Rainey made two speeches
in defense of the use of federal troops to ensure a fair election in South Carolina in 1876.
Charges had been leveled by Democrats that these troops prevented them from casting their
votes. On February 21, 1877, Rainey vigorously denied this charge and contended that the
danger to free exercise of personal freedom and political rights was so apparent that President Grant had no choice but to order federal troops to monitor the election.*

      I am well aware of and fully appreciate the great doctrine of our re-
publican form of government, namely, that the military must be subordinate to the

civil power, especially in times of peace. I know how deeply rooted this principle is in the hearts of the American people and how justly and properly they boast of this distinguishing feature of its fundamental law. But there are other principles of still greater importance and more essential to the perpetuity of our Government, and these are: that the citizens should enjoy their personal liberty and exercise fully and freely their political rights. This, Mr. Speaker, I regard as the first and most important duty of any government, without which no government is worth perpetuation. The framers of the Constitution comprehended the importance of this protection and provided for its exercise under certain conditions. These conditions existed in South Carolina, and the President, having been called upon by the executive of the State in accordance with the requirements of the Constitution placed the military forces of the Government in the State for the protection of life and liberty in the exercise of political rights.

The only question, it seems to me, that can properly engage our attention is this: Did the circumstances justify the action of the President in sending the troops to South Carolina? I answer the question in the affirmative, and will now proceed to state some of the reasons why I am of that opinion. There was a riot at Hamburgh last summer which has become known far and wide; the cold-blooded atrocity in shooting unarmed prisoners has awakened a just feeling of horror and indignation in every manly breast. That riot was looked upon in South Carolina by those who understood the true condition of the State as being of great political significance, on account of the time at which it occurred and the parties engaged in it, especially those controlling the affair. That riot was the key-note of the campaign. There were several political meetings held soon afterward by the republicans of Edgefield, Newberry, Abbeville, and Barnwell Counties whereat the governor of the State addressed the people on the political topics of the day. At these meetings there were large organized bodies of white democratic citizens, fully armed, who participated in, and in some cases took absolute possession of, the affair, and who by their violent harangues and threatening demonstrations plainly indicated that they intended to overawe and intimidate the republican citizens in the exercise of their political rights. These facts are notorious. It was this state of things that induced the governor to call upon President Grant for that protection to which every citizen of the Republic is justly entitled under the Constitution. The call was promptly responded to and troops were sent simply to preserve the peace between the contending political factions, and this was all they ever did.

I have scarcely patience to answer the charges that the presence of the troops prevented any democratic voter, or any voter at all, from voting. The charge is too absurd for serious consideration, much less refutation. Not the slightest evidence has been or can be adduced which is competent to prove such a ridiculous allegation. I cannot conceive of any one really and sincerely believing such a thing. I can and do understand politicians whose heated imaginations have been frenzied by defeat asserting such things upon insufficient proof and under such delusions who in their calmer moments would with contempt disregard all such allegations. I am perfectly well aware that the presence of troops with the well-known instructions given them exercised a great moral influence in South Carolina in preventing the democrats in that State from executing fully and effectively their carefully prepared plans for intimidating republican voters. This, I am sure, greatly exasperated them. . . .

―――――――――

Then, Rainey detailed incidents in a number of counties where Republicans were prevented from voting because of death threats. Any violations that occurred during the election were the results of actions by Democrats, not Republicans. In any fair vote, South Carolina Republicans had a substantial majority.

I do not know, Mr. Speaker, if it is necessary for me to add anything further to what I have already said, for if the unquestionable facts, here stated, fail to carry conviction to the minds of those who may somewhat differ with me on this question, then, indeed, they would not be convinced though one rose from the dead.

I have endeavored to show that there is a deep, an abiding objection to our exercise of the elective franchise, resulting from our former unfortunate condition of slavery. I have also stated that I regarded this slavery, which existed here for more than two centuries, as the primal cause of the unhappy and disturbed condition of our country, more or less, from its very foundation to the present day. I have thus proceeded, from these general remarks, into a minute and careful investigation of the charges of intimidation and fraud preferred against republicans at every election in our southern section. I have shown, I trust conclusively, that the charge of intimidation of democratic voters by the presence of United States soldiers at the polls is simply absurd and that the charge of fraud, as applied to democrats, is perfectly true. The pretended great reverence for law on the part of the democrats, by charging fraud and intimidation against the republicans, recalls to my mind these famous words:

O liberty! liberty! how many crimes are committed in thy name!

The sudden regard which these gentlemen manifest for the sacred forms of law, while ignoring justice, mercy, and truth, is enough to make one feel serious, very serious, when the future is thought of. He who spake as never man spoke has said:

Woe unto you, scribes and Pharisees, hypocrites! for ye pay tithe of mint and anise and cummin, and have omitted the weightier matters of the law, judgment, mercy, and faith: these ought ye to have done, and not to leave the other undone.

We ask only that removal of prejudice which denies us the right and privileges of citizens; that protection which every government, worth the name, is bound to give to its humblest subject; and that fairness, justice, and safety in the exercise of the ballot that make it a safeguard and bulwark of our political institutions, and not, instead thereof, an infernal machine in the hands of the newly enfranchised.

This being done, South Carolina will then be found with her sister republican States, standing steadfast for the perpetuation of our cherished institutions.

―――――――

The following week, on February 28, 1877, Rainey made his final remarks in the Forty-Fourth Congress on the election of 1876 in South Carolina. Reminding his colleagues that there had been a need for federal troops to ensure a fair election, he made one more plea for the subjugated black men and black women of the South—"I can only raise my voice, and I would do it if it were the last time I ever did it, in defense of my rights and in the interests of my oppressed people."

M̲r. Speaker, the brevity of the time allotted to me through the courtesy of the gentleman from Iowa [Mr. KASSON] to discuss this question will preclude the possibility of my entering into it as elaborately as I should have desired. This is a question in which I naturally feel a deep interest, not only on account of my State being the subject under discussion, but because I represent the constituency that has been unwarrantably assailed on this floor, and which in all the discussions appertaining to the southern question has been entirely ignored by the gentlemen on the other side of the House.

It is a matter of great surprise to me that in discussing this question the gentlemen on the other side of the House should not bear in mind or call to their recollection the fact that the Southern States are not composed now of the same voting element as they were composed of previous to the rebellion; that there has been an accession to the voting population of those States, and that that accession must necessarily have a tendency to wield an influence different from that which was wielded in the Southern States previous to the war. Sir, it is for that reason that I am here to-day; it is for that reason that I stand here to speak, not in defense of any one man, not in defense of any set of men, but to speak in defense of an enfranchised people, one and all, white and colored, in South Carolina, made to enjoy the immunities and privileges of citizens subsequent to the war.

It has been charged that on account of the military power being in South Carolina it was impossible to have a fair and honest election. That is the argument of the gentleman on the other side of the House. That was the argument before the commission yesterday. Now, if the whole of the argument as to that submitted here and submitted before the commission be taken for granted, why, sir, South Carolina was the very State in which military power should have been exercised. It has been declared that it had no government at all no government whatever. Why, sir, if it had no government, I ask you then must it not have been in a state of anarchy? And if it was in a state of anarchy, what was more essential than that that anarchy should be subdued by the strong arm of the Government? But I say that while it was not precisely in a state of anarchy, nevertheless it was so near to it in some respects that it was a godsend to my people, who were being assailed and murdered, that the Army did come down and by their presence exercise a moral influence that has saved the lives of many men in South Carolina.

I want now to say a word to the gentleman from Virginia [Mr. GOODE.]. He said that South Carolina had no voice on this floor. I say to the eloquent gentleman that I agree with him to a certain extent that she has no voice here. She has not the voice of the former slaveholder and oppressor, but she has the voice of one of the oppressed race who stands here to vindicate the rights of his people whenever an opportunity is accorded him on this floor. Sir, I am here to speak for South Carolina, and although the face of the gentleman from Virginia [Mr. GOODE.] is white and his mind cultivated and he is possessed of all the advantages belonging to his race, yet I stand here to-day and will endeavor to do my duty as one of the Representatives of South Carolina as well as I can, without comparing my record with his, or with that of Calhoun or any of the distinguished citizens of that State whose names he has mentioned here.

Sir, I love South Carolina. I am a native of the State, and, to add force to the emphasis of the argument I am trying to educe, I will take no background upon any question designed for the weal of South Carolina. I would not do anything that I believe to be wrong. I would not countenance fraud or intimidation on the part of my own people to deprive any one of their rights who was opposed to them.

But when I know we are assailed and oppressed and that attempts are made every day to drive them again under the heel of the oppressor, I can only raise my voice, and I would do it if it were the last time I ever did it, in defense of my rights and in the interests of my oppressed people.

I want to say to the democracy: Gentlemen, the colored people of the South do not hate you; they do not hate the democratic party, but I tell you that we always find our principal oppressors in that party. Therefore, we tremble with fear and apprehension when we are informed that a democrat is about to regain power, and it is for that reason that we want the State of South Carolina to-day to have a republican as governor, and rejoice that now, under the just decision rendered by the commission, we shall have a republican for President of the United States. [Applause.]

―――――――――

Reconstruction was over for these six black men. Their great hopes for its success had been replaced by feelings of sadness and resignation. John Lynch carried the banner of the Republican party for over a decade in Mississippi. As its only black congressman in the last four years of Reconstruction, he fought for and voiced black concerns but was the victim of ballot fraud in his effort for a third term. Joseph Rainey and Richard Cain of South Carolina and James Rapier of Alabama were eloquent in highlighting the continuing discrimination and the pressing need for enforcement of the Fourteenth Amendment and the civil rights laws, but they were also victims of discrimination and unable to continue their political careers. Blanche K. Bruce of Mississippi came late to the struggle for civil rights at the national level but continued his efforts until his Senate term ended in 1881; he, too, was not reelected. Frederick Douglass, the most important black leader in the country, wrote and spoke for the rights of all blacks in the South, urging the need for support of the Republican party. Unwavering in his commitment, he made an eloquent address at the Republican convention in 1876. But he, too, watched the erosion of the gains of blacks, and it deeply disturbed him. All six men could see that little could be done to reverse the policies of counter Reconstruction.

In the final analysis, however, the important decisions concerning Reconstruction and its future were not made by blacks. Instead they were made by northern white Republican politicians who had grown tired of the constant racial problems in the South. Attitudes in the North had changed, and few were prepared to argue for continuing occupation and control of the southern states. To Rutherford B. Hayes, governor of Ohio and soon to be president of the United States, the answer was the "let-alone policy"—let the South take care of its own racial problems. To veteran reporter James Pike, the answer was "the restoration of the predominance of the white population in the State [South Carolina] [that] seems to be only a question of time. . . ." The time was now at hand.

CHAPTER 12

CHANGED ATTITUDES IN THE NORTH

Republicanism has grown immoral in its old age . . .
—GEORGE TEMPLETON STRONG

George Templeton Strong, long a supporter of the Republican party and its principles, began to lose confidence in its policies. He was less certain that either of the two parties had answers to the problems now facing the country.

George Templeton Strong

June 25 [1873]. . . . There seems to be a prevalent feeling that a new party is wanted. Republicanism has grown immoral in its old age and survived much of its usefulness. But there are many thousand disgusted Republicans who remember the war times, and would as soon vote for the Devil as with the Democracy. They have no place as yet, but there are indications (at the West especially) that a new organism may be tending toward development with free trade for its vital principle.

There are signs, also, that Grant's friends are considering whether they can venture to put him up for a third term of office, and there are signs that a certain considerable number of "Democrats" would like to change the name of their party. Not that they are ashamed of it, as they ought to be, but because it is a "Scarlet Letter," and a badge of disloyalty, *incivisme,* [lack of civic responsibility] and infamy, which keeps them out of office and profit. New political combinations are almost certainly forming, but what they will be like no man knoweth. . . .

March 11 [1874]. . . . New Hampshire elections and opposition gains. Though this result is complicated with local issues, Grant's administration is losing ground, I fear. We are dissatisfied with many things, with corruption, extravagance, and Ben Butlerism at Washington, with the currency, the tariff, and the disgraceful customhouse spy system. Staunch Republicans would go over to the opposition in battalions if the opposition bore another name, but they cannot shake hands and rub noses with "Democrats" of 1860–65.

Died, Charles Sumner, an able, accomplished, and unwise man. The bludgeon of that caitiff and ruffian "Bully Brooks" made him a first-class confessor in the anti-slavery cause and has now promoted him to the dignities of martyrdom, for they say that memorable brutal assault was the remote cause of his death. But he never had much hold on the people. He was too self-conscious and, perhaps, too cultivated and scholarly for the American people. Ever since he deserted his party in 1872 he has been a lone man, out of humor with everyone, himself included. . . .

March 12. Flags at City Hall and everywhere else at half-mast in honor of Sumner. Who could have predicted this fifteen years ago? To do him justice, he shewed immense pluck in his fight for a principle when he seemed in a hopeless minority, and in enduring obloquy and hatred for its sake from all the South and half the North. . . .

March 23. . . . I am more disgusted every day with the inflationism, Butlerism, corruption, and fraud that rule at Washington. Grant is in bad hands. Were there an election tomorrow, I wouldn't vote at all.

March 24. . . . The House of Representatives by 168 to 77 inflates up to four hundred millions of greenbacks. Heaven help us! . . .

April 23. . . . *Vivat* Grant! He has vetoed the inflation bill. This veto will rank in his record with Vicksburg and Appomattox. Some say this will split the Republican party and destroy it. Never mind if it does. We want a new party founded on hard money, free trade, and home rule. Only let it *not* be called Democratic. . . .

One of Strong's greatest fears was the possible triumph of the Democratic party. He believed that a civil war might well occur if Democrats won the election of 1874. Perhaps "the good old days of 1860 have come back." At the same time, his confidence in the Republican party was rapidly disappearing, and he had few good things to say about Reconstruction in the South.

September 2. . . . Omens of "Democratic" gains this fall. God forbid the restoration of that party to power. But I should like to see the Republicans watched and menaced by a strong minority. They have enjoyed absolute undisputed control too long for their own good. Sporadic riots and lynchings among Southerners are exaggerated by the newspapers into a war of races and a reign of terror for effect on the fall elections.

In poor sorely-punished South Carolina, the doctrine of the rights of man and universal suffrage is settled by a *reductio ad absurdum* [reduced to the absurd]. Semi-brutal black voters are in a great majority and, under the leading of knaves and carpet-baggers, control the state and are sinking it into deeper ruin every day. Perhaps the unfortunate result of this experiment may open people's eyes and sooner or later bring about reaction at the North where it is sorely needed. As to South Carolina, it seems as if her white folks would have to emigrate in a body unless they can save themselves by a revolution. The nigger majority is confiscating all their property by fraudulent taxation for the benefit of political operators and demagogues, or rather "zoogogues." It may come to a war of races in bitter earnest.

September 4. . . . Southern symptoms are bad. Black spirits and white refuse to mingle for any political purposes. They distrust and hate each other worse and worse as time goes on, far worse now, I think, than nine years ago. An explosion may come any day and a social war. United States troops are ordered down to keep the peace, but they can't garrison the whole Southern country and watch thousands of square miles of powder magazine. . . .

September 16. . . . Order reigns at New Orleans, the bogus state government (so-called) having collapsed before the "White League," which will not much help the Northern "Democracy." The governments of South Carolina and Louisiana are, I fear, mere nests of corrupt carpet-baggers upheld by a brute nigger constituency. But have we here in New York any right to look down on them? Our civic rulers are, as a class, utterly base, and a Celtocracy is as bad as a niggerocracy, and in some respects worse. "When God will devast and punish a people or a kingdom . . . He bereaves them of wise, honest, and godly rulers and counsellors . . . then are the common people secure and merry, and they go on in all wilfulness. . . . Therefore, I fear the axe is laid to the root of this tree that it soon must be cut down. God of His infinite mercy, take us graciously away that we may not live to see such calamity!" Amen.

September 17. . . . Trouble not yet over in Louisiana, if it be true that Grant sides with the collapsed government and intends employing horse, foot, and dragoons to reinflate it. I don't clearly see how he can do otherwise, and there is probably not much to choose between the two gangs or factions, but we are steering close to another civil war, big or little as the case may be. . . .

October 19. . . . Western elections have disheartened the Republicans and also the third-termites, whoever they are. . . .

November 4, Wednesday. Yesterday's election was a Waterloo or Sedan to the Republicans. Total rout, North and South. General Dix was badly whipped. Some 80,000 votes changed in this state since 1872. Wickham is mayor, of course. New Jersey is Democratic, and so is the governor of Massachusetts! There has been no such discomfiture since Bull Run. One consolation is that Ben Butler's Massachusetts constituency invites him to try how the door of the house shuts from the outside and then to resume his seat by the domestic hearth. This revolution does not mean that people have changed their principles and gone over to Democracy so-called. It means that people are bored by the dullness of business ever since the panic of last year, that they are disgusted by abuses of power and bad management in Louisiana and other Southern states, by stories (half true, at least) of corruption and extravagance at Washington, and they are nervous about a "third term" and "Caesarism." . . .

November 6. . . . Election returns are painfully monotonous. As they come in more fully, they merely magnify the revolution of Tuesday. Some Northern Democrats and many downtrodden Southerners will probably misunderstand it. They will fancy that the good old days of 1860 have come back, and they will put on airs, exalt their horn, sharpen their bowie knives, and oil their revolvers. The amiable Isaiah Rynders, who crawled out into the light the other day, gave us a specimen of this kind of thing in certain rhetorical and parabolical allusions to "niggers." Very little of this would suffice to stir up an intense anti-Democratic reaction, which might possibly—and only possibly—carry Grant into a third term if he would take it. . . .

January 7 [1875]. Grant's Louisiana blunder is doing him and his friends great harm. Prominent Republicans denounce it, and indignation meetings are to be called here and elsewhere, "without distinction of party." Strange that the canny and politic Hamilton Fish can acquiesce in the wild capers of the Administration! That bold dragoon, Gen. Philip Sheridan, wants the President to proclaim all the white folk of Louisiana (except the carpet-baggers) "banditti" and to let him, General Phil, dispose of them as he did of Early and his men . . . I have stood up for Grant through evil report and good report for ten years, but he is "coming it rather too strong" now. There are reasonable people who think it Grant's deliberate purpose to stay in the White House after his term expires, if he can do so, *per fas aut nefas,* [by right or by wrong] but it seems preposterous. . . .

January 15. . . . Grant's Louisiana message is less truculent than was expected, but palliating and trying to excuse what seems a great wrong. . . .

January 20. . . . Grant has blundered again: "Federal myrmidons," that is, a squad of U.S. infantry, summarily eject the sheriff of Vicksburg from his shrievalty and install somebody else in his place. This is a cheap and easy substitute for the costly, tedious, and antiquated machinery of a *quo warranto* [writ establishing by what right one exercises an office]. But unless Grant is careful, he will be outflanked by an impeachment. . . .

March 5. . . . Congress adjourns and the sceptre departs from the hands of the Republican party. I bear the blow with resignation, for my faith in the party and in the Administration has been cooling off for some time.

Strong did not live to see the end of Reconstruction. He continued to make occasional entries in his diary until June 16, 1875. His health took a turn for the worse, and he died on July 21, 1875.

James Pike

In 1873 James Pike, veteran antislavery journalist and former ambassador to the Netherlands, visited South Carolina in order to write a series of articles on Reconstruction for the **New York Tribune.** *He completed his trip in two months (February and March). His articles were published during 1873, and his book* **The Prostrate State** *was published later the same year. Pike's writing, which was hostile to blacks, became part of the mounting evidence for a changed Reconstruction.*

Yesterday, about 4 P.M., the assembled wisdom of the State, whose achievements are illustrated on that theatre, issued forth from the State-House. About three-quarters of the crowd belonged to the African race. They were of every hue from the light octoroon to the deep black. They were such a looking body of men as might pour out of a market-house or a court-house at random in any Southern State. Every negro type and physiognomy was here to be seen, from the genteel serving-man to the rough-hewn customer from the rice or cotton field. Their dress was as varied as their countenances. . . . It is the dregs of the population habilitated in the robes of their intelligent predecessors, and asserting over them the rule of ignorance and corruption, through the inexorable machinery of a majority of numbers. It is barbarism overwhelming civilization by physical force. It is the slave rioting in the halls of his master, and putting that master under his feet . . . As things stand, the body is almost literally a Black Parliament, and it is the only one on the face of the earth which is the representative of a white constituency and the professed exponent of an advanced type of modern civilization. But the reader will find almost any portraiture inadequate to give a vivid idea of the body, and enable him to comprehend the complete metamorphosis of the South Carolina Legislature, without observing its details. The Speaker is black, the Clerk is black, the door-keepers are black, the little pages are black, the chairman of the Ways and Means is black, and the chaplain is coal-black. At some of the desks sit colored men whose types it would be hard to find outside of Congo; whose costume, visages, attitudes, and expression, only befit the forecastle of a buccaneer. It must be remembered, also, that these men, with not more than half a dozen exceptions, have been themselves slaves, and that their ancestors were slaves for generations. . . .

───────────

Pike was particularly interested in the behavior of the black legislators during the two-month session. At times he could see the progress being made by the newly freed slaves, but more often he was offended by the process.

. . . Sambo can talk on these topics [the arming and drilling of the black militia] and those of a kindred character, and their endless ramifications, day in and day out. There is no end to his gush and babble. The intellectual level is that of a bevy of fresh converts at a negro camp-meeting. . . . the negro is imitative in the extreme. He can copy like a parrot or a monkey, and he is always ready for a trial of his skill . . . His misuse of the language in his imitations is at times ludicrous beyond measure. He notoriously loves a joke or an anecdote, and will burst into a broad guffaw on the smallest provocation. . . . They are "quick as lightning" at detecting points of order, and they certainly make incessant and extraordinary use of their knowledge. No one is allowed to talk five minutes without interruption, and one interruption is the signal for another and another, until the original speaker is smothered under an avalanche of them. Forty questions of privilege will be raised in a day. . . .

But underneath all this shocking burlesque upon legislative proceedings, we must not forget that there is something very real to this uncouth and untutored multitude. It is not all sham, nor all burlesque. They have a genuine interest and a genuine earnestness in the business of the assembly which we are bound to recognize and respect, unless we would be accounted shallow critics. They have an earnest purpose, born of a conviction that their position and condition are not fully assured, which lends a sort of dignity to their proceedings. . . . Seven years ago these men were raising corn and cotton under the whip of the overseer. To-day they are raising points of order and questions of privilege. They find they can raise one as well as the other. They prefer the latter. It is easier, and better paid. Then, it is the evidence of an accomplished result. It means escape and defense from old oppressors. It means liberty. It means the destruction of prison-walls only too real to them. It is the sunshine of their lives. It is their day of jubilee. It is their long-promised vision of the Lord God Almighty. . . .

_____

One of Pike's main concerns was the corruption of the legislature. It seemed to him to be without limit.

So tainted is the atmosphere with corruption, so universally implicated is everybody about the government, of such a character are the ornaments of society at the capital, that there is no such thing as an influential local opinion to be brought against the scamps. They plunder, and glory in it. They steal, and defy you to prove it. The legalization of fraudulent scrip is regarded simply as a smart operation. The purchase of a senatorship is considered only a profitable trade. Those who make the most out of the operation are the best fellows. "How did you get your money?" was asked of a prominent legislator and lobbyist. "I stole it," was the prompt reply. The same man pursues his trade to-day, openly and unabashed. . . .

Not only are the residences of the white thieves who have stolen their half a million or more apiece, pointed out in Columbia, but here and there a comfortable abode of some sable ally, whose sole business is politics. But while the colored brother has had to be content hitherto with smaller sums than the white, which of itself would account for want of relative show, he is also more prodigal in his expenditures. Still his savings are not to be despised. Sambo takes naturally to stealing, for he is used to it. It was his notorious weakness in slavery, and in his unregenerate state he is far less culpable than the white. The only way he ever had to possess himself of any thing, was to steal it from somebody else. The white man is really the responsible party for his thefts. He may well turn and say to his former master, "The villainy you teach, I will execute." The narration I have given sufficiently shows how things have gone and are going in this State, but its effect would be much heightened if there were time and room for details. Here is one: The total amount of the stationery bill of the House for the twenty years preceding 1861 averaged $400 per annum. Last year it was $16,000. But the meanness of these legislative robberies is not less significant of the character of the legislation than their magnitude. Last year the Treasury was in great straits on one or two occasions for money to anticipate the taxes. Some of the banks came to its aid and advanced about $60,000. They were this year compelled to go before the Committee of Claims to get reimbursed. The shameless rascals refused to pay the claim unless they were allowed to bag some 15 or 20 per cent. of it for their share! Another class of men who are allowed to rob the State freely, comprises those who control the printing-offices. The influence of a free press is well understood in South Carolina. It was understood and dreaded under the old *régime*, and was muzzled accordingly. Nearly all the newspapers in the State are now subsidized. The State government employs and pays them *ad libitum* [as it desires]. One installment of $75,000 lately went to about twenty-five papers in sums ranging from $1,000 to $7,000 apiece, a list of which was published by order of a vote of the Legislature a short time ago. Down here these small weekly sheets can be pretty nearly kept going on these subsidies. Of course, none of the deviltry of the State government is likely to be exposed through them. The whole amount of the printing bills of the State last year, it is computed (for every thing here has to be in part guesswork), aggregated the immense sum of $600,000. . . .

Pike disagreed with many Northerners who felt that the answer to these problems was compulsory education. He agreed with many Southerners that blacks had never held the reins of government and had yet to show that they had the capacity for self-government. His views had changed significantly since his days as an abolitionist.

The question is often asked if education is not the remedy for the blackness of darkness that prevails in South Carolina. Yes, indeed, if that were possible. Make it compulsory then. But what is education? Is it the glib recitation of the alphabet, or the multiplication-table? Is it the knowledge of reading and writing? This is all that compulsory education can give, in its most successful forms. But here is a race to be educated in the very elements of manhood. They have to be taught positively and negatively. The education they require is the formation of a race the opposite of the existing race. They have to be taught not to lie, not to steal, not to be unchaste. To educate them properly is to revolutionize their whole moral nature. The groundwork of that education which will make them fit rulers of a republic will not even have been laid when they shall be taught reading and writing. It is the reading and writing negroes of the South Carolina Legislature who lead in its most infamous venalities and corruptions. This sort of education merely lends a cutting edge to their moral obtuseness. Education, to be what it ought to be with the existing race of negroes in the South, means to educate them out of themselves, means to undo the habits and practices and modes of thought and want of thought engendered by centuries of slavery. It means the moral enlightenment and regeneration of a whole people debauched and imbruted for ages. Such is the gigantic task demanded of an education suited to existing circumstances.

We do not mean to say that all this is necessary to entitle the colored man to the privileges of citizenship, but only mean it as a reply to the glib suggestion of compulsory education as a ready remedy for the existing disorders and crimes that disgrace republican government and menace its future. Neither is it any answer to say that other people are ignorant, and superstitious, and degraded. When the ignorant and superstitious and degraded subjects of other nationalities have shown themselves capable of governing the better classes of society, it will be time to plead their example and their qualifications for the functions of rulers. But they are the classes who have never yet in history exercised the functions of government. And thus the fact that they exist from age to age, and that their presence does not destroy governments, proves nothing. They have lived as pupils in the State, and not as its masters, as they now live in South Carolina. Let us not be misunderstood. We are not talking about denying rights of citizenship. We are denouncing governments of ignorance and vice, and demanding a remedy.

Again, there is no parallel to be drawn between the exceptional venality of Northern Legislatures and the corruptions of South Carolina government. They do not spring from the same causes. The former can be promptly remedied by exposure and by an appeal to the intelligence and virtue of the constituency; in the other case there is no such tribunal to appeal to. It is a moral morass in which there is neither standing nor holding ground. . . .

During his travels Pike developed a sympathy for southern whites. Many had suffered in the war because of the leadership of the old planter class. The war was not their fault. These men had been subjected to enough punishment; now they deserved fair treatment by the North.

We think there is full justification for the statement that a vast majority of the Southern people were entrapped by a handful of ambitious leaders, destitute of the first elements of sound statesmanship, into a war for which there was no provocation, and which they would never have deliberately confronted. But, war once begun, they were in a vise. A despotic military government was thenceforth their master. To that is to be imputed all that followed.

Considerations like these may lead us to inquire whether the South of our imagination, as seen through the smoke and the blood and the fire of civil war, is not something very different from the real South that was dragged into secession, or the actual South of to-day.

The war, the events of the war, the men of the war, hang like a thick, impenetrable curtain before the eyes of the present generation of Northern people, hiding from view a past history, and existing facts, and a present situation, all of which are profoundly essential to a proper understanding of the problem with which the statesmanship of the country has now to deal. There is in the South to-day an enormous mass of inherited worth, and virtue, and capacity, and wisdom, and every solid element of citizenship, that has an indefeasible right to demand recognition, and justice, and fraternal consideration. The commonest sentiments of humanity require it. The ties of a common lineage and a common government demand it. It is no more than we extend to the most worthless specimens of humanity of foreign birth that are annually landing upon our shores. Every generous impulse prompts it. The dictates of a wise statesmanship imperiously exact it. Nothing stands in the way of such recognition, but a blind, selfish, partisan hostility, that is as undying in its revenges as it is merciless in its judgments.

It is necessary to awake to the necessity of exterminating this hateful obstacle. It is time prejudice and enmity were put aside. In an eager desire to secure the natural rights of one set of people, we have quite overlooked the claims of another. In carelessness of the sufferings of the guilty, the heavy hand of injustice has been laid upon the innocent. . . .

Of even greater concern to Pike was the possible Africanizing of South Carolina. Unless the present Reconstruction policy was changed, such Africanizing was likely to happen. He believed that the entire Reconstruction policy was wrong and that the sooner it was ended, the better. White men in South Carolina must once again be put in charge of their state.

The Federal Government could do much, if it would take the necessary pains, toward correcting some of the worst practices of this corrupt travesty of a government. . . . It makes large appropriations for new public edifices in the State, as is attested by those which are now going up in Charleston and Columbia. It appoints to office the large body of revenue officers, both internal and external, the numerous postmasters, the Federal judges, attorneys, and special agents, and it keeps bodies of Federal troops in the State, which are everywhere welcome for the money they disburse. Through these and kindred influences, the Federal Government holds vast sway over the State. That for some reason it has not exercised its influence to any appreciable extent in the interest of good government, is evident. It might do much toward repressing many corrupt practices and raising the moral tone of the State government. It has not done this. And yet it would seem to be its interest to do it. Why should the Republican party of the country, composed so largely as it is of its best and most conscientious citizens, be compelled to endure the foul stain inflicted by the robberies and outrages of caitiffs, who deserve the State-prison? . . .

It would be a violent presumption against the manliness, the courage, and the energy of South Carolina white men, to allow the State to remain in the permanent keeping of her present rulers. . . . So that the restoration of the predominance of the white population in the State seems to be only a question of time, which can be abbreviated by suitable effort. . . .

Edward King

Edward King traveled through the southern and southwestern states during 1873 and the first half of 1874. The publishers of Scribner's Monthly *asked him to write about the social and political conditions of the people in those states. Originally his findings were published in fifteen articles. Later they were made into a book entitled* The Great South, *published in 1874.*

The first state that he visited was Louisiana, where he was both amused and disturbed by the "negro" legislature. It was run by blacks, but they were not the intelligent, well-to-do freedmen. Instead, the worst elements were voted into power. Corruption was everywhere. King was deeply troubled by the "horrible political condition."

A visit to Mechanics' Institute, the seat of the Kellogg Legislature, during the session, is a curious experience. At the doors stand negro policemen, armed with clubs and revolvers; and crowds of blacks obstruct the passage-ways. Mounting a staircase covered with old, tobacco stained matting, one finds himself in the House of Representatives, where sit the law-makers with their feet upon their desks. Nearly all the honorable members are black; some of them are so completely ignorant that they cannot follow the course of debate. But all are so drilled by the adventurers who control them that their opposition to anything likely to better the present horrible political condition is firm and determined. There are also many blacks in the Senate. When a colored man is in the chair, he is always falling into profound errors with regard to his rulings and decisions. He finds it difficult to follow the course of any bill the moment half-a-dozen members are speaking of it, and constantly submits to corrections and suggestions from some lean white man, dressed in new clothes, who smiles contemptuously, as, from a carpet-bag point of view, he superintends this legislative farce. And this scene has been enacted for six weary years—the State meantime sinking deeper and deeper into the abyss of crushing taxation. It is not wonderful that "White Leagues," in opposition to negro government, are springing up throughout Louisiana. . . .

During a visit to New Orleans, in March of 1874, my attention was called to a number of notable instances of the rapid decline of property. One gentleman pointed out a house which, in 1868, he would have been glad to purchase for $12,000; a little later it was sold for $8,000; then for $6,000, and now no one could be found to take it at $4,000. Many houses are given rent free to persons who will occupy them, that they may not be allowed to fall into decay.

The sheriff is the prosperous man in New Orleans. His office has been made worth $60,000 yearly.

The annual session of the Legislature, fortunately limited by the Constitution to sixty days, is a terrible trial. The state government cannot be depended upon. Earnest men, on the conservative side, are deterred from conciliatory action by the insincerity of those in power. At one time the dominant party seemed really desirous of inaugurating reform in the management of certain affairs, and called for a committee of investigation to be composed of the property-holders. But as, at nearly the same time, it voted away $500,000 worth of State bonds for a doubtful enterprise, the property-holders could not be made to believe that there was, in truth, any desire for "retrenchment" and "reform."

Time and time again the legislature which the Federal Government placed in power in Louisiana has sworn in as members men whom the returning-boards did not even pretend had been elected; and these men have been allowed to sit as representatives of people whom they have never seen.

One of the worst features of the situation in Louisiana is the entire absence of the intelligent and well-to-do negroes from politics there. It is only the rascals and the dubious who get into power; and they are more terrible than the white rogues. They practice all the vices in the calendar; they take the thousands of dollars diverted from their proper channels, and lavish them upon abandoned white women; they enrich themselves and boast of it. . . .

A trip to Georgia confirmed King's growing conviction that Reconstruction was a failed policy.

Certainly reconstruction is null and void in Georgia. It has been a complete failure there. That there have been instances of glaring injustice practiced on both sides no fair-minded man can for an instant doubt. The Republican administration lasted scarcely three years; and the legitimate results of the war were not maintained so long as that after 1868. Out of the 90,000 colored voters in the State, scarcely 30,000 vote to-day; free schools are almost unknown outside the large cities and towns; and there has not been a Republican inspector of election since the Democrats assumed power. To judge from the testimony of native Georgians who are Republicans, and who have never been suspected of any dishonesty or untruth, the negroes are very grossly intimidated; and the Ku-Klux faction still exists as a kind of invisible empire. This is naturally to be expected after the occurrences in Louisiana, South Carolina, and Alabama; it is the revulsion from tyrannical ignorance and carpet-baggery; and may prove as baneful in its results as has its degraded and disreputable opposite. The Democrat of Georgia talks with all the more emphasis of a white man's government in his commonwealth, because he feels that there is a black man's government in a neighboring State; if he has ever had any exaggerated fears as to a too free assumption of civil rights by his ex-slave, those fears are accented ten-fold since he has seen the real injustice practiced by negroes where they have attained supreme, unrestricted power. . . .

The attempt to establish free common schools throughout Georgia has thus far resulted in failure. Prior to the war there was but little effort made for the education of the masses. A small sum was appropriated as the "indigent school fund," but the majority of the poorer classes in the back-country remained in dense ignorance. In the present State School Commissioner's office I was informed that there had been no common school open outside the large cities for some time. It was alleged that the school fund had been diverted to unlawful purposes during the "previous administration," and that the State had been much embarrassed by a debt of $300,000, incurred in prematurely putting schools into operation. There seems no doubt of a sincere desire on the part of the Georgia Conservatives to maintain free schools; and it is, by the way, noteworthy that three of the Southern States that are Conservative in politics are leading all others in education. Local taxation is the principal bugbear. The farmer dislikes to be taxed for schools. . . .

In the South Carolina legislature, King saw similarities with the political conditions in Louisiana, but in South Carolina black leadership was of a higher quality. Thus, he foresaw the possibility of a better future if "the dreadful question of race against race" could be set aside.

There are men of real force and eloquence among the negroes chosen to the House, but they are the exception. In the Senate I noticed decorum and ability among the members. Several of the colored Senators spoke exceedingly well, and with great ease and grace of manner; others were awkward and coarse. The white members, native and imported, appeared men of talent at least. The black pages ran to and fro, carrying letters and documents to the honorable Senators; and a fine-looking quadroon, or possible octoroon woman, and the ebony gentleman escorting her, were admitted to the floor of the Senate, and sat for some time listening to the debates.

To the careless observer it seems encouraging to see the negroes, so lately freed from a semi-barbaric condition, doing so well, because their conduct is really better than one would suppose them capable of, after having seen the constituency from which they were elevated. One cannot, of course, prevent reflections upon vengeance and retribution drifting into his mind,—it was, doubtless, to be expected that some day the negro would lord it over his master, as the law of compensation is immutable,—but there is danger in the protraction of this vengeance. We must really see fair play. Ignorance must not be allowed to run riot. If we saw it consummating, as a Commune assembled in Paris, one thousandth part of the infamy which it effects as a Legislature in South Carolina, we should cry out angrily for interference.

But this is an epoch of transition. When the negro is a little older as a politician, he will be less clannish. The masses of the blacks will divide more fully into parties. Then there will be some chance for the setting aside of the dreadful question of race against race. At present the blacks in the State move solidly together. Their eyes are fixed on the spoils which the white men have taught them to gather. They have not yet begun to understand that in stripping the State, compromising her credit and blackening her reputation, they injure themselves much more than they harm their old masters. They will learn in time that they have committed a grave error in allowing the whites to be virtually excluded from representation, and that both races will be forced to labor together, honestly and faithfully, to save the State, and to insure their own future prosperity.

I visited the University a day or two after the revolution caused there by the entrance of the first colored student, the Secretary of State himself. In the library, where the busts of Calhoun and Hayne seemed to look down from their niches with astonishment upon the changed order of things, I saw the book from whose lists the white students had indignantly erased their names when they saw the Secretary's round, fair script beneath their own. The departure of the old professors and scholars was the signal for a grand onward movement by the blacks, and a great number entered the preparatory and the law schools. They have summoned good teachers from the North, and are studying earnestly. The University attained its present title in 1866. It was founded as a college at the beginning of the century, but now consists of ten distinct schools, and is rich in libraries and apparatus for scientific studies. While I was in the library, a coal black senator arrived, with two members of the House, whom he presented to the head of the faculty as desirous of entering the law class. I was informed that dozens of members were occupied every spare moment outside of the sessions in faithful study; but this has been the case for a short time only. . . .

A few days later King visited the legislature in North Carolina, where he found similar conditions. The situation was not as severe as in South Carolina, but Negro suffrage had dramatically changed the legislative process in Raleigh, North Carolina.

The evils of universal suffrage have been very great in this State. The great mass of densely ignorant and ambitious blacks suddenly hurled upon the field created the wildest confusion, and crushed the commonwealth under irredeemable debt. The villainy and robbery to which the white population of the State was compelled to submit, at the hands of the plunderers maintained in power by the negro, did much to destroy all possibility of a speedy reconciliation between the two races. Still, the citizens are loyal to the Union, and are anxious to be on friendly terms with the North; yet continue to regard Northerners as in some way the authors of the evils which have befallen them. They do not, however, reproach the North with having sent them a carpet-bagger; as the man who did them most harm, and whose conduct has been most sharply criticised, was a citizen of their own State.

The reconstruction convention in 1868 was a singular gathering. Its proceedings bordered on the ridiculous. It finally secured a Constitution which has since been much amended. The judges and other officers placed in power were notoriously incompetent; and Mr. Holden, who was appointed first provisional Governor of the State under reconstruction, was the author of so much questionable work that he was successfully impeached and removed. There was, at one time, imminent danger of civil war in the State; several counties were in insurrection; the Ku-Klux flourished and committed all kinds of infamous outrages. Holden was an original secessionist, and his newspaper, the *Standard,* printed at Raleigh, was the mouth-piece of the Democracy until 1860, when this unblushing "scallawag," as the South-erners call political renegades, threw his Democratic sentiments out at window, and went in for the Union cause. Of course he did this with an eye to future plunder. Mr. Holden was, in 1873, Postmaster at the State Capitol, and seemed but little af-fected by his forcible removal from the executive chair.

At the close of the wild carnival of robbery and maladministration which marked the career of the first reconstruction government, North Carolina found that her debts were between $36,000,000 and $40,000,000. This was an appalling exhibit, for the mere payment of the interest was enough to stagger the impoverished and strug-gling agriculturists. The money had gone, alas! none save the thieves knew where. The plundered people only knew that out of $16,000,000 voted by the Legislatures for "public works of improvements," but $500,000 had ever been devoted to that purpose; and the ignorant negro himself was puzzled to discover what had become of the resources which, at the outset of his political career, he had imagined to be unfailing.

The main villainies had been consummated at a time when the mass of the white natives who took part in the war were excluded from office, and when the negro vote was overwhelming. As soon as Governor Holden was impeached, the white popula-tion succeeded in gaining a fair share of influence again, and when he was removed they came into power, Governor Caldwell, Holden's successor, working pretty har-moniously with them. The political troubles may now be considered as nearly over, and if the industrial opportunities of the State are improved, there will be a return to some degree of prosperity. Many of the most influential citizens believe that an attitude of perfect frankness on the part of North Carolina toward its creditors will be the only thing that can save the State. They are anxious to see a compromise ef-fected as speedily as possible, that both white and black may know just how they are situated, and may set their shoulders to the wheel in earnest. . . .

━━━━━━

Near the end of his travels, King mused over the conditions that he had seen and the possi-bilities for the future. The North must make corrections in its Reconstruction policies which would involve "the removal of the more odious Carpetbaggers." Southern whites and blacks would need to work together to find a mutually acceptable solution. Beyond that, he was un-willing to speculate.

There is much that is discouraging in the present condition of the South, but no one is more loth than the Southerner to admit the impossibility of its thorough redemption. The growth of manufactures in the Southern States, while in-significant as compared with the gigantic development in the North and West, is still highly encouraging; and it is actually true that manufactured articles formerly sent South from the North are now made in the South to be shipped to Northern buyers.

There is at least good reason to hope that in a few years immigration will pour into the fertile fields and noble valleys and along the grand streams of the South, assuring a mighty growth. The Southern people, however, will have to make more vigorous efforts in soliciting immigration than they have thus far shown themselves capable of, if they intend to compete with the robust assurance of Western agents in Europe. . . .

As soon as the negro vote in the South is divided, and the black man learns to respect the merits of a candidate in spite of his political complexion, there will be but little of the trouble now-a-days so conspicuous in Louisiana, Alabama, and some of the other States. Within the last few months the South Carolina conservatives have frankly allied themselves with those of the negroes who have shown a disposition to encourage honest government in the State, and this is a movement which will be general throughout the South as the abuses of reconstruction are corrected, and some of the more odious carpet-baggers, who have arrayed the negro wrongfully against the principal property-holders, are summarily dismissed from the arena of politics.

The South can never be cast in the same mould as the North. . . . but it will be progressive, more progressive and liberal every year. Its provincialisms will fade gradually away; its educational facilities, despite the occasional hindrances imposed by such unwise manoeuvres as the projected passage of the Civil Rights bill, will increase and flourish. The negro will get justice from the lower classes of whites as soon as those classes are touched by the liberalizing influences of the times. There is, of course, still much objection to sitting with him on juries, or otherwise acknowledging his equality.

It is not the province of this volume to indulge in theories as to the grave dangers which many politicians fancy still environ the Southern question, nor is it important to speculate upon the possible determination on the part of the planters to demand compensation some day for their emancipated slaves, or to hint that they may try to establish a labor system which shall relegate the negro to serfdom. Time alone can disclose the rôle which the Southern Conservative will play when he returns to power. . . .

Rutherford B. Hayes

Rutherford B. Hayes, former Republican congressman and two-term governor of Ohio, was losing confidence in the policies of the Grant administration. His earlier enthusiasm for Reconstruction programs had faded into doubt and disillusionment. Now these programs seemed too radical and punitive. In 1875 he was approached about running for a third term as governor. He hesitated because of his doubts about an increasingly corrupt Republican administration. Though it would not be an easy race, it was too tempting to refuse.

March 28 [1875] . . . The Republican caucus at Columbus last Thursday, according to report, was unanimously for me for governor. A third term would be a distinction—a feather I would like to wear. No man ever had it in Ohio. Letters tell me I am really wanted. But the present condition of my money matters requires attention. The chance of an election is not good. More important still, I do not sympathize with a large share of the party leaders. I hate the corruptionists of whom Butler is leader. I doubt the ultra measures relating to the South, and I am opposed to the course of General Grant on the third term, the civil service, and the appointment of unfit men on partisan or personal grounds. I wouldn't hesitate to fight a losing battle if the cause was wholly and clearly good and important. I am not sure that it is in all respects what it should be, and as to its importance, I am more than in doubt. Hence I have said decidedly *no* to all who have approached me.

April 14, 1875.—I am still importuned in all quarters to consent to run as Republican candidate for governor. Several suggest that if elected governor now, I will stand well for the Presidency next year. How wild! What a queer lot we are becoming! Nobody is out of the reach of that mania. . . .

April 18. Sunday.— . . . The prospect of an election seems to me to be not good. The third-term talk, the Civil Rights Bill, the partisan appointments of the baser sort, in other words the *Butlerism* of the Administration, are all bad, and weights on us. . . .

———————

As Hayes campaigned, he began to think about Reconstruction in the South. He was opposed to the Reconstruction policies and especially the Civil Rights Act of 1875, which was meant to end racial discrimination in juries and all forms of transportation and public accommodation, because these policies had their major impact on the South and its segregated facilities. Hayes wanted to find ways to reach out to Southerners and even considered including a few former Confederate soldiers in a ceremony on Decoration (Memorial) Day in Toledo in May 1875.

*M*ay 11. . . . I am asked to speak on Decoration Day in Toledo. I am inclined to accept. May I speak of uniting with Confederates in this ceremony?

I would honor any man who dies in obedience to his convictions of duty, who dies for others. The conductor, the engineer, the brakeman, who dies at his post; the captain, the sailor who goes down at sea to save his passengers; the fireman who perishes, the policeman who is killed in the line of duty. But how of those who died in an effort to destroy the good? Does he believe in his work? Martyrs of false religions?

Every age has its temptations, its weaknesses, its dangers. Ours is in the line of the snobbish and the sordid. . . .

———————

Hayes was nominated in early June and commenced a grueling campaign. In the midst of politicking, he wrote a letter to a friend in Texas about his Reconstruction views. He was now considering the "let-alone policy" that would abandon all Reconstruction efforts in the South.

Fremont Ohio,
July 27, 1875.

My Dear Guy:—I send you a copy of my campaign speech to be delivered next Saturday. It was prepared under great difficulties. Two of my children were down with scarlet fever. One is still in bed but we hope slowly recovering.

Thinking of you I put in a word about Texas. As to Southern affairs "the let-alone policy" seems now to be the true course; at any rate nothing but good-will now exists towards you. The future depends largely on the moderation and good sense of Southern men in the next House of Representatives. If they are like Lamar, of Mississippi, all will be well. If like Preston, of Virginia, all will be "fuss and fury" for a time. But I think we are one people at last for all time.

As ever,
R. B. Hayes.
Guy M. Bryan
Texas. . . .

═══════

In October Hayes won the governorship of Ohio and was inaugurated on January 13, 1876. Immediately he became a leading Republican candidate for president. On June 16, 1876, he was nominated on the seventh ballot. In the next four months his every word and action were carefully scrutinized, especially as they related to Reconstruction. In response to a letter from Carl Schurz concerning Reconstruction, he wrote:

June 27, 1876. . . . I now feel like saying something as to the South, not essentially different from your suggestions, but am not decided about it. I don't like the phrase, by reason of its Democratic associations, which you use—"local self-government"—in *that* connection. It seems to me to smack of the bowie-knife and revolver. "Local self-government" has nullified the Fifteenth Amendment in several States, and is in a fair way to nullify the Fourteenth and Thirteenth. But I do favor a policy of reconciliation, based on the observance of all parts of the Constitution— the *new* as well as the old—and, therefore, suppose you and I are substantially agreed on the topic. . . .

═══════

However, as the campaign continued, Hayes began to worry about an election result that could be contested. As early as October 22, Hayes referred to this possibility. It alarmed him because it might lead to another Civil War.

Columbus,
October 22, 1876. Sunday. . . .

Another danger is imminent: A contested result. And we have no such means for its decision as ought to be provided by law. This must be attended to hereafter. We should not allow another Presidential election to occur before a means for settling a contest is provided. If a contest comes now it may lead to a conflict of arms. I can only try to do my duty to my countrymen in that case. I shall let no personal ambition turn me from the path of duty. Bloodshed and civil war must be averted if possible. If forced to fight, I have no fears of failure from lack of courage or firmness. . . .

It was as Hayes had feared—a contested election with no winner. Tilden had a majority of electoral votes but was short one vote. Hayes and his wife tried to reconcile themselves to the imminent loss. He worried about its impact on the South.

Saturday, November 11. . . . I went to bed at 12 to 1 o'clock. Talked with Lucy, consoling her with such topics as readily occurred of a nature to make us feel satisfied on merely personal grounds with the result. We soon fell into a refreshing sleep and the affair seemed over. Both of us felt more anxiety about the South—about the colored people especially—than about anything else sinister in the result. My hope of a sound currency will somehow be realized; civil service reform will be delayed; but the great injury is in the South. There the Amendments will be nullified, disorder will continue, prosperity to both whites and colored people will be pushed off for years. . . .

However, the next day it became clear that the election was not over. Three states in the South—Louisiana, South Carolina, and Florida—plus Oregon could yield a majority of electoral votes. The votes were contested and would be decided by a commission. During the long wait Hayes continued to receive visitors and to write. Southerners began to contact him to express their views about the election and Reconstruction. They said what Hayes wanted to hear: "We will favor measures to secure the colored people of all their rights." He was happy to hear these words and wanted to believe them.

December 1, 1876.—Colonel Roberts of [the] New Orleans *Times* wanted an interview with me. Had lunch at Comly's. After lunch he said he called on me to give me the views of Lamar, of Mississippi, General Walthall, ditto, Wade Hampton, of South Carolina, and probably [General] Gordon, of Georgia.

"You will be President," [he said]. "We will not make trouble. We want peace. We want the color line abolished. We will not oppose an Administration which will favor an honest administration and honest officers in the South. We will favor measures to secure the colored people all of their rights. We may not, and probably will not, leave the party of opposition, but such an Administration as you can have, we will support as men of the opposite party can. We want nothing of you in the way of promise or pledge."

This was the substance. I replied by saying I was gratified to know it. That my Letter of Acceptance covered the whole ground; that it meant all it said and all that it implied. This was the substance.

In case of my election there will be further conference, and I hope for good results. . . .

Columbus, Ohio,
December 16, 1876.

My Dear S——: . . . I am very hopeful that much good will come from friendly relations with good men [in the] South—sooner or later . . .

Sincerely,
R. B. Hayes
Honorable William Henry Smith. . . .

In January 1877, a special electoral commission was appointed by Congress. It was composed of five congressmen, five senators, and five associate justices of the Supreme Court. It was to be seven Democrats, seven Republicans, and one undecided, but it ended up being seven Democrats and eight Republicans. The "undecided" justice, David Davis, resigned from the commission, and a staunch Republican, Justice Joseph Bradley, took his place. By a series of 8–7 votes, all the disputed electors were awarded to Hayes.

In a letter to Carl Schurz on February 4 Hayes expressed his concerns about developing a policy toward the South. Schurz warned him to slow down in his efforts to pacify the South. Hayes agreed that he had been too enthusiastic and would try to be more cautious.

Columbus, Ohio,
February 4, 1877.

My dear Sir:—I have your note of the first. It impresses me strongly. My anxiety to *do* something to promote the pacification of the South is perhaps in danger of leading me too far. I do not reflect on the use of the military power in the past. But there is to be an end of all that, except in emergencies which I can't think of as possible again. We must do all we can to promote prosperity there. Education, emigration and immigration, improvements occur to me. But the more I think of it, the more I see in what you say. We must go cautiously and slowly.

The result of the great lawsuit [conflict over the election of 1876] will, perhaps, relieve me from all responsibility. I am, fortunately, not anxious to assume it. If it comes I want to be ready. You will see, from what I write you, that the South is more on my mind than anything else. Perhaps we must be content to leave that to time — taking care not to obstruct time's healing processes by injudicious meddling. I will think of it. Thanks.

Sincerely,
R. B. Hayes. . . .

With his election virtually guaranteed, Hayes began to complete his plans for ending Reconstruction. If the South would give assurances that the Thirteenth, Fourteenth, and Fifteenth Amendments would be observed and enforced, he was ready to abandon northern Reconstruction policies. Troops would be pulled out, and possibly a southern Democrat would be appointed to the cabinet. Hayes believed that the word of southern congressmen was a sufficient guarantee that the amendments would be enforced in the South.

February 17.—Last evening Louisiana was decided by the Commission in our favor. There is still some doubt, but apparently very little, of the result. The inaugural and Cabinet-making are now in order. I would like to get support from good men of the South, late Rebels. How to do it is the question. I have the best disposition towards the Southern people, Rebels and all. I could appoint a Southern Democrat in the Cabinet. But who would take it among the capable and influential good men of those States? General Joseph E. Johnston occurs to me. I must think of this. . . .

February 18. Sunday.—The indications still are that I am to go to Washington. I talked yesterday with Fred Douglass and Mr. Poindexter, both colored, on the Southern question. I told them my views. They approved. Mr. Douglass gave me many useful hints about the whole subject. My course is a firm assertion and maintenance of the rights of the colored people of the South according to the Thirteenth, Fourteenth, and Fifteenth Amendments, coupled with a readiness to recognize all Southern people, without regard to past political conduct, who will now go with me heartily and in good faith in support of these principles. . . .

February 25.—Yesterday the Commission decided Oregon to be for Hayes and Wheeler. This is the last of the disputed and doubtful States. The only apparent chance of defeating us now is the revolutionary conduct of the Democrats in the House. The Southern members of that party, who have hitherto been conservative and favorable, are disturbed by an article in the *Ohio State Journal* unfriendly to them, which is charged to have been inspired by me. The truth is I stand on my Letter. If I speak at Fremont or elsewhere during the next few days, I may say:

"My Letter [of Acceptance in July last] expressed what I thought were just sentiments on the leading questions which then interested the country. I thought its doctrines were sound before the election. I think they are sound now that the election is over. And if the issue pending in Congress shall be decided in our favor, those principles will be the standard by which my official conduct shall be guided. If I were to write that letter now, I would give that part on the Southern question greater emphasis. The great body of the people of this country earnestly desire a wise and just settlement of that question. They want peace, they long for repose.

"What is required is: First, that for the protection and welfare of the colored people, the Thirteenth, Fourteenth, and Fifteenth Amendments shall be sacredly observed and faithfully enforced according to their true intent and meaning.

"Second, We all see that the tremendous revolution which has passed over the Southern people has left them impoverished and prostrate, and we all are deeply solicitous to do what may constitutionally be done to make them again prosperous and happy. They need economy, honesty, and intelligence in their local governments. They need to have such a policy adopted as will cause sectionalism to disappear, and that will tend to wipe out the color line. They need to have encouraged immigration, education, and every description of legitimate business and industry. We do not want a united North nor a united South. We want a united country. And if the great trust shall devolve upon me, I fervently pray that the Divine Being, who holds the destinies of the nations in His hands, will give me wisdom to perform its duties so as to promote the truest and best interests of the whole country." . . . [No occasion for the delivery of such a speech presented itself.]

Hayes was inaugurated on March 5, 1877. Among his first acts was the ending of northern occupation of the two states still under military control. He also appointed Frederick Douglass as marshal in the District of Columbia, and a Southerner, D. M. Key of Tennessee, as postmaster general.

*A*pril 22.—We have got through with the South Carolina and Louisiana [problems]. At any rate, the troops are ordered away, and I now hope for peace, and what is equally important, security and prosperity for the colored people. The result of my plans is to get from those States by their governors, legislatures, press, and people pledges that the Thirteenth, Fourteenth, and Fifteenth Amendments shall be faithfully observed; that the colored people shall have equal rights to labor, education, and the privileges of citizenship. I am confident this is a good work. Time will tell. . . .

It had been apparent for several years that only the use of federal troops could stop counter Reconstruction. Southern white conservatives were unwilling to accept the Reconstruction governments, and only the united efforts of the North had any chance of protecting the legal rights of black citizens in the South. However, by the mid-1870s the North was tiring of Reconstruction—in part because of the writings of journalists like James Pike and Edward King—and President Grant was not willing to use the army to put down the "annual autumnal outbreaks [riots] in the South." George Templeton Strong, in the last months before his death, wrote of his lack of confidence in the Republican party and its Reconstruction policies: ". . . my faith in the party and the Administration has been cooling off for some time." Other Republicans in the North wanted each state to enforce its own laws. This would mean that ex-slaves would have to fend for themselves because the federal government would no longer protect them.

Rutherford B. Hayes had been opposed to Reconstruction policies and the Civil Rights Act of 1875. He looked for a way to reach out to Southerners. In his letter to a friend in Texas, Hayes summed up his attitude and that of the North: "As to Southern affairs, 'the let-alone policy' seems now to be the true course. . . ." With his election and inauguration as president in March 1877, federal troops were withdrawn from the South, and the Reconstruction period was officially ended.

Reconstruction officially ended when **Rutherford B. Hayes** ordered federal troops to leave Louisiana and South Carolina in April 1877. Their removal signaled the end of the Republican governments in the South. In the following months, Hayes closely watched the situation in the South, hoping that his "let alone" policy of pacification would work. In order to build support in the North, he toured the New England states urging "a union of hearts and hands in all parts of the country." Later Hayes traveled through Ohio, Kentucky, Tennessee, and Georgia, stressing the importance of harmony among the sections. "Our aspiration is for the reign of peace and good will over the whole of our recently agitated and afflicted land." He was pleased with the response.

By the end of the year Hayes was satisfied that his measures were indeed working. In a message to Congress in the fall of 1877, he congratulated the country on the success of pacification. Later, in March 1878, he noted in his diary that safety and order existed in the South "to an extent not known for half a century." In May he visited Hampton Institute in Virginia to encourage its efforts at educating and training freedmen and freedwomen. He made a few remarks stressing the importance of "industry, self reliance, self control and economy" for Negroes and was impressed by their progress.

However, in the fall of 1878 Hayes was told that whites were resorting to intimidation and violence to prevent colored people from organizing for the elections. His response was to make another statement that he hoped would settle the issue. On October 26 he wrote, "I must make a clear, firm and accurate statement on the Southern outrages, and restoration to the sound opinions I have long held on the subject. What good people demand is exact justice, equality before the law, perfect freedom of political speech and action, and no denial of rights to any citizen on account of color or race—the same to colored as the white."

Despite his best efforts, Hayes had a protracted struggle with the Democratic Congress over federal supervision of elections in the South, and by his last year in office he had serious reservations about the willingness of Southerners to abide by the Thirteenth, Fourteenth, and Fifteenth Amendments. He expressed dismay in particular over the failure of the South to faithfully observe the provisions of the Fifteenth Amendment which was the main reason for his failure to complete the pacification policy. "It is on this hook that the bloody shirt hangs." He laid the responsibility for this state of affairs on the Democratic party. Too late Hayes realized that it had not lived up to its earlier promises to him.

At the end of Reconstruction, **Marshall Twitchell** was in New Orleans helping the Republican party organize the new legislature. His presence was essential to maintain a one-vote majority. With his help the legislature was organized, the state government continued to operate under Republican control, and W. P. Kellogg was elected senator. Kellogg's election gave the U.S. Senate a one-vote Republican majority. The Louisiana Democrats withdrew and formed a separate government that continued until April, when a compromise brought the two governments together. This compromise was the conclusion of the work of a special presidential commission that went to New Orleans to work out a satisfactory settlement. Those Republicans and radicals whose seats had been contested were allowed to keep their seats in the legislature. The Democrats agreed to abide by the Thirteenth, Fourteenth, and Fifteenth Amendments and to provide money for Negro education; also the Democratic party promised that no further action would be taken against the Republicans. Hayes accepted these promises and ordered the federal troops back into their barracks. Thus, Reconstruction was over.

On April 23 Twitchell was sworn in as a state senator, along with the others who had been elected by their parties. He was elected leader of his faction and worked closely with many Confederate veterans for the remainder of the legislative sessions.

When the legislature concluded its business, Twitchell returned to the North. President Hayes met with him and asked that he serve one more term, after which he would receive a federal appointment. The president stressed that the presence of the Republican senators was important in guaranteeing that the courts would not be used for the persecution of Republicans.

Twitchell returned to the South in January 1878 for his final legislative session. Having become used to "revolutions," the session seemed routine and uninteresting. It went off smoothly, and he left Louisiana for the last time. On April 1 he was appointed consul at Kingston, Canada. It was near his home and considered a comfortable place for him to work in the final years of his life. Once again he surprised those who thought that he was near death. As he later wrote, "People had always been deceived about my vitality." He served for twenty-seven years at his position in Kingston and died in 1905 at the age of sixty-five.

Charles Hays, four-term congressman from Alabama, lived only two years after Reconstruction. Now out of office, he suffered rapidly deteriorating health (Bright's disease), his political world was in a shambles (his district was gerrymandered), and he was virtually insolvent. In his last political speech on July 4, 1878, he called the Republicans to do battle. He promised to fight on despite "terrible odds" and finished by pledging that "we shall not falter in the struggle to this end." Hays expected the eventual vindication of the Republican party but realized that he would never see it. He died on June 24, 1879.

During these same years **George Browder,** a presiding elder in the Louisville Methodist Conference, was busy with his church and family. His career prospered, and he remained active until his death in 1886. Occasionally he would reminisce about the good old days—"It is sad to think how the old family servants were scattered and the ties of the olden time will not be known by the rising generation." He still employed Negroes to work his fields but was distressed by their unwillingness to work at his demand. Referring to one Negro and his wife, he wrote, "he and his wife and all hands insist on going to the show and leaving the tobacco down in the ground." Until his dying day, Browder had trouble adjusting to this kind of behavior. He longed for a return to the days of slavery.

Frances and James Leigh left their Georgia plantation for good in 1877. Falling prices, flooding, and constant difficulties in finding reliable labor—plus the death of an infant son—convinced them to make the move. Six months after they left, their property agent died, and the next year a terrible storm swept over the area at harvest time. Fortunately, the appointment of a new manager worked out, and the Negroes were able to save most of the damaged crops. James visited it once more and was satisfied with its operation.

Frances's last visit to Georgia came in 1883 while she was finishing her book, *Ten Years on a Georgia Plantation.* Apparently pleased with work on the plantations, she gathered records for the appendix to her book. Clearly her views on the abilities of Negroes had changed over the years. Previously she had believed that Negroes were capable of being raised to a position of equality with whites without a loss of their morality. Now her views lacked the hopefulness of those earlier years: "The Negroes are so like children and easily influenced . . . Children they are in nature and character, and children they will remain until the end of this chapter." She blamed the excesses in Reconstruction on "Northern 'carpet-baggers' and Southern 'scalawags,' who have used him [the Negro] as a tool to further their own nefarious ends." Negroes received the vote before they were ready for it. Her book was published in 1884. She never again saw her plantations, living in England for the rest of her life. In 1908 the plantations were sold, and two years later she died at the age of seventy-two.

Albert Morgan, his wife, and three children left Mississippi for good in 1875 and lived in Washington, D.C., for the next ten years. He had been indicted for murder on trumped-up charges by his Democratic opponents; it was unsafe for him to return to Mississippi. In the spring of 1876 he testified before a Senate subcommittee investigating the Mississippi election of 1875. He recounted his ten years in Mississippi and his unwillingness to raise black troops to protect the election. It would have meant a race war. Without federal troops it was impossible to have a fair vote.

By the early 1880s he had received a $1,600 a year job as a clerk in the Pension Office; he also had a $13-a-month soldier's pension. He practiced law for several years, but because of malaria contracted in the Civil War and his war wounds he asked for and received a clerk's position, which required less exertion. During those years he was able to write a lengthy book on his life in Mississippi—*Yazoo; or, On the Picket Line of Freedom in the South*—which he self-published in 1884. It was his effort to "set out a simple and truthful narration of the principal incidents and events" in his life in Mississippi. Unfortunately for him, Grover Cleveland, a Democrat, was elected to the presidency in 1884 and upon inauguration appointed L. Q. C. Lamar, a bitter opponent of Morgan, as secretary of the interior. As was expected, Lamar quickly removed Morgan from his position. After some thought Morgan decided to leave Washington, D.C., and take his family to Lawrence, Kansas, a place that he had considered before going to Mississippi in 1865. It was an unfortunate move. He tried a number of jobs with little success, barely able to feed his family on his $13-a-month pension.

Finally in 1890 Morgan went to Colorado, without his family, to try to make a fortune in gold and silver. Living in Denver, he continued to have trouble making any money; but the silver issue intrigued him, and he switched to the Democratic party and campaigned for William Jennings Bryan in 1896 and 1900. Though the silver issue died away, Morgan continued to run a "School of Money," publishing three books on the gold-silver issue. Again, his efforts were financial failures. During these years Morgan lived apart from his wife, four daughters, and one son. In fact, they did not live together in the last thirty-two years of his life. He contributed little to their support and on occasion borrowed money from several of his children. He died in Denver on April 15, 1922, and was buried in Indianapolis. His son said of him after his death, ". . . my father never made a success, and he became so disheartened that he was really ashamed to come home."

In the remaining seventeen years of his life, **James Alcorn** maintained an interest in politics, although his career as a scalawag made election to high office unlikely. The national Republican party was busy courting southern Democrats and had little interest in southern Republicans. He did receive four votes for vice president on one of the ballots of the Republican party in 1880; it was the result of a protest vote by four Mississippi delegates. In 1883 his interest and expertise in levees resulted in his election to the Coahoma County Board of Supervisors.

His last political position was as a delegate to the Mississippi Constitutional Convention in 1890. Alcorn was successful in ending the leasing of convicts to private contractors, a reform that he had unsuccessfully supported as governor. He also secured a clause that allowed the state to accept federal aid for levees. However, he failed to realize that his support of an "understanding clause" guaranteeing white supremacy had the unintended effect of disfranchising Negro voters in Mississippi. Alcorn had hoped that this would mean a return to the early years of responsible Whig rule. Instead it led to the rise of the Democratic party and its "rednecks" under James K. Vardaman and Theodore K. Bilbo. It was not what he had intended. His health failed in the last four years of his life, and he died on December 20, 1894.

During the 1880s **Rutherford Hayes,** as a private citizen, continued to work for the improvement of conditions in the South, especially as they related to Negroes. He accepted appointments to the executive board of the Peabody Education Fund (1877) and the State Fund (1880), the latter "to educate young men to teach the colored people of the South." Until his death in 1893 he was active in this work. His diary has numerous references to his trips to board meetings, to efforts to provide equal education for "colored youth," and to efforts to support the financial needs of Negro schools and their teachers. One interesting example of this work was contributing to the financial support of W. E. B. DuBois (later founder of the NAACP):

> April 15, Friday [1891]. At breakfast received a card from DuBois, the colored scholar from Harvard. President Gilmore [president of Johns Hopkins] and I arranged to give him seven hundred and fifty dollars—one-half cash donation, one-half on his note—to support him one year in Germany at some university. Very glad to find he is sensible, sufficiently religious, able and a fair speaker.

In the last four years of his life, Hayes made two special trips in behalf of his pacification policy and the interest of the Negro in the South.

On May 4, 1889, Hayes attended a semipolitical symposium on conditions in the South. It was held in New York City and included a number of former Civil War generals, two of whom had become governors—Generals Gordon of Georgia and Buckner of Kentucky plus Senator Evarts, General Butterfield, and General Howard. Southerners made several speeches answering criticism of the South and its treatment of Negroes. Hayes was asked to make a few remarks. He stressed the absolute necessity of protecting the Negroes' rights and of providing equal representation for all states, small and large—a point of concern to many Southerners. He ended with a call for "one country, one constitution, one destiny." The response was gratifying to him.

The second trip was a tour of the South in November 1891. He made a number of speeches about the value and necessity of education for Negroes; he also visited Fisk College, where students were "making telescopes," and to Clark College, where Negro students were making wagons and carriages. Later he wrote to a friend, "The trip South gratified me. The corner seems to be turned."

Hayes remained hopeful to the end. He died on January 17, 1893, at the age of seventy.

Frederick Douglass remained an active spokesman for Negro rights for the remaining eighteen years of his life. He held several governmental positions—marshal (1877–1881) and recorder of deeds for the District of Columbia (1881–1886) and minister to Haiti (1889–1891), but his major interest was the welfare of Negroes, especially in the South. As conditions worsened in the South after Reconstruction, many Negroes despaired, urging a wholesale migration to the North or the West. With this, Douglass vigorously disagreed. Negroes must remain in the South and work hard to achieve freedom and equality, he believed. He still believed that the federal government would act to remedy the problem if given enough time.

But the Supreme Court decision in 1883 declaring unconstitutional the Civil Rights Bill of 1875 made him angry. He denounced this decision "as a further illustration of the reactionary tendencies of public opinion against the black man." He also referred to "moral weakness in high places which has attended the conflict between the spirit of liberty and the spirit of slavery from the beginning."

His indignation increased greatly when he visited South Carolina and Georgia in 1888 and realized how little he knew of the true conditions of blacks in the South. These conditions were much worse than he had imagined. The Negro was "minimally free" but actually a slave. In a speech on the twenty-sixth anniversary of the emancipation in the District of Columbia, he told the country: "I here and now denounce his so-called emancipation as a stupendous fraud—a fraud upon him, a fraud upon the world." He bitterly attacked the federal government for abandoning Negroes, ignoring their rights, and leaving them, in reality, slaves.

Again in 1891, after his resignation from the position of minister to Haiti, he took up the cause of protecting Negro rights in the South. For the next four years, until his death, his pen and voice remained active. Blacks were being lynched across the South. The pretext was that they were raping white women. Douglass did not mince words. "The men who break open jails and with bloody hands destroy human life are not responsible. These are not the men who make public opinion. . . . It was the men of wealth and respectability, who by raising the cry of an outrage of a Negro upon some white woman offered the excuse for the lynchers yet for two hundred years or more, these very men had committed this offense against black women, and the fact excited little attention. . . ." In an address entitled "The Lesson of the Hour" he argued that there was no Negro problem. Rather, it was a national problem. The nation had to protect its citizens against fraud and violence. Instead of people's looking for ways to restrict the suffrage of Negroes, Negro rights guaranteed by the Constitution had to be protected if they were to be more than high-sounding phrases. It was his last public address. On February 20, 1895, he collapsed and died. He was seventy-eight years of age.

After four and a half years in the South, **Peter Randolph** returned to Boston, his former home. There he found hundreds of Negroes from the South searching for homes and employment. They were "like sheep without a Shepherd, leaving their churches behind them and having no church affiliations here." After talking the matter over with friends, Randolph decided to build a Baptist church in the South End of Boston.

His first church was in a rented hall in Washington Street, but as the numbers grew there was a need for a new building. The congregation moved to a larger and more comfortable church edifice on West Concord Street. Soon it was renamed the Ebenezer Baptist Church.

Unfortunately, the new church had no pool for baptism. Arrangements were made for the use of a pool at the nearby Clarendon Street Baptist Church. When Randolph appeared with twenty-one candidates for the first baptisms, accompanied by a large part of his congregation, the white congregation became interested in "the colored baptism" and remained to see it performed. Randolph had cautioned his candidates to be calm and respectful, but their excitement grew until some "got happy in the water." The white minister, uncomfortable with the liveliness and zeal, dismissed his congregation, indicating that it was "best for us [the whites] to be alone as we had some ways peculiar to ourselves."

The Ebenezer Baptist Church continued to increase in numbers and influence until it became one of the largest "colored" churches in Boston. Randolph served as pastor until his retirement, when he entered the law office of E. G. Walker and read law "for a while." He hoped to get a clearer understanding of common law in order to better serve his people. This resulted in his appointment as justice of the peace under Governor Washburne and his reappointment by Governors Long and Ames, respectively. In time he tired of this work—"this was not my 'calling'"—and went back to occasional preaching and work for the Baptist church.

Writing in 1893, Randolph expressed satisfaction over the unity and good feeling between the North and South since the Civil War. However, he was "ashamed of the present condition of our colored Americans, in this great country." The white South seemed to believe that the freedmen had few rights to be respected. The North was turning the "Negro question" over to the South to be taken care of. Still, Randolph believed that freedmen had made progress and were ready to be intelligent and industrious citizens. The freedman must be left alone with "all impediments out of his way and encouraged to make progress." It would take time, and Randolph counseled patience. The only answer was the Golden Rule—"Do unto others as you would have others do unto you. On this rests the joy or sorrow of America." He remained optimistic about the future of race relations in the United States.

There is no record of his life after 1893.

Hiram Revels accepted the presidency of Alcorn Agricultural College in 1876 and served until 1882, when he resigned for reasons of health. He left the independent African Methodist Episcopal church and joined the segregated Methodist Episcopal church. He continued his religious work in the 1880s and 1890s. Revels died on January 16, 1901, while attending the Upper Mississippi Annual Conference of the Methodist Episcopal church at Aberdeen, Mississippi.

Blanche K. Bruce served as a Republican in the U.S. Senate from March 4, 1875, to March 3, 1881. During those years he fought for integrated army units, raised money for four hundred of his constituents who wanted to emigrate to Liberia, and opposed proposals to ship illiterate poor blacks to Liberia. Bruce was a delegate to the National Republican Convention in Chicago in 1880. On May 23, 1881, President Garfield appointed him registrar of the U.S. Treasury, making Bruce the first black man to hold this position, which he filled until 1885. In 1888 he was nominated for the vice presidency on the Benjamin Harrison ticket and received eleven votes. In 1889 President Harrison appointed him recorder of deeds for the District of Columbia, a position that he held until 1893. In 1896 President McKinley reappointed Bruce as registrar of the Treasury. He died on March 17, 1898.

James T. Rapier turned away from politics for the rest of his life. He successfully managed his plantations, adding acreage and employing a number of black tenants. In July 1878, over the protests of conservatives, Rapier was appointed collector of internal revenue for the Second District of Alabama. He was the first black man to serve in such a position in Alabama. Rapier began to support emigration of southern blacks to the West and on May 6, 1879, made a powerful speech at the Southern States Emigration Convention describing the continuing injustices in the South and the impossibility of true political and civil equality. For the rest of his life he strongly advocated this movement. In 1880 he was a delegate to the National Republican Convention, supporting John Sherman for the presidency. Continuing opposition by white Republicans resulted in his suspension from the position of collector of internal revenue in September 1882. His health declined, and he resigned the position. Appointed federal treasury officer for a new government building in Montgomery, Alabama, he died before construction began on May 31, 1883.

Joseph R. Rainey completed his fifth term as a congressman on March 3, 1879. Two months later, on May 22, he was appointed internal revenue agent of South Carolina; he served until July 15, 1881, when he resigned. For the next five years Rainey engaged in a banking and brokerage business in Washington, D.C. In 1886 he returned to his South Carolina home in Georgetown and died there on August 2, 1887.

Richard Cain was reelected to Congress in 1876 and served until March 3, 1879. He continued to minister in the African Methodist Episcopal church and was successful in enlarging its membership. One of the churches that he organized, the Emmanuel church in Charleston, became the largest church of that denomination in

South Carolina. In 1880 Cain was made its fourteenth bishop, serving in the Texas-Louisiana conference. In 1884 Cain returned to Washington, D.C., to serve as director of the first Episcopal conference. He died on January 18, 1887.

Robert B. Elliott was elected attorney general of South Carolina in 1876 but under pressure from Wade Hampton's Democratic government resigned on May 1, 1877. For the next two years he and two other black attorneys ran a law firm in Columbia. The firm dissolved in the fall of 1879, and Elliott was in desperate financial straits. Fortunately, a friend contacted John Sherman, secretary of the Treasury, and Elliott was appointed special investigator of customs in Charleston. This resolved his financial problems. In 1880 he was a delegate to the National Republican Convention in Chicago and was in charge of gaining black support for John Sherman. The following year Elliott was transferred to New Orleans over his protests. On April 29, 1882, eleven months after the move, he was removed from his customs position. With few financial resources, he remained in New Orleans practicing law. On August 9, 1884, he died of malarial fever.

John Lynch held elective office for only one year after the end of Reconstruction. He won a disputed election with James Chalmers and served from 1882 to 1883. However, he still maintained an interest in politics in the following years as a delegate to five Republican conventions and as temporary chairman of the convention in 1884. In later years he received two presidential appointments: one as fourth auditor of the United States—by Benjamin Harrison—and the other as paymaster of the army—by William McKinley. He remarried and moved in 1911 to Chicago, where he practiced law for the rest of his life.

In the latter years of his long life (he lived to age ninety-two), Lynch turned his attention to correcting what he considered to be inaccurate accounts of the Republican governments in the South after the Civil War. Writing from firsthand experience and considerable research, he argued—in *Facts of Reconstruction* (1913) and numerous articles and letters over a twenty-year period—his views on Reconstruction. He believed that the Republican governments, although not perfect, were the best governments ever in the South, that Negroes never dominated any state governments, that Negroes, always a minority, were as honest and competent as the whites, and that the mistake was allowing the Southerners to use force and violence to overthrow these governments. Granting that the problems in the South were enormous, he believed that the federal government should have supported law and order instead of deserting the Republican governments in their time of need.

The views of Lynch were diametrically opposed to views held by a group of young southern scholars who studied with John W. Burgess and William A. Dunning at Columbia. These views, which were later called the "traditionalist view," held that Reconstruction was a failure because blacks were incapable of responsibly using the freedom given to them. They belonged to a race that had never subjected "passion to reason, had never, therefore, created any civilization of any kind." The only valid principle upon which to found the southern society was inequality. Because Reconstruction failed to recognize this truth, these historians' view was that Southerners "literally were put to the torture" by blacks and by carpetbaggers whom they [the historians] called "emissaries of hate." The result was violence and assaults on southern womanhood until the white Southerners regained power and ended the tragic era.

The efforts of Lynch to share his views with James Ford Rhodes and Claude Bowers, two leading historians, proved unsuccessful. Rhodes read several of Lynch's articles with interest but disagreed with his findings. Bowers had even less interest in Lynch's work. Other efforts to have his work published in the *American Historical Review* and the *American Political Science Review* also failed. The only scholarly journal that published his work was *The Journal of Negro History*, but it reached a small audience.

Thus, in the early 1930s Lynch, in his mid-eighties, wrote another book, *Reminiscences of an Active Life*, which incorporated chapters of *Facts of Reconstruction*. Throughout the few years left to him, he dictated his story to his niece, who wrote it down. He continued to revise it until his death on November 2, 1939, at the age of ninety-two. The night before his death he was still rewriting the manuscript. Lynch was buried with full military honors in Arlington National Cemetery on November 6, 1939. His long battle over Reconstruction was finally over.

COPYRIGHTS AND ACKNOWLEDGMENTS